WHERE THE HELL IS AFRICA?

The author in 1959.

Where the Hell is Africa?

Memoirs of a junior naval officer in the
mid-twentieth century

PHILIP SEYMOUR

The Pentland Press
Edinburgh – Cambridge – Durham – USA

First published in 1995 by
The Pentland Press Ltd
1 Hutton Close,
South Church
Bishop Auckland
Durham
United Kingdom

ISBN 1-85821-300-2

Typeset by Carnegie Publishing, 18 Maynard St, Preston

Printed and bound by Lintons Printers, Crook. Telephone: (01388) 762197.

To Mike and Nina, with Love.
May you long enjoy the Peace and Freedom
your fathers went to sea to fight for.

CONTENTS

ACKNOWLEDGEMENTS

It may be said that almost everyone named in this book and still alive has contributed information and encouragement. All contributions have been valuable. I should, however, make special mention of Rear Admiral John Carlill, who proved a mine of information and a valuable link with Ministry of Defence (Navy) Archives Department. I am particularly indebted for information and encouragement from the known surviving four of the original seven, including myself, around whose naval careers the book is written. These are Mike MccGwire, Mike Kersey, Mike Vaughan and Gavin Wemyss. Peter Hoare is dead and Joe Lungley has disappeared. I am especially grateful to Mike MccGwire, who has been happy to allow me to tell almost as many outrageous stories about him as tales in praise of him; but I must advise that he does not vouch for the accuracy of my reports of him.

I am highly appreciative of advice and encouragement from Cdr. Bob Gaunt, whom I chanced to meet for the first time on a short train journey in England in 1994. I would like to express my special appreciation of Jill Rowena Cole of Pentland Press, without whose warm and enthusiastic encouragement I would not have gone ahead with publication.

Support has also been strong for me in Australia. I must thank my son Michael for persuading his sixty-five-year-old father that there was no magic in working a simple Personal Computer, and my wife Patricia for suffering all the chores and home responsibilities I have avoided whilst writing the book. Darcy Caldbeck and Colin Varcoe, of Craftsmen Type & Art, have been more than helpful in reproducing photos, etc. for me, as has Andrew Rodger of MITA (Aust.) who has assisted with a great deal of copying. Finally, I am enormously indebted to Professor John Sheppard who has steered me towards writing grammatical English.

FOREWORD

BY ADMIRAL SIR BENJAMIN BATHURST GCB ADC
CHIEF OF NAVAL STAFF AND FIRST SEA LORD

AFTER THE EXCITEMENT of youth and war, Philip Seymour's time as a Lieutenant might seem, from the perspective of nearly half a century, to have occurred in a rather drab era. The rapid demobilisation of a Navy which had totalled over three-quarters of a million men and women at its wartime peak quickly reduced the great fleets of 1945 to a nucleus, in which only the most modern ships remained in commission – only one of Seymour's ships, the corvette *Flint Castle*, had been first commissioned before VE Day! Money and men were in short demand – by far the largest fleet was the Reserve Fleet, with over two hundred cruisers, destroyers and frigates, few of them more than ten years old. Only the 'front-line' ships were up to complement and by the late '40s only in the Mediterranean was there what could be regarded as a truly 'front-line' fleet, for the Home Fleet's sea time was devoted largely to training. Elsewhere, the business of Empire or 'Commonwealth', as it was coming to be known, was sustained mainly by cruisers and frigates, in the West and East Indies, the South Atlantic and the Far East, showing the flag, one day deterring those who tried nibbling the moribund lion, the next helping them after devastating earthquakes or floods.

It is difficult for those of us who came later, and benefited from the experience of those who went through those lean years, to think of a Navy without NATO. The 'Cold War' had undoubtedly begun, but the Soviet Union posed little threat at sea in the early post-WWII years; the Navy had a breathing space in which it could think seriously about catching up with technology – how to catch snorting submarines and land jets on aircraft carriers were technicalities, but coping with nuclear weapons meant a new mentality. The Alliance was created in 1949, but the rebirth of the RN's relationship with the US really happened in the next year, when war began in Korea. From 1950 to 1953, the Eastern Fleet was the 'front-line' Command but support for the UN armies was not preparing the Navy for the next phase, which followed on quickly from the end of the Korean War.

The rise in Soviet ocean seapower, represented by submarine and surface ships, was fortunately matched by sufficient funds to complete the first generation of ships incorporating post-war experience. 'Full employment' had not helped naval manning and Reservists had to be recalled to man the Fleet during the Korean War, but it did mean that the national economy was sufficiently strong to support a building programme which concentrated on aircraft carriers and new frigates and minesweepers. In 1955, for example, no fewer than 56 frigates and 'sweepers' were launched and the carriers *Bulwark* and *Ark Royal* became operational.

The Navy which the 'Class of 39' bequeathed proved to be soundly-based and it lasted long enough to be tested in recent times, when the remaining handful of us who were taught by them were fortunate enough to contribute to the naval operations in the Falklands and the Gulf.

PREFACE

NEVIL SHUTE prefaced one of his novels with the observation that the world would never be free of the threat of war until all those who had had such fun in World War II were dead. Of course, he was not serious, being well aware of the horror, suffering and misery resulting from war.

On the other hand, all veterans know that War Service was not unmitigatedly grim. Furthermore, events experienced—tragic, emotional, unexpected or ridiculous—all widened the horizons and helped develop character. This was particularly true of young regular Naval Officers who were thrown straight into active service afloat, having just turned seventeen. They had three formative teenage years facing 'the dangers of the sea and the violence of the enemy'. With this went the freedoms and responsibilities of adult life, before they were strictly adult.

This was nothing new to the Royal Navy. Back in Nelson's time, Midshipmen often found themselves at sea at thirteen. In World War I, all RN College, Dartmouth, Cadets—aged fifteen—were sent off to sea at the outbreak of war. A number of these were to die within a year at the Battle of Jutland. One, who survived, wrote an article for *Blackwoods Magazine*, entitled 'War Babies'. This officer went on to serve through World War II, earning two DSOs and three DSCs. He was the father of one of my closest friends in the RN. I was privileged to meet him in 1989, when he was aged eighty-nine.

This book follows a small selection, of half a dozen members of the last pre-World War II entry into RNC Dartmouth—the Term of May 1939. The narrative does not attempt to be a definitive historical record of all the members of this group (originally numbering forty). They are now too scattered, world-wide, for me to research their stories. Nor do those included constitute a studied cross-section. Rather, they happened to be those who were close friends of mine and with whom I have been able to maintain some contact. Nevertheless, they are reasonably representative. A few others who were close—but not exact—contemporaries have also been included.

The intention of this story is to convey an impression of just what a splendid world-wide Club officers serving under the White Ensign belonged to in the mid-twentieth century. The period is from 1939 to 1959 with an epilogue giving an account of the Reunion, held thirty years later.

That was fifty years after the principal characters in the book joined the RN as thirteen-year-old Cadets and tells how the lives of the survivors present had turned out.

The narrative has not been consciously contrived to make it more colourful. The material is derived from the recollections of the writer and his friends, with research limited to only readily available records. There may be some inaccuracies, but there are no total fabrications. I have made an honest attempt to capture the spirit of the times.

Philip Seymour

HAPPY HOOLIGAN DAYS

'WHAT ON EARTH have you got there, Mike—and where the hell did you get it?' I asked my friend, Sub Lieutenant Mike MccGwire.

'What does it look like? It's a Baby Duck, of course, and it's a long story how I "won" it.'

He was not talking about a fluffy little yellow handful of duckling, nor was he speaking in some sort of code. In 1945, in the last stages of World War II, everyone in the Allied invasion forces knew exactly what a Duck was. The name, DUKW, was an improbable acronym signifying an American conveyance that could carry a dozen troops as a propeller-driven boat. It could also carry on up a beach or river bank on its six-wheel drive. There was a smaller version generally described as an amphibious jeep or, to MccGwire, a Baby Duck.

Sub Lieutenant MccGwire was the First Lieutenant (being the only other officer after the CO) of Motor Torpedo Boat 476 of the 30th Flotilla currently based on Ostend in Belgium. A Sub Lieutenant RN myself—and some eight months junior to MccGwire – I was taking over from him, as 'No.1' of this vessel. It was not my first acquaintance with this remarkable man—and certainly not my last. I had known MccGwire for several years at Dartmouth, where he had captained the 1st XV and was Chief Cadet Captain of the College—two Terms ahead of me.

On passing out, collecting an armful of prizes and the King's Dirk, MccGwire had already shown indications of outstanding ability. He became a Russian Interpreter, served as Assistant Naval Attaché in Moscow and later headed the Russian Section of British Naval Intelligence, before taking early retirement from the Navy, foregoing almost certain further promotion. He was awarded an OBE in the next honours list. As a genuine altruist, he had his heart set on applying his talents in, and for the benefit of, the Third World. But he found the relevant UN agencies were already over-subscribed. He moved to Canada with a wife and five children, but no job. However, he was soon occupying the Chair of Strategic Studies at a Canadian University. He then spent eleven years as a distinguished Senior Fellow of the acclaimed Washington 'Think Tank', the Brookings Institution, where he was active in the debate about Soviet military and foreign policy, writing two books on the subject.

An individual of such evident talents and a 'watch-him-he's-supposed-

to-be-good' reputation, might well have been an arrogant, even insuffer-
able, person. Happily, Mike MccGwire was not. He was disarmingly
unassuming, and possessed an engaging personality and good looks with
athletic build, sandy hair and guileless boyish grin. Accordingly, he was
well loved by all who served under him and practically everyone else.
Only a few pompous Senior Officers in later years suspected that his views
on the Russians indicated he was some sort of 'pinko'. Rather, he was
intensely patriotic, but had an infinitely deeper insight into Russian thinking and their ever-changing political scene than many of his critics.
MccGwire was no Anthony Blunt, nor secret admirer of Communism. He
simply had a much broader view of the world scene than most people,
and I had noted that, in action, he was quite fearless. When he was aged
nineteen, I already regarded him as a hero.

Over the years, I was to come across MccGwire in many parts of the
world. But, after leaving the Navy, I lost track of him for twenty years,
until Des Ball of the Australian National University told me he was at the
Brookings Institution. I wrote and reminded him of some of the experiences—and escapades—we had shared. He wrote back '. . . Loved your
wander down Memory Lane. Those were Some Days—we were Happy
Hooligans.' My mental reaction was 'Speak for yourself, MccGwire!' But
I found myself longing to see him again.

He finally retired in 1990 and lives with his charming wife Helen, with
occasional visits from his grown-up offspring—brilliant in differing ways,
if a trifle eccentric. Their home is in the beautiful Durlston locality of
Dorset, England. I cannot envisage Mike vegetating, or even slowing
down. As recently as 1989, in Washington, he was striding along the
sidewalks at a pace a fit person would struggle to match, and he still
ordered beer by the jug—not the pint. This was notwithstanding a double
by-pass operation and a heart pace-maker—perhaps to slow down this
mighty and generous heart. Certainly, the fortitude of the man is such
that one envisages him as indestructible. My life has been the richer for
knowing Mike MccGwire.

To return to the Baby Duck, it seems the story was: MccGwire and
his friend Tony Bowen chanced to meet up and have a few drinks with
two US Marine officers. Both were considerably older and of higher rank
than MccGwire and Bowen. One was a Lieutenant Colonel who had
evidently suffered war stress and, perhaps as a consequence, was no match
for MccGwire when it came to holding his liquor—in this instance, Mumm
'Cordon Rouge'. This was not because Mike was an affluent Champagne
Charlie. Far from it—he was usually broke and champagne was the only
drink he could afford. This was because we had taken over the German
Schnellbooten (E-Boat) officers' mess, which was stocked with almost limitless
quantities of this admirable beverage, looted from Rheims.

Late in the evening, the Americans asked the two young British officers back to their quarters. They took the remnants of a dozen-case of champagne, which saw them through to the not-so-small hours of the morning. Eventually, our two young Navy Hooligans realised that they ought to be heading back to their quarters—and their duties. 'Take a jeep from the pool,' said their hosts. Accordingly, they picked out an interesting looking conveyance—the Duck. Unfortunately, MccGwire, having been sent to sea at seventeen, had never learnt to drive a car—let alone a vehicle with four-wheel drive options and/or a propeller. As a result, there were a few expensive-sounding metallic crunching noises before they roared out of the barracks.

By now the Colonel had sobered up enough to wonder if he would ever see the amphibious jeep again and decided to give chase in another jeep. Mike had an appalling blood/alcohol level—and no previous experience as a driver. Nevertheless, he quickly mastered the controls and led the Marine on a 'cops & robbers' car chase around the narrow streets of Ostend. MccGwire knew these well—including which canal bridges the retreating Germans had blown up. As a result, the chase ended with MccGwire making a last minute turn-off from a bridge which simply was not there. He watched the unhappy pursuing Colonel's jeep become airborne and splash into the canal. Fortunately, the water was shallow and Mike last saw the poor man sitting motionless and stupefied, still holding the steering wheel and the water up to his armpits. He was unhurt—but he never saw his amphibious jeep again.

Minutes later, the vehicle was being painted navy grey by willing sailors from MTB 476. They were gleefully encouraged by the author and several close friends from Dartmouth days, happily together again as officers of the 30th MTB Flotilla.

This narrative will recount episodes shared with these and other contemporaries, around the world. Few will be as outrageous as that of MccGwire's Duck. The characters were not heroes but typical high-spirited young naval officers of the mid-twentieth century. The question is, were young individualists, with a certain devil-may-care attitude and disregard for Establishment mores, attracted to the Royal Navy or did the Navy develop them that way? I suspect the latter—noting the honours heaped on MccGwire by RNC Dartmouth—where a certain nonconformity about him would hardly have passed unnoticed. Dartmouth assessments of MccGwire were sound—he served his country with distinction. A common characteristic amongst his comrades was a certain eccentricity. Whilst imbued with the best traditions of the RN, they tended to have something of an iconoclast streak. One of the finest officers in this book was Gavin Wemyss (a gleeful witness to the Duck incident). At Dartmouth, he had been known to exclaim, 'No! Not another picture of the death of the Immortal Nelson!'

Naval officers were not a celibate monastic group; nor a cult like the French Foreign Legion—divorced from the mainstream of society. Most married and had happy family lives, yet the call of duty came first. It was said—in jest, but with a grain of truth—that a naval wife had to accept a bigamous marriage, knowing her husband was already married to his ship—or the Service.

Recalling my own relatively brief naval career, in war and in peace, I can but echo MccGwire's sentiments: 'Those were Some Days!' It was with reluctance that many of us took voluntary early retirement in the late fifties. The fleet was a tenth the size of the one we had joined in '39 and there simply was not enough employment to go round. The Royal Navy had been like a caring but tolerant parent to us and, in return, we gave our unqualified devotion. We parted sadly but on good terms, when such parting became inevitable. The reader is invited to share some of the author's memories of Those Days.

CHAPTER I

JOINING

AT 3.35 P.M. on Monday 4 May 1939, as an excited, but anxious, thirteen-year-old, I stood on a station platform in my brand new Naval Officer Cadet uniform. With me were my mother and father. The train pulled in. There were hurried farewells—a clasp on the shoulder by my father and an embrace from my mother, from which I disengaged as quickly as possible. I was acutely conscious of a hundred eyes of like-uniformed boys looking out of carriage windows. Quickly boarding the train and with a cheery, but unconvincing, wave of bravado, I was on my way to join the Royal Navy.

My childhood had differed from what would be considered the norm today but was not uncommon in the pre-World War II days of the British Empire. My father's career in the Colonial Service had taken us to several parts of the world. I was born in Ceylon (Sri Lanka), my elder sister in France and my younger brother in Fiji. At nine and eight, my sister and I had been packed off to boarding schools in England. For the next five years, until my father's retirement in 1939, we were to see our parents only occasionally.

It was, therefore, not altogether surprising that planning my future life was left very much in my own hands. Career advisers were unknown in those days. The only view my father had expressed was that it would make him happy if I should turn out to be a classical scholar. With this in mind, he had put my name down for Winchester. But my prep school days had given no indication that I would excel at Latin or Greek and the academic world held little attraction for me. Instead, I fancied the Navy. By the age of eight, I had completed two circumnavigations of the globe and, by eleven, had crossed the Atlantic to Trinidad and back. My peripatetic childhood had given me a taste for travel around the oceans of the world. Furthermore, I had recollections of white-uniformed officers aboard gleaming warships visiting Fiji. With no other serious options suggested to me, I decided it was the Royal Navy for me.

I had already learnt that the most direct route to a naval career was through 'The Cradle of the Navy'—RN College, Dartmouth. This meant entry at the age of thirteen and applying whilst still twelve. Somehow, formalities were completed (with my parents on the other side of the Atlantic—and no air mail to the West Indies in those days). I then

The author aged 13, keen and eager to start his naval career.

discovered that selection and entry for Dartmouth was not as easy as I imagined. In 1939, Britain still had the mightiest Navy in the world with an intake of two hundred officer trainees, through several channels, each year. For Dartmouth, there was an intake of about forty cadets every Term (hence the reference by naval officers for many years to their Term—not Year—at Dartmouth). In April 1939, there were 150 candidates for the forty-odd places. The selection was in two stages— an initial interview and medical, which reduced the number to ninety—who then sat an exam, from which forty were accepted.

In my case, it was the interview which proved the biggest worry. My school had done little to prepare me for this. In the sixty year life of the school, no one had ever asked to take the Navy Entry before. There was nothing wrong with my prep school except that it had rather an odd name—although it had never seemed so to me whilst I was there. This name was to affect me significantly—perhaps for the rest of my life. It was Bigshotte School, so called, as the rambling old house had been named 'Bigshotte Rayles' by the old Dowager Duchess of Reading who had built it nearly a hundred years before. To this day, I have no idea how she arrived at that name. Once I had gained entry to Dartmouth, after a few days, a fellow new entry—a 'character', one Gavin Wemyss— chortled out, 'There's the boy from Bigshot, ha ha ha!' Little did I realise that I would be stuck with this as a nickname for the rest of my naval career and hear it used by many people who had no idea how it had originated. Indeed, fifty years later, in 1989, on landing at John Foster Dulles International Airport, Washington and being met by an old Navy contemporary, I heard behind me a hearty hail of, 'Hi, Bigshot'!

My interview was held at what was the Admiralty at the Trafalgar Square end of the Mall. This is still an imposing edifice. To this boy from the South Pacific, the whole of London was awe-inspiring and the inside of the Admiralty was positively terrifying. I found myself listed as the first interviewee after lunch—no doubt a pleasant repast for the Board Members, whereas I had not lunched, but had no appetite anyway. My spirits sank as one interviewer after another, of the five, appeared, shot a speculative glance at me and disappeared behind a large oak door opposite. At last, I was called in. A large ruddy faced man with an impressive air of authority chaired proceedings from the end of the table and posed the questions. Some were reasonable (Why do you want to join the Navy?) and others quite perplexing (Here is a round field with long grass in which you have lost your cricket ball—draw on this paper the course you would take to search for the ball).

Michael MccGwire aged 13, in 1938.
'Butter would not melt . . .'

From the looks on the faces of my inquisitors, I was simply not 'winning' and was about ready to throw in the towel. The next question was to give me some heart. 'Tell us what the Navy did in the last war' (World War I). I had, of course, shown enough interest in the Navy to have read quite a lot about the RN 1914 to 1918. I rattled off all the surface actions I could think of: Coronel, Falkland Islands, Dogger Bank, Heligoland Bight and Jutland, with a slight feeling of inner smugness. My chairman looked reasonably pleased—but evidently not satisfied. 'Was that all?' I later learnt I was supposed to mention the RN at Gallipoli and the exploits of the Naval Brigade in Belgium. I was now desperate.

Happily, I suddenly remembered a magazine article I had read. 'Ah yes, there was the action in the English Channel in 1917 in which the destroyers *Broke* and *Swift* routed six German destroyers.' The effect was astonishing. The entire Committee let out a guffaw, the chairman slapped his side and roared with laughter. (What could I have said?) When decorum at last returned, I was asked the seeming non-sequitor, 'What do you know about Antarctic explorers?' 'Not a great deal, I am afraid, Sir.' Then, after more laughter, 'Very well, that will do. Off you go! Send the next candidate in.' Those familiar with early twentieth century naval history will have guessed that my civilian-clothed chairman was none other than Admiral Sir Edward Evans KBE DSO, etc. As a Lieutenant, he had been second-in-command of Captain Robert Falcon Scott's ill-fated expedition to the South Pole, and led the relief party which found the bodies of Scott and his companions. As captain of HMS *Broke*, of the Dover Patrol, he had become a hero. In a night action with the *Swift* he had rammed one of the six destroyers, and his crew had engaged the Germans in hand-to-hand fighting before the enemy vessel finally surrendered. This was a very different naval warfare from today's Exocet missiles coming from over the horizon and crippling a warship.

Lord Mountevans, as he finally became, was assuredly the most distinguished naval officer of the inter-war years. However, in April 1939, Philip Seymour had not the slightest idea who this impressive man at the end of the table might be. Later, I could only conclude that my Board decided that this candidate was not as dim-witted as he appeared. Clearly, he had taken the trouble to find out who was to be in charge of his interview panel. He had looked up his story and had an ace to play—when the moment was right. Obviously a boy of considerable initiative, just the type for the Royal Navy! How lucky can one get? So it came about that I was boarding that train on 4 May 1939.

Once aboard the train, I noted that every other Cadet in sight appeared much older and bigger than myself. I realised that I was in a carriage allocated for so-called Special Entry Cadets, joining the Navy at seventeen or eighteen straight from senior schools. This carriage may well have included Prince Philip of Greece and Denmark, as he then was, and a Cadet by such entry.

After a short time, I did find one other diminutive Cadet, with whom I was soon in conversation. His name was Joe Lungley and, through the years, he was to prove one of my closest friends. It seemed his background was similar to my own. His family were in Batavia, capital of the Dutch East Indies. We could not know that, within three years, he would never see his family again. His father, sister and mother were all brutally murdered by the Japanese.

It was only fourteen miles by rail from Torquay to Dartmouth, and could have been done with less trouble, from door to door, in the family car. But this was unacceptable. Joining Instructions had been specific about the train. Arrival by any other means would have deprived me of my first taste of naval discipline and the rigours of the training that lay ahead. Across the Dart, it was a case of: 'Fall in . . . Right Turn . . . Quick March.' We went at a brisk pace under the hot summer sun for the up-hill mile to the imposing buildings of Naval College. Before we completed our time there, the RNC would be severely damaged by aerial bombardment. For the moment, such a possibility never entered our minds. This was the pre-war Navy, with officers in frock coats for Sunday 'Divisions', whilst senior Cadets wore bell-boy type short 'Round Jackets', with buttons up to the neck.

CHAPTER 2

Dartmouth 1939–42

PRE-WAR SALAD DAYS

OUR FIRST TERM was pre-war Royal Navy in all its splendour. It had been a shock, coming from prep schools where we had been prefects and privileged seniors to an establishment where we were the lowest form of animal life. Discipline was strict and routines demanding. Nevertheless, I was unaware of any bullying, or 'bastardisation'. The rules were tough and most of us were caned quite often for relatively minor offences, but never felt crushed or humiliated. This has made me reflect on the value of corporal punishment. I feel it seldom did much harm—nor much good. It is inappropriate for particularly sensitive children, when the effects may be harmful. Conversely, later experience taught me that, alone in the case of bullies, scornful of any other punishment, a few strokes of the cane could achieve remarkable behavioural improvement.

After finding we all had to smarten up, new horizons were opening up all the time. There were superb sports facilities and boat-sailing on the River Dart. The curriculum included fascinating new subjects such as 'Seamanship', embracing everything from knots and splices through signalling to warship organisation, and 'Engineering' in the College workshops. Sport was not excessively glorified, although a blazer badge signifying membership of a College First Team certainly carried prestige. Rather, on reflection, I believe the activities were so structured that almost everyone could develop self-esteem through shining in some field. Such could vary from boating to beagle whip, handling the hounds of the Britannia Beagles. But, naturally, distinction in any of the sports would only come to us as more senior Cadets.

Notwithstanding the glamour and excitement of pre-war Dartmouth, in the summer of 1939, the clouds of war were gathering. Yet the ominous developments indirectly led to the most exhilarating event of our first term.

Our House Cadet Captain explained to us, in June 1939, that the Admiralty now regarded war with Germany as inevitable. Reservists were being mobilised and the Reserve Fleet prepared for active service. It was planned to have all ships worked-up by late July. This fleet would be reviewed by the Sovereign at Portland. It would then take part in serious exercises with the regular Home Fleet, to be ready for anticipated hostilities by the end of September. In the event, predictions were close, and the Navy was almost fully operational when war was declared on 3 September 1939.

To us, as New Entry Cadets, this advice constituted a dramatic, if chilling, forecast. More immediately exciting was the news that, following the Portland Review, the King and Queen and the young Princesses Elizabeth and Margaret would be coming to Dartmouth. They were coming aboard the Royal Yacht *Victoria and Albert* for a three-day visit to inspect the Naval College and other local institutions. This was to be at the very end of our first term.

This Dartmouth Royal Visit took place, and proved a tremendous success—at least to our eyes. One small incident, of which the writer was entirely oblivious at the time, may or may not have been of importance to the future of the realm. During those three days, the thirteen-year-old future Queen of England first came face to face with the seventeen-year-old Cadet Prince Philip of Greece and Denmark—who was about to receive the King's Dirk as the most outstanding Cadet of his entry. Much was made of this meeting in years to come. Speculation as to its significance in 1939 now seems pointless. I simply record that the encounter occurred.

The highlight of the Royal Visit was the spectacular departure of the *Victoria and Albert* at dusk on 22 July. Every boat the College possessed and practically every civilian craft in the port was manned and milling round the Royal Yacht. The scene could best be described as a miniature version of the Australian Bicentennial Harbour Spectacular. It seemed almost possible to step from one boat to another right across the River Dart.

Minutes before the *Victoria and Albert* sailed, one of the College rowing boats was called alongside and given a message for the College Captain aboard the yacht *Amaryllis*. The missive was duly read out: The King had graciously seen fit to award the College four days extra summer leave. A mighty cheer went up from all the Cadet-manned boats. The Royal Yacht steamed slowly out to sea to the sound of every steam whistle and horn that could be operated, and tumultuous cheering. This was not only from Cadets but from the populace of an ancient naval port for their Sailor King. He had been formally re-visiting the place of learning, where he had undergone the greater part of his own education.

Fifty years later, at our reunion dinner aboard HMS *Belfast*, we were delighted to receive a reply to our message of loyal greetings to Her Majesty. This came in the first person (not 'Her Majesty has asked me to convey to you . . . '). It concluded: 'I RECEIVED THIS MESSAGE WITH MUCH PLEASURE AND SEND MY BEST WISHES TO ALL CONCERNED FOR A MOST ENJOYABLE OCCASION ELIZA-BETH R.' We liked to think that the Queen had actually recalled her own visit to Dartmouth, that Term—or had been reminded of it by Prince Philip. He would have been one of the cheering Cadets, with what private thoughts, we may never know.

DARTMOUTH AT WAR

After the excitements of our first term, the Naval College, now at war, steadily adapted to wartime conditions. Total blackout was imposed and Air Raid Precautions instituted. These were rudimentary to start with, but were steadily built up until each of the five hundred Cadets had an 'Action Station'. Such might be as a fire engine crewman, stretcher bearer, messenger, even manning ancient machine guns on the high roof of 'D' Block at the back of the College. There were a number of air raid warnings, with everyone taking cover or assuming their allotted duties, but no actual attack ever tested this elaborate organisation.

Other less dramatic changes occurred. There were new uniform regulations; pre-war, the everyday 'working dress' for Cadets comprised white flannel trousers, reefer jacket, cap, etc. The trousers were a curse as after one fall in the long polished corridors—which Junior Cadets were required to cover at the double—knees were marked with brown smudges. For wartime, we wore black shoes, long navy socks and navy drill shorts—an altogether more practical turnout.

After a time, and sleep lost as the result of occasional air raid warnings, the authorities decided we should not sleep in the vulnerable upper floor dormitories. Instead, the Cadets should use three-foot high bunks in converted ground-floor boot locker rooms, with brick blast walls outside.

Another wartime innovation was the establishment of the RNC Special Service Corps. This involved arming the senior Cadets (fifteen-year-olds plus). We underwent basic training in the use of rifles, bayonets and hand grenades and elementary tactics such as concealment and covering fire. Whether we would have materially impeded the war-hardened troops of the Wehrmacht or German paratroops is debatable. Certainly we had no doubt we would prove more than a match for the might of the German Army. At least this was in the spirit of Churchill's rallying speech of 'We shall fight on the beaches, . . . in the streets . . . We shall never surrender.' There were occasional exercises defending the College against units of the Army proper, in which we, at least, considered we acquitted ourselves well. There were also exercises in which we played the German invaders, pitted against the local Dartmouth Home Guard. These were more fun, allowing us to show enterprise and initiative. One party infiltrated to the waterfront of Kingswear along a dozen passenger coaches in the railway sidings. An even more venturous team entered the Dartmouth sewer, emerged out of a manhole in the centre of the town and declared Dartmouth captured. We all got a great kick out of these activities.

Notwithstanding the foregoing diversions, we were aware that there was a real war going on. In the winter of 1940–41, the Luftwaffe launched its savage *Blitzkrieg* against the cities of Britain. Before long, it was the turn of Plymouth—subjected to four successive nights of bombing. The Civil Defence Forces were overwhelmed. The fires started the previous night would not be under control, casualties collected and treated, streets cleared of rubble or emergency supplies of water, gas and electricity restored, before the next night's onslaught. By the fourth night, the authorities decided the only option was to tell all the population who could, to flee the city. At night, only thirty-five miles away, we could see the ruddy glow of the city burning. Before Plymouth and Devonport were devastated, many of us were taken there to view the battle-scarred, but victorious, cruiser *Exeter*—back from the defeat of the *Graf Spee* in the River Plate.

Further evidence of the war was the arrival of the Belgian fishing fleet of 114 craft. These proved an embarrassment to the authorities. They were not allowed to fish locally, in the mined and defended coastal waters, and were suspected of harbouring possible German spies. Indeed, such would have been a relatively simple way for the Germans to get some spies into Britain. Their local popularity was not increased when none of the fishermen were prepared to return with their boats to help rescue the BEF (British Expeditionary Force) from the beaches of Dunkirk. In fairness, we do not know how harrowing a time these people had had in getting out of Belgium at all. Nevertheless, thousands of small craft, from luxury cabin cruisers to open fishing boats, did go, constituting the famous armada of 'Little Ships' which saved the British Army from annihilation. Even the old steam ferry, the *Mew*, which had carried generations of Dartmouth Cadets across the Dart, set off. But, sadly, she got no further than Dover before her ancient engine broke down.

Occasionally, unexpected large merchant ships appeared, including the former cruise liner *Arandorra Star*—sunk soon after, carrying internees to Canada. There was excitement when Captain Lord Louis Mountbatten came in with his magnificent flotilla of brand new 'J' and 'K' Fleet destroyers. The Captain of the College prevailed on him to address the Cadets. Many of us would serve under 'Lord Louis', in years to come. But this was the first time we would fall under the spell of this extraordinary charismatic leader of men.

From time to time, grim news would reach us of another warship sunk. This would be the more distressing when Midshipmen, whom we had known as Cadets at Dartmouth, were reported lost. This was particularly true in the case of the *Hood*—a ship we all knew as the biggest and most powerful warship of the fleet. Only three of the Ship's Company of 2,500 survived. In late 1941, in 5th Term (last of 'Junior College'), I had been fag (although not so-termed at Dartmouth, there being many privileges attached to the job, and keen competition for the position) to a Cadet Captain named Dundas. He was good to me and performing small services for him was in no way onerous. It saddened me, knowing that he had gone from Dartmouth straight to HMS *Hood*, to be sunk within five months. Amazingly, I soon learned that Midshipman Dundas was one of the three—and the only officer—to survive this disaster. I was not to meet him again for seventeen years, when both of us were Lieutenant Commanders at Royal Naval Air Station, Eglinton in Northern Ireland. He told me that he had been the sixth man out of a porthole as *Hood* went down. None of the others were ever seen again.

The years 1939–42 had excitements and sorrows but, generally, our schooling was little changed from the normal—work, study, sport, achievements and disappointments, but plenty of fun. I had an easier time than most, as my home was only fourteen miles away by road—and half an hour by train. I was allowed to take friends home on day leave at week-ends. This easy-going pattern was to be shattered in September 1942.

DARTMOUTH BATTERED BUT NOT ABANDONED

We had always realised that the Naval College and those under training there constituted a legitimate military target. But, by now, this was of little significance to the Germans, who were bombing cities indiscriminately. It took the enemy three years of war to make a deliberate attack on Dartmouth. A very well executed raid was made by six FW190 fighters, each carrying a 1000lb. bomb. They approached low over the sea and were undetected by radar. Accordingly, all six planes attacked their selected targets and were out to sea again before the air raid siren was sounded or an anti-aircraft gun had opened fire. Six bombs were dropped. Two destroyed a large workshop at the shipyard where mine-sweepers were being built. One hit and sank a cargo ship. One (the only unsuccessful attack) was a near-miss on a tanker. The other two scored direct hits on the College. Major damage was done to the RNC and almost every window was smashed.

Mercifully, not a Cadet was even injured. This was simply because we were all away on our summer leave. The bombs fell around 1030 just when we would all have been streaming across the 'quarterdeck'—in the centre of the College—on our way to get our morning-break bun and mug of cocoa. One bomb fell on the corner of this hall, bringing down two of four massive two-storey stone arches and leaving the whole quarterdeck a shambles of broken masonry. The Germans had not kindheartedly decided to try to knock out the College while the Cadets were away. In fact, they had good reason to suppose we would be there. Happily, they had not done their homework thoroughly. When we first arrived at Dartmouth some all-knowing Cadet had advised us that we would score a week's extra leave in our last summer holiday from the College. Why? Because every school, having a standard number of weeks of terms and holidays starting and ending on the same days of the week, gets one day out each year. Two are lost in a leap year and a one-week adjustment must be made every now and then. This is usually an extra week of holidays. It so happened that Dartmouth needed to do just this in the summer of 1942 (war or no war). The Germans did not know this and bombed the College during our one fortuitous extra week's leave.

Home on leave in Torquay and, standing by the harbour down in the town, I heard the distant 'crump' of exploding bombs. This was something I had become used to, as the Germans were now making quite a number of hit-and-run raids on the coast of south-west England. I looked to the south, whence the sound seemed to have come. Across Torbay and from beyond the hills behind Brixham, I saw mushrooming clouds of smoke and dust rising several hundred feet. I said to myself, 'That has to be Dartmouth—I wonder if they have hit the Naval College.' I was not left wondering long. A telegram arrived that day instructing myself, and the other eighty cadets of the two senior Terms, to remain on leave for a further two weeks. This was to give enough time to make about a fifth of the College habitable so that the two senior Terms could go back there for our final term of studies. The remaining Cadets were told to remain on leave indefinitely, until arrangements were finally made for them to go to Eaton Hall, seat of the Duke of Westminster in Cheshire. The Naval College remained there until after the war.

At Dartmouth, there were a number of casualties at the shipyard. At the College, sadly, one Wren was killed but no one else was injured. There were two bizarre incidents resulting from the raid. The Captain of the College had convened a meeting of officers to review the standing Air Raid Precautions Orders, in the light of the new German hit-and-run tactics. The meeting had just started when the bombs struck, breaking all the windows of the room in which they were conferring. The story goes that, once the dust had settled, Captain Cunliffe decided to carry on with the meeting. 'Give me those orders,' he said and promptly threw the book into the waste paper basket. 'The new orders are: Any person, on hearing an air raid siren, gun fire, bomb explode or recognised note of a hostile aircraft engine, shall drop whatever he is doing and run as far and as fast as he can—to the woods.'

Something even stranger occurred in the office of the Naval Officer In Charge, Dartmouth—responsible for naval movements in the area and for local defence. The HQ was in a first floor room to the rear of the main frontage of the College. When the bombs struck, the back wall fell outwards but none of the duty staff in the room was hurt. Nevertheless, the floor appeared to be about to collapse. Accordingly, the personnel quickly moved out—just before the floor did fall away. Moments later, the telephone on the wall of this (floorless) room rang. The Duty Officer somehow managed to climb round the wall and answered it. A blasé voice in Operations HQ in Plymouth advised, 'There seem to be a few hostiles [aircraft] in your area, old boy.' I have no record of the Dartmouth officer's reply—'Fancy' perhaps?

Our last term at Dartmouth was rather disorganised. With much of the College damaged and the main central hall in ruins and even with only eighty-odd Cadets instead of the usual five hundred, many changes were needed. There were further interruptions to our studies caused by air raid scares but the College itself was not again attacked.

There was one small incident which caused me some personal distress— of minor significance, and only recorded here because it also involved one of my close and life-long friends. Even with so few Cadets, there were insufficient usable classrooms. Accordingly, the canteen pavilion, up amongst the playing fields, had been utilised. One morning, a class of about twenty of us was standing around in this improvised classroom, waiting for our teacher to appear. To our delight, we found that the canteen manager had left out a half-full quart tin of ice cream. As sixteen- and seventeen-year-old still-growing boys, we were engaged in a great deal of physical training and strenuous sporting activities. But we were on the same reduced rations as everyone else in wartime Britain, and we were perpetually hungry. I need hardly say, most of us were soon digging into the ice cream. Not a great deal was taken by any individual—perhaps a dessert-spoonful by myself—but together, we significantly reduced the ice cream in the tin. The Canteen Manager, Mr Laver, a congenial man against whom we bore no ill will, found his depleted ice cream tin and, rightly, felt he had been robbed. He reported the matter to the Commander. The whole incident was then magnified out of all proportion.

All Cadets were mustered and the Commander ordered the ice cream thieves to step forward. No one moved. Dire threats were then made and we were told that all privileges would be cancelled until the criminals came forward. I could stand it no longer and put my hand up. Immediately, my close friend, Michael Kersey, felt obliged to do the same. Sadly, no one else felt so moved. Thus it was concluded that Cadets Seymour and Kersey had guzzled all the missing ice cream. The Commander considered, with the culprits now found, that the incident could be closed. I was sentenced to six strokes with the cane by one of the senior Cadet Captains. The physical pain was no more than in the case of my many beatings as a junior Cadet. But I had not been caned for at least two years and this punishment, administered by one of my peers, left me feeling both crushed and humiliated—but only for a day or so! As for Kersey, as he was a Cadet Captain, it was felt that to beat him would be inappropriate and some other punishment was considered. In the event, Kersey insisted that, if Seymour was to be beaten, then he must be similarly punished. Many years later, discussing this incident, Mike said, 'The trouble with you was you were always so damned honest.' I can only comment that at least he had just as high a sense of honour.

The perceived morality of this story is complex. We were beaten for stealing perhaps a penny-worth of ice cream. Yet three years later, we all cheered Mike MccGwire for succeeding in highjacking an American amphibious jeep worth US$1000 in those days. The difference was that the first theft was entirely for personal benefit and satisfaction—the other was seen as for the common good, albeit for a limited community. Relativities should also be considered. In 1942 Britain, food, in any form, was precious (but we were not suffering malnutrition). On the other hand, by 1945, Allied-occupied Europe was almost choked with American war material, little of which could possibly be used in the Pacific theatre against the Japanese.

Furthermore, once that war was concluded, billions of dollars of American war material would be simply dumped. I watched two whole squadrons of 'Martlet' fighter aircraft simply pushed over the forward 'round-down' of HMS *Venerable* into the Atlantic off Gibraltar in August 1946. The Americans just did not want their planes back. All this would not have passed through MccGwire's mind when he relieved the Americans of their jeep but he would have been aware of the general background. I suspect MccGwire would have had few qualms over the ice cream—but would have confessed at once, on being questioned. As for the jeep, if asked if he was guilty, I suspect he would have replied, 'That's for you to find out.'

We managed to conclude our last term at Dartmouth with something of a blaze of glory. Traditionally, the Passing Out Term staged a grand end-of-term dance with decorations and other arrangements planned months ahead. Such events had always been held in the quarterdeck. By now, this was no more than a rubble-filled shell, and the hosts numbered fewer than ninety, instead of the usual five hundred. Accordingly, the dining room was fixed up as our ballroom. What we lacked in numbers was more than made up in enthusiasm. A good band was engaged and young hearts beat with fancied romance as the dancing continued to the scheduled closure at midnight. Thus the curtain came down on an important act in the story of Royal Naval College, Dartmouth—no more Cadets would be seen there until after the war.

There may have been similar happy scenes that night for young gradu-
ates at the German Naval Officers' School. The tide of war was turning
against the Third Reich. Rommel's Afrika Corps had been defeated at
Alamein two months earlier and the German Army had finally given up
their assault on Stalingrad only two weeks before. Nevertheless, the Axis
powers were still near the limit of their conquests. The U-Boats were close
to winning the Battle of the Atlantic and their Japanese allies had still to
be turned around. If there were parallel German naval celebrations, I fear
there would have been very few survivors of the Class of '42 for a reunion
in 1989 or whenever, given the toll on the U-Boats over the next two and
a half years.

CHAPTER 3

People at Dartmouth—
Staff and Contemporaries
(with some Reflections)

1   It is to be accepted that in this, or any other, enterprise, the fundamental key to success is PEOPLE.

2   The ideal to which all levels of Management must aspire is a situation in which anything less than the best endeavours of any individual will be seen by him as letting down his immediate superior.

THESE WERE NOT PRECEPTS spelt out for me at Dartmouth, but nonetheless they were consciously or subconsciously 'taken aboard' by the author at the RNC. Many years later, I wrote them into, and they constituted, the standing orders of the manufacturing company of which I was the managing director after I had left the Service. It was people who made the Naval College, and the officers trained there played a large part in making the Royal Navy such a fine Service. I can pay tribute here to only a few of the people who contributed to making the Naval College the 'successful enterprise' it undoubtedly was.

Much credit must go to the successive Captains, Dalrymple-Hamilton and Cunliffe. After Dartmouth, the former was given command of the battleship *Rodney*. Her mighty 16″ guns contributed to the final destruction of the hitherto-invincible *Bismarck* in swift nemesis for the sinking of the majestic *Hood*, three days before, in May 1941. He finally retired as Admiral Sir Frederick Dalrymple-Hamilton KCB.

Captain Cunliffe achieved no further fame or glory but was well loved. Forty-seven years after leaving Dartmouth, at our reunion, we resolved to send our old Captain a message of greetings—he was then aged ninety-four.

The two Commanders during my time were Addis and Weir but somehow their impact on our lives seemed less than in the case of the Captains. But both proved effective Executive Officers of the College.

Of rather greater impact on the lives of Cadets were the House Officers. Pre-war, these were usually picked from the brightest and most promising younger officers available. When the war came, such were judged to be of greater value commanding small ships. Accordingly, they tended to be replaced by older and less active, although still capable, officers. Nevertheless, it was not long before the College started to acquire a few brilliant younger officers. Such had all their mental faculties but had been severely wounded and declared unfit for sea service, at least for the time being. Among these was Lt. McKendrick who had a ramrod-straight bearing and great personal drive. Unfortunately, he had a disfiguring scar, right up the back of his head. But the Cadets were much too impressed by the strength of his personality to be put off by this. Another fine officer was Lt. Mellor, who had been severely wounded in the head on the bridge of a destroyer at Dunkirk and left for dead on the deck. When the action was over, he was found to be alive and, after brilliant surgery, made an almost complete recovery. His only perceptible handicap was a slight speech impediment. This only tended to make his many words of wisdom the more memorable. One, which most of us never forgot, was, 'Good organisassion makes an effissent ssip—an effissent ssip is a happy ssip.'

There were two incidents concerning Cdr. Weir and Cadet Seymour, neither of which was to my credit. One (already recounted) was the saga of the Great Ice Cream Robbery of '42. The other, somewhat earlier and of an absurd nature, also involved my friend Kersey. Neither of us had a background of huntin', shootin' and fishin' but we had been co-opted to be part of the 'field' for a hunt with the Britannia Beagles. Technically, I suppose, this was a 'blood sport', but in practice, I cannot recall any report of this pack ever actually catching a hare. On this occasion, however, Kersey, Seymour and other members of the field felt we had a chance to outsmart the quarry. I cannot recall the details but we were able to work out that if we took a short cut into another field we could cut the hare off. To our surprise, we found ourselves standing in line with the hare running straight at us. The quarry was hotly pursued by the beagles and the rest of the field, including the Commander mounted on his hunter. Hares, of course, are proverbially swift and even the athletic Mike Kersey—College 1st XV fly half—failed with his flying tackle and the hare ran between the legs of another 'defender'. The result was another win for the hares. What we were not prepared for was the positive torrent of abuse from the Commander, for ruining the scent and causing the whole hunt to be called off.

As with the naval officers at Dartmouth, the civilian school teachers were mostly drawn from the cream of the teaching profession. Furthermore, they often made teaching at the College their lifetime career—in the tradition of *To Serve Them All Our Days*. It is hard to pick out only a few names. The Headmaster, Mr Kempson, commanded great respect and others had distinguished themselves in various fields. Mr Mark Sugden had been a rugby international and coached some of the teams. Another noted teacher was Mr (later Professor) Parkinson—who was to achieve world-wide acclaim for his splendid book, *Parkinson's Law*. Perhaps best known was my tutor, Mr C. H. Grenfell. CHG, as he was known, had taught French to decades of Cadets.

If we learned nothing else, everyone knew the little speech we had to make if we arrived late for his class: *'Monsieur, je regrette infiniment d'arriver si en retard. On m'a retenu malgré moi. Jamais je ne le ferai plus. J'ai fait tout le trajet à la course et je suis hors d'halène* (puff . . . puff). *Je n'en peux plus. Je ferai de mon mieux pour ratrapper le temps perdu'*—invariably followed by *'perduuu'* (nasal) *'perduuu'* . . . *'Asseyez-vous.'* Some two years after leaving Dartmouth, I was aboard the destroyer *Orwell* in the English Channel after the Normandy landings. We had a rendezvous with the Free-French destroyer *La Combattante*. But owing to an accident, involving two minor casualties who had to be put ashore at Newhaven, we arrived two hours late. The French Captain was owed some explanation. 'Leave this to me,' said my Captain Lt. Cdr. Hodges. 'It so happens I have a good command of French . . . Signalman, take down this message: "*Monsieur, je regrette . . .*"' In the event, the unfortunate non-French-speaking signalman became so bamboozled that the message had to be abandoned. This was just as well or, I am sure, the Frenchman would have concluded that the English were even crazier than he had always thought.

For the last Term of '42, with only ninety cadets still at Dartmouth and the remainder elsewhere, the teaching staff had to be split. Recruiting suitable teachers had already proved a problem, with so many young schoolmasters away at the war. Ever older teachers were recalled for service at the College. The oldest of these was Mr P. T. Harrison, who, I noted (from the pictorial biography of Mountbatten), had signed the Passing Out Report on 'Lord Louis' as his tutor in 1915. I do not know how old 'PTH' was. To us, he seemed incredibly ancient. But he was still a competent teacher of maths and greatly assisted me to come to terms with differential and integral calculus. He would sometimes pass a few minutes before starting the class to discuss some news item relating to the war. He might well remark, 'I remember young Cunningham well—he was a good boy.' It can be imagined how staggered we would be to realise that our teacher was speaking of the illustrious Commander-in-Chief, Mediterranean, soon to be made Viscount Cunningham of Hyndhope! With advancing age, PTH's voice had become a little slurred, but unhurried. If a distant aircraft was heard, he would ask with great deliberation, 'Do you conshider that to be the shound of the engine of a hoshtile aircraft?' The immediate reply would be, 'Yes Sir' . . . 'Very well. Clear the classroom.'

There were many other devoted staff, mostly naval pensioners, looking after the grounds, buildings etc, who had helped make the RNC the splendid place it was.

There were other aspects of leadership that inevitably brushed off on us. I was conscious of the commendable advice contained in Rudyard Kipling's memorable poem 'If'. I feel PTH calmly ordering, 'Clear the classhroom', instead of yelling, 'Run for your lives!' typified 'If you can keep your head when all about you are losing theirs . . . . ' Much later, it will be told how the author failed to live up to this in a moment of minor crisis, during the Suez operations. At least, on that occasion, it will be seen I was *trying* to follow Kipling's dictum! In my years of Naval Service I certainly had ample opportunity for trying ' . . . to walk with Kings—nor lose the common touch' as well as ' . . . to meet with Triumph and Disaster and treat those two imposters just the same'.

Other qualities instilled into us were Honour and Respect for Tradition—but not at the expense of innovation or initiative nor even a sense of humour ('Not another picture of the death of the Immortal Nelson!') The two incidents involving the author and the Commander represented occasions when, in this imperfect world, there was some loss of a sense of proportion.

I return to the second of my 'Standing Orders' quoted at the beginning of this chapter, about individuals not letting down their superiors. I suggest that Horatio Nelson would have been wasting his time with his famous signal before Trafalgar, 'England confides [expects] that every man will do his duty', if he was not aware that he had virtually achieved the ideal state I defined before he made his signal. In fact, Lieutenant (later Admiral) Pasco, who executed the signal, recorded that the original message was to be 'Nelson expects . . . ' and was changed because 'Nelson' would require more flags. Pasco also records that, contrary to popular belief, the word used was 'confides' rather than 'expects', in a usage uncommon today.

An improbable incident during my last year at Dartmouth has some bearing on this matter. In April 1942, for the first time ever, it was decided the RNC would enter a team in the Inter-Public Schools 7-a-Side Rugby Competition. Our side was drawn from such players from the previous (Christmas Term) rugger season with the squad completed by Mike Kersey and myself who had been in the previous season's Colt's team, both as reserves. However two star members of the last 1st XV were available, having just left Dartmouth and not yet joined their first ships. These were Uvedale Wood and the one-and-only Michael MccGwire as captain. Unfortunately, the odds were stacked against us as the Dartmouth Team was made up of sixteen-year-olds and just seventeens. On the other hand, most of our opponents were around a year older and this makes a big difference at ages when youths are still growing.

The nine of us were simply given return rail tickets and some money and told to get on with it. There was no coach or supervising officer or master. We made our own accommodation arrangements and I was kindly put up by Term-mate Mark Ross and his family, who lived at Hampstead.

The football proved a disaster. Our two star players, MccGwire and Wood, never even made the match, having taken a taxi which got lost between the West End and Richmond. The result was that Kersey and I, who had been hoping like hell we would not be needed—after seeing the size and power of the players in other matches—had to take to the field. We were thrashed. The arrangements, made on the hopeful assumption that our team would go through to the finals, were that we should spend three nights in London. This meant three nights of totally unsupervised living it up by a crowd of sixteen- and seventeen-year-olds, let loose in the metropolis. We took in restaurants, musicals, the Windmill Theatre, etc., with MccGwire leading the charge. We returned home penniless but it had all been tremendously stimulating for me—having known nothing of the Big City before.

In early 1942, although we did not stop to think about it, the war was close to being lost. The flood tides of Axis aggression in Europe and Japanese in the East were close to high water. Britain was emerging triumphantly from what Churchill called 'Her Finest Hour' but the tide had yet to turn. Back on the personal level, Mike MccGwire told me—fifty years later—that he still felt ashamed that he had 'let down' Mark Sugden, who had arranged the event, by failing to make the match.

Finally, there were my Term-mates and friends, made at Dartmouth. Lifelong friendships may have strange beginnings. They often start through individuals being thrown together in unfamiliar surroundings. Other people, despite much in common, could well remain acquaintances, rather than close friends, simply through having less close initial association. I believe this is particularly true of boarding school friendships. Those arriving at a school a year (or a Term) ahead of another group will initially be regarded as notionally superior, and the following intake as inferior. Those who arrive together will regard each others as peers.

In my case, I might easily have been a member of the preceding Dartmouth Term. For Dartmouth, eligibility was strictly governed by date of birth. I was born in Ceylon in the early morning of 1 August 1925—still 31 July in England. For my Term, the threshold was 1 August 1925. In other words, had my birth certificate shown my birthday as 31 July, rather than 1 August, I would have had to enter the previous Term—or not at all—and would not have made the same lifelong friends.

With forty newcomers more or less equally 'at sea' in their new environment at the College, it was inevitable I would get to know some of my contemporaries before others. I have already recounted my meeting with Joe Lungley, on the train. My next series of contacts would be those occupying neighbouring and nearby beds in the dormitory, individuals one naturally talked with, going to bed and getting up. The new-entry Cadets were located in beds in strict alphabetical order. Thus, with the name Seymour, I chanced to find myself placed between two of the leading lights of the term. These were Michael Ryland and Michael Vaughan. Ryland was to prove the unchallenged academic and intellectual leader of my contemporaries, and Vaughan became Chief Cadet Captain (and winner of the King's Dirk). Both became close friends and visited my home for many a half-day's leave, over the ensuing years. Michael Vaughan remains a close friend to this day. I attended his wedding and became godfather to his son David, now himself a Commander in Submarines and headed for Flag Rank. My association with Michael Ryland was sadly much shorter, but more on that anon.

Also close by, because of alphabetical proximity, were Mark Ross and Gavin Wemyss. I would not see much more of Ross, but in addition to staying with him whilst in London for the Sevens we were also partners in a 'bomb' of a car, whilst on our Sub Lieutenant courses in late '44. Another in our car syndicate was Oswald Cecil, with whom my friendship grew stronger over the years. 'Oz' retired from the Navy in the early eighties as Rear Admiral Sir Nigel Cecil KBE CB and, for a time, was Lieutenant Governor of the Isle of Man. Why he was not Sir Oswald, he has not told me. Gavin Wemyss remains one of my closest friends. He was, and is, unquestionably regarded as the No.1 'character' of the Term. Michael Kersey, another life-long friend, was my best man and godfather to my son. Another Term-mate of whom I saw little for many years but became very friendly with, when we were shipmates aboard HMS *Bulwark*, was George Freer. I was George's best man and our two families have kept in close touch since, with their daughters staying with us in Australia in recent years. We have enjoyed delightful and hilarious reunions in UK.

It was, of course, coincidence that so many of my friends were named Michael—Kersey, MccGwire, Ryland and Vaughan (all known as Mike except Ryland, who somehow remained Michael). With my wife also knowing one or two Michaels, it is hardly surprising that our son is Mike Seymour.

After our first term at Dartmouth, we split up amongst the five Houses of the College. This led to a further sifting of close associates. But of the nine of us who went to St Vincent House, I found my Term-mates included Mike Kersey, Joe Lungley and Gavin Wemyss. The four of us had already become close friends. The names of these will appear repeatedly in this narrative as we kept running across each other from Mombasa to Sydney.

Of the friends I have mentioned, Mike MccGwire was not of our Term, but of that two before ours. It will be recounted how, with most of my other friends, I would be thrown together with MccGwire, at various times, around the world during the next twenty years. Accordingly, I feel he should be included in the small 'band of brothers' covered in this narrative. I like to regard Mike as another of my lifelong friends—although MccGwire, as the archetypal extrovert, probably has more lifelong friends than anyone else I know.

Another outstanding personality, slightly senior to my Term, quite as audacious and even less conforming (other than in the ethos of non-conformity) than MccGwire, was one Joe Brooks. But as I only came to know him well some years later, I will introduce him properly anon.

CHAPTER 4

OFF TO WAR—JANUARY 1943

CHRISTMAS 1942 had been spent happily with my family. This comprised my father (retired from the Colonial Service, now a Sergeant in the Home Guard or 'Dad's Army'), my mother, my sister, and my brother, still at school. My sister June—hereafter referred to as MSJ—was in the Foreign Office, working for Naval Intelligence at Bletchley Park.

I awaited my first appointment. At Dartmouth, we had been allowed to name one other friend with whom we would like to serve. Michael Vaughan and I had coupled our names. Thereafter, one had no say as to preferred type of ship or station. In due course, I received the fateful telegram. I was appointed to HMS *Mayina*, with the accompanying cryptic instruction: 'Report to "J5P", King George V Dock, Glasgow at 0900 on 6 Jan, 1943.'

I had never heard of HMS *Mayina*. Aided by my father, I combed dictionaries and the *Encyclopaedia Britannica*, in a vain search for some clue to the significance of the name, which might identify this ship. I asked MSJ, in Naval Intelligence, about the *Mayina*. She could not help me—but I could hardly expect her to know the name of every ship in the Royal Navy. My next step was to phone my friend Vaughan. Yes, he also had been appointed to HMS *Mayina* and 'J5P'. Fortunately, his personal Intelligence Service was better than mine. He had probably simply phoned the Admiralty and asked. He was able to tell me that *Mayina* was the name of the Base at Mombasa, where the British Eastern Fleet was now located. 'J5P' was the code name of the ship that was to transport us there. So a few days later, my family farewelled me—off to fight, not the Germans, but the Japanese. They did not expect to see me back for two years, and then only if not drowned or captured. They were in for a surprise.

I packed all my gear—uniforms, blue and tropical, modest civilian clothing (one Harris tweed jacket and pair of grey flannel trousers), some navigational text books and minimal personal belongings. With a trunk and a suitcase I set off into the world.

After an overnight stop at my friend Vaughan's home (near Croydon, South London), where a farewell party was held, we were off on the overcrowded night train to Glasgow. We grabbed what sleep we could, sitting on suitcases in the carriage corridor. From Glasgow Central station, bleary-eyed, on a cold damp winter morning before sunrise, we took a taxi to King George V docks. We anticipated we would soon be aboard some great ocean liner, now a troopship, and about to sail for warmer climes—and adventure. In the docks, we spotted a number of large liners, some of which I recognised—*Stratheden, Nieuw Amsterdam, Capetown Castle* and others, painted a dull grey all over. Our excitement rose, wondering which of these would prove to be 'J5P'. Sadly, she turned out to be the smallest and least imposing of all the ships present—the SS *Antenor*, 10,000 tons, cargo-passenger steamer of the Blue Funnel line. Her normal passenger complement was about fifty. We learned that she was now to carry two thousand servicemen on a six-week voyage round the Cape of Good Hope to the Middle East. The two thousand comprised some two hundred Army officers, eighteen naval officers (including twelve Midshipmen of our Term from Dartmouth), two hundred naval ratings and the balance in Army other ranks. Our accommodation was very different from the luxury liners aboard which I had travelled around the world. We were six to a cabin, with our only washing facilities an old-fashioned tip-up basin for which (if we were lucky) someone brought an occasional can of hot water. Yet, by comparison with the lot of the 'troops', we were in luxury.

Having found our quarters, we asked a ship's officer when we would be sailing. 'Tomorrow?' 'Heavens no—in about two weeks.' 'In that case, can we go ashore again?' 'Certainly not!' 'Why not?' 'Security, of course,' and so it was to be. For most of the passengers, it would be three months without setting foot on dry land. They would suffer privations, perhaps worse than the convicts transported to Australia in the First Fleet.

After four days, one by one, the ships left their berths—down the River Clyde to the Tail of the Bank, off Greenock and Gourock, where the Firth of Clyde is several miles across. It was exciting to see the armada of ships assembled there. Our convoy of twenty-odd liners had the battleship *Malaya* assigned to escort us against German warships and 'commerce raiders'. There was the majestic *Queen Elizabeth*—the largest and fastest liner in the world. She and the *Queen Mary* would cross the Atlantic completely unescorted, relying solely on their speed (of 30 knots) for protection against submarines. In addition, there were other convoys arriving and departing. Another two weeks were to pass before we were ready to sail.

When the day came, we steamed down the Firth of Clyde and past the Isle of Arran. The convoy assumed its planned formation and a dozen escorting frigates and destroyers were deployed around us. The convoy rounded the Mull of Kintyre and headed due west into the open Atlantic. It was judged necessary to steam 600 nautical miles west before turning south, in order to give the U-Boats based on the French Biscay Ports as wide a berth as possible. Unfortunately, the convoy rounded the Mull of

Dominion Monarch. *Post-war—very different from war-time grey-giving glimpses of 50 feet of keel under bows in Force 10 Western Ocean gale.*

Kintyre into the teeth of a mid-winter North Atlantic Force 10 gale. It was soon evident that our planned convoy speed of 18 knots could not be sustained and had to be reduced to 10. I recall the awe with which I watched large ocean liners, like the *Dominion Monarch*, rear up until 50 feet of keel showed clear under the bow. Moments later, the bows would fall through 60 feet, until the sea was at hawse-pipe level. If this was what was happening to the big liners, it can be imagined what it was like aboard the little *Antenor*, struggling along at the same speed.

It is not my intention to dwell on hardship and suffering in this narrative. On the other hand, I feel I owe it to those less fortunate than myself aboard SS *Antenor* to record some of the misery they had to go through.

The sailors on passage were mostly young conscripts, at sea for the first time, as were nearly all the Army other ranks. For their accommodation, decks had been built into the holds and racks of three-tier bunks erected for the men to sleep in. Washing facilities and latrines were in makeshift wooden sheds in the well decks between the forecastle and the midships superstructure and between the latter and the poop, as were the galleys, or field kitchens, to feed nearly two thousand men. Unfortunately, driving into the 30-foot waves, *Antenor* was taking 'green seas' over the bow. This meant that the forward well deck was more or less continuously awash.

The cooks struggled valiantly to keep the galley fires going, but, for three days, the troops had to survive on little more than ship's biscuit, cold bully beef and a little hot cocoa. Practically everyone suffered miserably from seasickness. The two ends of the ship were heaving up and down through 40 or 50 feet in violent motion as the bows crashed down on succeeding waves. Towards the stern, there was also hideous vibration and noise, as the propellers 'raced' half out of the water. Nearly all the passenger officers were seasick—I was sick myself. I think this was the only time I actually succumbed to the malady during my naval career. I held out longer than any of the other Midshipmen, having spent more of my life at sea than any of my comrades. But by the third day, the all-pervading smell of wet seaboot stockings (of unscoured wool), and the inevitable stench of vomit, finally got to me.

Notwithstanding our own wretchedness, we Midshipmen felt we had a duty to go down to the sailors' mess deck, and do what we could to keep up their morale. Later, when the gale had blown itself out, we were allowed to get the sailors up in the sun and fresh air. We arranged an hour or so exercising and games on the boat-deck each day. I fear that little was—or could be—done for the soldiers but we felt our duty was to the sailors. I am certain our efforts, little though they were, were greatly appreciated by the ratings. I believe the soldiers might well have mutinied, had the men below decks had enough strength or spirit left to do other than 'hope death would come quickly'. As it was, the Senior Naval Officer on passage, a recalled retired Commander for whom, I fear, we Midshipmen had scant respect, went so far as to warn the ship's Captain of the possibility of mutiny. He suggested the posting of armed guards.

There was another activity for which we had very limited enthusiasm, I suspect, thought up by this same Commander. The theory was that our chances of being torpedoed might be reduced if a really good look-out was kept for submarine periscopes. Who should perform this duty? The Midshipmen of course! Accordingly, two of us had to stand watch, one on each side of the boat deck under the wing of the bridge. We were unsheltered from the gale, in the corner of the guard rail, in duffle coat and sea-boots with binoculars around our necks. As might be imagined, the visibility was such that there was no chance of spotting a periscope. In any case, the 30-foot waves made it impossible for any submarine to operate at periscope depth. We failed to see what good the binoculars were to us, especially at night. This activity was abandoned when there were no longer enough active Midshipmen to keep the watches.

Such were the first three days of hell, being our initial taste of 'seatime'. However, nothing goes on for ever. On the third day, the storm abated dramatically and the sun came out. Unfortunately, at this point, the old steam engines of the *Antenor* decided to break down. The ship lost speed until, one after the other, all ships astern of us overtook *Antenor*. Finally, the ship was stopped altogether, dead in the water, as the convoy disappeared over the horizon. Lying there motionless, in clear weather with a high column of smoke still coming out of the funnel, we were a sitting duck for any U-Boat within twenty miles. Mercifully, there was none—or this story would probably not have been written.

At this stage, our thoughts turned to the chances of survival, if we should be torpedoed. In theory, there was a place aboard at least a life raft for all on board. Mike Vaughan and I found that we were fortunate to have berths in one of the lifeboats. Whether or not there would be time to launch our, or any, lifeboat, we did not know. We also reflected that, with only half a dozen Deck Officers aboard the ship, there would be too few for one for each lifeboat. Mike, having passed out a few places ahead of me at Dartmouth, was senior to me. He could, therefore, well find he had his first Command after only a few days at sea, aged only seventeen. Under the circumstances, we felt the least we could do was uncover our lifeboat and check it out. We looked to see what stores and rations there were on board and what spars and sails or other means of propulsion. Where we thought we would be going from six hundred miles out in the Atlantic, did not occur to us.

Happily, this question did not arise. I had no idea why the engines had failed but was ready to cheer the engineers who, after two hours, somehow managed to coax some life out of them. A faint mechanical sound could be heard from below decks. Over the side, the ship was again seen to be moving through the water, albeit very slowly—a mere 3 knots for the first day. Furthermore, the ship had turned and was headed east once more, towards land. Gradually, more and more speed was achieved until, four days later, still wholly unescorted, we limped back round the Mull of Kintyre to safety. We had spent our first week at sea in the RN—one we would not forget but would also not wish to live through again. Hardships, however, are relative. Service was far tougher on Russian convoys, but perhaps those involved had got used to the idea that life at sea in wartime could be tough. We had been thrown in at the deep end—almost too literally.

The anchor was dropped at the Tail of the Bank around 1000 and the whole naval contingent—officers and men—were told they could have two weeks' leave. With commendable efficiency, railway warrants and ration books were issued and, within two hours, we were on the train to Glasgow. Sadly, for the soldiery, there was to be no leave—even to the pubs of Greenock. The authorities had concluded (probably rightly) that, once ashore, a great many of these unfortunate beings would not be seen again. I am happy to report that, to the best of my knowledge, all of the sailors came back.

That evening, Mike and I once again boarded the overnight train to London, but not before enjoying a luxurious hot bath—our first for weeks—at the Central Hotel, Glasgow. Next morning we took an equally relaxing shave, shampoo and manicure at Simpsons, Piccadilly (being what any self-respecting veteran back from the war should do—according to Vaughan). I returned to Torquay by rail and, unannounced, knocked on the door of my home, just over three weeks after stepping aboard 'J5P'. It seemed like three months.

TRYING AGAIN

There followed two weeks of enjoyable and wholly unexpected leave. We had no telegram to wait for this time, having simply been told to be back in two weeks' time. Accordingly, there was no speculative anticipation, nor related excitement; we knew exactly what was ahead of us but could, at least, ensure we had plenty of warm underclothes.

After the familiar journey—overnight at Vaughan's and night train to Glasgow—it was back to Greenock. We returned aboard *Antenor*, to the envious looks of the soldiers. The engines were repaired in under three weeks but the ship had to wait for the next Middle East convoy. Happily, much thought had been given, and action taken, to making life more bearable for all concerned should we encounter another Force 10 gale, which, mercifully, we did not.

The next convoy proved relatively uneventful. There were just as many large ocean liners, and the cruiser *Sussex* to escort us. No ships were lost, or even attacked by U-Boats. Whilst the voyage was uneventful for the convoy, we failed to notice that *Sussex* left us for two days. A German 'Ultra' signal had been intercepted and decrypted at Bletchley (MSJ may have been involved), giving a mid-ocean rendezvous for U-boats to refuel from a tanker sent there for this purpose. *Sussex* found and sank the latter—reported as having been located by Coastal Command aircraft. This had baffled those aboard *Sussex* as the weather had been such that Coastal Command would have been highly unlikely to have found anything.

It was, of course, essential not to let the Germans know the Allies were intercepting and decoding their secret messages. I only learnt of this incident in 1991, when entertaining, in Sydney, another old Term-mate, Paddy Langran (visiting from Canada—the old RN remains a good Club). Paddy was a Midshipman aboard *Sussex*. Strangely, our fathers had known each other back in Ceylon in the early twenties, before either of us were born.

This must have been one of the last large round-the-Cape convoys, as the Eighth Army had linked up with the Americans who had landed in French North Africa. The Afrika Corps was confined to Tunisia and the Mediterranean would soon be clear for shipping. Nevertheless the war was far from being won.

Strathaird *in company in ex-Glasgow convoy February 1943.*
The funnels had an air of mystique!

Our convoy was soon in tropical waters and steaming into the Sierra Leone River at Freetown for refuelling. Security was no longer a problem. It was unlikely there were any spies in Freetown and, even if there were, they could see and identify the ships that had entered port. Furthermore, no man in his right mind was going to jump ship in Freetown. Nevertheless, there was to be no shore leave and, frankly, there was very little to go ashore for—at least not for twenty thousand or more servicemen at a time.

As for the Midshipmen aboard *Antenor*, we longed for any break to the monotony of our life on board. Happily, we were able to do something different. We persuaded the Captain to allow us to take the ship's one powered lifeboat and cruise round looking at the other ships (the fast running tide made it impractical to sail one of the bulky ordinary lifeboats). To view the same ships that we had been gazing at for weeks, even if from closer quarters, does not sound like a big thrill. There was, however, one liner that had a particular fascination for us, namely the *Strathaird*. Why this ship? We had somehow learnt that, alone amongst all the troopships, *Strathaird* was carrying women passengers—some fifty 'Wrens' bound for the Eastern Fleet base at Mombasa. We could not claim we had not seen a girl for months, but still felt it would be nice to see some again—even from a distance. We made straight for the *Strathaird* and, sure enough, there was a handful of white-uniformed girls leaning over the guardrail high above us. We shouted greetings (which they could not hear) and waved furiously. To receive friendly waves back from these charming creatures made us feel good and that our afternoon had not been wasted.

There was a story I believe to be true which we were to hear a few weeks later, that was the talk of the *Strathaird* for some time. The ship was one of the earlier P & O 'Straths' and had three funnels. Only one of these actually served as a 'smoke stack', the other two being merely for effect. It was possible to go up the inside of the dummy funnels to platforms, from which aircraft lookouts could function. The story goes that one of the servicemen (from which Service is not stated) and one of the Wrens had formed a 'personal attachment'. In a ship with five thousand souls on board, finding a secluded spot for any amorous dalliance was almost impossible. Our Romeo thought he had the answer—the top of the dummy funnel. The couple found their way in and bolted the door behind them. Their privacy would now be assured—so they thought. Unbeknown to them, there was an intercom system with a loudspeaker on the bridge—doubtless for reporting attacking aircraft—and the microphone in the funnel had been left on. The amplified sounds coming out on the bridge may be left to the reader's imagination. I do not know whether any action was taken against the young lovers or whether they were even identified. Moralists may feel dismayed but it is difficult to envisage just what charge could have been brought against the pair. Suffice it to say that there were many 'cracks' referring to funnels, and those of the *Strathaird* retained an air of mystique and fascination.

The voyage continued without incident to Cape Town. We did not enter harbour but the convoy marked time for a few hours, while some escorting destroyers and frigates changed over or took on more fuel. The scene was the picture-postcard one of spectacular Table Bay, with the towering mass of Table Mountain behind the city of Cape Town. The weather was fine but there was a low swell—the tail of the 'Cape Rollers' which drive on inexorably round the Cape of Good Hope, the year round. This swell gave the ships of the convoy no more than a gentle lolling motion. Whilst waiting to move on, we were entertained to what I regarded as a splendid piece of showmanship. One of our new escorts was the destroyer *Racehorse*. She came out weaving through the troopships at 25 knots with her loud-hailer relaying the ship's signature tune—the Posthorn Gallop. Moving at that speed, the swell gave *Racehorse* a lilting motion. Certainly, to me, the general swashbuckling air was quite as impressive as it was intended to be.

On to Durban, still without incident. On our arrival, to our surprise, we found ourselves ordered to transfer to another troopship, the Dutch motorship *Christian Huygens*. In a strange way, we had become fond of the poor old *Antenor* but, by comparison, the *Christian Huygens* was truly a luxury liner. We did not rate cabins but had sleeping berths on camp beds in what had been the promenade deck dance floor. Folding doors opened each side to admit cooling breezes once we again approached the tropics.

Furthermore—we could hardly believe our luck—our fellow passengers included the detachment of Wrens from the *Strathaird*. Sadly the *Christian Huygens* was torpedoed and sunk a few months later but, fortunately for us, not on this voyage. It was only a week's voyage to Mombasa but one of unalloyed bliss. The food was far superior to that aboard *Antenor* and we soon struck up friendships with the Wrens, friendships we were to follow up once ashore at Mombasa. There were no dummy funnels on *Christian Huygens*.

We entered the beautiful harbour of Kilindini, the port of Mombasa, and were impressed by the sight of the Eastern Fleet, although decreased in size since its peak strength of the previous year. Present were the battleships *Resolution* and *Revenge* and three or four cruisers and armed merchant cruisers, as well as a number of smaller ships. Naturally, we wondered to which of these we would be appointed. We disembarked to the base barracks, HMS *Mayina*, itself. We were in the War Zone at last—so we thought—unaware that there were no Japanese within five thousand miles of us, and further from any fighting than we had been since the outbreak of war.

CHAPTER 5

EASTERN FLEET—MOMBASA—*REVENGE*

HAVING DISEMBARKED, we found ourselves housed in the pleasant officers'
quarters of *Mayina*. We were comfortable in our airy thatched huts
amongst palm trees and grassed areas, with colourful tropical hibiscus and
other exotic shrubs. The food was good, with unaccustomed fresh fruit,
served by Kikuyu servants who spoke no English. Accordingly there was
a rather strange procedure whereby the steward presented one with a
menu. After a selection of a course had been made by pointing to the
offering, the native placed his own finger on the chosen item and ran off
to the kitchen.

We expected to be directed to various ships of the fleet immediately.
When a few days went by with no instruction reaching us, our thoughts
turned to the newly arrived Wrens. My friend Vaughan was far more
worldly than myself, and so he made the plans. 'Ask some of the girls we
have met to come swimming with us.' The only bathing beach was some
miles away, so we would have to have a car. We soon found a garage
that had a few veteran American soft-top vehicles for hire, and asked if
we could have one for the day.

'I assume you have UK driving licences.'

'Well, not actually with us.'

'I tell you what—just go round to the police station, explain your
position and I'm sure the Inspector will fix you up with provisional
licences.'

At the station, after preliminary enquiries: 'I think I had better give
each of you a test. Here's an authority to hire the car. Come back in an
hour and we will do the tests.'

I admit that, by now, I definitely had cold feet. The fact was, I had
never even tried to drive a car before. There had been no opportunity at
Dartmouth and our family car had been laid up on bricks since the start
of the war. Mike Vaughan had somehow learnt the essentials of driving
and tried to assure me there was nothing to it. Thus, after fifteen minutes
briefing as to which pedal did what, etc., I found myself behind the wheel
of our hired car with an examiner beside me. Amazingly, I managed to
move away and navigated slowly round a block. My tester then said, 'Now
let me see you do a three-point-turn.' I could not imagine what this was
but somehow picked up what he wanted. Alas, at this point, I managed

to back the car into a ditch—from which it took about twenty minutes to extricate. This happened to be close to our starting point.

'I think that's enough. Let's see what your friend is like.'

Mike Vaughan climbed in with supreme confidence and completed the test with aplomb—even double-declutching.

'That's OK; you can have a licence—but I'm afraid your friend . . . '

So, we had one driver and a car. We soon had charming Wren partners and were off to the beach, where we had a pleasant afternoon.

Unfortunately, our subsequent socialising was somewhat curtailed. We were not allowed to take Wrens (as opposed to Wren Officers) to the Officers' Club. But, more importantly, we had little money for entertaining anyone.

In those days, Midshipmen were paid a mere five shillings a day (about ninety pounds a year). This had to cover monthly payments to Gieves (naval tailors) to whom naval officers' indebtedness steadily increased throughout their careers. Gieves did, however, generously waive outstanding accounts of all officers killed in action. One also had to pay a mess bill to supplement officer's fare over and above the Admiralty allowance to feed every sailor from Ordinary Seaman to Admiral. We also had our 'wine bill' to pay.

To put these sums of money into perspective, one may apply a concept our son told us he had learnt when studying economics, which he rather fancied at school. It is called MB Economics—the MB standing for 'Mars Bars'. It seems there has been no product over the last sixty years less changed in character, packaging, or real manufacturing cost, yet known the world over, than Mars Bars. Accordingly, it was most meaningful to value everything in terms of the number of Mars Bars it cost, at any given time. In 1939 in England 1 MB equalled 2d. Thus, the ice cream stolen by Kersey and Seymour together was about 1 MB. MccGwire's jeep was tens of thousand MB. A Midshipman's daily pay was about 30 MB. But his best uniform (@£50) cost some 6000 MB—nine months' worth of Mars Bars. Suffice it to say, most Midshipmen had little cash to spare. I was more fortunate than some, in having 'private means'—though not enough to make me a 'baron' (naval slang for anyone who had money 'to throw around'). My father had settled on me an allowance of £50 a year on becoming a Midshipman, until the age of twenty-one. The relative impact of this diminished with my rising pay and inflation. Nevertheless, to start with, my income was augmented by 6000 MB a year—or about 16 a day. It was not enough to pay my account with Gieves, but was a great help. I really have no idea how many of my comrades received any subsidy from their parents. It may be said that none were perceived to be wealthy and, unlike officers in the Brigade of Guards, a private income was not a necessity in the Navy.

Enough about money. Returning to our sojourn at *Mayina*, three weeks passed quickly and no one had told us to join a warship. Mike Vaughan and I called in at Naval Headquarters and simply asked what was to happen to us. We were then shown a list of three ships to which the twelve of us had been appointed. Vaughan and I, together with Term-mates Skene and Terrell, were to join the battleship HMS *Revenge*. It seemed that there had been an administrative oversight and no one had thought to tell us. In the light of these circumstances, the four of us hired a boat out to *Revenge*. We asked the Officer of the Watch (OWW) whether it would be all right if we joined. The answer was, 'I suppose so—but you had better make it snappy as the fleet sails tomorrow morning.' So, in quick time, we hurried back to our quarters, packed our gear, and by taxi and another hired boat repaired aboard *Revenge*, at 1630. At Dartmouth we had absorbed the proper protocol and procedure for joining our first ship. At 0900 sharp, one ascended the gangway and saluted the Quarterdeck and the OOW, reporting 'Midshipman Seymour—come aboard to join—Sir.' In the event, we found all the officers except the OOW off duty, mostly without shirts on and playing 'Deck Hockey' on the quarterdeck. In other words, no one was worried about protocol. A Midshipman was told to show us where to put our gear and where the Gunroom was located. We had taken up our first appointments at last and the fleet sailed next morning.

As complete rookies aboard this great ship, we had a fast learning curve to achieve. First of all, we had to find out where everything was and how to get from A to B. This was complicated by the fact that, under wartime damage control states, most watertight doors were clamped closed. It was often necessary, therefore, to go up one or more decks and down again to reach an adjoining compartment. There were our duties as Midshipman of the Watch at Sea to be learnt. We soon discovered that the most important of these was making mugs of cocoa for the more senior officers on the bridge during night watches. This was not as simple as it sounded, as I learnt a few months later *en route* to Durban. The OOW declared, 'Now, Seymour, I want my cocoa good and strong with plenty of sugar in it—I want to see the spoon stand up in it.'

Weakly, I replied, 'Sir, I'm afraid we have used up the sugar for the bridge and the Pussers [Supply Officers] won't issue any more for the present.'

'Don't tell me what the Pussers have said. I want my cocoa good and sweet—or there is no leave for you in Durban.'

Even more weakly, I said, 'Aye aye, Sir.'

So I had to go right down to the Captain's quarters at the stern and bribe the Captain's steward to slip me some of his master's sugar. One senior Lieutenant Commander decided that Midshipman Seymour might be of some use after all!

On the more serious side, we all had our appointed Action Stations and had to learn quickly what was expected of us. The training emphasis was all on night actions as this was where the RN was felt to have the 'edge' over the Japanese, who had proved the superiority of their carrier aircraft in daylight. My Night Action Station was as Searchlight Control Officer (SCO). I had two huge (44″ diameter) searchlights to control on each side of the ship. These were remote-controlled from the bridge and their operation did appear an exciting job. The procedure was: Radar picked up an enemy on an approximate relative bearing and the SCO peered through the (remote-control) searchlight sights fitted with powerful binoculars. As soon as he saw the enemy and centred the target on crosswires in his binoculars, he shouted out: 'Searchlight Target!' Meanwhile the Starshell Control Officer went through a similar procedure, as did the Main Armament Director (a central-control sighting system—for more information, see Appendix 2). 'Director Target. All guns follow Director.' Around would swing eight 15″ guns. 'Ready to open fire, Sir' . . . (from the Captain), 'Engage.' On would go two powerful searchlights, 4″ guns would illuminate the enemy with starshell, the Director Layer and Trainer would adjust their aim 'drawing a bead' on the target—perhaps ten miles away. All this would only take seconds, in an efficient ship. The Main Armament would open fire, hopefully before the enemy had realised he had been spotted. This was the pattern at the Battle of Matapan, in which three heavy Italian cruisers were blown out of the water. For this, Midshipman Prince Philip was 'Mentioned in Despatches' for the efficient performance of his duties as Searchlight Control Officer aboard HMS *Valiant*.

The foregoing gives some idea of the sort of training in which we were involved in our first few days aboard *Revenge*. It was all stimulating stuff— but only exercising. We just hoped we would be able to do our bit under action conditions—under fire ourselves. The fleet spent four days at sea, undergoing intensive training, the climax of which was the actual firing of our mighty 15″ guns. This was more dramatic than anything I had expected. All pictures in the Gunroom were taken down and glassware carefully stowed. When the guns fired, the whole 30,000 tons of solidly-built ship (with 12″ thick armour-plated sides) was shaken, as in an earthquake. The noise was deafening.

Five days later the ship was back in Mombasa and settling down again to the almost peacetime routine of sporting activities and socialising, including the usual Sunday night film show for the officers on the quarterdeck. For the Midshipmen, however, this did not mean a soft life. We had numerous ship's duties and daily instruction in gunnery, signals, navigation etc. Also, *Revenge* was an old ship—having actually fought at Jutland—and was far from comfortable. Midshipmen still slept in hammocks, unchanged since the days of Nelson's *Victory*. These could be

Midshipmen Vaughan and Seymour, aged 17, on quarterdeck of Revenge *at Mombasa, 1943.*

slung almost anywhere, and my billet was the after capstan engine flat—a dark and greasy machinery space three decks below the quarterdeck. I soon acquired a small stretcher camp bed in which I could sleep on deck.

All in all, it was a good life at Mombasa, infinitely preferable to the cold dank winter in the Firth of Clyde. Furthermore, the climate of Mombasa was more agreeable than that of Freetown, on the other side of Africa, about as far north of the equator as Mombasa was south. At the former, it had been unbearably hot and humid and, as I was to discover later, many buildings were damp and mouldy. The place appeared to me altogether depressing. Mombasa, on the other hand, usually enjoyed clear blue skies and fresh sea breezes. The Sierra Leone river was always a dirty muddy colour, whereas the port of Killindini, between the mainland and the Island of Mombasa, had cleansing tides running through, leaving relatively clear water. In fact, routinely at 1600, the order 'Hands to Bathe' would be 'piped' and five hundred or more officers and men would be over the side for a swim. Sharks were a notional hazard, but precautions comprised an armed Marine sentry with orders to open fire on any shark seen and a bugler to 'Sound the Retreat'. I have no recollection of a shark alarm.

Mombasa was generally a healthy place and the climate did not preclude vigorous sporting activities. Vaughan and I played several lively rugby matches for the *Revenge* at the Mombasa Sports Club. I also recall a gruelling cross country race, which I did not enjoy—but then, I do not think I enthused about cross country races held anywhere else.

Although Mombasa seemed a healthy and pleasant place, the fleet as a whole did suffer one epidemic of malaria although *Revenge* had relatively few cases. I believe the malaria was not of a particularly virulent strain. This was before the days of Mepacryn (Paladyn to the Americans) which, later on in SE Asia, rendered servicemen almost immune from the disease. Indeed, returned patients amongst the sailors swore that the illness was well worth catching. It was said that one only had to pay a small fee to an entrepreneur on board who kept a bottle of 'trained malaria mosquitoes'. One was then off to the hospital ship *Tjitchalenka* for a week of having a beautiful nurse placing her hand on your fevered brow. This was followed by two week's sick leave in Nairobi—reported to be like heaven on earth.

Mike Vaughan and I soon found we had something else to cheer us. After our first few weeks aboard *Revenge*, the cruiser HMS *Newcastle*, flying the flag of Rear Admiral Tennant, joined the fleet. This ship had formed the surface escort of yet one more Round-the-Cape troop convoy. Who should we find as Midshipmen on board but our old mates from Dartmouth, Mike Kersey, Gavin Wemyss, Joe Lungley and Mark Ross. We began to realise what a splendid world-wide Club we had joined, and that we could well meet up with some old friend or shipmate anywhere in the world.

The ship-visiting to renew friendships can be imagined. We had all only been separated for little over four months but it seemed much longer. One of these reunions proved rather more damaging to our healths—in the short term—than intended. Mike Vaughan and I had invited Gavin Wemyss to *Revenge* for our Sunday night quarterdeck movie. Our ship had HMAS *Napier* berthed alongside to utilise our more extensive sick bay and Medical Officers and staff—her crew being decimated by malaria. The officers from the Australian destroyer who had not succumbed were naturally welcomed aboard *Revenge* for the film. Most were entertained in the Wardroom before the show. The *Napier*'s one Midshipman, however, headed for the Gunroom (Junior Officers' Mess). As no one else stepped forward to welcome our Australian cousin, Vaughan and I took it upon ourselves to look after him. It turned out that this young man—admittedly a year or so older than us—had an unbelievable capacity for alcohol. Most young naval officers in those days drank to excess, but there was some curb on the amount we could buy, our monthly wine bills being limited to 10*s*. (At duty-free prices, this bought a great deal of liquor. Beer was relatively expensive at about 4*d*. a glass. Midshipmen were not permitted to buy 'spirits', i.e. whisky, brandy, rum or gin but, inexplicably, were allowed liqueurs. At 3*d*. or less, these were our favourite tipple. We were not connoisseurs of good French cognac—most Midshipmen did not mind what they drank, provided it was sufficiently alcoholic. The wine caterer was given a simple directive: 'See what liqueurs are cheap—put a match to them and, if they light, buy them.' So the bar was stocked with sloe gin, cherry brandy, and Van der Hum.)

On this particular night, through entertaining Wemyss and our new found Australian friend, we never actually got to see the film. By 2300, we had considerably reduced the bar's stock of liqueurs and, more importantly, had to admit that, although it was early in the month, both Vaughan's and my 10*s*. limits had been reached. At this point our Australian guest came out with a few well-chosen (but not pejorative) expletives. He declared, 'If

Revenge *as finally configured, but numerous 20mm Oerlikon AA guns and radar arrays not shown.*

you Pommies haven't any grog aboard your bloody ship, you'd better come aboard my bastard.' So we did, and made a bad error of judgement—but, by this time, our judgements were impaired anyway.

Four hours, half a dozen bottles of beer and several bottles of whisky later, Vaughan and I were back aboard *Revenge*. Wemyss had passed out an hour or so earlier, and an unfortunate boat's crew had been turned out to take him back to his ship. He had come-to enough to mumble '*Newcastle.*' Unfortunately, the Aussie coxswain had not heard of this newly arrived warship and spent over an hour combing the harbour and (adjoining) Reitz Bay, looking for a Union Castle liner. *Newcastle* was moored just two ships astern of *Revenge*—five minutes by boat. As for Vaughan and myself, we made a superhuman effort to pull ourselves together, walked gingerly across the gangway to our ship and, very deliberately, to the quarterdeck. Here we struggled to make some coherent statement to the OOW—so it would not be on record that we had returned drunk—a condition in which we certainly were. After making my way to the 'heads', where I was violently ill, I retired to my own little hidey hole—the after capstan engine flat. I hoped I would be quietly left to die, or at least remain for as long as possible that day (by now almost dawning). I had no one but myself to blame for the mother of all hangovers while I slowly recovered. But, recover I did—as did my friend Vaughan.

The only lasting effect on me was the belief that all Australians and particularly RAN officers were incredibly hard drinkers. This impression was reinforced by further encounters with HMAS *Napier*. The notion was to persist for years—so much so, that I was really worried, some years later, about volunteering for Exchange Service with the RAN. Would I be able to handle the drinking? Subsequently I learnt that *Napier* was exceptional in this respect. Someone once asked, 'Does the bar ever close in this ship?' to which the Aussie replied, 'Certainly—No.1 will not allow drinking at breakfast'!

I have to record that heavy drinking was not limited to Australian warships. Indeed, aboard *Revenge*, the Commander (Executive Officer) had quite a name in this respect. Cdr. St John-Cronyn RN was said personally to consume a bottle of gin a day, at sea or in harbour (many officers made it a rule not to drink when their ships were at sea). Our Commander was a short balding stout man, but there was no doubting his sharp intellect—which I never observed impaired by his intake of alcohol. I do not believe he really disliked Midshipmen but he delighted in exercising his vocabulary and invective on them when they displeased him. I would later incur his full wrath when I damaged one of the ship's beautifully-kept picket boats.

There was a story that the ship's previous Captain (our highly regarded Captain Middleton had joined shortly before us), who was a somewhat straight-laced officer, suspended the Commander's wine bill. This occurred when *Revenge* was last refitting in Durban. Such a suspension was unprecedented—rather like ordering the beating of a Cadet Captain. In the event, an interesting constitutional situation enabled St John-Cronyn to resolve the matter quite satisfactorily. A 'C' Class light cruiser was berthed alongside *Revenge*. Her Commander was an old friend of St J-C's. Accordingly, the latter exercised his prerogative, as President of the Wardroom mess of *Revenge*. He granted his old mate honorary membership of the mess and the Commander of the cruiser reciprocated. Thus they each had a wine account in the other's wardroom—and carried on drinking as before. It should not be supposed that Commander St John-Cronyn was not well thought of as a professional naval officer. He was later promoted to Captain and, immediately after the war, given command of HMS *Devonshire*—the Cadet Training cruiser—a very highly regarded appointment.

One other officer aboard *Revenge* should be mentioned, not because of any particular distinction attaching to him, but rather because of our attitudes, as Midshipmen, towards the man. This was our so-called 'Snotties' Nurse'—officer-in-charge of the Midshipmen. He was just thirty years old, and a Lieutenant on the point of promotion to Lieutenant Commander. He was not a particularly outstanding personality but we had no reason not to respect him. Nevertheless, we regarded him as a rather dreary individual. If this view was expressed, however, someone would always say something that at least implied, 'He is thirty and "over the hill". He has had his life.' This was an attitude of youth I felt it would be salutary for me to remember in future years.

CHAPTER 6

To South Africa

A MONTH LATER, *Revenge* had another week at sea, exercising with the rest of the fleet, with the new Midshipmen now feeling much more confident about their duties. Our third sailing from Mombasa was in company with our Flagship (and sistership) HMS *Resolution*—bound for Durban and a six-week refit.

The reader will have grasped that our lives and routines at Mombasa were remote from the war raging elsewhere in the world. Steaming south with *Resolution* seemed even more like a peacetime passage. The ships' companies did stand-to for time-honoured Dawn Action Stations each day—traditionally to ensure that warships were not caught napping as visibility increased with daybreak. In fact, no one seriously expected to find Japanese warships waiting to catch us off guard, nor did we anticipate surprising any enemy.

Indicative of the lack of wartime concerns, I remember the Captain asking to be called at the sighting of the first albatross. This was something I would look forward to when nearing the southern oceans in future years. Anyone who has seen these majestic creatures in their seemingly effortless soaring, dipping a wingtip to the waves, will be aware of the fascination there is in watching them. Nevertheless, it was a measure of our removal from the most awesome conflict the world had known that, steaming through the Mozambique Channel, the sighting of the first albatross should be uppermost in our minds.

On arrival in Durban, the two battleships were soon in Dockyard hands—with little work for the ship's companies, especially the Midshipmen. Everyone was granted two weeks' local leave, in addition to liberal routine shore leave, to enjoy the delights of Durban, which seemed untouched by war. There was no sign of the food rationing to which we had become accustomed in England, and other restrictions were minimal. A large number of the young men were away at the war (many having been captured at Tobruk). We, on the other hand, were in for six weeks of not even earned rest and recreation.

In Durban, we were hospitably entertained in the beautiful homes in the hillside suburb of the Berea. We enjoyed tennis, surfing, yachting, theatres, cinemas and a performance by the Durban Symphony Orchestra. This last was of Tchaikovsky's Piano Concerto in B Flat Minor and the tone poem 'Death and Transfiguration' by Richard Strauss, the first such concert I had ever attended. It made a lasting impression.

We had a chance to observe the politics of South Africa at that time. We saw little evidence of serious tensions, but soon realised that the country's racial problems were—and still are—far more complex than most outsiders imagine. The nature of the problems also differed widely between one province and another. I did my best to study the history of South Africa and something of the racial problems that beset the country. Suffice it to say that these were very much less evident in 1943 than they became in later years. I do not propose to discuss the politics of South Africa, then or today, thereby buying into heated arguments on issues outside the main theme of this book.

Returning to our carefree youthful days in 1943, the time came for Vaughan and me to take our two weeks' leave. Arrangements were in the capable hands of a splendid organisation called SAWAS (South African Women's Auxiliary Services) which matched servicemen's stated preferences with offers of hospitality. We decided to take up a kind offer to spend two weeks staying with a couple on a sugar plantation in Zululand. We were to be the guests of Mr and Mrs (Cliff) Currie, near the small town of Amatikulu. Native South African place names seemed to sound more musical than Aboriginal names in Australia—Gingindlovu, Empangeni, Umbogintwini, compared with Wagga Wagga, Mudgee, Yamba, Dapto. But perhaps I am being too selective.

We went by train from Durban across the historic Tugela River—said to have 'run with blood' during the Zulu Wars in the 1870s. It now formed the border of Zululand proper with the rest of Natal. We were soon disembarking at Amatikulu. Apart from the kindness of our hosts, the Curries, and the friendliness of their faithful Zulu houseboy, December, I principally recollect the relatively primitive life in this sugar-growing land. This did not mean that life was hard for the planters and settlers in the area. The pace was, not unnaturally, a little slower and less hectic than in the cities. Nevertheless, Zululand did have something of the air of the Mid-West of America at the turn of the century. In the whole of Zululand there was only ¼ mile of sealed road—the Main Street of Eshowe, the regional centre for the territory. Furthermore, many people still moved about on horseback. Such included Vaughan and Seymour.

We learnt that Amatikulu, a neat little town centred on its sugar mill, did not boast a pub. The nearest town that did was Gingindlovu—only eight miles away across country but nearly twenty round by road. Cliff Currie kindly provided us with mounts and we set off on horseback. As with most things, Vaughan was a better rider than myself, but, unlike my total incompetence with a car, I had been taught to ride as a boy, in Fiji, and felt quite happy in the saddle.

We had a most enjoyable outing to Gingindlovu, marred only by one sad event. In Zululand, we were wearing plain clothes for about the first time since leaving England. I therefore set out wearing my Harris tweed. It was a beautiful day but I realised I would be much too hot in this jacket, cantering along the tracks between the canefields of the undulating country. I had no saddle bag into which I could bundle my coat. Accordingly, I took it off and carefully hid it behind a bush, for collection on our ride home. Our arrival at Gingindlovu seemed like a fantasy. The township was in a dip between low hills and looked for all the world like a movie set from a Hollywood Western. There was the railway station and lines running, unfenced, alongside the one dusty street. We rode down this at a trot, until we came to the one pub with the splendid name of the Imperial Saloon. It had wooden slatted half swing doors and a hitching rail for the horses out front. To complete the illusion, at that moment a train went by and made the characteristic Western whistle call—a sort of deep throated 'Wrooo-Wroo-Wrooo'. After watering our horses, we entered the 'saloon', expecting to find a barman with curled moustache and traditional white apron round his waist. We were to be disappointed in this but not with the thirst-quenching pint of the ubiquitous 'Lion lager'.

Gingindlovu was a slightly larger town than Amatikulu and could claim to be called a railway town. Whilst not exactly the Crewe of Natal, it did boast the one and only junction in Zululand, connecting the Eshowe branch line to the main line, running north-east parallel to the coast to the sizeable town of Empangeni. Having seen all there was to see in Gingindlovu, we remounted and headed back to Amatikulu. Sadly (as the reader may have guessed), my Harris tweed had vanished. No doubt some Zulu long treasured it, although it would have been too hot to wear except in the highlands of Zululand, away from the coast. For me, alas, I had lost my scarcely worn and most-prized article of civilian attire—worth at least 1000 Mars Bars.

Our fortnight in Zululand was full of interest. The production of sugar was fascinating. In Australia and some other places, ripe canefields are burnt off leaving just the sugar-bearing canes to be harvested, mechanically these days. In Zululand, some cane was burnt off but, with adequate labour to do it, growers preferred to slash the cane by hand and cut off the trash. Evidently this left a higher sucrose content and provided fuel for firing the boilers that powered the sugar mill. On the Currie plantation, the cane was brought in, not in lorries or tractor-drawn hoppers, but by ox carts. Each cart could transport several tons of cane and was only fitted with old fashioned cart wheels, without pneumatic tyres and easily bogged when fully laden. For traction, however, two 'span' of oxen—sixteen beasts—were employed.

Such would pull almost anything, almost anywhere—but only if skilfully handled. The trick was to persuade all the animals to pull at the same time. In Australia, 'bullockies' knew, and still know, how to do this, no doubt as the result of careful training of their teams and judicious use of the stock whip. In the South African canefields an entirely different system was used and proved a marvel to watch. Each cart with team of oxen was managed by an old and experienced Zulu accompanied by a young boy of nine or ten. When the beasts were required to pull, the old fellow gave out a deep throated and rhythmic chant, at which the animals all plodded to the time he set. But when he sensed the oxen needed a spell, he would stop his chant and his young mate would take over with his own high-pitched song. All the animals knew that this meant they could take a rest and immediately stopped pulling—until the old boy started up again. Vaughan and I asked if we could have a go at this. One of us tried to mimic the deep throated rhythmic chant and the other the falsetto 'resting song' as required. I regret to say that the oxen were singularly unimpressed and would not budge an inch. Later, we studied every step of the processing of the cane through to the mill to the point of being raw sugar—white sugar but a little dirty—to be refined elsewhere.

We had considerable contact with the Zulus and picked up some elements of their language, but mostly only 'Kitchen Kaffir'. Such was used for giving instructions to December, e.g., *Ngey funa* (I want, or it is needed) *shissa manzi* (hot water—the Currie home had running cold, but not hot, water). There were some splendid onomatopoeic words. An aeroplane was an *ndizi-machini*. There were traps, however. Vaughan and I, out walking one day, were greeted by a Zulu, with what sounded like '*Okosahn.*' To this we replied, '*Okosahn* to you, old boy!'—only to receive a very sour look. It seems this greeting freely translated to 'Hail White Chief'. Evidently we should have said '*Salagahli*' or '*Hamagahli*' (according to whether the person spoken to was coming or going).

I was to be the house guest of the hospitable Curries when I returned to Durban two years later, but by then they had moved to near Empangeni. Meanwhile, we were to have one more week-end of leave before our ship left Durban. This time, we resolved to view some entirely different South African scenery. With more bravado than sense, we said, 'Why don't we go off and climb the highest mountain in South Africa [then thought to be Mont aux Sources, of nearly 11,000 feet]?' Just why such mountain should have a French name, we did not know. But this is just as reasonable as Australia's highest mountain, Kosciusko, being named by a Pole. Strangely, almost exactly fifty years later, in 1993, Vaughan and I would ascend Kosciusko and drink a toast in Australian wine to the memory of Count Strezlecki, the explorer who named the mountain.

The map showed our mountain to be near the border of the Orange Free State and that the rail-head was a little town named Bergville.

Accordingly, on the Friday, we bought overnight rail tickets to this place. Unfortunately, I developed violent toothache that evening and we had to delay our departure until the next day, after I had had the offending molar extracted. We really had no idea what our mountain was going to be like. We were not mountaineers, though regarding ourselves as reasonably fit. Neither had we imagined how cold it would be after Durban, which was only 7° outside the tropics. Next morning, we awoke to find the air outside below freezing and the great mass of the Drackensberg Mountains still thirty miles away, entirely covered with snow and ice. As a result, we booked ourselves into Bergville's one hotel. Here we were very comfortable, in front of a huge log fire quaffing pints of the celebrated Lion lager. Sadly, we got no closer to Mont aux Sources but judged it very beautiful to look at—from a distance. Always keen to see what there was to see, we looked around Bergville's dairy and cheese factory.

We felt we had had a remarkably pleasant stop-over in a friendly community and our week-end had not been wasted. As my wag of a friend, Gavin Wemyss, would have said (as one of his *bons mots*), 'All torpedoes missed astern—useful lessons were learnt.' We had seen the beauty and grandeur of the Drackensbergs in their winter glory, an experience not too many people have had—just as I have never gazed upon the Matterhorn, let alone Everest. Mountains were to retain a certain fascination for me, as will be recounted later. Now it was back to Durban, the Navy, our imminent departure, and the war, about which we had now become quite oblivious.

CHAPTER 7

Back to UK, Home and War

TO CAPE TOWN

With our refits almost finished and the ships fully painted, we realised we would soon be leaving. Whither, we did not know, but assumed it would be back to Mombasa.

One morning, we were surprised by the appearance of two more battleships—not of the Royal Navy, but of the French Fleet—of the *Lorraine* Class. These had been 'Vichy French' vessels but the port where they had been holed up had been reoccupied and they were rejoining the Allied team. To our eyes, they looked old and unimpressive; after two years of inactivity, they probably were far from ready for war. Nevertheless, they were of similar size and vintage (World War I) as *Resolution* and *Revenge*. I never heard what further part, if any, they played in the war. Our Captain made an enigmatic remark: 'Gentlemen, you will note that we have company!' This was not very profound, perhaps, but the appearance of two battleships anywhere had to have some significance—they might be about to reinforce the Eastern Fleet at Mombasa.

Shortly afterwards, *Resolution* and *Revenge* steamed past the Bluff, at the entrance to Durban's magnificent harbour, out into the Indian Ocean. At this point, however, the ships turned 'right', not 'left' (towards Mombasa). We wondered why—but not for long. The Captain announced we were now bound for Cape Town and thence to UK. A cheer went up throughout the ship, most of the ship's company having been away from home for far longer than the recently joined Midshipmen. Our voyage was to prove free of major drama but far from uneventful.

En route to Cape Town, we were to experience blue skies and light winds, but also those huge Cape rollers. These were waves forty feet high and four hundred feet long with their surface only faintly rippled by the gentle following breeze. I had seen something of these waves, coming round the Cape the other way, aboard *Antenor*. But now the size of the swell was greater than anything I was ever to witness in my naval career. The effect of this swell on a 30,000 ton battleship, moving in the same direction at nearly the same speed, was fascinating to watch. As the bow dipped into each wave, the water level would slowly rise up, up, up and up until the fo'c'sle disappeared under water. The sea closed over the bow, with only the top of the jackstaff support showing like the periscope of a submarine. Then, equally slowly, the bow would steadily rise. A thousand tons or more of water started to cascade over both sides of the fo'c'sle, while a massive wall of water broke over 'A' and 'B' Turrets. Even then, the bow would continue to rise until our fore-foot must have been almost visible, although the ship drew 30 feet. The motion of the vessel was so gentle that it could not have been in the least sea-sickness inducing. On the other hand, it became very hot and stuffy below decks forward as, of course, all ventilator inlets on the fo'c'sle had to be clamped firmly closed.

There were no other interesting sights before Cape Town except for several whales, dolphins, the beautiful albatross and other sea-birds. The two battleships had five days in Cape Town, with the crew enjoying more hospitality. I was personally entertained to dinner by one of the Province's winery families in a beautiful old Dutch Colonial homestead, nestling below Table Mountain. The officers and men spent nearly all their pay buying up food-stuffs to take home to their severely-rationed families in Britain.

Our ship was fully fuelled and provisioned for a long voyage. We took on an unexpected passenger, whom we were merely told was 'Mr Smith'. The 'word', however, was that this gentleman was an Italian spy being taken to UK for trial for espionage. He was certainly under guard, but not in a cell, and he did not look too worried. I never heard the full story or what became of the curious 'Mr Smith'. Of perhaps greater significance, the day before sailing, the ship loaded a prodigious quantity of gold—300 ingots in individual wooden boxes. Each was heavy enough to require two men to carry. Their value was said to be £3,000,000 sterling. I am unsure of the actual quantity or value, but in today's values, it would represent a very large sum perhaps as much as a billion Mars Bars! This gold was carefully stowed in one of the magazines. Extra padlocks were fitted and a Marine sentry posted outside. The floating Bank of England sailed next day.

TO THE CONGO AND FREETOWN

On clearing harbour, we had other ships in company; we were joined by two liners, both regarded by me as old friends. One was the *Dominion Monarch*, which I had watched with fascination as we headed into our North Atlantic gale, just seven months before. The other was the aging Union Steamship liner, *Aorangi*, aboard which, aged six, I had been a passenger across the Pacific from Fiji to Vancouver. Finally, as we were, once more, in the U-Boat infested waters of the Atlantic, we had an escort of eight destroyers.

We speculated in the Gunroom as to where our next port of call would be. Evidently this question had also caused some concern to the naval Staff. We knew that 'R' class battleships, designed to counter the German 'High Seas Fleet' in the North Sea in World War I, could not carry enough oil to steam from Cape Town to Freetown, non-stop. Furthermore, we would be expected to fuel our escorts at sea, *en route*. These battleships had originally reached the Indian Ocean via the Mediterranean, but this was still felt to be too hazardous a route back to UK. I was not very strong on geography, but could think of no deep-water harbour (to take a battleship drawing 30 feet) short of Freetown. Someone on the Staff doubtless asked, 'Why not the River Congo?' This question would be answered in due course. As usual, we were not told our next destination until after sailing. But, sure enough, we were bound for the River Congo for a rendezvous with a fleet oiler, for refuelling.

This leg of the voyage was pleasant and uneventful. The weather became hotter and we bade farewell to the albatross, but had flying fish to watch instead. One day, the sapphire blue of the ocean gave way to muddy coloured water and we were steaming into the wide mouth of the mighty river Congo. The banks near the entrance were ten miles apart. The two battleships alone went up-river (the first and last battleships ever to steam up the Congo). The two liners and the escorting destroyers remained at sea cruising back and forth for two days. We found the fleet oiler *Olna* waiting for us in the Congo.

Since leaving Mombasa, we had taken our orders from *Resolution* whose Captain was senior to ours and therefore assumed the acting rank of Commodore–commanding the Third Battle Squadron. (The term Battle Squadron would die soon after the war, with the passing of battleships.) Even the temporary posting as Commodore (theoretically equivalent to Brigadier) entitled an officer to carry the single broad gold stripe on his sleeve (or shoulder strap). He was treated as a Flag Officer and his ship wore the 'Broad Pendant' of a Commodore, at the masthead.

The 'Why-not-the-River-Congo?' question, rhetorical or not, was about to be answered. Midshipman Seymour was to be the first person to be disenchanted by this river. I had recently been put in charge of one of the ship's two beautiful 'picket boats'—35 foot sleek, enamelled and polished power boats—the pride and joy of the Commander. One, regrettably, was now headed for trouble.

As soon as the two battleships had anchored, my picket boat was hoisted out and sent over to *Resolution* for 'despatches'—a routine procedure on entering harbour. The trip to our Flagship and back was quickly completed and the mail-bag handed up the gangway. The next move was to secure my picket boat at the starboard 'lower boom'. Normally, this was a simple enough procedure and I felt I was quite competent at boatwork. We had handled motor boats at Dartmouth and I had taken charge of other craft at Mombasa. The ensuing mishap was no one's fault but mine. But I had not been previously entrusted with a picket boat of such size and power. Furthermore, the River Congo, with its swirling 8-knot current, was not the best place to get the hang of my new command. I cannot describe exactly what happened, mainly because I am unsure how it occurred, but the small 'bridge' of the craft, on top of the engine compartment, became snarled in the boat-rope leading forward from the boom. The boat was soon nearly side-on to the current, caught with this rope round the bridge and unable to move. The next moment, the whole bridge structure was torn off the boat, clean over my head and into the water. Fortunately, the engine controls and helm were still intact, although I was now standing on the smooth top of the engine compartment. I was able to manoeuvre the boat back to the boom and secure it properly this time. I had been very lucky not to have been carried overboard with the bridge structure, as the craft had been heeling heavily, but bobbed back violently when released by the departing bridge. I feel I must have stayed aboard by holding the wheel and ducking as the bridge coaming passed over my head.

Had I gone overboard, I would probably have drowned; I heard of similar drownings in the Sierra Leone river. The current would have carried me a mile or so down the river in a matter of minutes. No other boats had been hoisted out, no others being seen to be needed. The 'seaboat'—an oar-driven whaler—could have been lowered in a minute but would have been of little use in the fast flowing current. All the battleship's other boats had to be painstakingly hoisted out with the main derrick. This had a powered hoist and topping-lift, but needed sixty men to work the guys, so it took twenty minutes to hoist out each boat. There were no local boats of any sort in sight. In fact, there was no sign of civilisation whatsoever.

Back on the quarterdeck of *Revenge*, as might be imagined, I felt considerably relieved, after this alarming incident. Commander St John-Cronyn appeared. What did he say? 'Thank heavens you are all right—you did well to save yourself and the boat'? Not on your life—rather, 'Come here Snottie. Are you the fat bloody arse of an incompetent idiot who has just smashed up the picket boat?' (The more hurtful as I regarded myself as no fatter than the average second-row forward.) Happily, the sting would be taken out of any tirade from the Commander, no matter how strong his invective, as there was always the suggestion of a glint in his eye as he abused you—but you had to look him full in the face to see this. Fortunately, the shipwrights had the boat repaired by Freetown, our next port, where, regrettably, I was to have another mishap with this craft. This time, I incurred even more displeasure from the Commander, even though no damage befell the precious boat.

I will jump ahead and recount the story of the second unfortunate incident. As the anchor went down, on arrival in Freetown, my picket boat, crew and myself were, once again, being swung out and onto the water. We stowed away the heavy wire slings and I manoeuvred towards the port after gangway, to come alongside. In this, however, I was thwarted by the picket boat from *Resolution*, the Midshipman in charge of which made a dash past me, to get to the gangway first. As a result, my bows just clipped his stern. In any Court of Enquiry, I am sure I would have been cleared, under one of the basic 'International Rules for the Prevention of Collision at Sea': 'Overtaking vessel must keep clear'. No damage was done to either craft but, for so-called Pouncer Patrols (in case of midget submarine attack), both boats carried two full size depth charges (each with 500 lbs. of High Explosive) on the stern. The slight collision was just enough to knock one of these charges off the stern of the other boat, down into deep water almost under the stern of *Revenge*. It happened that Captain's rounds had been scheduled for that morning and a dozen officers, waiting for the Captain to appear, were watching the two boats from the quarterdeck guard rail. In a flash, they were all gone. I knew there was no danger, as the depth charges were not 'armed'—had no primer in them. But the miscellaneous officers on the quarterdeck did not know this.

Soon, my fault or not, I was standing in front of Commander St John-Cronyn receiving the full blast of his most powerful invective. There was, in fact, a serious aspect to this. Although the depth charge was theoretically safe, it was sitting somewhere on the bottom of Freetown Harbour and the water was too muddy and too deep and the current too strong to allow searching for it with divers. So, there it had to stay, where it could conceivably explode after a year or so if the explosive had become unstable, if some ship dropped an anchor on it. I imagine that it became the subject of a Notice to Mariners, with the time-honoured opening of 'Mariners are warned . . . ' At least, after over fifty years, I would like to think that 'my' depth charge no longer menaces anyone.

Returning to the matter of fuelling the battleships up the River Congo, a start was made by *Olna* making fast alongside *Resolution* and starting pumping. Unfortunately, within half an hour, the current proved too strong to hold the tanker alongside. All the lines holding her parted and the tanker broke loose. The operation was abandoned, and not even attempted with *Revenge*. Clearly, refuelling in the River Congo had not been a good idea. Nevertheless, the ships still had to be fuelled.

Next morning, both ships weighed anchor and returned to the open sea, where another system was tried. Both battleships again anchored, and our escorting destroyers prowled around for possible submarines (an anchored battleship in the open sea would make a perfect target). *Olna* then anchored ahead of *Resolution* and veered her cable until her stern was close ahead of the battleship's bow. Hawsers held stern to bow and oil hoses were passed across to the fo'c'sle of *Resolution*. This time, all went well and fuelling was completed in an hour.

It was now *Revenge*'s turn, but this operation was less successful. The same procedure was followed and more than half the required fuel pumped. But although our anchor held, that of the tanker dragged, until *Olna* was lying at right angles to *Revenge*—beam-on to the current. Within a minute, two steel wire ropes three inches thick had twanged like violin strings breaking, two four-inch thick manila hawsers parted and two oil fuel hoses under pressure burst. The fo'c'sle was deluged with thick black oil fuel. Several seamen and the boatswain were covered from head to foot and the Commander himself, in his white uniform, was spattered. Even St John-Cronyn's elaborate vocabulary of expletives was inadequate to express his feelings. By now, it was judged that we had enough fuel to get *Revenge*—and escorts—to Freetown. All ships weighed anchor, got under way and headed west. On arrival in Freetown, *Revenge* still looked as though the forward fifty feet of her topsides on both sides had been painted black.

Sadly, this was not to prove our last mishap concerning oil fuel before Freetown. We had to fuel escorting destroyers at sea. By 1943, the drill for this exercise had been well worked out and normally presented no problems. That was for ships with fully powered cranes to take the weight of the oil hose between the two ships. Aboard *Revenge*, we had to rely on our hated main derrick—with sixty men manning the guys. The first two escorts were fuelled successfully. On the next one, however, the oil hose-end being passed across was allowed to drop into the water and was dragged aft by the two ships, doing 12 knots. Unfortunately, there was a steadying-line from the hose-end to inboard on *Revenge*. As this thin rope ran out, it somehow snagged around the ankle of one of the seamen assisting the operation, dragging him to the guard rails. These prevented him from being pulled overboard. But, after agonising seconds, the poor man had his foot pulled right off his leg at the ankle before, mercifully, he passed out with the shock. I witnessed this accident from only fifteen feet away, on the deck above. This was distressing as it happened in slow-time but there was nothing I could do.

Into Freetown, with memories of *Antenor* (and *Strathaird*); but this time I was no longer a spectator passenger. We were allowed shore leave, but this only confirmed my suspicion that we had not missed much when we had not been given leave from *Antenor*. Throughout our stay, the weather was hot, humid and unpleasant and, on the day we went ashore, the rain bucketed down. Here we could find no mountains to gaze at, ox-carts to try driving, sugar mills or cheese factories to inspect, or Wrens to take to the beach—there did not even seem to be a beach. I think we got no further than the overcrowded Officers' Club and drank some tepid beer from glasses made out of cut down beer bottles. My shore-leave companion, as usual, was Mike Vaughan. Doubtless, today, he would tell me that my assessment of Freetown was unfair. This is because, many years later, he was to serve as Naval Attaché to Sierra Leone and Adviser for their fledgling Navy. But then, the impressions one can form of a place as an impecunious Midshipman, ashore for one day in the rainy season, could well be very different from the perspective of someone with the rank of Commander, air-conditioned office and full Diplomatic Corps privileges.

Our presence in Freetown gave rise to a naval occasion that seemed unremarkable at the time but, with hindsight, represented a unique event. In addition to *Resolution* and *Revenge*, in port was our sistership *Ramilles*, fresh from a refit in UK and looking very smart (in contrast to poor old *Revenge*, with sailors struggling to remove the black fuel oil from our fo'c'sle and topsides). Smart looking or not, this must have been the first and last time three proud battleships would honour the relatively unimportant port (or base) of Freetown. Also, it was almost certainly the only occasion during World War II, when as many as three 'R' Class battleships would be in harbour together. Of the original five, *Royal Oak* was torpedoed and sunk in Scapa Flow in the first weeks of the war and *Royal Sovereign* remained UK-based until 1943. The latter was then given a major refit before being handed over to the Russians and renamed *Archangelsk*. The Russians did not treat her well, as the ship was in a dreadful state when returned to Britain in 1950. This was a sad end to a warship bearing a name so illustrious in British naval history, notably as Vice Admiral Collingwood's ship, which became the Flagship in place of the *Victory* upon the death of Nelson at Trafalgar.

There would certainly be no future such meeting as *Resolution* and *Revenge* were to pay off and not be recommissioned for active service after our arrival in UK. *Ramilles* was headed briefly for the Indian Ocean and the Eastern Fleet, before returning to UK and Force D for bombarding Normandy.

TO GIBRALTAR

Before we left Freetown we took on some more unexpected passengers. These were the surviving CO, officers and crew of a U-boat recently sunk in the Atlantic and put ashore at Freetown. I believe there were four officers and a dozen crewmen. The latter were given a small mess of their own up forward and kept under guard. The officers were accommodated (in considerable comfort) in the Captain's quarters, right aft, complete with own galley, etc. Our Captain was content to use his sea cabin up on the bridge. The German officers were confined to their quarters and had a Royal Marine sentry posted outside. (The Marines were having a busy time—keeping an eye on 'Mr Smith', several million pounds worth of gold and now German naval POWs.) The passage given to these last would hardly be worth recording, if it was not for the contact my friend Vaughan had with them. Mike was one of the few of us who had studied German (as well as the obligatory French) whilst at Dartmouth—he was later to qualify as a German interpreter. (There must be something that I could do which Vaughan could not, before this book is finished. But he certainly was, and is, a 'man of many parts' although his superior ability to myself, in nearly everything, never harmed our friendship and I like to think we are as close friends today—fifty years on—as ever.)

Back aboard *Revenge* in 1943, Vaughan was delighted that we had some real live Germans on whom he could try out his language skills. Naturally, orders had been given that no one was to communicate with these enemy officers. Mike Vaughan was undeterred. He either evaded, or talked his way past, the RM sentry, and slipped into the Captain's quarters at night. Bringing chocolate and cigarettes, he soon had the Germans talking and was delighted to find he had no problem with the language. The U-Boat CO was particularly talkative and proved to be a die-hard Nazi, with a thoroughly Teutonic view on life. He did have a high regard for the Royal Navy and went on to say, 'Our nations should not be at war. You have the finest Navy and we the greatest Army—together we could conquer the world!' Vaughan would make some such remark as 'Quite so' and try some other subject.

In today's world, it seems improbable that a seventeen-year-old Midshipman should have the self-confidence to engage in unaccompanied conversation with a seasoned U-Boat Commander. On the other hand, the latter was probably only in his twenties, himself—yet still perhaps half as old again as the Midshipman. The truth was that young men grew up very rapidly in war, and time on active service was much more significant than age.

The passage to Gibraltar was uneventful and we parted company with the two troopships before our arrival. 'The Rock' had long been, and would remain, a popular port-of-call for RN warships. The ethnic Spanish populace (who, nevertheless, fiercely asserted their British citizenship) were lively people. The bars and night spots of the town, frequented by officers and ratings, made for a stimulating 'run ashore'. The local 'vino' was cheap and frenzied dancing by narrow-hipped men and black-frilled dressed women provided entertainment.

A happy feature of wartime Gibraltar was: no black-out. The base was within range of enemy aircraft but it was felt that concealment of The Rock was impossible with the Spanish coastline a blaze of light from

Algaceiras to La Linea. Throughout the war, there was only one minor air raid on Gibraltar—not by the Germans, but by Vichy French aircraft as a measure of retaliation for the British bombardment of their ships at Dakar in 1941. But times had changed. All of French North Africa was now in Allied hands, the invasion of Sicily was getting under way and Anglo-French animosities were (almost) forgotten.

Messrs Vaughan and Seymour joined in the general night-time revelry. Nevertheless, our natural curiosity led us to see what else we could learn about Gibraltar, when we had an afternoon off. I had visited the place ten years back, aged seven, as a passenger aboard an Orient liner headed for boarding school in England. Accordingly, I had some clear memories of The Rock—though not of the vino or the castanet-clacking dancers. For Vaughan, this was to be the first of many visits to the famous Naval Base.

We were curious to see what we could of the military defences of Gibraltar and assess their effectiveness—with the almost unbelievable presumption on the part of two seventeen-year-olds, whose knowledge of Army tactics, etc., was limited to our experience in the Dartmouth Special Service corps. Undaunted, we called at Fortress Headquarters and asked if we might be shown round the Defence Installations. The Deputy Fortress Adjutant was doubtless facing another afternoon of boredom (on the premise that the time was long past since any enemy could be expected to attack Gibraltar). Perhaps he was heartened that anyone at all from the Navy should show an interest in defence matters at The Rock and cheerfully agreed to show us around. I am not sure that we were much wiser about Gibraltar's defences by the end of the day. But we had a splendid conducted sightseeing tour, taking in the celebrated Rock apes and the North Face Galleries with the ancient naval cannons pointing across the isthmus towards La Linea. It was these fortifications that had enabled Admiral Rooke to withstand the siege and attacks on Gibraltar nearly two hundred years before.

We never saw any more modern weapons pointed towards Spain, whereas there were some formidable coastal defence batteries around Europa Point at the southern tip of The Rock, designed to command the Straits of Gibraltar. We suspected that, had anyone tried to attack the place from the landward side, it would have been another case of Singapore—with all the guns pointing the wrong way. Realistically, however, had the Germans (or any other foe) occupied Spain and the shores of Algaceiras Bay, Gibraltar would have been useless as a base, as the town and dockyard would have been within easy artillery range from all round the bay. Fortunately, this never occurred and Gibraltar remained a valuable naval base for the repair of warships and a jumping off point for Malta convoys. By mid 1943, the base was perhaps more valuable than ever—particularly from the Air Force viewpoint. From the Rooke

Galleries we were able to look down on feverish activities at the Air Base, with the runway already extended well into the bay. Planes of every sort were arriving and departing more or less continuously—doubtless staging towards the Sicily invasion operations.

BACK HOME

The two battleships, with escorts, sailed from Gibraltar on 6 September 1943, headed for UK and paying off. *En route*, we were alarmed by news reaching us of radio-controlled bombs which the Germans were launching from their long range Dornier 177 4-engined bombers. They had already made some successful attacks—from outside the range of anti-aircraft guns. Three days later we anchored off Gourock on the Clyde, whence we had left UK seven months back.

The gold was unloaded and our various 'passengers' were soon on their way. Within a few days and without waiting for the ship to pay off, the Midshipmen left the ship for the last time, for leave and reappointment. After one more overnight journey from Glasgow and on by rail to Torquay, I was home again. My family (other than my sister, who knew exactly where I was) had no indication that I was not still in the Indian Ocean. We could not even hint in letters as to where we were writing from, let alone where we were going (assuming we knew). There was no Services airmail—although we could send brief airgraphs (I believe they were called). I had written home from Durban and I find it hard to imagine that my letters would have failed to have indicated I was not at Mombasa. My parents may have guessed we were refitting in Durban. But if they had, I did not myself know where we were headed next. From Durban onwards, all letters were probably carried as mail aboard *Revenge*. I could have rung home from Greenock—and probably should have. But I could not resist the temptation, once more, to simply knock on the front door. Needless to say, my parents were delighted to see me and hear that I was now to have at least three weeks' leave.

Just twelve months back, I had still had one more Term to do at Dartmouth, yet to be bombed. It was less than eight months since I had last left home, for my second embarkation aboard SS *Antenor*. But, in that time, I had been nearly round Africa and back, and lived in another world. Now, recollections of Wrens at Mombasa, the 'flesh-pots' of Durban, primitive Zululand, beautiful Cape Town, the hated River Congo, Freetown and Gibraltar were but memories, soon to be overshadowed by new excitements. I still had not seen any action or a gun 'fired in anger'. But I was soon to do so—with a vengeance—before the year was out. Meanwhile, I had three weeks of wonderful leave to enjoy.

Enterprise

THERE HAD BEEN twelve Midshipmen in the Gunroom of *Revenge*: four 'Darts' from the Term before mine, two South Africans and one Indian Midshipman named Valladares, with whom we had become close friends. There had been a reservist named Lyons who had somehow enrolled in the Royal Indian Navy, having volunteered in India, where his father was serving with the Indian Army. Finally, there were the four of us who joined at Mombasa—Mark Terrell, Malcolm Skene, Mike Vaughan and myself. We had been a happy crew and were sorry to see the team break up. Nevertheless, our *Revenge* days were over and we knew not what lay ahead for us. But, for the moment, it was three weeks' leave.

My time at home, with my mother, father and—briefly—sister and brother, passed happily, but all too quickly. I took stock of how things had changed in eight months. In late summer of 1943, Torquay seemed a most attractive home-town. The hit-and-run air raids had long ceased. Bomb damage (along Tor Hill Road, at the top of the town, the great gap in the Palace Hotel, which had been used as a hospital for severely wounded RAF aircrew, the gas works on the road to Paignton and other spots) had all been tidied up so that Torquay looked almost its usual peacetime self. Food rationing was as severe as ever and there were very few private cars about—but taxis could be hired. The food shortage was eased by our garden being largely turned over to growing vegetables. Surplus produce of all sorts, including greenhouse tomatoes and cucumbers, could be given to friends or traded for a few eggs from people with chickens (the ration was one egg each a week). We also ate rabbit and good locally-caught fish. Missed, however, was tropical fruit; no one had seen a banana for four years.

People looked cheerful and one sensed we were winning the war at last. A new aspect was the increasing number of American servicemen—a reassuring sight, as we knew these were allies come to help us win the war. But inevitable social problems were starting to manifest themselves, with man-starved wives and girlfriends with menfolk away at the war. Now, there were large numbers of 'available' Yanks—'Over-paid Over-sexed and Over Here'. In reality, many, no doubt, badly missed their own sweethearts back home. My personal sensitivities were bruised when, on revisiting Dartmouth College, I found the place, not repaired, but the habitable part used as a barracks by a unit of the US Rangers. I suppose I could not expect these visitors to be conscious of the Royal Naval heritage enshrined in the RNC, even if badly damaged. But I was dismayed to hear a callow Lieutenant (Junior Grade), who had seen no active service, declare, 'Jeez—all I can say is this is a pretty goddam place to have as a Naval Academy.' Do not worry, gentle American reader—I do love Americans dearly.

I gained a clearer picture of the general progress of the war than we had been able (or had found time) to acquire amongst the 'fleshpots' of Durban, five thousand miles away. During our eight-month absence, the tide of war had markedly turned. The Afrika Corps had been driven out of North Africa and then Sicily. On 3 September 1943, exactly four years after Britain declared war, Allied forces set foot on mainland Europe with a landing at Reggio, on the 'toe' of Italy. Mussolini was a fugitive and a new Italian government, under their king and Marshal Badoglio, not only surrendered to the Allies but pledged Italy to fight for the Allied cause. As earnest of this, on 8 September their fleet made a dash from Genoa and Spezia to Malta. *En route*, one of their biggest and latest battleships, *Roma*, was hit and sunk by a new type of German radio-controlled bomb. This was the weapon that had, justifiably, alarmed us aboard *Revenge*. On land, the long and hard-fought campaign to drive the Germans out of Italy had begun. (On a personal note, during this campaign, my cousin, Douglas Seymour, was wounded leading a fighting patrol behind enemy lines but earned a Military Cross.)

In Russia, the Germans had been forced back from Stalingrad on the Volga and were now withdrawing to a new defence line, based on the Dneiper—giving up half the Russian territory they had occupied—after losing over 800,000 men killed on the Russian Front.

The British and US bombing offensive against German cities had reached an intensity of hitherto unheard-of proportions. One raid in late July saw over 2,000 tons of bombs dropped on Hamburg in three quarters of an hour, devastating eight square miles and killing 42,000 Germans. This exceeded the death-toll of the entire 'Blitz' on British cities.

On the oceans, where the Germans once looked like defeating Britain in the Battle of the Atlantic, U-Boat losses were running at nearly one a day. (The Germans started the war with a mere 56 submarines but had 760 sunk during the whole war.) In the war with Japan, most of New Guinea had been regained and the Americans were steadily rolling the invaders back from successive islands in the Western Pacific.

Naturally, as an eighteen-year-old with information limited to BBC news broadcasts, I was unaware of the full extent of the enemy's woes. However, as official bulletins were not given to minimising Allied successes, it was easy to believe that the war was nearly 'all over bar the shouting'. In reality, this was far from the case. The Wehrmacht—battered though it might be—was still the largest, toughest, most battle-hardened and best-equipped army in the world and showed every sign of fighting to the finish. The Battle of the Atlantic was not over. The Germans had developed a new type of submarine (the Type XXI) which, though conventionally propelled, had enormous battery power, giving short bursts of underwater speeds of over 20 knots. This was faster than the hunting escorts and certainly than the speed at which any surface ship could operate Asdics (Sonar). Before the war-end, the enemy built three even faster small submarines with propulsion using concentrated hydrogen peroxide (H_2O_2). Had the Germans been able to build more of these super U-Boats (especially the Type XXIs), before their army was defeated on land, they would have stood a good chance of winning the war—at sea.

The Germans were also pinning their hopes on new secret weapons ranging from the atom bomb—which they were racing to develop—to jet fighters, ram-jet medium-range missiles (V1s) and ballistic rockets (V2s). All of these except the atom bomb were in service, or ready, by the war end.

German civilian morale showed no sign of cracking under the awesome bombing by the Allied air forces, which were themselves sustaining heavy casualties in their onslaughts. Despite the unprecedented destruction at Hamburg, almost unbelievably, production from factories there was practically back to normal within three months. It is not altogether surprising, therefore, that the agony of the war in Europe would continue for another eighteen months. I had a final thought about the changing world scene—but on a relatively trivial plane. If our 'Mr Smith' from Cape Town really had been an Italian spy, what should be done with a secret agent of a country to which we were now allied?

Shortly after my leave, on 23 October, a minor operation ended in disaster for the Royal Navy. The new cruiser *Charybdis* with several destroyers attempted to intercept a reported west-bound blockade-runner amongst the (German-occupied) Channel Islands. In the ensuing engagement with destroyers from Brest the *Charybdis* was torpedoed and sunk. There was heavy loss of life but little effect on the war overall. It did, however, have a bearing on the next year of the life of the author. The destroyers of the German Navy had consistently fought with determination and valour, even though overpowered by superior RN forces in the second Battle of Narvik in 1941. There were to be several brushes between British ships from Plymouth and the two German flotillas now based on Brest. In one of these engagements a powerful Canadian Tribal Class destroyer was sunk. The RN developed a healthy respect for these Brest flotillas.

I soon learned that, together with ex-*Revenge* shipmates Terrell, Skene, Vaughan and our genial friend Lyons, my next ship was to be the light cruiser HMS *Enterprise*, to which we were to 'repair on board' at Dalmuir

West, Glasgow. The telegram, this time, told much more than that appointing me to HMS *Mayina*. Nevertheless, joining the ship had an element of '*déjà vu*'—train to London, overnight with Mike Vaughan and family, and night train to Glasgow, then on to Dalmuir West.

I already knew a good deal about the *Enterprise* and was soon to learn much more. She was not a new ship, but was ten years newer than *Revenge*. *Janes Fighting Ships* showed she had been laid down in 1919 but not completed until 1925. *Enterprise* and her similar but differently configured sistership, *Emerald*, although developed from the smaller and less powerful 'C' and 'D' light cruisers, were built to a radical design. They were the last cruisers in the RN to have their main-armament 6″ guns in open-shield mountings, as opposed to twin (and later, triple) turrets—much to the discomfort of guns' crews, on watch for long periods in cold weather. *Enterprise* did, however, have an experimental two-gun turret (prototype for the secondary armament 6″ turrets aboard *Nelson* and *Rodney*). This was on the fo'c'sle instead of the two-tier, single, open-shield 'A' and 'B' guns of *Emerald*. The rearrangement forward permitted a larger and more modern design of bridge. There were more guns than in earlier light cruisers—seven 6″ in all—six to a broadside, three single 4″ Anti-Aircraft (AA) guns and a number of new-type power-operated twin 20 mm Oerlikon close-range AA guns.

The main difference between these two ships and their 'D' Class forerunners was that their size was increased from 5,000 to 7,000 tons displacement, permitting not only extra guns but also further boilers and more powerful turbines. The main engines developed 70,000 shaft horse power (to propel a 7,000 ton ship) compared with only 40,000 in *Revenge* (of 30,000 tons of broad-beamed battleship, as opposed to the slender-lined cruiser). *Enterprise* and *Emerald* were the fastest cruisers proper (as opposed to the lightly-armed Manxman Class, so-called cruiser minelayers) the RN ever had. They were said to be capable of 33 knots, compared with *Revenge*'s lumbering 21. We were soon to learn that *Enterprise* was indeed very fast, but also that a 7,000 ton ship with 70,000 h.p. driving her at speeds in excess of 30 knots could be extremely uncomfortable to live aboard. This was especially true for the Midshipmen. From the scuttle (porthole) of the Gunroom the 'A Bracket' and starboard outer propeller were visible twelve feet under water. Another manifestation of *Enterprise*'s extra power and more boilers was a third funnel, just abaft the mainmast. The only other three-funnel cruisers in the RN were the stately County Class heavy cruisers, with three near identical funnels in a neat row. The two 'E' cruisers had a slender funnel abaft the foremast, a thicker one behind that and the third, another slender one, a long way back, abaft the mainmast. This configuration lacked any symmetry and one would have to call the ships 'ugly ducklings'. But speed and power were obviously more important than beauty.

HMS Enterprise, *as refitted and modernised in 1943. The principal modifications were: Fo'c'sle—previously terminating at after end of bridge—extended to abaft the two side-mounted 6″ guns, amidships. After two sets of torpedo tubes removed. New modern light-weight tripod masts, forward and aft. Latest AA Director, with Type 285 Radar, fitted—for control of the three 4″ AA guns. Numerous power-operated twin 20mm Oerlikon AA guns installed. Latest Surface and Air Warning Radar fitted. Fewer boats—more Carley Floats—carried.*

The ship had originally carried sixteen 21″ torpedoes, but these had been reduced to eight, in two quadruple torpedo tube mountings (one on each side). This reduction was later to prove a disappointment to me, in action as Torpedo Firing Officer. It had been necessary to reduce top-weight to permit new radar aerials mounted aloft on the two tripod masts. The ship was now fitted with the latest radar. Finally, it was exciting to find our ship carried a catapult-launched seaplane (an American Vought-Sikorsky 'Kingfisher'). For recovery there was an efficient crane—also useful for other purposes. This meant no more hated main derrick.

Enterprise was completing a major refit/modernisation when we joined her at Dalmuir West. If not the latest thing in cruisers, this ship was about to be handed back to the Navy in good shape. We had no idea for which fleet or even theatre of war we would be headed but, wherever, this cruiser clearly had great potential and we hoped would acquit herself well.

Even before commissioning and starting to 'work-up', we were told our duties. I was to assist the Torpedo Officer and my action station was to be on the bridge, under his orders.

In 1943, the Electrical Branch of the Navy had yet to be formed. The system was that the Engine-room Department was responsible for the generators (steam turbine or diesel). Power distribution and all electrical equipment was looked after by 'executive' (non technical) officers and seamen. Accordingly, at Dartmouth our instructors had tried to initiate us into the mysteries of ship's 'High Power' and 'Low Power' systems. In particular, there was a clever device called a 'Twin Ring Main Dynamo Fuse Release Switch'. I am not sure I was ever quite clear what this did—but one remembered it because it rolled off the tongue and sounded impressive. (It should be pointed out that the Gunnery Branch—always the great rivals of the Torpedomen—contrived to string together even more involved word-combinations, of which, I feel, the 'Latch-Retaining-Catch-Retaining-Breach-Mechanism-Lever-Housed' took the prize.) Seriously, however, the rapid wartime development of technology had already made the formation of a new technical Electrical Branch unavoidable. Nevertheless, for the moment, all clever new electrical equipment remained under the Torpedo Officer. Yet he was still expected to have the Seaman Officer's skills of navigation, ship-handling, signals, and executive command, in addition to the operational control of his main weapons—torpedoes.

For Midshipmen generally, our overall instruction was in the hands of the 'Snotties' Nurse'. In my case, the Torpedo Officer also felt he should do what he could to teach me about new electrical equipment. This officer—Lt. Foord (sic)—was older than most Lieutenants, having come up the hard way, from the lower deck. He was quiet-spoken and competent. He had already received one decoration for gallantry and I was to develop great respect for him. I recall his having the civilian representative of Metropolitan Vickers spend several hours trying to explain to me the intricacies of things called Metadynes—being the remote power units of our electrically operated twin Oerlikons. I did my level best to absorb these mysteries, but confess I only had a modest grasp of the equipment at the end. Not only was technology in ships leaping ahead at an unprecedented rate, but our 'engineering' training at Dartmouth—conducted by old pensioners—was generally of the pre-World War I era. Well do I recall wrinkled old blacksmiths shouting at us in their Devonian accents, 'Put 'n back in the fiere—'eat 'n up to a cherry-red 'eat.' I simply hoped that the ship had electrical artificers who understood the new technologies (which, happily, it had).

After a week of feverish activity by a host of shipyard technicians and other civilian workers, *Enterprise* was commissioned and left in the hands of the Royal Navy. Now it was up to us. I would later learn that, even in peacetime, with a full ship's company of regular personnel, working up a ship with a new crew is always a difficult time. It was much harder after four years of war, with so many experienced men lost, but ever more ships entering service. Four-fifths of the crew were 'Hostilities Only' conscripts, many going to sea for the first time. Even the experience amongst the officers was diluted and everything became harder as the cold and wet northern winter drew closer.

The birthpangs of the commission were as painful as could be expected.

There were inevitable teething troubles and many human errors, as we carried out trials and functioning tests in the Firth of Clyde, including a full-power trial over the 'measured mile' off the Isle of Arran. It was exhilarating, seeing the speed the ship could do, but the amount of vibration involved was alarming. There was one near mishap, at the end of a day's activities as the ship dropped anchor in the Holy Loch. A misunderstanding between the bridge and the engine room, with the fault at the bridge end, led to more and more astern speed being 'rung on' for the main engines, but the ship simply not losing ahead speed. The anchor cable ran out uncontrollably until the so-called bitter-end took the strain at the very end of the cable. Stopping the inertia of 7,000 tons of ship in this manner is not to be recommended—not to put too fine a point on it! The whole ship juddered, so that personnel below thought we had hit a rock. Fortunately, the cable did not break, nor was the bottom pulled out of the cable locker. Some heavy sighs of relief were heaved, but there were more tribulations to come.

In due course, we steamed out of the Firth of Clyde, round the Mull of Kintyre, into the open Atlantic (or Western Ocean, as old salts liked to call it). Happily, no Force 10 gale greeted us this time, but the sea was rougher than in the sheltered waters of the Firth. Accordingly there was widespread seasickness amongst our fresh young sailors. Naturally, though aged eighteen ourselves, we ex-*Revenge* Midshipmen with eight months seatime under the belt did not regard ourselves as rookies. We felt no seasickness—just that it was good to be at sea again. We knew we were headed for the main Home Fleet base of Scapa Flow in the Orkneys where we assumed we would soon meet many old friends.

Enterprise reached Scapa in early November for our work-up proper. There was a thrill in arriving at this base, steeped in the history of World War I, as well as the current conflict. We were greeted by the sight of many powerful warships. The Home Fleet was not facing the same degree of menace from German surface ships as had the Grand Fleet of World War I, looking out for the German High Seas Fleet and Admiral Hipper's battlecruisers. There were more than just the ghosts of the Great War adversaries. Beached near Lyness on the Island of Hoy was HMS *Iron Duke*, Admiral Jellicoe's flagship at Jutland. Pre-war, this fine old vessel had been used as a sea-going training ship and was to return to active service when the war broke out. Unfortunately, *en route* to Scapa Flow in the first days of the war, she was mined. Casualties were small and she was able to reach Scapa, but the ship's back was broken. For the rest of the war, *Iron Duke* lay in shallow water, visibly little damaged, and was used as an accommodation ship and for Fleet Base offices. Not far off, in a nearby inlet, afloat but completely upside down, was the German World War I battle-cruiser *Derfflinger*, the last of the surrendered ships of the High

Seas Fleet, scuttled in Scapa Flow and later salvaged for scrapping, but in this case still waiting to be towed away.

Returning to our war, as *Enterprise* steamed through the Boom Defence gate of Hoxa Sound we were to view much of the might of the RN of the time. Battleships included *King George V* (Flagship), *Duke of York* and *Rodney*—about to be joined by the most powerful French battleship still operational—the *Richelieu*—back in our team once again. (We had last heard of *Richelieu* in 1940, when her guns had repelled the attempted seizure of Vichy French-held Dakar, West Africa, hitting and damaging *Revenge*'s recent consort, *Resolution*.) The battlecruiser *Renown* (of Force 'H' fame) was there, an *Illustrious* Class fleet carrier and a dozen cruisers. Round the corner of the island of Flotta lay more than twenty destroyers, a number of depot ships and fleet auxiliaries.

Many of these ships would soon be taking part in the Normandy landings and, thereafter, the more important units would be headed for the Pacific. Nevertheless, there were enough major surface ships of the German fleet, either undamaged or potentially menacing, to require constant vigilance by the Home Fleet. The *Tirpitz* had been damaged by midget submarines in Alten Fjord two months earlier but the extent of her disablement was uncertain. What was known was how much effort—and the loss of *Hood*—it had cost to deal with her sistership, *Bismarck*. The battlecruiser *Scharnhorst*, the 'pocket battleship' *Scheer* and the heavy cruiser *Hipper* were still around and posing a serious threat to Russian convoys. Furthermore, several of these had shown the havoc they could cause if they cut loose in the Atlantic. Any one of them, intercepting the *Queen Mary* or the *Queen Elizabeth* could sink such a ship in a matter of minutes. This would also dispose of a whole US Army Division of 15,000 men. Within two months, the largest and most dangerous ship still operational, *Scharnhorst*, was sunk off North Cape by units of the Home Fleet. *Tirpitz* had been so damaged by the midget submarine attack and a carrier-born aircraft strike in April 1944 that she was never operational again, being finally sunk by RAF bombers in November 1944. The demise of the *Tirpitz* and *Scharnhorst* was to be after the departure of *Enterprise* from Scapa Flow.

JOE BROOKS

Leaving the strategic situation, it is time to look at the story of an individual once more. Earlier, it was mentioned that Joe Brooks would be introduced later as another example of a brilliant but non-conforming young man. Joe joined Dartmouth a year before I did but he was one of those whom everyone seemed to know—better, perhaps, than his elder brother Sam. The latter had a distinguished naval career, but was not the dashing eccentric, even rebel, Joe was. The younger Brooks was exceptionally fit and athletic, yet I do not recall his being outstanding in any of the College sports except sailing racing. This, of course, did not require exceptional physique. He was one of the few Cadets who had his own boat at Dartmouth—a 'National 12', being about the most racy and sophisticated of pre-war sailing dinghies.

He was always a brilliant dinghy sailor and later racing yachtsman. Nineteen years later, despite a severe physical handicap, he was to be the tactician/navigator of Britain's first post-war challenge for the America's Cup aboard *Sceptre* in 1958. Three years after that, shortly after I had left the Navy, I was privileged to find myself sailing with him aboard the 12 metre *Flica*, of which I was the 'sailmaster'. *Flica* was the pace-maker for Tony Boyden's subsequent challenge for the America's Cup. I had, however, sailed with Brooks a number of times whilst we were still serving and we had both specialised in the Torpedo/Anti Submarine Branch.

Regressing back to Joe's Midshipman's time, aged seventeen he was serving aboard the cruiser *Dorsetshire*, present at the final destruction of the *Bismarck*. Once the latter had gone down, there were hundreds of German survivors, including many injured, in the oily water. *Dorsetshire* was the principal ship involved in picking up survivors. So-called scrambling nets were placed over the side for survivors to clamber up. However, it was beyond the capability of many, particularly the wounded, to struggle up the 20 ft. ship's side of a County Class cruiser. In an action in character for Joe Brooks at the guardrail, without hesitation he flung off his jacket, leapt over the side and started saving drowning Germans.

No one had told him to—nor had they told him not to. Unfortunately, at this moment, a destroyer on the screen detected a submarine. A 10,000 ton cruiser lying stopped was a target a U-Boat commander would dream of—picking up German survivors or not. The Captain of the *Dorsetshire* at once decided he must abandon the recovery of *Bismarck* survivors and get under way. This resulted in there being only 96 survivors instead of 200 or more.

On the bridge of *Dorsetshire*, the scene can be imagined as the Captain was told Midshipman Brooks was over the side—just as he was about to order full power on all engines. A muttered oath, perhaps? Then the frightful dilemma—should this brave young Midshipman be simply abandoned to almost certain death by drowning or should the Captain place at risk his 10,000 ton ship and her crew of a thousand men for a moment longer than necessary? Happily for Brooks, the Captain delayed a minute or two, giving orders to get Brooks out of the water as quickly as possible. Joe rapidly heeded the shouted instructions and, because of his strength and agility, he was able to fight his way through dozens of Germans and was up the netting and over the high topsides in a flash. But he doubtless had a sense of remorse at abandoning to virtually certain death so many men he had just been struggling to rescue. *Dorsetshire* was quickly under way, gathering speed and zig-zagging. Much later, the U-Boat in question was identified. Her Commander had sighted the 'sitting duck' cruiser but could make no attack as the submarine was returning to base and had no torpedoes left. Such are the chances of war. For Joe Brooks, this was the first of at least four occasions on which he came close to drowning or other death in the water.

However, this was not the only aspect of the sinking of the *Bismarck* involving Joe. Amongst his many accomplishments, he was a competent sketcher and illustrator. Few photographs had been taken of the sinking of the *Bismarck* or of the picking up of survivors. Accordingly, despite the hypothermia no doubt caused by his time in the North Atlantic in winter, he went ahead and made several commendable sketches. He sent them to the *Illustrated London News*, in which they were printed—to the considerable annoyance of his Captain.

Within two years, Brooks—now a nineteen-year-old Sub Lieutenant—was to be in the news again. He had joined the group of midget submarines which had disabled the *Tirpitz*—temporarily altering the whole balance of naval power in Northern Europe. Of the six craft in that venture, only three managed to complete their attack and escape from Alten Fjord; two of the COs (both captured by the Germans) were awarded the Victoria Cross. Joe was not in that attack but took part in a similar sortie in Bergen Fjord, where a tanker was sunk. It took an exceptional type of young officer—aged just nineteen—to volunteer for this service. Joe was such.

Two further dramatic incidents occurring after the war will be reported later. These nearly cost Brooks his life. We shall also see a remarkable defiance of authority—which he managed to get away with. Suffice it to say RNC Dartmouth was turning out some remarkable young men in the early 1940s.

ENTERPRISE—SCAPA FLOW WORK-UP

Before returning to the story of HMS *Enterprise* herself, it is now appropriate to introduce some of the people on board. In a narrative of this nature, it is possible to mention only a few. Our Captain's name was Grant, a Canadian who was, or had recently been, the youngest 'Post Captain' in the Navy List, soon to prove himself a very fine officer. He held the respect of the whole ship's company. Yet even Captain Grant, who had not commanded as big a warship as a cruiser before, had a learning curve to negotiate. I imagine he was not pleased with himself over our Holy Loch anchoring mishap, whether or not it was he who had given the wrong orders to the engine-room. He would soon also realise that a mixed bag of young conscripts and officers of limited experience is not transformed overnight into an integrated team running like clockwork.

Our Executive Officer, the Commander, was also a fine man. But he was now past the age when he should normally have been expected to tackle the problems of turning *Enterprise* into a finely tuned fighting machine in short time. He had a full set of World War I medals—something we all respected and associated with aging officers recalled to the colours. Understandably, however, such were not usually possessed of the same fire and spirit as younger men. He must have been ten years older than our Captain. Nevertheless, there was no questioning his bravery and he was to be severely wounded in action, bombarding the forts of Cherbourg, before another year was out.

I have already described Lt. Foord, the Torpedo Officer, with whom I was to be closely involved. Naturally there were fewer officers than aboard the battleship we had come from. Many of these served with distinction but I had little association with them and so feel unqualified to write about them.

Our team in the Gunroom was, of course, also smaller than aboard *Revenge*. There were only eight Midshipmen—the five from *Revenge*, now the senior group, and three Special Entry Midshipmen fresh from Dartmouth. These were the same age as Skene, Terrell, Vaughan and myself, but eight months junior and, of course, an important eight months less experienced. Nevertheless, we were all regulars, except Lyons, whom we had come to regard as 'one of us'. There were, however, four Sub Lieutenants in the Gunroom: a Paymaster Sub Lieutenant named Feuerhert, whom we regarded as highly intellectual; the pilot and the observer of our seaplane; and THE Sub Lieutenant (executive and regular). He was the President of the Mess and a 'tin god' over the Midshipmen, if he chose to be—which he did. This young man had been a year ahead of us at Dartmouth where he had failed to impress as a fine upstanding individual. In the Gunroom of *Enterprise*, he appeared as an even less attractive personality. He left us in no doubt that he expected complete subservience from the Midshipmen. If any of us was seated in one of the three armchairs when the 'Sub' came in, we were expected to vacate this for him. He might even demand a magazine we were reading if he wanted it, or simply to underline the power he sought to exercise over our lives. In other words, we could not stand this petty tyrant and had no respect for him whatsoever. The reader will no doubt have detected that Dartmouth had done nothing to engender subservience, but rather had sought to convey the meaning of the word 'leadership'. Sadly, our bullying young overlord had failed to get the message. It was not altogether surprising that within a month I found myself in direct confrontation with this—my 'Superior Officer'—with the matter represented as insubordination and a serious breach of discipline. But this was for the future.

Of our two aircrew Sub Lieutenants, the observer was a large genial fellow who was prepared to take life as he found it. On the other hand, the pilot was an RNVR airman who took his aviation very seriously. One could almost say he lived to fly. In those days, there was always a certain antipathy between 'fly-boys' (Fleet Air Arm Officers) and 'fish-heads' (Executive, or Seaman, Officers). In this instance, I fear we were rather insensitive towards this somewhat introspective young man who, we felt, tended to take himself rather too seriously. This was quite unjust on our part as he was a very competent flyer and practice launchings and recoveries of the seaplane were always executed with impressive efficiency. This could not be said about too many of the evolutions we undertook in our work up. In winter in the Orkneys with only about seven hours of daylight each day it was hard to envisage the potential usefulness of our aircraft. But it had immense potential value for scouring the South Atlantic or Indian Ocean for blockade runners or armed merchant cruisers. Such a ship was the *Kormoran* which sank HMAS *Sydney* in December 1941. Secretly, I longed to go up in our plane but was never able to. In the event, because of altered plans for *Enterprise*, the seaplane never did have a useful role to perform—but this was in no way the fault of the pilot. The observer's name was Brooker and the pilot's, Chevalier—pronounced as in cavalier, not the French way as with Maurice.

Regarding the work up generally, *Enterprise* plodded ahead with gunnery practices—surface 'shoots' at towed battle practice targets and AA firings at 'drogues' towed by aircraft. The control of the 4″ AA guns was the special duty of our colleague Midshipman Lyons. We fired and recovered torpedoes, practised taking other ships in tow, etc. Whilst these activities were all worked through after a fashion, all sorts of things seemed to go wrong and many equipment malfunctions occurred. Our gunnery appeared unimpressive with very few hits on the target and few if any drogues shot down. Certainly, there seemed little in common with the highly efficient night action exercises we had taken part in with such enthusiasm in *Revenge*. The worst mishap occurred during one of our 6″ gunnery practices. Our one smart motor boat had accidentally been left 'swung out' (on its old-type swivelling davits) as opposed to being fully inboard and resting on crutches on deck. The result was that one of the 6″ guns fired so close to the motor-boat that the 'flash' from the gun blew the stern right off the boat.

By this time, the engine of our only other powered boat—the pinnace—was broken down and we had the greatest difficulty moving any persons from one ship to another in the Flow. There was a routine whereby a daily boat had to report to the flagship for despatches (recalling my misadventures doing just this up the River Congo). Aboard *Enterprise*, I had no gleaming picket boat to command, just the 'whaler' propelled by five oarsmen or sail. Accordingly, the Commander declared that Midshipman Seymour would proceed to the Flagship with the whaler. I got quite a kick out of sailing my boat gingerly up to the quarterdeck gangway of HMS *King George V*. This caused considerable astonishment amongst the senior officers pacing the deck above. I also recall paying a similar visit to HMS *Renown*—the RN's one surviving battle-cruiser (after the sinking of the *Hood* and *Repulse*). Unlike the other two, *Renown* had undergone major modernisation, along the lines of the treatment given to the battleships *Queen Elizabeth* and *Valiant*. But *Renown*, being larger, with two funnels, looked more impressive and had three twin 4.5″ turrets on each side (as opposed to the two on the battleships) although, as a battle cruiser, *Renown* had less armour-plate.

We did have occasional free days and some time for sporting activities. Shore leave for us at Scapa meant only a visit to the Officers' Club on Flotta, where one drank copious quantities of beer and had 'tea'—of which the main feature was boiled eggs. It will be recalled that on my last leave I had found the ration was one egg per person per week. In the Orkneys it seemed there were vast numbers of chickens laying huge quantities of eggs, but no means of distributing these to the egg-hungry mainland. Accordingly, it was routine to have four eggs each at a sitting for tea at the Officers' Club—but this novelty soon wore off. Also, with only one or two afternoons ashore and no social visits to other warships (because of lack of boats), I cannot recall meeting a single old comrade.

I remember only one sporting event ashore. I have mentioned that the Home Fleet was joined by the French battleship *Richelieu* which had been afforded a less than tumultuous welcome. We were still a little wary of Frenchmen who had remained loyal to Petain's Vichy France. *Richelieu* was a huge ship of 45,000 tons and a ship's company of over 1,500. Seemingly, the Frenchmen decided that a good way to 'break the ice' would be a friendly rugby match with a British warship. Did they challenge a ship of their own size, like the *K.G.V.* or the *Renown*? Not on your life! They looked round the fleet anchorage and picked out the smallest cruiser they could see—*Enterprise* of 7,000 tons with 500 crew—and issued us a challenge.

Once again, Mike Vaughan and I found ourselves representing our ship. The last occasion had been at the splendid Mombasa Sports Club. The venue now could not have been more different. To call the ground a rugby field was paying it an undeserved tribute. The ground sloped down from the two goal lines towards the centre line, of which little could be seen, as it was partly covered by a sizeable shallow lake. It never was going to be a 'friendly' match and proved a disaster—at least for Anglo-French relations. The ground was so muddy that no one's colours were distinguishable within five minutes and the situation was made worse by snow starting to fall by half time. There was never a chance of any serious tactical football and the match soon deteriorated into a general free-for-all, with scant attention paid to the ball. Nevertheless, we somehow struggled over the opponents' line and were awarded one try. Some fifteen minutes into the second half, with no score to the French, the light was fading and the snow falling more heavily than ever. Even the referee had now had enough, and blew the whistle for 'full time'. Both teams broke off the brawling and, battered, bruised and teeth chattering with cold, hurried off the field. Without so much as an attempted '*Monsieur, je regrette . . .* ' we sullenly made for the waiting 'drifters' (commandeered fishing boats) to get back aboard respective ships for a hot shower. Later, Vaughan and I reckoned we were entitled to a stiff drink to celebrate our 'thrashing' the Frenchmen—and from the mighty *Richelieu* at that. Nelson would have been proud of us—and England judged that we had 'done our duty'. This proved the only occasion in the war when I was engaged in hand-to-hand combat. It was a pity it had to be with allies! Fortunately, the Marquess of Queensbury's Rules—if not those of rugby football—had been generally adhered to and there were no serious injuries.

As for the French, I could imagine some of them concluding that it had been a mistake for them ever to have left tropical Dakar. This was where their ship had remained idle for most of the war (other than the brief interlude when their 15″ guns had repulsed the warships of Perfidious Albion in 1940). I have to say that any sense of superiority over the French on the football field I might have had was to be well and truly obliterated seven years later. The Destroyer Squadron team, in which I was playing, was comprehensively trounced by the battalion side of the *Chasseurs Para-troop* at Philippeville, Algeria. These were some of the toughest troops of the French army, in North Africa at the time. Do not worry, gentle Francophile reader—I have since come to love La Belle France and her people. Also—*Vive le Rugby!*

CHAPTER 9

ENTERPRISE OPERATIONAL—
READY OR NOT

IN THE EARLY SIXTIES, many years after the war and after my departure from the Navy, I listened to a wise man. His name was John Marsh, and he was the Principal of the UK Business Staff College, Henley, England. His point was that the only real way to learn management was to do some managing. His colourful analogy—which he did not claim as original—went, 'It has been said that you can read the entire works of Freud, but, sooner or later, you've got to go out with a girl.' With hindsight, I believe much the same is true for any fighting unit. I still have no wish to glorify war, but if there has to be fighting, it is best done with the most effective forces possible. Any unit, such as a warship, becomes effective most quickly through seeing some action. This was to be the case with *Enterprise*. It applied to the ship as a whole and to individuals, including the author. Experiences *en route* to Mombasa, in South Africa and back to UK had been mind-broadening and, with my contemporaries, I now regarded myself as a seasoned mariner. On the other hand, we had yet to see action. Until a man has been under fire, hearing enemy shells on their way towards him and half scared out of his mind, he is not an experienced serviceman. All this was to happen to us sooner than we expected—and I, for one, had not stopped to think what it might be like.

Meanwhile, at Scapa Flow the time allotted for our work-up had expired and the ship must now begin operational service. We knew that the ship was far from being a well-oiled fighting machine. No one had had a proper 'run ashore' for two months and the last few weeks had seen the almost constant cold, wet and misery of Scapa in winter. Tempers had frayed and morale in the ship was low. We had no idea where we were headed, but clearly it was away from Scapa—which was the only good news.

I never imagined that within a year I would enjoy being back there, and later, envious of other ships returning to Scapa Flow, while my ship remained patrolling the Straits of Dover. We had perceived that we were not joining the Home Fleet, as we had not exercised with the fleet. Furthermore, *Enterprise*, with her open gun-mountings and lack of special equipment, was unsuitable for Russian convoy escort duty in the Arctic.

We were also too small and lightly armed to fight any of the remaining German surface ships.

Once at sea, we were told our first port would be Plymouth. This raised morale as the ship was Devonport-manned and many of the crew were from the West Country. I was personally delighted as I would be within easy distance of my home at Torquay.

More of the general picture began to unfold. It seems it had been planned for *Enterprise* to work up and then join the Eastern Fleet, now shifting from its rear base at Mombasa to Trincomalee in Ceylon. But this was not to be our lot. It would have been pleasant enough, but we would have had another nine months far removed from the action of the war. This was the lot of our friends Lungley, Ross, Kersey and Wemyss who served out their Midshipmen's 'big ship' time aboard *Newcastle*. They were then reappointed to Eastern Fleet Destroyers for their four months' small-ship time before Sub Lieutenant courses in UK.

The reason for this change for *Enterprise* was that one cruiser had long been stationed at Plymouth. This was for the interception of blockade-runners (from Japan) and possible commerce-raiders (heavily armed merchant ships disguised as neutrals). The cruiser was also to back up the Plymouth destroyers against the Brest flotillas, if required. The ship given this role had been the ill-fated *Charybdis* which, as we have noted, had been sunk in the Channel Islands in late October, just when *Enterprise* was about to start her work-up at Scapa Flow. There had been no Plymouth cruiser for six weeks. Our ship was now to take on this duty—which was to prove a busy one for the next few months. Indeed, our new role looked like starting immediately.

Shortly after leaving Scapa, as we entered the Irish Sea, we felt the quickened throb of our powerful engines as the ship increased to full speed. We learnt that a Coastal Command aircraft had located a blockade-runner, or commerce-raider, approaching the Bay of Biscay and we were to intercept her. This meant reaching this ship before the Brest destroyers coming out to meet her. The German ships were nominally faster than us but, as we were much larger, we could maintain speed in heavier weather. The race was important as it had been tacitly accepted that if the destroyers from Brest reached our quarry first, they had 'won'. We should then keep out of the way and run for Plymouth, otherwise we stood every chance of suffering the same fate as *Charybdis*. In this opening game of the match, we appeared to be winning—about 'Forty-Thirty'—with a good chance of dealing with our prey before the destroyers got there.

Accordingly, all burners in the boilers were full on and, for the first time, the ship logged an average speed of 32 knots in a twenty-four hour period. But life was hell trying to snatch some sleep when off watch down aft. Meals in the Gunroom were reduced to the steward serving food that could be eaten by hand, as cutlery and crockery rattled off the dining table within seconds, even with the table-cloth laid over wet blankets. This existence persisted through the first night and following day. All the while, the approaching enemy ship, and the destroyers speeding to meet it, were plotted from aircraft sightings.

The surface ships, however, were not the only players in the game. Once within range of bombers, the RAF took a hand and their bombing attacks damaged and slowed the incoming vessel. Nevertheless, we still expected to rendezvous during the night and administer the *coup-de-grâce*. In the event, within three hours steaming of our planned interception point, the RAF informed us we need not bother—the ship had sunk as the result of their bombing. This outcome for us was an anti-climax but we high-tailed it towards Plymouth before we became entangled with the powerful destroyer force.

Enterprise steamed into Plymouth Sound the following afternoon. Everyone was tired and irritable but looking forward to some shore leave at last. As we approached harbour, something prompted me to commit my misdemeanour—or act of insubordination. On hearing the pipe 'Special Sea Dutymen close up, Cable Party muster on the fo'c'sle', I set off for my station for entering harbour—at the whaler on the port side abaft the bridge. I knew the whaler would be lowered with 'buoy-jumpers' to take the picking-up wire from the fo'c'sle to the buoy. I would then oversee the buoy-jumpers shackle on the ship's heavy anchor cable—a procedure I had performed many times at Scapa and which posed no particular problems.

In order to reach the whaler from the quarterdeck level, I had to ascend a ladder leading up to the fo'c'sle deck. When I reached this ladder, I found it blocked by my heartily-disliked Sub Lieutenant, carrying on a conversation with a seaman. I waited, for perhaps half a minute, with the Sub showing no sign of moving. Fed up, I decided I had had enough and might as well 'take the bull by the horns'. I called out, 'Are you going to move or not?—I haven't got from now till Christmas to get to my station.' My adversary was simply not used to, or prepared to stand, being spoken to like that by a Midshipman. He came back with, 'I'll take as long as I f . . . ing well like—go round and use the other gangway.'

'And, if I don't,' I said, 'will you charge me with insubordination?'

'Yes, that's just what I'll do. Either you use the other gangway or I'm running you in.'

I waited stolidly until His Lordship decided to move and then went on up to my station at the whaler. I realised I had been highly provocative but felt it was time for a show-down.

The ship entered harbour and, with the services of my whaler, secured to the buoy. An hour or so later, I had almost forgotten about my confrontation with the Sub. He had not. Upon meeting me in the Gunroom, he told me, in a matter-of-fact manner, 'I'm sorry, old boy, but your leave has been stopped indefinitely.'

I could hardly believe my ears. This punishment might be justified, but I knew that he had no authority to hand down such a penalty. I therefore asked, 'On whose orders?'

He replied, 'The Snotties' Nurse's of course—you can see him if you want to but it won't do you any good.'

Filled with righteous indignation—although I knew I was in the wrong—I declared I would see the Snotties' Nurse anyway.

I sensed that this had to be out of line with King's Regulations and Admiralty Instructions and/or the Naval Discipline Act. I was being convicted and punished, without the judge even hearing what the defendant had to say. My plan had been to rely on a plea of guilty of insubordination—in mitigating circumstances. These were that I had disobeyed an order that had nothing to do with the performance of the Sub Lieutenant's duty but was hindering the performance of mine. Also, as the order had been couched in obscene and offensive language I had not felt obliged to obey it. This might not have got me off the hook, but at least I was going to see to it that the Sub was also in strife. In defiant mood, I knocked on the door of the wardroom and told the steward to tell the Snotties' Nurse that Midshipman Seymour requested to see him. The former was having a drink at the bar and sent a curt message back that he did not wish to see me. As I could negotiate no further by messages passed via a wardroom steward, there was nothing more I could do—at least for the present.

After he had dined, the SN did consent to see me and hear my story. He gave me a lecture—which I took to heart—on the foolishness of petty quarrels when we might all be blown to bits tomorrow. My respect, previously low, for this man, rose markedly. He said, 'If you will apologise to the Sub for your disrespectful language, we will forget this incident.' This seemed fair enough, so I sought out the Sub and made a full apology. To my dismay, the latter (possibly sensing this was the first crack in the edifice of his authority) flatly refused to accept my apology. By now, I was tired, dispirited and sick of the whole deal. I told my mate Vaughan the full story and asked his advice. His unexpected answer was, 'All I can think of is to get drunk. I'll help you. We will do it together.' With the horrors of my 'hang-over' following our drinking bout aboard *Napier* at Mombasa a faded memory, this seemed as good an idea as any. I would soon regret this and swear that never again would I drown my sorrows, however grievous, in alcohol. (I was eighteen and four months.)

For the next few hours, Mike and I steadily worked our way through the gunroom liqueurs. For a time, the plan seemed to be working. My *angst* subsided and I found myself in an unnatural state of conviviality. Inevitably, I eventually started to feel unwell and simply wanted to go to bed. Then came my nemesis. Unbeknown to us, events were occurring outside the world of the Gunroom. Subsequently, I reflected that I could hardly expect a public warning: 'Midshipmen are advised not to get drunk this evening because they will be required for duty later.' Nevertheless, those at the top undoubtedly knew that things were happening and some hint would have been invaluable to me. Moored in Plymouth Sound on a stormy winter night, with no way of communicating with the enemy, there could be no security risk.

What we had not known was that, for two hours, we had had a fleet oiler tied up on our port side pumping oil fuel into our tanks at full pressure. We were already preparing for another sortie into the Bay of Biscay, only six hours after our arrival in harbour. To my utter dismay, at about 2300, the pipe was made: 'Special Sea Dutymen close up, Cable Party muster on the fo'c'sle.' With a sense of shock, I realised that this meant I had to man my whaler and get the ship unmoored from the buoy. I was not immediately galvanised into action and I staggered in the dark to the whaler's location. On arrival, I was distressed to find that my boat had just been lowered without me. I was now really worried. I might get away with being disrespectful to the Sub Lieutenant, but absence from my place of duty could end my naval career—or so I reckoned. The whaler had just reached the water but was still hooked onto the 'falls'. I felt I had to be in that boat at all costs. Without considering the danger— my cerebrations being well and truly dulled by alcohol—I climbed over the guard rail and leapt six feet in the near-total darkness. I had to grab one of the lifelines hanging from the wire pendant between the davits. I caught one, slithered down and landed in a crumpled heap in the stern sheets. This was just in time to hear the coxswain ordering, 'Bear off forward—give way together.'

That man was Leading Seaman Frampton, whose name I shall never forget. We had come to know each other well during our various whaler missions around Scapa Flow and had established bonds of mutual respect. He was able to see the state I was in but did not scorn me for it. For my part, I knew he was quite capable of taking charge of unshackling the cable from the buoy, with no help from me. But I sensed he somehow recognised the effort I had made to be in the boat at all. We were later able to laugh about the incident—strengthening the bonds of goodwill between one Midshipman and one Leading Seaman.

The ship was quickly un-moored, the whaler hoisted and *Enterprise* once again working up to full power as we steamed out of Plymouth Sound. Not rostered for Midshipman of the Watch that night, I was in my hammock by 0100 and 'out like a light' in minutes, the 70,000 h.p. engines notwithstanding. Not only had I been up late, on top of excessive consumption of alcohol, but I had had little sleep since leaving Scapa Flow three days before.

Needless to say, the RAF had found us another ship to intercept. I believe I would have had no difficulty sleeping the clock round—but such a luxury was out of the question at sea in wartime. In the event, I had just four and a half hours before being roused by the bugle call for Action Stations. 'Oh no!' I thought. Surely, I was not going to have to face my first action in the physical state I was now in. I cursed the Sub Lieutenant and would have signed a pledge of total abstinence, there and then, if offered the paper. I pulled on my reefer jacket and trousers over my flannel pyjamas, wrapped a scarf round my neck, donned seaboots and duffel coat and made for the bridge. It was still dark and there was no one shooting at us. It was just another routine Dawn Action Stations. But this was not the mere time-honoured ritual to which I had first been introduced aboard *Revenge* steaming down the Mozambique Channel. The growing light might reveal hitherto undetected Brest destroyers on the horizon—even with our efficient modern radar. Happily, it did not and, once it was light, Action Stations were stood down and I returned to the Gunroom for some breakfast—by hand. A few hours later, once again, the RAF told us we could go home now—they had sunk the ship anyway.

Next time we returned to Plymouth we did have a few days in port, even though still at our buoy in the Sound. For the first time in six weeks, shore leave was granted. Regrettably, discipline and morale were not of a high order and our libertymen got themselves into all sorts of trouble. There were many cases of drunkenness and disorderliness and some 'absent over leave'. At this point our Captain decided it was time for him to step in personally and get his ship's company into shape. He addressed the whole crew, declared he knew everyone had had a hard time since commissioning but such were the exigencies of war.

He promised he would do all he could to secure recreational and sporting facilities for the ship while we were in harbour. In the meanwhile, the ship had to smarten up and improve efficiency. The chances of survival of everyone depended on each man doing his job to the utmost of his ability. He would be fair but would stand for no more hooliganism ashore. Such would be dealt with, if repeated, with the utmost severity. Furthermore, if the ship's company were to perform well in action, everyone had to be physically fit. Accordingly, there would be Physical Training for all personnel, including officers, under the age of thirty-five for half an hour every morning. Some leadership was at last being exercised. None of this was resented by the men and almost overnight morale and efficiency improved out of sight.

As we were still on standby, with the ship remaining in the Sound, only short leave was granted. I now found myself as one of the Midshipmen taking my turn to run the pinnace, the engine of which was working once again. There was nothing very special about that except we had to cross the take-off and landing paths of the Sunderland flying boats of Coastal Command from Mount Batten at the entrance to the Hamoaze.

These were the aircraft which were finding the ships for us to hunt. But I had some anxious moments at night, wondering if there was time to cross the flare path before a circling flying boat came in to alight on the water. As the result of representations by the Midshipmen, and to encourage closer liaison between the two Services, some of us were invited to Mount Batten for short flights in the Sunderlands. This was the first time I had been up in any sort of aircraft and it was a big thrill. It has been said that the difference between looking at the view from a train and from an aircraft is that, from a train, you can lean out of a window. I was amazed to find one could actually lean out of the 'window' of a Sunderland. There was a large 3 feet long by 18 inch high port, wide open—for throwing out flares.

ACTION

Enterprise was at sea for another sweep within a few days. Once again, no enemy ships were encountered and the three days out were unremarkable except for Christmas Day 1943. We were in the Bay of Biscay, but already headed for home. The weather was fine for a change and the sea almost calm. I was Midshipman of the Watch in the afternoon and the whole scene appeared remarkably peaceful. One of the lookouts reported an aircraft on the starboard beam. The Officer of the Watch turned his binoculars in the direction indicated and made out a four-engined plane. 'That will be another Liberator,' he said. We had seen several during the day. 'Call him up, Signalman, and make "Happy Christmas".' 'Aye aye, Sir,' and his Aldis lamp started flashing. The plane turned towards us with an answering signal lamp blinking. Nobody was able to make out the message sent and within half a minute the aircraft was nearly overhead. In the last ten seconds of approach, however, the OOW suddenly realised this was not another Liberator but a German Focke-Wulf Condor. There was no question of a 1914 Christmas Day fraternisation. The alarm buzzers had crews swinging their guns round as quickly as possible as the order was given: 'Engage.' By the time the 4″ AA guns were aimed the plane was already out of range. A few rounds of 6″ were fired at the retreating plane, but quite ineffectually. No other aircraft were seen but a much more alert state of readiness was maintained thereafter. This incident was not significant, except for Mike Vaughan remarking to me, 'We can recall in future that we saw our very first gun "fired in anger" at sea on Christmas Day 1943.' Three days later we would see our guns blazing, almost continuously, for more than an hour.

After another quick turn round at Plymouth on the 26th, *Enterprise* was in the Bay of Biscay again on the 27th. This time, we felt certain we would intercept the incoming blockade-runner, being constantly shadowed by the RAF and reported to be well armed. The interception was expected at midnight, although, once again, we received reports that the ship had been damaged by bombing. Nevertheless, action stations were sounded at 2200 to prepare for the anticipated action. Once more, around 2300, we learnt that our quarry had sunk. Action stations were stood down but after five hours sleep we were at our quarters again for Dawn Action Stations. Well before dawn, we were able to see that we were now in company with another ship. The Captain explained that a night rendezvous had been arranged with the *Glasgow* which happened to be on passage from Gibraltar to UK. *Glasgow* was a larger and more heavily armed cruiser than *Enterprise*—with a main armament of twelve 6″ guns.

In a coded exchange by radio, the two captains decided that with two cruisers it was worth taking on the Brest flotillas. It seemed these were unaware the ship they were to meet had been sunk and they were still heading west. The exact strength of the enemy force was not known. In fact, it comprised five heavily armed destroyers—known to the RN as Narvik Class, as they had first been encountered in Narvik Fjord. Six more were so-called Elbing Class (for reasons I did not know, as all German destroyers merely had a letter and number designation). The Narviks had the heaviest guns ever fitted aboard destroyers. They were 5.9″—almost the same as the 6″ of *Glasgow* and *Enterprise* and were said to have a greater range than the old 6″ of our ship. The Narviks had five 5.9″ compared with the seven 6″ for *Enterprise* (six on a broadside, i.e., only six could be fired at a target on one side) and twelve 6″ for *Glasgow*. In other words, in terms of fire power the two cruisers had an effective total of eighteen 6″ guns against twenty-five 5.9″ aboard the five large destroyers alone. The Elbings, between them, had another twenty-four 4″ guns. Whilst it would take many hits with 4″ to knock out a cruiser, they could make a mess of a ship like *Enterprise*.

The chief menace of the Elbings lay in their torpedoes, of which they carried a total of forty-eight. If all were fired together at a single target, they could hardly fail to sink a cruiser (as in the case of *Charybdis*). The two cruisers, being bigger ships, made more stable gun platforms in the moderately rough seas. But this was offset by being larger individual targets and each cruiser could only engage one ship at a time. So other destroyers could shoot deliberately with no hostile fire disturbing them. It will be seen, therefore, that Captain Clarke of *Glasgow* and our own Captain had made a bold decision to throw down the gauntlet to these destroyers. This was also why *Enterprise* had not been game to tackle these ships until now.

After dawn broke, reconnaissance reports indicated that the enemy were still at least two hours steaming away. Action stations were therefore stood down but every possible preparation was made for impending action. Sub Lt. Chevalier was keen to hear if his seaplane would be wanted. He was told to have it fuelled up ready—only to be ordered to defuel it. Some hundred gallons of 100 octane fuel were judged too big a fire hazard and we were getting all the enemy reports we needed from Coastal Command.

The German destroyers were sighted shortly after midday. Battle ensigns were hoisted and all hands were at action stations. I do not know what the dispirited Chevalier decided to do. He probably took up a position where he could keep an eye on his precious plane and prayed that it would survive the day.

The author has no record of the track charts of the ships involved, only a general impression of what happened amid all the smoke and noise of the next two hours. The two cruisers manoeuvred independently and, for the most part, fought separate actions, although remaining within sight of each other. Likewise, the Narviks acted as one unit, battling it out with *Glasgow*, whilst *Enterprise* took on the six Elbings. We were still within 5 cables (half mile) and astern of *Glasgow* when she opened fire on the Narviks to starboard at 1355. I was impressed by her twelve-gun broadsides but could not see if she was hitting.

A few minutes later, my heart sank as I saw *Glasgow* receive a direct hit herself, at the after end of her bridge structure, on the top of the aircraft hangar starboard side. I had no idea what a hit with a 6″ (or 5.9″) shell would be like and was appalled by the explosion and accompanying smoke and flame. The damage appeared worse than it was because the ship, partially obscured by shells falling round her and the smoke from her own guns, appeared to be on fire. Thick black smoke was billowing from amidships. My immediate reaction was, 'If *Glasgow* can be knocked out as quickly as that, what hope is there for us?' Shortly afterwards, I was reassured to see that our consort was not on fire and the smoke was belching out of the fore funnel. I later learnt that one of the fanshafts for the forced draught for the forward boiler-room had been damaged, cutting the air pressure to the furnace. This briefly caused incomplete combustion of the oil fuel, with consequent making of thick black smoke.

My attention was distracted from *Glasgow* as our own ship was now in action, having opened fire on the Elbings on our port side. We soon had a hail of 4″ shells coming at us from the twenty-four guns of these ships. It was still long range for the 4″ and we were not being hit—but I wondered for how long. Through my binoculars, I could see our own shells sending up great spouts of water close to one of the destroyers but we had not scored any hits either. This exchange of fire seemed interminable and I confess to feeling terrified as I heard successive salvoes tearing the air on their way towards us. I took comfort from endless chain-smoking of cigarettes but could not resist the reflex action of ducking below the rail, with canvas screen dodger laced to it. This, of course, afforded no protection whatsoever. My impression was of all hell let loose. It can be imagined what it was like, being in action for the first time. The ship was juddering from our own guns, with attendant deafening noise, and thirty or forty high explosive shells a minute were bursting all around. I had not so much as a foxhole to take cover in. It was certainly an experience I have no wish to repeat. I was heartened by observing Lt. Foord who seemed to be watching all this mayhem with detachment. I assumed he had been through this sort of thing before and was, no doubt, calmly evaluating just when he would have the chance to use his precious torpedoes.

During all this time, with *Enterprise* under intense fire, the ship was weaving a tortuous course, as the Captain ordered the helm 'Hard-a-Starboard' and 'Hard-a-Port' alternately. With each turn under full rudder at 32 knots she would heel 15 degrees, as she was handled like a destroyer. The subsequent consensus was that the Captain's personal conning of the ship during this period was principally responsible for no direct hits being sustained. Certainly, our erratic course would have made the resolution of fire control problems by the enemy almost impossible. Our ship would be on a 45 degree different course when shells arrived compared to that when they were fired. On the other hand, the violent movement of the ship would have made it harder for our own Director Layer and Trainer to keep sights levelled on the target. It would also have been more difficult for individual guns to 'follow director', perhaps explaining why we were not scoring hits.

After perhaps fifteen minutes, the number of shells bursting around us appeared to have dropped dramatically. On peering through the smoke with my binoculars, I saw that the enemy destroyers had formed into line-ahead and were steaming at full speed almost directly towards us. This greatly reduced the number of their guns that could be brought to bear. I recall having vague thoughts about the time-honoured tactic—going back to Nelson's time—of 'crossing the enemy's T'. We were, in fact, doing just this—to our tactical advantage, in terms of gunnery. It took me longer to realise that the enemy was now making a formation torpedo attack on us, to give us the *Charybdis* treatment.

In theory, if the destroyers launched all their forty-eight torpedoes in a tight fan, it would be almost impossible for *Enterprise* to survive. Such attack had to be delivered at relatively close range or our ship would have time to turn away to 'comb the tracks'. At 32 knots, we would be beyond the 10,000 yard range of the 40 knot torpedoes before the latter caught their target up. Accordingly, the enemy probably intended pressing home their attack to 5,000 yards (two and a half nautical miles). This was a brave move, because that range would be almost point-blank for our 6″ guns.

In the event, the enemy failed to execute the manoeuvre efficiently. Their ships should have been on more of an intercept course, rather than steaming straight for us. The former would have increased the time they were at risk from our close-range gunfire, but in quarter-line they could have kept more of their own guns firing. Furthermore, when the moment came, they could have turned together, launching torpedoes simultaneously to achieve the maximum concentration. As it was, with all our 6″ guns firing as fast as the crews could load them, a hit was at last scored on the leading destroyer, right amidships. I was able to observe what looked like the fore funnel blown off and somersaulting through the air. This vessel was disabled and almost immediately stopped. Those following had to veer out of line to avoid the stricken ship and the formation attack was effectively broken up, the other five deciding to withdraw at high speed. I do not know whether or not any torpedoes were launched. If they were, none passed close enough for their tracks to be seen from *Enterprise*.

For the first time we were now clearly 'ahead on points'. The time had come for a knock-out. This was the moment Lt. Foord had been waiting for—perhaps through his whole naval career to date. The Captain asked, 'Do you think you can sink this ship with your "fish", Torps?' Foord gave an affirmative reply and advised how he would require the ship manoeuvred. (Torpedo tubes are not aimed like guns; the ship—or submarine—is turned and the weapon launched as the target comes into the torpedo sight.) The general rule is that if an enemy is judged to be a torpedo target, all available torpedoes should be fired, to ensure hitting. This was when we regretted the removal of a set of four tubes from each side of our ship. Foord felt certain he could guarantee hitting with two of the four of the port side torpedoes—on a stopped target, beam-on, only 6,000 yards away. He sensed that more torpedoes would be called for before the day was out. Accordingly, depth and other settings were ordered and reported checked through myself. *Enterprise* was duly turned (slowly, this time) to bring the target on to the sight, aimed abeam. 'Fire one . . . Fire two,' ordered Foord. I operated the firing switches to his commands; two torpedoes slipped out silently and were seen to be running and on their way. There followed an agonisingly long wait—in fact an anticipated four minutes.

Sadly, the calculated running time was well and truly expired and no explosion occurred. Whether both torpedoes had just missed or there had been a malfunction of the warhead firing system we will never know. For Lt. Foord, however, the failure was devastating—his quiet air of self assurance was replaced by one of utter dejection. The Captain was aware that his Torpedo Officer was a highly conscientious and reliable man. Whatever the reason for our failure to torpedo this ship, it was most unlikely to have been the result of any failing on the part of Foord. Fortunately, he was able to declare something to the effect of, 'Don't worry, Torps. We've got another one for you to tackle on the starboard side. We'll come back and deal with this one later.'

Glasgow had disabled one of the five Narviks she had been fighting and the other four had made off. This ship had been abandoned and had clearly taken a battering. Once more, arrangements were quickly made to launch torpedoes—from our starboard tubes.

Foord's faith in himself and his 'tin fish' was not shaken and he was determined to show that no more than two torpedoes were required. Everything was doubly checked and the torpedoes launched with the target precisely in the sights. There was another long wait, but this time there was a big explosion and a column of water in the air, followed by the crippled Narvik sinking stern-first. A look of quiet satisfaction spread over Foord's face with a word of congratulation from the Captain. I even had time to savour a moment of relief. Less than half an hour back, I could see little hope of *Enterprise* surviving the afternoon, although I had avoided thinking about the prospect of my ship being sunk. Now, one enemy ship had been destroyed, another was waiting to be sunk and the enemy was fleeing. Furthermore, a second Elbing had been disabled—whether by our guns or those of *Glasgow*, I do not know. The rest of the action was simply mopping up. We sank one of the Elbings by torpedo and *Glasgow* despatched the other by gunfire.

It was now nearly 1600 and night would soon be falling. Pursuit of the remaining destroyers was judged impractical. However, our two ships were not yet out of danger. We soon had half a dozen of the long-range four-engined Dorniers circling us. These were the planes that carried the deadly radio-controlled glider bombs. The official Naval War History records that aircraft supporting the German ships 'released glider bombs at the RN cruisers'. On the bridge, we saw no German aircraft until the late afternoon and when we did we were watching very closely for any sign of glider bombs—but saw none.* There was, however, one air attack, which may have occasioned the report.

---

* I was unaware of any such attack. But in 1992, Malcolm Skene told me that he saw (from his superior viewpoint to mine—the Air Defence Position) a glider bomb hit the water 500 yards astern of *Enterprise*.

The circling bombers were keeping their distance and we fired occasional ineffectual 6″ salvoes at them. As the light faded, however, we observed the rearmost plane break off and head towards us. Both ships let fly with every gun that would bear. It was soon evident that *Glasgow*, rather than our ship, was their target. There were AA shells bursting all round this plane and tracers from *Glasgow*'s pom-poms, but on it came. A stick of bombs was dropped but fell well short. Only then was the bomber identified not as a Dornier but as a Liberator—of the US Army Air Corps.

That was the last of the action and we were thankful to be shrouded by darkness and headed back to Plymouth. Brave men had died on both sides. The Germans had lost the destroyers Z 27, T 25 and T 26 with about 360 lives. *Glasgow* had five dead as the result of the hit I saw her take, which claimed the entire multiple pom-pom crew on top of the starboard hangar. *Glasgow* had been 'peppered' by shrapnel from near misses, particularly one near the starboard quarter, but no major damage was sustained. Aboard *Enterprise* we were fortunate, losing no lives. There had been a number of near misses with shell splinters coming aboard. One of these chanced to hit the firing mechanism of one of the 6″ guns, putting it out of action, but a happy Sub Lt. Chevalier was able to report that his beloved 'Kingfisher' seaplane appeared to be unscathed. One splinter had hit our brave young (fifteen-year-old) Royal Marine bugler in his backside, inflicting a nasty but not serious wound. This lad had sounded his bugle (into the PA System) for General Alarm to call hands to action stations. If still alive, like the writer, he would now be in his sixties—I would like to hope that he no longer has any discomfort sitting down. Our Commander also suffered an unpleasant but not serious head wound. *Enterprise* had more equipment failures through the ship being violently shaken by our own gunfire over a long period than were inflicted by the enemy. When we ceased firing we had only one 6″ gun still 'firing by director', the others only able to fire under 'local control'. It could be said that by the end of the day, *Enterprise* had shot her bolt but, for an old ship, lightly armed and lightly armoured, she had acquitted herself well.

Shortly after the Biscay action, word came that Captain Grant had been awarded the DSO. On hearing this, the whole ship's company mustered on deck to cheer our Captain as he crossed the gangway. This was for the commanding officer who had initiated stern disciplinary measures only a fortnight before. *Enterprise* was to see more action, bombarding shore positions after the Normandy landings.

Sadly I must report one discreditable performance aboard *Enterprise* in action—told me years later by a fellow Midshipman at the time, namely: 'Another incident you may recall was when the Sub [named] wanted to shoot up German survivors in the water—after spending the battle cowering behind his pom-poms, clutching his private parts.' I had not known this but it was in character for this man we so heartily disliked and in marked contrast to his Dartmouth contemporary, Joe Brooks, heroically leaping overboard to help rescue injured survivors of the *Bismarck*. I had naively believed that all the 'stinkers' we heard about in the war were on the other side. At least I never even heard of any other such stories by our people. Perhaps this man had suffered child abuse at an early age.

There were two minor—and improbable—sequels to the action that day. *Enterprise* was alongside in Devonport dockyard next evening, the 29th. The following day, I was home on leave at Torquay. My sister had leave from Bletchley (where she had followed the course of our action blow-by-blow) and on the 31st, as her younger brother, I found myself taking her to the New Year's Eve Ball at the Imperial Hotel, Torquay (as I had done exactly a year earlier, before setting off to join *Antenor*). This year we found a host of free-spending bemedalled officers of the US Army Air Corps. We were soon in conversation with a group of these airmen. One of them was recounting—without modesty—how he had been out bombing German destroyers as part of the action in the Bay of Biscay, three days back. I had to tell him I was there and ask if he was sure they were German destroyers he was bombing. He said, 'Well, I can't be sure of that. As we ran in the flak was so thick we had to just let the bombs go anyhow. My co-pilot said, "Jesus Cap'n, with flak like that, I guess those weren't German destroyers at all".' I said, 'I feel your co-pilot was right—let's have another drink.'

The other sequel occurred fifteen years later. On my last appointment in the Navy, I was teaching Anti-Submarine Warfare to Fleet Air Arm A/S aircrew at a naval air station in Northern Ireland. Sundry squadrons from NATO countries came for training. Amongst these were the 1st and 2nd *Unterseebootenjagstaffel*—German anti-submarine Gannet squadrons. Most of the officers were older than our aircrew and ex-Luftwaffe airmen—Iron Crosses and all. One, however, happened to be ex-Kriegsmarine. Noting that I had no 'wings' and was not an aviator, he asked me what warships I was aboard in the war. I was not keen to pursue this line of discussion but did answer his question.

'Ah ha.' he said. 'Were you aboard *Enterprise* in the Bay of Biscay in December 1943?'

I had to admit I was.

He continued, 'I was on one of the T destroyers. We tried to make a torpedo attack on you.' (They liked such discussions, as if talking about a friendly football match.)

'Yes, I was aware of that,' I replied.

'We never pressed home our attack. If we had, we would have sunk you.'

I could only say, 'I am very glad you did not,' and, with some of the few German words I had, putting on (I hoped) a disarming smile, '*Wünchen sie ein Gin, Herr Kapitän.*' I refrained from telling him that I had fired the torpedo that sank his Flotilla Leader.

Now, thirty-seven years on from the conversation reported above, I would like to feel my days are over, at last, of social contacts with people who had done their best to kill me—whether allies or enemies. Gin, with which to shut them up, is getting too expensive.

CHAPTER 10

ENTERPRISE 1944—OTHER ACTIVITIES

IT TOOK MOST OF JANUARY 1944 to make good the defects that had developed during our action in the Bay. There was a great deal of maintenance necessary in the engine room after the boilers and turbines had been flogged harder and longer in three weeks than those of *Revenge* would have been in a year. It was greatly to the credit of the Engine Room Department that no major break-downs had occurred. There was also much work to do to smarten up the ship above decks. With continuous steaming at full power, and the funnels constantly too hot to place a hand on, the spray had left them coated white with salt, and rust was appearing on upper deck fittings and the topsides. There was insufficient time for a complete paint-ship, but rust was scoured and painted with red-lead and a coat of the appropriate blue-grey for our camouflage scheme. The Midshipmen were kept busy with routine duties and catching up on our instruction, of which we had received none since Scapa.

We also had time to explore Plymouth and see, for the first time, the full extent of the destruction wrought by the Luftwaffe in 1941. Whole blocks of the main shopping area had been flattened. Indeed, when post-war reconstruction was undertaken, a totally new street plan was laid out. A poignant sight was one of the larger churches, St Anne's, which stood as a completely gutted shell. But a painted sign over the opening that had been the West Door bore the one Latin word RESURGAM. However, the broad grassed area between the city and the cliff top, overlooking the Sound, and the buildings fronting it appeared unmarked. This is still known as Plymouth Hoe and includes the legendary green on which Sir Francis Drake leisurely finished his game of bowls before boarding his ship to fight the Spanish Armada.

There was a great deal of interesting activity in Devonport Dockyard, which was working at full pressure fitting out and repairing all manner of warships. At the northern end of the yard, alongside each other, were *Revenge* and *Resolution*, paid off for the last time. These two old war-horses were no longer useful and the personnel who might have manned them were badly needed for new ships entering service every day. Out of nostalgia, I went aboard *Revenge* and up to the bridge, now totally neglected and grimy. I saw no point in conjuring up ghosts, such as my old Captain watching albatross in the Mozambique Channel. But I did have a moment of reminiscence, on looking in the Operations Room, which had been stripped of everything usable and was littered with rubbish. On one bulkhead was an operational state-board blackboard, on which was written in chalk, 'We are headed for Home. E.D.A. UK 9 September. Whacko!'

In due course, we were ready for sea again. We had no more forays into the Bay at high speed and saw no more of the Brest destroyers. We did make one voyage somewhat further afield—paying a visit to Horta on the Island of Fayal in the Azores, where the ship spent two days and two nights. I cannot remember being told why we went there, but believe it had some improbable connection with a meeting of Allied leaders in North Africa. It was, however, an experience I will never forget. The island with its lush sub-tropical vegetation was incredibly beautiful, in sharp contrast to the windswept, almost treeless Orkneys. The Azores were, and are, of course, Portuguese and therefore neutral territory. This was the first and only neutral port I visited during the war. In fact, apart from Latin America, there was precious little of the world still neutral—in Europe, there were only Sweden, Switzerland, Spain and Portugal. I am sure very few of the crew of *Enterprise* spent much time wondering what we were doing in this improbable harbour. It was only just big enough to take our ship at head-and-stern buoys. Everyone was simply prepared to enjoy our brief stay in this sub-tropical paradise.

Shore leave was granted to each watch (half the ship's company) over the two days in port. The little town must have been swamped by hundreds of sailors ashore each day and the various bars almost drunk dry. The local fortified wine, of the Madeira variety, was strong and free-flowing. There were few, if any, acts of hooliganism, but it must be admitted that many libertymen were the worse for wear on returning to the ship. Once again, the engine of the pinnace was out of action, and local craft were not forthcoming for moving several hundred men between ship and shore. Initially, the cutter under oars was used, but only a small number of sailors could be carried in the stern sheets. Then, when it came to trying to get the men back—mostly drunk—late at night, the cutter, with oars, proved impossible. The eventual solution was to rig long ropes from ship-to-boat-to-shore. The oarsmen were taken out of the boat and manned the line on shore. As many libertymen as possible would then be piled aboard and the cutter physically hauled across to the ship—an undignified and unedifying procedure, but effective.

Midshipmen Vaughan, Lyons and Seymour explored the place together and chanced upon a delightful small restaurant with the imposing name of the Café Internationale. Here, from the terrace, we could look down on the harbour and the bows of *Enterprise*, the clear blue water beyond, and across to the Island of Pico. The channel between the islands was five miles wide and only another five away was the summit of the magnificent mountain of the same name as the island—not surprisingly, Pico. This peak is 2351 m. (almost 7,000 ft.). The lower part was obscured by cloud and, far above where the eye looked for the summit, was the top 1,000 feet of the mountain—a magnificent sight. I believe the peak of Tenerife (of 3718 m.—on a rather larger island) has a similar appearance. The three of us dined well and sat late under the stars, sipping the local wine and, between us, solving all the problems of the world. The one purchase I made and brought back from the Azores was half a bunch of bananas—which proved a matter of wonder and delight at Torquay.

We were soon back at our mooring in Plymouth Sound, still at short notice for steam but not again to be called to speed off at full power into the Bay of Biscay. Henceforth, *Enterprise* would be occupied with quite different activities. The build-up for the opening of the 'Second Front'— the assault on Hitler's 'Fortress Europe'—was well under way. For all we knew, this operation could be launched at any time. The whole of south-west England was packed with hundreds of thousands of army person-nel—these were mostly American—and every harbour and inlet crowded with landing craft from 4,000 ton 'Landing Ships, Tank' (LST) down.

I could not know that eighteen months later I would find myself second in command of one of these large ships—some 10,000 miles away. It soon became clear that there was to be a role for *Enterprise* supporting the invasion of Europe. Naturally, we had no idea where the main landing would be made, or when. Not being privy to such code words as Operation Overlord, sailors generally had to find some term to use when discussing the forthcoming operation. Wartime servicemen tend to develop a rather macabre humour. The feeling was that even establishing a foothold on European soil was likely to be a most exacting undertaking with an assumed heavy loss of life. Accordingly, the operation we were preparing for became known simply as the 'Bloodbath'. Frequent usage of the word brought a familiarity which took away any harrowing overtones to the term. Each time we sailed at dead of night and found ourselves amongst a large armada of landing vessels and many other warships, men would ask each other, 'Do you reckon this is the Bloodbath—or just another exercise?'

Enterprise took part in several large-scale rehearsals. The practice land-ings would take place at Slapton Sands—a three-mile long beach only five miles from my 'starting point'—RN College, Dartmouth. At the southern end of the beach was a hamlet called Tor Cross, to which many Cadets used to make Sunday afternoon cycle expeditions for a 'Devonshire Cream Tea'. By 1944, the whole area, covering many square miles, was made a Prohibited Area for civilians. The exercises would involve pre-dawn land-ing of mine-clearance teams, heavy aerial strafing and bombardment by warships and rocket-firing landing craft—with live ammunition—and then landing some 40,000 men. Through binoculars from the bridge, we could see all the little lanes and woods we had known so well. It seemed terrible to be pouring so much high explosive into one of the loveliest stretches of the English coast.

However, we knew this was necessary. After the war the whole area was restored so that today the only evidence of the tremendous and fearful activities of early 1944 is a stone obelisk with a bronze plaque commemorating the invasion rehearsals. In general, the exercises appeared to proceed smoothly. However, on one of them, an audacious formation of German torpedo boats (*Schnellbooten* or simply E-Boats to the Allies) infiltrated the 'Invasion Fleet' at night and torpedoed two LSTs. In both cases one torpedo hit the bow and the other the stern—blowing both ends off, so that the ships sank very quickly—with the loss of 570 lives. This incident provided much food for thought. If the enemy could wreak this havoc, 100 miles from their base, what could they do close to their own shores, presumably swarming with E-boats? In the event, the German Coastal Forces did put up a hard fight—mainly countered by RN Coastal Forces, including the 30th MTB Flotilla which I was to join later at Ostend.

The four Midshipmen who had served together aboard *Revenge* and *Enterprise* would not be aboard the latter on D-Day. In mid-April, the time had come for us to be sent to destroyers for our four-month Midshipman's small ship time. We bade farewell to *Enterprise* at Plymouth and would not see her again.

CHAPTER II

ORWELL

UNLIKE FOR OUR PREVIOUS APPOINTMENTS, the ex-*Enterprise* Midshipmen now had a much clearer idea as to where we would be headed. We knew we would be split up and each would be sent to a destroyer. Furthermore, we had been told, we would be joining our new ships at Plymouth. The only destroyers we knew of at Plymouth were the Canadian 'Tribals'. These were powerful modern destroyers and I felt it would make a pleasant change to serve aboard a Canadian warship. Accordingly, during three more weeks' leave, my father helped me research (through *Encyclopaedia Britannica*) names of various Red Indian Tribes—Athebaskan, Haida, Huron, etc. In the event, this was of little value—other than briefly widening my knowledge of North American Indians.

In due course, I was appointed, not to a Canadian Tribal, but to HMS *Orwell*. The 17th ('O' Class) Flotilla had arrived in Plymouth during our absence. I was happy to find Mike Vaughan was joining *Offa*, of the same flotilla. But, as it turned out, I was to see little of him for the next four months as our ships were given different assignments. The magnificent 'J's and 'K's of Mountbatten's flotilla, the 'M's and half the 'N's (including HMAS *Napier*) had been laid down pre-war. They were armed with twin 4.7″ guns and beautifully fitted out, whereas the 'O's were very much 'wartime-austerity' destroyers. The Flotilla Leader, *Onslow*, together with *Offa*, *Oribi* and *Onslaught* had single 4.7″ mountings. But, for *Opportune*, *Obedient*, *Obdurate* and *Orwell*, the only guns that could be found were the short-barrelled 4″ dual-purpose, currently being fitted to anti-submarine frigates. These four ships were equipped for mine-laying, although I never heard of them actually laying mines—certainly, none were carried whilst I was in *Orwell*. All eight ships survived the war, one transferring to the Turkish Navy and three to Pakistan.

I soon discovered that anything these ships lacked in glamour was more than made up for in morale and fighting spirit. The 17th had escorted more Russian convoys than any other Home Fleet flotilla and, on one occasion, had had to tackle *Lutzow* and *Hipper* with no other support. The odds were far worse than those of the eleven destroyers from Brest against *Glasgow* and *Enterprise*. Furthermore, the 'O's could not simply run for home when they had had enough—they had a vulnerable convoy to defend. The occasion was, perhaps, the finest destroyer action of the war,

Scale model of the German cruiser Admiral Hipper—*a big Ask for four destroyers to tackle!*
(Model, Imperial War Museum.)

with Captain Sherbrooke commanding the flotilla from *Onslow*. In that action the puny collection of 4.7″ and 4″ guns of the destroyers posed little threat to the two heavily armoured ships and their 11″ and 8″ guns. Sherbrooke's one 'long suit' was the eight torpedoes aboard each ship. He knew, however, (and the Germans knew) that once these torpedoes were fired, his ships would represent no further menace to the big ships. Sherbrooke also knew that one hit from an 11″ or 8″ shell could put paid to any of his destroyers. The merchant ships, with their vital war cargoes for Russia, could be quickly disposed of, once the destroyers were out of the way.

Captain Sherbrooke's tactics were to make a series of feint torpedo attacks, at great risk to his ships as they ran in to close range. But, unlike our opponents in Biscay, his ships were resolutely and skilfully handled. As a result, none of the 'O's was seriously damaged but *Onslow* was hit, resulting in seventeen dead and twenty-three wounded, including Captain Sherbroke who lost one eye, but continued to exercise command. However, each time the Germans judged the destroyers were at torpedo firing range, they were compelled to turn away at high speed to avoid sixty-four possible torpedoes coming their way. Sherbrooke had ordered the ships of the convoy to disperse and flee at full speed.

Every lunge he made at the two heavy ships drove them further away from their would-be prey. There were losses on both sides. As part of the general action which was named the Battle of the Barents Sea, in addition to the damage and casualties aboard *Onslow*, the destroyer *Achates* was sunk with only eighty-one survivors, and the minesweeper *Bramble* with all hands. The Germans lost the destroyer *Friedrich Eckholdt* with all hands.

But, most importantly, the tactics employed were so successful that not a single merchant ship was lost. Sherbrooke was awarded the Victoria Cross for this action.

Most of the officers and men present that day were still aboard the destroyers two years later. For instance, our Gunnery Control Officer—a genial RNVR Lieutenant named 'Bertie' Binch—stoutly maintained that *Orwell* scored one hit with a 4″ on *Hipper*. If this were true, it probably scarcely dented the armour plate. Nevertheless, he told us that after the war—if *Hipper* was still afloat—a plaque in the engine-room would read 'Here entered one 4″ shell from HMS *Orwell*'! No one wished to dispute this claim—rather, people would say *Hipper* was lucky not to have been sunk by *Orwell*'s 4″ guns! Another intriguing little anecdote involving *Orwell* is given in Appendix 7 of this book.

Despite my immediate impression of a happy and efficient ship, I viewed the prospect of Russian convoys with very little enthusiasm. In fact, losses on summer convoys to Murmansk—with long arctic days of exposure to enemy aircraft—had been very heavy. Accordingly, by April, the season for convoys to Russia was considered closed. The last such run had been made for the winter. I was 'saved by the bell'. In any case, attention was now focused on preparations of the invasion of Europe.

The 17th Flotilla returned to Scapa soon after I had joined it. The Flow seemed a pleasant place in spring and we had many opportunities for catching up with old comrades spread among the forty destroyers there. I even recall a day-leave visit to Kirkwall, which proved an attractive little town, even having a few trees around it. It had not occurred to me that people actually lived in the Orkneys. It was fascinating to discover that the 'natives' did not even speak with Scottish accents—they were quick to explain that they were not Scots, being of Nordic ancestry. Another diversion for us was an ENSA troupe that came to Scapa to entertain the fleet. Two of the star performers were John Mills and Bernard Miles. Both had had major roles in Noel Coward's celebrated film *In Which We Serve*. As a personal tribute to Fleet destroyers, they wished to perform for destroyer men—although much bigger audiences would have been assembled aboard, say, an aircraft carrier. Accordingly, a stage was rigged across the midship sections of *Orwell* and *Opportune* alongside and the concert given in the open air.

Practically all the cruisers and destroyers were undergoing intensive training in shore bombardments—hardly surprising in view of the anticipated operations; but not *Orwell* nor her 4″-armed sisters *Obedient* and *Opportune*, nor *Savage*. This last was an unusual destroyer, with a prototype twin 4.5″ turret forward and single 4.5″ guns aft (all the other 'S's had four single 4.5″ mountings). It looked as if we were to be the Cinderellas for the coming invasion, but it was hard to see why *Savage* was omitted.

After a short time, these four ships were detached from the Home Fleet and sent to Invergordon from where we carried out a series of Night Encounter Exercises, not unlike those we had practised so diligently aboard *Revenge*. Radar played a greater role and searchlights were no longer used, illumination being by starshell. I found my action station was on the bridge, as Starshell Control Officer. I could not imagine what this training was leading to—but we would soon find out.

In the last days of May, *Orwell* steamed south through the North Sea. *En route*, our Asdics detected a possible submarine upon which we made a slow and deliberate depth charge attack. Whether or not this was a submarine and if so whether we damaged it, was not established. *Orwell* had already been present at the sinking of one U-Boat by a Sunderland aircraft, itself shot down in the process. *Orwell* picked up the survivors from both plane and submarine—including the latter's dog. It is hard to imagine how a dog lived aboard a submarine—or was taken for a walk. Be that as it may, this Belgian fox terrier was adopted by our CO, Lt. Cdr. Hodges, and renamed Adelbert, the name of the U-Boat Commander. He felt no qualms over changing allegiance and was happy to become one of *Orwell*'s ship's company.

Returning to the depth charge attack made in the North Sea, the charges had been dropped with shallow depth settings when the ship's speed was too slow. The result was a small split in the steel plating of our stern. The damage was not serious and pumps controlled the leak into the steering compartment, but it had to be fixed before we embarked on any operations. Accordingly, *Orwell* sailed for Sheerness (on the Kent side of the Thames Estuary) straight into dry dock, where the damage was repaired in a matter of days.

A totally unexpected outcome of our days in dock at Sheerness was the First Lieutenant sending for me at 1130 and telling me I could have twenty-four hours leave—back by noon next day. The dates were the 1st and 2nd of June. It seems absurd, but I simply did not know what to do with my twenty-four hours of leave. There was no point in hanging around Sheerness, where I was a total stranger, but it was only an hour by rail to London—whither I headed. However, what should I do in the metropolis? It was now obvious that the long awaited D-Day could only be a few days off at most. There was so much movement of shipping of all sorts that there was no question of another exercise, there being nowhere to exercise in south-east England anyway. The 'Bloodbath' was at hand. The turmoil in my mind may be imagined. This might well be my last-ever leave before being killed or maimed. I should try to make this twenty-four hours memorable—but how?

I knew no one in London and hardly knew the city, my knowledge being restricted to the three hectic nights of our Seven-a-side football there, during which I had simply followed the mob. I might have tried to visit MSJ at Bletchley (one hour north of London by rail) but had no idea how to get there, or even how to contact her—and there was no time to find out. In any case, so-called Station X was at its peak of activity intercepting and decrypting enemy radio transmissions. Were this a novel, I would structure a story line about meeting an 'old flame'—or a glamorous new one—pouring my heart out to her in a scene of heavy drama, with her seeing me off, giving me a talisman to keep close to my heart as I departed to storm the battlements of Agincourt. Sadly, nothing like this occurred and my leave pass proved totally anticlimactic. With little money, I could not 'live it up' with a night at the Savoy. I cast about for some kindred spirit to drink with at a bar but found no stimulating company. All the active young fighting men were already on the move and preparing for battle. I had to content myself with a couple of reasonable meals, a good hot bath and a comfortable night's sleep in a hotel bed. I returned to duty next morning, back at Sheerness, on schedule.

Once on board, I had no time to ponder my unenterprising leave. The next forty-eight hours for me would be both busy and exciting. Until now, I imagine, only our Captain—and possibly the navigator—had any idea where the landings would be. We had mostly assumed the Pas de Calais, as, fortunately, had the Germans (through elaborate deception initiatives, including bogus reports from supposed German spies). I did not know the exact date planned, nor what role *Orwell* was expected to play. Within twenty-four hours, I would have the answers to these questions and a great deal more—whilst still in Sheerness dockyard. Operational security up to the last minute was essential—yet there was a vast amount of information to be disseminated. *Orwell* had two heavy sealed mailbags stuffed with volumes of secret orders, maps, special codes, numerous subsidiary operational orders, etc., etc. These had been received on board and placed under tight security upon our arrival at Sheerness, having been made up and despatched perhaps a week before. As a result there was another half bag containing literally hundreds of amendments to the main orders. All these amendments had to be inserted before the operation started. The Confidential Books Officer was a young RNVR Sub Lieutenant (Jamie Cockburn) with a heavy load of responsibility. It was arranged for this officer, the other Midshipman (RNVR) and myself to be be locked up in the Captain's quarters aft and told to get on with the amendments. Our meals were passed in to us and we slept there for two nights without seeing the light of day. I was briefly reminded of our U-boat POW officers similarly constrained aboard *Revenge*—but had little time for such reflections.

I could not resist looking at the maps first and immediately learnt that the landings were to be in Normandy, between the Seine and the Cherbourg Peninsula. The full pattern of the Mulberry harbours was set out and a mass of detail covering the whole undertaking. The scale of the overall operation was staggering—so many thousand tons of bombs from so many hundred aircraft were to be dropped here and more thousands somewhere else. There were also to be naval bombardments of undreamt of intensity. The phasing of huge invasion convoys along swept channels through minefields was truly elaborate. Some idea of the scale is given by the fact that 325,000 troops were put ashore in the first four days. Naturally, we only had time to read a piece here and another there, as we had to work fast to cut out and paste in the endless amendments. The vast mass of intelligence about the enemy was staggering, pin-pointing every coast defence gun, pill-box and defending troop formation. The location of practically every German aircraft was given and just what ships, E-Boats, etc. were based on each port. The remarkable thing was that, while our forces knew almost everything there was to know about the German order of battle, they knew practically nothing about ours. They continued to believe the main thrust was coming in the Calais area and that the Normandy landings were a feint to draw divisions away from the Pas de Calais for more than a week after D-Day. Bletchley had played a major part in both the gathering of intelligence and misinformation for the enemy. Clearly neither MSJ, nor any one else, would have been keen to see me the day before.

It was some time before we came upon the orders for the special operation (with its own code name) planned for the three 'O's and *Savage*. Naval Intelligence believed that the Kriegsmarine had only one large warship still operational, namely the *Hipper*—the old adversary of *Orwell* and her sisters. With Allied air superiority and the great naval strength at the disposal of the invaders, *Hipper* could not be expected to survive for long. Nevertheless, should she cut loose for even one day, amongst the landing craft headed for Normandy, she could sink dozens of vessels and inflict tens of thousands of casualties. Special plans were made to ensure *Hipper* never got close to Normandy. A factor that had escaped my notice was that our ships were the last destroyers in the fleet still fitted with eight torpedo tubes. In all others the after set had been replaced by an extra 4″ AA gun. Accordingly, our orders were to wait for *Hipper* to turn round Cap Gris Nez and reach a pre-determined spot where sandbanks would restrict her manoeuvrability, and sink her with torpedoes. I did not relish the prospect of four destroyers against a 14,000 ton heavy cruiser with eight 8″ guns. *Enterprise*—of half the size and effectively six 6″ guns—had thwarted a torpedo attack by six destroyers and *Hipper* had far superior gunnery control systems than *Enterprise*. Perhaps our superiors felt seven 'O's had not been too frightened to take on two heavy ships (including *Hipper*) once before and so four should be able to take care of one of them. Certainly the prospect did not daunt the others aboard *Orwell*; indeed,

Lt. Binch swore that *Orwell* would not let *Hipper* off lightly with only one 4″ hit this time.

Aside from my anxieties regarding the *Hipper*, the overall impression was that, with such overwhelming force being brought to bear, this invasion would be irresistible. Even the E-boats, that had worried me, were provided for—with hundreds of aircraft to blast their bases, and flotillas of our own coastal forces arrayed against them.

OPERATION OVERLORD

D-Day was never a firm date that was immutable. It was originally planned as 1 May 1944, but various circumstances had ruled this out. Thereafter, the next acceptable combination of moon and tide conditions was around the first week of June—but the operation could only proceed if there was not a gale blowing. Planning went ahead based on sea-borne landings at dawn on 5 June. Many vessels actually sailed from English ports on the evening of the 4th. Aboard *Orwell*, we watched a motley collection of old coasters and small ships set off down the Medway. These were to be scuttled off the Normandy beaches to improvise a breakwater to protect landing craft on the open beaches prior to the arrival of the Mulberry harbour. The weather on the 4th, however, was touch-and-go, with strong westerly winds blowing. At the last possible moment the entire operation was put on a twenty-four-hour hold, and the coasters came plodding back into the river. Next day the weather had improved, although further strong winds were expected. The decision was taken and the die was cast. The following day, 6 June, was to be D-Day. Overnight, a thousand bombers dropped five thousand tons of bombs on the coastal defences and over 3,000 ships were on their way, in the greatest amphibious operation ever known. A hundred and fifty thousand troops went ashore on the first day.

It is not the purpose of this narrative to retell the story of Operation Overlord, which has been well chronicled. The foregoing has been related to give background to the small part in the overall story played by HMS *Orwell*.

The morning of 6 June found us somewhere south-west of the Straits of Dover, but still a hundred miles from the Normandy beaches. We therefore neither saw nor heard the heavy aerial bombing overnight nor the subsequent massive naval bombardment. We had seen ships and landing craft moving in the distance but, for *Orwell*, the day was something of an anti-climax. Our knowledge as to how things were going on the beaches was no better than that of any civilian hearing the regular BBC news bulletins. The only matter that concerned us was whether or not

Hipper was at that moment preparing for sea and a last glorious fight for the Third Reich. In fact she was not—and was not going to. Unknown to us, *Hipper* was not even operational, Hitler having ordered her paid off and her crew sent to man the U-Boats. If only MSJ and her Ultra friends at Bletchley had intercepted some message telling us this, *Orwell* and her consorts might have been spared a great deal of worry over the next three months.

Hipper or no *Hipper* our time spent in the English Channel was not uneventful. The daylight hours were quiet enough, as the RAF (or the USAAC) could be relied on to deal with any hostile surface craft. At night, it was another story. Despite heavy bombing of their bases, there was still plenty of night activity by E-Boats and other German small craft. Accordingly, *Orwell* had to be ready for instant action through the hours of darkness. Our activities would not have been unlike those of Cdr. Evans and the *Broke* on the Dover Patrol in World War I—except that we had radar. This did not make life much easier as we spent much time chasing shadows.

We had one near disaster. There was a friendly destroyer, which shall remain nameless, known to us as being something less than the supremely efficient unit that we considered *Orwell* to be—not to put too fine a point on it! As outlined in the description of Night Encounter Exercises aboard *Revenge*, the principle was that if one detected or sighted a probable enemy vessel, all guns ready to fire were aimed on the other craft before revealing one's own presence. One night, we came upon just such a potentially hostile ship. Round swung the guns and I was poised to give the order that would light up our target with starshell. In case of doubt, however, there was an established system of 'Challenge and Reply'—a secret two-letter Morse signal to which any 'friend' should immediately respond with two other flashed letters (which changed every few hours). In theory, the challenge was only made if one was ready and willing to open fire at once, failing a correct reply. Any delay would give time to alert the enemy and allow him to open fire first. The act of making the challenge, therefore, always caused a few moments of intense anxiety. On this occasion, the challenge was made, but no light flashed in reply. 'You don't suppose that could be the — ?' asked someone. 'Shouldn't be,' said the Navigator, 'they aren't supposed to be anywhere near here.' Hideous dilemma for the Captain, who (against all the rules) ordered, 'Make the challenge again.' Once more, there was no reply. Now what? 'Well, at least nobody has fired back at us—I reckon that must be the —' (on the assumption that the Germans were more efficient than that). Subsequent investigation revealed it was, in fact, HMS —.

There were a few minor incidents during daylight, including our picking up survivors from a crashed American bomber, some severely wounded.

There was another time when we came upon a capsized, but still floating, landing craft possibly mined or caught by an E-Boat during the night. Survivors had evidently been picked up but this floating wreck represented a serious navigational hazard. Accordingly, we fired our pom-pom into it until it sank. Unfortunately, our torpedo derrick had been left stowed pointing forward instead of aft, placing it in the arc of fire of this gun. This caused the incident, reported early in the narrative, of our late rendezvous with FFN *La Combattante* and our CO's attempt to signal that ship in French.

Once the first few days were over and *Hipper* had shown no signs of making a move (having learned *Orwell* was waiting for her, perhaps), the four ships settled down to a routine of three ships only on patrol each night—each of the four having a night off at anchor in Spithead every fourth night. I do not recall shore leave being granted—it would have been difficult making the long trip to Portsmouth and back by boat. In any case, my chief concern was to catch up on sleep. At sea, we had to be at immediate alert all night and ready to fire starshell to illuminate hostile E-Boats and other enemy craft. This meant my standing by on the bridge on full alert half the night, and the other Midshipman the other half, as duty Starshell Control Officer. Furthermore, if action occurred, a second Officer of the Watch was needed on the bridge. This had to be the other Midshipman. The result was that I and my fellow Midshipman had six hours on duty as SCO but also spent much of the time conning the ship on an anti-submarine zig-zag course, as the assistant to the Officer of the Watch. It would be 2000 to 0200 one night, alternating with 0200 to 0800 the next. But when not on actual duty, we remained on stand-by and could only sleep on the steel deck of the bridge (not the most comfortable of beds) in our duffel coats—until the next alarm, whether false or real.

It was hard to get much sleep on the night in harbour as my only allotted sleeping billet was the wardroom settee. Unfortunately, the other officers liked to have a party there until midnight—and reflect how much better it was to have a night in harbour in Spithead than in Murmansk. Still only 18½, I suffered increasing fatigue under this routine. I was so weary one night, that almost mechanically, I called down the voice-pipe to the wheelhouse the helm-order, 'Starboard twenty.' The quartermaster acknowledged and the ship started the intended 40 degree turn to starboard. I then slumped over the compass; the ship kept turning, until a voice from below called out, 'Still got twenty-a-starboard wheel on, Sir.' I woke with a start to realise the ship had turned through 180 degrees. The OOW I was assisting was nearly as weary as I was and had not noticed either. There was nothing for it now but to complete the circle—an unusual form of anti-submarine evasive steering.

The one time I always felt keen and eager was before dawn on our third night out. Lt. Cdr. Hodges had complete faith in his navigator—one Lt. Scrymgour-Wedderburn (known as Scrym). The captain would retire to his sea-cabin on the bridge with a final instruction: 'As soon as it's light, you may pack up and head for Portsmouth at 25 knots. Call me when we reach the Nab Tower [at the approach to Spithead].' Somehow, I always seemed to be on watch with Scrym on these mornings. He was nearly three years older than me and I remembered him from Dartmouth, but he was now a real veteran of numerous Russian convoys and other operations. I regarded him with enormous respect. Nevertheless, after much watchkeeping together on the bridge, a certain bond had developed between us. Furthermore, he was the first Lieutenant (other than Foord of *Enterprise*) I had known who was prepared to talk to a Midshipman other than as to an infinitely lesser mortal.

We would consult as soon as there was a glimmer of dawn in the eastern sky as to whether one could now say that 'it was light'. It has to be admitted that the moment of 'first light' tended to be a little earlier each time, as we turned west and set off at 25 knots. After a time, however, a complication arose as for several weeks there tended to be quite dense morning fog when we were turning for home. Scrym and I were cautious over this to start with but soon developed a technique about which we both felt completely confident. The system was that Scrym took the 'con' whilst I watched the surface radar display in the charthouse at the rear of the bridge. Our course was necessarily restricted to quite narrow swept channels through the minefields, along which were passing a succession of cargo ships, LST and landing craft convoys in tight formations. This meant we often found ourselves weaving our way at 25 knots through twenty or more vessels coming the other way, with visibility down to 300 yards. Without really good radar (which *Orwell* had) this would have been impossible. In passing I should record that *Orwell* had probably the best performing Type 276 Surface Radar in the fleet. This was due largely to the expertise of PO Radio Mechanic Harry Wade, who had joined *Orwell* aged forty, having been an advertising bill sticking agent as a civilian. Scrym recommended him for his DSM—and kept in touch with him until he died twenty-four years after the war.

Even with our superb radar, this manoeuvring was a hazardous business demanding intense concentration. Nevertheless, Scrym and I felt we had the game down to a fine art, and claim we never even had a near-miss. It was rather like consistently driving a car over the speed limit—personally convinced one was doing nothing seriously wrong, but outside the rules, nonetheless. For some time, nobody objected to our behaviour. But, in due course, our much respected and affectionately regarded captain, Lt. Cdr. Hodges DSO, was moved on and we had another CO. Our new

Aorangi—an old friend of mine since the age of 6! White-hulled here (1947) as legacy of recent war service as a Hospital Ship. (Photo, Wellington Maritime Museum.)

skipper was to be well thought of in the Service and was a competent and respected destroyer CO. But (perhaps because of only short acquaintance with him) I never had the same warmth of feeling towards him that I had for his predecessor. Following our usual back-to-Portsmouth routine, Scrym and I both forgot we had a new CO. He happened to appear on the bridge in the half light in a thick fog in time to see a cargo ship pass down the port side at a relative speed of 35 knots no more than 200 yards away. Our new Captain practically exploded, as he leapt to the wheelhouse voice-pipe and yelled down, 'Stop both engines—half astern both.' The two of us were threatened with court martial if we were ever found hazarding the ship like this again. Scrym, of course, took the main force of the blast as he was clearly in charge at the time. We exchanged sheepish glances—but the days of back-in-Spithead-in-time-for-breakfast were over.

There was always a big concentration of shipping in Spithead but one large ship always attracted my attention. It was my old friend, so to speak, the *Aorangi*, that had conveyed me across the Pacific at the age of six and been with *Resolution* and *Revenge* on our voyage north from Cape Town, including our unhappy visit to the River Congo. *Aorangi* now had an important role as the Headquarters Ship for the small fleet of tugs of

Operation Overlord. These were for towing the floating concrete Mulberry breakwater units across to Normandy. In due course, this operation was completed and *Aorangi* was no longer needed as a Headquarters Ship. She was then turned into a Hospital Ship. I recall the strange sight of this 20,000 ton liner half painted in camouflage patterns, with the other half newly painted white with red crosses. I remember idly thinking, 'I suppose the enemy are allowed to bomb the forward half of the ship only.'

It will be clear to the reader that, by now, most of the excitement in the Channel was over. However, on 26 June, *Enterprise*, as part of a force of British and American cruisers, bombarded the forts of Cherbourg, after the now cut-off Germans there had refused to surrender—or rather had been forbidden to surrender. Their failure to surrender cost them heavily in lives, against very few Allied casualties and only a day or two longer occupation of Cherbourg. There was little further naval activity. The Home Fleet destroyers, having used all their ammunition—and almost worn their guns out—in shore bombardments, had nearly all returned to Scapa Flow and relative peace and quiet. How we envied them. The action thereafter was nearly all on land, with Montgomery's Army group breaking out of the bridgehead, liberating Paris and driving the Germans back to the Rhine.

There was, however, one RN loss on the night of 20/21 July, which was a matter of great personal sadness to me. This was the loss of the destroyer *Isis* and my two Term-mates Ryland and Nicholson, both of whom had been among our brightest mates at Dartmouth. It will be recalled that Michael Ryland had been a particularly close friend of mine as well as being the most brilliant and intellectual of our contemporaries.

Initial reports of the loss of *Isis* were sketchy, suggesting the ship had been mined whilst at anchor in the Seine Bay. Her disappearance had seemingly gone unnoticed for eight hours until HMS *Hound* had picked up twenty survivors at 0209. Recent research by the naval historian (Author of *War Losses*), initiated through my friend and Term-mate John Carlill, has thrown new light on the matter. The historian has advised:

> [*Isis*] was on A/S patrol off the western beaches when a large explosion, followed by two others, occurred abreast the starboard side of the forward boiler-room. The ship was also holed in the port side abreast B gundeck; the forward galley caught fire. Although she trimmed by the bow and took a heavy list to starboard, flooding almost immediately up to the upper deck, *Isis* took about 20 minutes to sink. The survivors believed that she was mined; she was certainly not torpedoed by a U-Boat or a 'human torpedo'. The position of the initial explosion and of the hole in the port side argue against a magazine detonation and it is possible that secondary explosions were caused by the forward boilers.

I agree with the historian that 'human torpedo attack' (against a ship under way) can be ruled out and no doubt there were good reasons to dismiss a U-Boat torpedo (or attack by E-Boats—which could hardly have gone unnoticed). However, it is strange that there were at least five damage locations : 'large explosion followed by two others . . . abreast starboard side of forward boiler room', 'ship holed in the port side', ' . . . split in starboard side abreast B gundeck' and, finally, the galley fire. It is surprising that all these should have occurred as a direct result of striking a mine. Another puzzling factor was the loss of (presumably all) ten officers. Those on the bridge might be expected to survive a mine explosion underwater and those off-duty could be expected to be in the wardroom or cabins aft—that part of the ship furthest from the reported damage. With the ship taking twenty minutes to sink, it is surprising that no officers from the stern survived.

A more eerie matter to me was that Michael Ryland, who was a devout Catholic, had spoken to several people, including my sister—but not to me—of a premonition he had that he would die in the war. The sad thing for me is that I never saw him after we left Dartmouth; our ships never seem to have been in port together.

I will not try to write a belated obituary to Michael Ryland but feel compelled to make some observations about this outstanding young man. I only knew him until we left Dartmouth having just turned seventeen. Whilst I claimed him as a close friend, I was never on the same intellectual plane as Michael. His tangible distinctions at Dartmouth included passing out top of our Term, with the Howard Crockett Memorial Prize. He was the House Cadet Captain of Grenville House and had made a name for himself in several College theatrical productions, taking a succession of leading dramatic roles. He was, however, also athletic and earned his colours in several sports. He was remarkably good looking, with the Lesley Howard type of good looks, rather than those of the 'macho he-man'. Most girls who met him (including my sister) found him very attractive— but he was a 'man's man' as well. He was a deep-thinker but was also quick-witted and possessed of a delightful sense of humour. He exhibited signs of the iconoclast streak of so many of his contemporaries, extending to extremists of his own religious faith. In Ryland's case, I cannot say whether his character, in this respect, was engendered by the prevailing Dartmouth ethos or that his innate personality contributed to it. He possessed great artistic sensitivity and enjoyed classical music. Had he lived, it is difficult to imagine that the shrinking peace-time Navy could have held him for long. He could have distinguished himself in any field he chose—but what this would have been is anyone's guess. Suffice it to say, his death at the age of eighteen was a sad loss and deeply mourned by all who knew him. Strangely, I never met any other member of his family, although his younger brother—who later joined the priesthood— stayed at my home at one stage when I was overseas.

CHAPTER 12

Sub Lieutenant Shore Training

By the end of August 1944, our appointed twenty months of Midshipman's time had passed. I had turned nineteen and on 1 September acquired a full gold stripe on my sleeve as an Acting Sub Lieutenant. The 'Acting' would only be for four months—until the completion of our professional shore courses in Gunnery, Torpedo, Signals, Navigation, Anti Submarine, Fleet Air Arm and one or two minor one-week courses. Effectively, we were now proper officers in the Royal Navy—and were entitled to be saluted by any Serviceman in uniform. There would, of course, be new responsibilities, and, in the case of my comrades and myself who went straight on to Motor Torpedo Boats, these would be immediately apparent. Coastal Forces represented something of another world in the RN and we would be only one bullet away from command of a fighting unit. There were other differences which all of us would only come to realise in the fullness of time.

The status of seagoing Midshipmen in operational warships was a unique one, with an indefinable ambivalence as to whether a Midshipman was an officer or not. One had many of the privileges of officers, yet, under training, undertook practically every arduous or dirty task expected of lower deck ratings. Such included running boats at all hours in all weathers at Scapa Flow (perhaps missing one's evening meal as a result) and, the toughest I recall, Engine-room Training aboard *Enterprise*—specifically boiler cleaning. Shortly after those days, mechanical systems were developed for this work, but not in time to spare the 'Middies' of *Enterprise*. The ship had half a dozen so-called Admiralty Three Drum boilers with 'superheaters'. Cleaning was in two parts: 'Internal' and 'External'. The former involved climbing right into the (upper) steam drum and 'searching' (passing descaling articulated rods down every one of a thousand odd tubes between this drum and the two (lower) water drums. As the steam drum was only about 20″ diameter one had to work in extremely cramped quarters—especially if 6′ 1″ tall, like myself—and not be subject to claustrophobia. If this 'internal' cleaning was not much fun, the 'external'—in the furnace part of the boilers—was infinitely worse. This involved cleaning out all the filthy oily soot from the outside of the tubes we had reamed out 'internally'. Furthermore, this exercise had to be continued through the funnel uptakes. After a day's work of this, even in overalls and one's face swathed as much as possible in muslin, one came out blacker than any coal miner leaving the pit. Furthermore, it took a week to work the oily grime out of the pores of one's skin.

I mention such things because this training was valuable. It was not important for Midshipmen to make detailed physical study of boiler construction—such could have easily been taught by diagrams or cut-away models. On the other hand, it was highly desirable that the 'Young Gentlemen' (as Midshipmen used to be called) should be made fully aware of all the unpleasant tasks lower deck ratings were called on to perform. Later, as Officer of the Watch, in harbour, one would be far more reluctant to provide a boat to take an officer to another ship, if the boat's crew had not had their supper.

Another aspect of the special status of Midshipmen was that sailors would have watched and heard Midshipman Seymour on the receiving end of the wrath of Commander St John-Cronyn. Such would have included language no officer would ever use towards a rating. The men knew that the life of a Midshipman was not a 'bed of roses' and would feel a certain sympathy towards him. The upshot would be that sailors would confide in Midshipmen thoughts they would never communicate to any officer with gold braid on his sleeve. Such might be about some real, or imagined, injustice a man had suffered at the hand of an officer. The cause of the complaint might have seemed so trivial that the officer who caused it had been wholly unaware of having upset the man. Importantly, the Midshipman had the chance to make a mental note to avoid such an action or remark himself. In the view of the author, the Navy was the poorer when the system of Midshipmen at sea (except as trainees) was abandoned.

Since I have lived in Australia, I have acquired great respect for the so-called Jackeroo System—of young men learning about becoming graziers (sheep or cattle farmers). They had, and still have, very much the same status as Midshipmen, but on the land—working long and hard with station hands on jobs as varied as cleaning out cowsheds, dealing with fly-blown sheep and clipping evil-smelling sheep's feet for foot-rot. The same young man would still be included in the social life of the station owner to whom he was apprenticed, so to speak. He is expected to 'scrub up', be well turned out and hold his knife and fork properly at a dinner party the family employing him might be holding. Any man—or woman— managing a property should benefit greatly by taking an agricultural degree, but skills such as animal husbandry and—even more important— employer/employee relationships need to be learnt in the field. Once again I recall the words of John Marsh: 'You can read the entire works of Freud . . . ' But you have also got to get practical experience. Enough philosophical observations—back to Acting Sub Lieutenants in late 1944.

For the first time since leaving Dartmouth, the whole of my Term (with the sad exceptions of Ryland and Nicholson) were ashore again in UK. We were joined by our Special Entry contemporaries, as well as 'opposite numbers' who had come up from certain Commonwealth Naval Colleges, such as Flinders Naval College, Australia. This collection of young officers ashore for further professional training was split into seven or eight groups and sent to different specialist schools. All had 'Ship Names' such as HMS *Excellent* ('Whale Island') for Gunnery, *Vernon* for Torpedo, *Dryad* for Navigation, *Mercury* for Signals, etc.

We would never be altogether at one place. But as most of these establishments were in or near Portsmouth, we were soon meeting up with most of our old buddies. In the case of the group in which I found myself, our first course was Torpedo. HMS *Vernon* at Portsmouth had long been the 'Home' of Specialist Torpedo (and, later, Torpedo-Anti/Submarine) Officers—and would be again. But, during the Blitz, *Vernon* at Portsmouth had been largely destroyed. Accordingly, other accommodation had been found near Brighton. When invasion threatened in 1940, many schools and other establishments on the coast of south-east England were evacuated to places further removed from the 'front line'. One modern building, dominating the landscape behind the little village of Rottingdean, which had been vacated and then occupied by the RN, was St Dunstan's Home and Rehabilitation Centre for the Blind. This was to be the first shore accommodation in which I was quartered, since the RNC. However, we were merely housed there. Each day, a bus took us to another unlikely establishment, now designated HMS *Vernon II*, where we were taught about torpedoes and associated equipment. For a great many years, this had been one of England's finest and most prestigious girls schools—Roedean. There is little to record about that course, except an apocryphal story—which I cannot confirm or deny—that the new occupants were delighted to find, in the former dormitories, a bell with sign: 'Ring once for Mistress'!

Our next course was at Worthing, at another commandeered school, now designated HMS *Royal Arthur II*—for a so-called Divisional Course. The establishment had been set up for induction training of reservist Midshipmen and Sub Lieutenants for their introduction to concepts of Naval Discipline and Officer-like Qualities. This involved a great deal of marching about a parade ground—with a brief church service each morning, for which the hymn number was hoisted in naval numeral pendants. It was evidently felt this would serve the dual purposes of invoking the protection of the Almighty, whilst at the same time engendering familiarity with naval flag signalling. It might have been thought beneficial to mix New Entries with Midshipmen of about the same age, but who had seen nearly two years of war service at sea. Sadly, this concept proved a failure from all points of view. The place was probably run as it should have been, for the purpose intended, but we could not understand what we were doing there. We were hardly good role models for the New Entries. Our uniforms were rather weather-beaten, compared with their shiny new outfits from Gieves. Also, we could not understand our need for further 'square-bashing'—apart from the somewhat irreverent and critical attitudes, inexplicably developed in us at Dartmouth.

Most of the rest of our courses were in or around Portsmouth. The city itself had suffered severe bombing but everything had been tidied up, although not rebuilt. This was the heartland of the Royal Navy and, even though new to the place, I felt at home there, particularly with so many friends, last seen at Dartmouth, Mombasa or Scapa Flow. My group included few of my close mates, but they were nearly all people I at least knew and we were a cheery bunch.

Excellent, on Whale Island, amongst the mudflats of Portsea Harbour, north of Portsmouth itself, had a number of points of interest. As a relic of the Great War, there was an old army tank of the parallelogram shape that had stood on a concrete slab for twenty-five years. However, with invasion believed imminent in 1940, to support the Home Guards—some armed only with pikes—an enthusiastic Engineer at *Excellent* had managed to restore the engine of this monster to working order, so that it could offer rather more resistance to German invaders than the pikemen of 'Dad's Army'.

If not already perceived, it will be found that this narrative is something of a kaleidoscope of places, people and ships that keep reappearing—sometimes unexpectedly. In a mud-berth, bows towards Whale Island, what ship should I behold, but the former Royal Yacht *Victoria and Albert*. We had last seen her steaming out of the River Dart in a blaze of glory five years back in July 1939. It had long since been obvious that this sixty-year-old wooden-hulled vessel's days as a Royal Yacht were over. But the ship-breakers had been too busy 'scrapping' irreparable warships for their steel to have had time to break up the venerable '*V & A*'. By now, the gold leaf was fading and the black enamel paint dull and peeling. However, with much of Portsmouth flattened by bombing, accommodation was at a premium, yet, with so many men under training, the population of Whale Island was now several thousand. Accordingly, rather than fill up remaining space with Nissen huts, why not utilise the old Royal Yacht for accommodation?

So it came about that Sub Lt. Seymour found himself in a beautiful walnut-panelled cabin aboard this remarkable old ship. I was able to explore the inside of the ship—but, sadly, found the engine and boiler rooms locked. I was told that, in the late nineteenth century, raising steam with the ancient coal-fired boilers would involve the two yellow funnels belching great clouds of sooty black smoke. Accordingly, the furnaces would be stoked like fury until the arrival of the Royal Train and Queen Victoria at Portsmouth Harbour Station. Not another shovelful of coal would then be added, but the ship would have enough head of steam to make Cowes *en route* to Her Majesty's beloved Osborne House. What did provoke speculation was just which of the vast old-fashioned wood-surround baths was used by the Queen Empress. Perhaps she waited until she reached Osborne. My three weeks living aboard a former royal yacht was interesting—and fun.

It was soon apparent that, if humanly possible, one needed to have at least a share in a car at Portsmouth. Our pay now came to a few more 'Mars Bars' but scarcely enough for a car. Nevertheless, I teamed up with old Term-mates Mark Ross, Oswald Cecil and a genial Special Entry colleague named John Fisual, as a partner in a tiny 1933 clapped-out Morris Minor (not to be confused with the post-war Minor of the fifties), for the princely sum of £28. This vehicle conveyed us around a few of the pubs but was about as minimal a car as one could imagine. The self-starter had not worked in years and the crank handle was missing. It could therefore only be started by pushing and, if on one's own and not already on an incline, this meant right-foot-out-of-door-propulsion, until the engine fired. Breakdowns were frequent, particularly punctures, yet this vehicle was better than nothing—but only just. About the last straw came when I was driving it off Whale Island while several hundred Libertymen streamed 'ashore' on foot. At this moment, the off-side rear wheel decided to leave the vehicle, overtake the car and cut a swathe through the sailors—fortunately not hurting anyone. After a month, we decided to scrape up all the cash we could muster and buy ourselves a better car. This time it was a new-looking (repainted) little 1935 Morris Eight. It was a splendid machine and really worked—most of the time— but so it should, as it had cost us £70. The only slight drawback was that it was a tourer, it was now winter and when it snowed there were no side screens to keep the weather out. Nevertheless, our 'new' car carried us far and wide around Portsmouth and even up to London. We were allowed a small petrol ration—but one should not question too closely where all the petrol we used came from. I can still recall what it was like having accidentally swallowed some petrol after a suck/syphon operation—with an occasional belch of petrol fumes.

It was during this period that my close friendship with 'Os' Cecil developed. I was a frequent guest at his home at Botley, not far from Portsmouth. His father was a retired Commander and specialist Signals Officer with particular achievements in the pre-war field of wireless, being credited with the development of the 'Queen Bee'—radio-controlled pilotless aircraft. Os also had a delightful sister who was a Wren. Although

Oswald Cecil had not been particularly brilliant academically at Dartmouth, he was possessed of great charm and personality, not to mention
an unflappable disposition. These characteristics would have fitted him
well for the Diplomatic Corps, on the fringe of which he did serve—as
Flag Lieutenant, first to the British Naval Representative on the Western
Union Defence Council in Europe—the forerunner of NATO—and later
as the aide to the British Naval Attaché in Washington. Whilst these
appointments indicate the degree of polish that Os always possessed, he
had real ability as a naval officer. This became evident later when a shrewd
senior officer appointed him as the First Lieutenant of a ship which had
been on the verge of mutiny. Within six months, this vessel was the most
efficient unit, with the highest morale in the squadron—the sailors loved
him. It was with good reason that he went on to retire as Rear Admiral
Sir Nigel Cecil KBE CB. I was delighted to catch up with him at our
1989 reunion and still like to regard myself as a good friend of Os—even
if he does now prefer to call himself Nigel.

Our last course was the Flying Course at RN Air Station Arbroath in
Scotland. It was also the only really unpleasant one. It was now December
and few places in Britain are colder than the east coast of Scotland in
winter and, of course, the hours of daylight were short. This would not
have been important had we been on a course in warm well-lit classrooms
and had comfortable accommodation. As it was, we were quartered in
Nissen huts and our time was mostly spent trying to learn to fly in
open-cockpit Tiger Moths and Swordfishes. Added to our disenchantment
with this course was the near total lack of enthusiasm shown us as visitors.
Indeed, I have to say that the officers of the *Unterseebootejagstaffel* were
afforded a considerably warmer welcome at RN Air Station, Eglinton,
(fourteen years later) than we were at Arbroath.

The wartime antipathy between 'Fish-heads' (Executive, or Seamen,
Officers) and 'Fly-boys' (Fleet Air Arm Pilots and Observers) has already
been recorded. Happily, this soon evaporated after the war. But with
hindsight, the wartime ill-will is understandable. With very few exceptions
FAA Officers were Reservists or Short Service Commission Officers,
recruited for no other purpose than to fly naval aircraft. They were brave
young men with as much patriotic fervour as regular Seaman Officers.
But they were Airmen first and Naval Officers second. Indeed, their
personal loyalty would be to their Squadron rather than to the aircraft
carrier, in which such might be embarked. They had not had years looking
at pictures of the Death of the Immortal Nelson.

Their life expectancy was very much shorter than non-flying officers.
Before the advent of angled decks and mirror deck-landing aids, they were
taking their life in their hands to some extent every time they landed on
a carrier. Although RN aircraft carriers were arguably the finest in the

world, the planes the aircrew were given were unquestionably second-rate. The Swordfish was a biplane ten years out of date, yet remained the principal FAA aircraft for most of the war. They scored a spectacular success crippling the Italian Fleet at Taranto in November 1940 (on the anniversary of Trafalgar). But in February 1942, all ten Swordfish sent to torpedo the *Scharnhorst*, *Gneisenau* and *Prinz Eugen* in their dash through the English Channel were shot out of the sky without achieving one hit. It was not until the last two years of the war that the FAA began to receive American Navy fighters, which could hold their own against Japanese carrier-borne aircraft. There were political reasons—which need not be gone into here—as to why the RAF had priority over new aircraft. Suffice it to say that it must have been extremely depressing for FAA officers to be constantly losing good friends and fellow airmen from their squadrons. They had few duties on board when not flying and it was not surprising that many drank alcohol to excess. From the viewpoint of the Fish-heads, however, the aircrew officers were a crowd of unsociable drunken lay-abouts. This was a wholly unfair assessment, as was their assessment of us as a crowd of toffee-nosed dilettantes who really had no idea what fighting a war was about. No one had made them clean out a cruiser's boilers!

Needless to say, there were many level-headed and tolerant individuals on both sides. Sadly, however, our Instructor Officer at Arbroath was not one of them. This RNVR Lieutenant Commander could not stand Fish-heads generally and hated regular Sub Lieutenants most of all. This was most unfortunate as the course was designed to enthuse us about Naval Aviation. It has to be said that this individual had some character defects anyway. He felt it necessary to impress us by carrying a silver-headed malacca cane and gloves all the time—except when actually flying.

We were given about half a day's instruction on the theory of flight and aircraft controls, little more than the instruction Mike Vaughan had given me on how to drive a car. Then it was up in a Tiger Moth. This initial experience of actually flying a plane oneself and finding it respond-ing to one's own movement of joy-stick and rudderbar was initially both exciting and stimulating. Unfortunately the pleasure would be shattered by the instructor in the rear cockpit calling through the voice-pipe, 'I have got her now,' and proceeding to put the plane into a spin so that, looking up at what should have been clear sky, one saw only the ground below, gyrating in a completely unnatural manner—in fact quite terrifyingly. At this point, a voice through the pipe screeched in a crescendo, 'You are in a spin now—remember what you were told to do to get out of a spin "left rudder—right aileron". Hurry up, if you stay in a spin too long you'll never get out of it . . . ' Needless to say, by this time I simply did not want to know what the plane was doing and was crouched down with my head ducked inside the cockpit. Back on the ground, I was told, 'Well, one thing that's for certain is you'll never be a pilot—you couldn't even handle a Tiger Moth.' This idiot had one or two other tricks like putting a Swordfish into a steep power-dive, such as the aircraft was never designed for, and calling out, 'What the hell are are you doing? Everyone knows the wings come off a Swordfish at 200 knots.'

By this time, we no longer worried about such things, rationalising that our instructor would make sure the plane would not crash with him in it. Subsequently, I was not sure that this assumption was valid. Regrettably, some months later, this maniac, showing off by trying to fly his plane between the funnels of a cruiser, made a misjudgement and was killed.

We finished our course at Arbroath with a sigh of relief. Nevertheless, just one year later, 10,000 miles away in Singapore, I would be presenting myself at RNAS Sembewang and asking to be accepted for training as a Fleet Air Arm Pilot.

CHAPTER 13

30TH MTB FLOTILLA

LOWESTOFT AND OSTEND

FOR THE FIRST TIME in our careers, we were given some choice regarding our next appointments. In almost every case it would be one Sub Lieutenant to one ship. So it was a question of what jobs were going, and who would like them. There was just one posting for which five of us were required—namely as No.1s of MTBs in the 30th Flotilla. It might be asked why this number for one particular flotilla but no other vacancies in the whole of Coastal Forces, with a total of over a thousand craft. To answer this, one must briefly regress through the wartime history of Coastal Forces. The RN had started the war with a handful of MTBs, manned, of course, by regular personnel. However, nearly all the original officers and ratings had moved on or been killed, yet the number of craft in Coastal Forces grew rapidly. In addition to Motor Torpedo Boats, similar sized fast craft with more guns but no torpedoes were known as Motor Gun Boats (MGBs). They were developed mainly by Vospers and the British Power Boat Co. A third Co.—Fairmile—developed the ubiquitous Fairmile 'B' Motor Launches (simply known as MLs). These were of relatively slow speed but had longer endurance and better sea-keeping qualities. Truly 'maids of all work', they were found as far afield as the Pacific, as units of the RAN. One of these was commanded by a future good friend of mine, Marsden Hordern, about whom we will hear more anon.

In European waters the MLs were mostly employed escorting coastal convoys against submarines and aircraft. The Fairmile Co. also brought out the Fairmile 'D' MTBs which were 120 ft. long, carried four torpedo tubes, had two 6-pounder guns and were powered by four V-12 aircraft engines. There was a large number of these powerful craft built. Unfortunately, they were simply not fast enough to do battle with the E-Boats (*Schnellboote*). The latter were of aluminium construction with four torpedoes but light gun armament and powered by superb Mercedes Benz supercharged diesel engines. Amongst the British craft, the smaller, faster Vospers and British Power Boats were generally described as Short Boats.

By D-Day (Normandy), Coastal Forces comprised many dozen flotillas of small craft. As the war had progressed, both weapons and tactics had

Model of 71ft. 6in. British Power Boat MTB—476 was the number of the author's boat. (Model by B. Hunt, West Beach, South Australia.)

steadily evolved, so that Coastal Forces operations had become a highly specialised and sophisticated form of warfare. Yet nearly all the development, special training and technology had been done by RNVR officers. By Normandy, senior officers at Admiralty realised that the end of the war might well be in sight. Unless something was done, all the accumulated know-how could be lost as the reserve officers were demobilised, leaving the regular Navy with no one experienced in CF Warfare.

In May 1944, steps were taken to rectify this situation. Unlike the Army, the RN had always resisted the concept of elite units. Naturally, some types of warship were more glamorous than others, e.g. fleet destroyers compared with armed trawlers, but no attempt was made to make up 'crack' destroyer flotillas. The 30th MTB flotilla, however, was to be something rather special, but not elite for the sake of elitism. The theory was that if young regular officers were to be given war experience in coastal forces, they had better learn from top practitioners of this specialised art. Accordingly, a new flotilla was commissioned under the command of a highly respected Senior Officer, Lieutenant Peter Magnus DSC* RNVR. Two of the other COs had previously commanded their own flotillas, and bore many gallantry decorations. There were nine boats in the flotilla. The other eight COs were Lieutenants, RNVR: The Hon. Frederick ('Freddie') Shore, Peter Standley, 'Red' Thompson, Paul Watkins, Geoff Aimers, Graham Bradley, Ross Campbell (RCNVR), and

Sub Lt. (RAN) 'Bob' Lang. Three experienced RNVR No.1s were included, but the remaining six First Lieutenants were RN Sub Lieutenants straight from their shore courses—all ex-Dartmouth, of two Terms before ours. Two of these were introduced earlier—the inimitable Mike MccGwire, and Uredale Wood, who was the other star footballer, supposed to help win the rugby 'Sevens' for the RNC. The other four were also prominent members of that Term—Tony Bowen, David Norman and two others, of whom I recall little, named Maslem and Freer-Smith.

Their boats were the latest British Power Boat Co.'s 71 ft. 6 in. MTBs—armed with two 18″ torpedoes, a power-operated 6-pounder gun forward, twin 20 mm Oerlikon aft, twin Vickers machine guns, depth charges and chemical smoke equipment. Power was provided by three Rolls Royce Type V12 'Merlin' supercharged aero engines as fitted in Spitfires (American-built by Packard) to give a top speed of 40 knots at full 'boost' of 12 p.s.i. The flotilla was operational in time for the Normandy landings and saw plenty of action with the German E-Boats and the more heavily armed 'R-Boats'—acquitting themselves well.

Eight months later, it was considered that the five bright young regulars had had enough experience and they were needed elsewhere in the fleet. Also, it would be a good idea to let a few more regular Sub Lieutenants have some similar experience. By this time, it was no longer thought necessary to hand-pick the brightest and best of the newly qualified 'Subs'. Rather, it was a question of who would like this posting. The offer was no sooner made than four close friends from Dartmouth snapped it up. They were Joe Lungley, Mike Vaughan, Gavin Wemyss and myself and we were joined by Term-mate Jeremy Gurney. Second in command of a motor boat of some seventy feet does not sound impressive. In fact these craft were very formidable fighting machines. The 4,500 hp of aero engines can be related to the 40,000 of *Revenge*, 400 times as big, and every foot of boat was packed with lethal weaponry. The glib (American-inspired, and facetiously used) catch-phrase was 'Seventy-one foot six of Snarling Death'. We were only to be the 2 i/c but could easily find ourselves in command at any time.

To set the war background (in January 1945), the German's last desperate (Ardennes) offensive, threatening the vital port of Antwerp, had been thrown back in December 1944. The British and American armies were on the Rhine, with practically all France and Belgium liberated, although 20,000 Germans had been by-passed in Dunkirk. As they had no capacity to break out, the Allies merely contained them and pressed on; they remained there until VE Day. As far as Coastal Forces were concerned, there was still much to be done. The E-Boats and other craft were doing their best to harry the stream of shipping beginning to pour into Antwerp. In order to provide better cover for convoys in the Scheldt

Estuary (approach to Antwerp), a forward base for MTBs was established at Ostend and designated Coastal Forces Mobile Unit No. I (CFMU I)— the 'I' was superfluous as there were no further CFMUs. Three flotillas of MTBs arrived and started operating but disaster struck only a few weeks later. The Board of Inquiry concluded that a boat had been pumping bilges in harbour with some 100 octane aviation spirit in the bilge-water. This petrol surfaced at once and a cigarette-end carelessly thrown into the harbour was all that was needed to ignite it. The fire spread quickly across the water and exploded the full fuel tanks of MTBs and most of their ammunition and torpedoes. Twelve MTBs were blown up and others damaged. Sixty-one lives were lost and there would have been more had many crewmen not been ashore.

Of this disaster, the official RCN History records:

> At the end of the day the 29th Flotilla had ceased to exist. Five of its eight boats had been destroyed. Seven British boats had been lost and many more damaged. Twenty-six Canadian and thirty-five British sailors had been killed. The disaster was a stunning blow to the men of the small craft everywhere; and only the 65th Canadian Flotilla now remained to carry on the war with perhaps the most colourful, most closely knit and the most thoroughly 'allied' of all the forces (namely Coastal Forces) in which men of British, Canadian, French and many other nationalities worked together.

At this time, the 30th was kicking its heels at Lowestoft—after tough fighting off Normandy and the French coast of the Channel (See Appendix 3). However, following the Ostend disaster, the flotilla was ordered there to take the place of the (Canadian) Short Boat flotilla that had been wiped out. This was about the time our little group reached Lowestoft.

Before any of us could join the flotilla, we had to undergo intensive specialised training. This came as something of a shock to us, imagining we were now well trained in almost everything. In fact, we had much to learn. For instance, we could all read Morse (by light) reasonably well but now had to do it at twice the speed. We knew something about machine guns but now would be expected to completely strip and reassemble a Vickers machine-gun lock in quick time—blindfold. At sea, all our action would be at night and we had to know almost everything there was to know about the boats and all the equipment carried. Such included where all the controls were—from communications equipment to the methyl bromide fire control system for the fuel tanks which held 3,500 gallons of 100-octane petrol. It all had to be thoroughly memorised as things happened very quickly aboard MTBs. Functions would have to be performed in the dark and there would be no one to ask what to do.

There was an image of MTB officers as dashing heroes. In reality, the key to success lay in dedicated, painstaking and thorough training so that people could act instinctively under stress. Nobody was a greater exponent of this concept than our Senior Officer, Peter Magnus. To illustrate his personal mental agility and ability, on one occasion, infiltrating his boats through a large number of escorts to attack a convoy, he was challenged (by light) by one of the escorts. Before this moment, however, Peter had been silently stalking an R-Boat on the other side. The Germans used exactly the same Morse two-letter Challenge-and-Reply system as the RN—as previously described aboard *Orwell*. On being challenged, he instantly seized the signal lamp and made the same two-letter challenge to the other boat he had been watching. On receiving the two-letter reply, he swung round and made these two letters back to his challenger—all within seconds. This sort of thing was not heroics but quick-thinking and competence. He expected the same dedication from the officers of his flotilla. I did not have a great deal of contact with Peter Magnus as his boat was refitting at Lowestoft most of the time I was in Belgium. I would next meet him fifteen years later at the Royal Sydney Yacht Squadron (where we were both members) and became a good friend of Peter and his wife Helen, whom he had first met as a Wren at Lowestoft.

Training at Lowestoft included intricate tactical games in a simulator training centre. Each trainee would be a CO on a simulated bridge, or a No.1 in a simulated chart-room. To these would come a mass of R/T (voice) and W/T (written) signals, together with a stream of slips of paper advising events occurring. The CO would decide where to steer, at what speed and when to fire torpedoes. Meanwhile the No.1 (in his capacity of Navigator/Operations Officer) would have to keep track of where the boat had got to in relation to enemy and friendly craft. As can be imagined, this sort of 'game' really kept us on our toes—but it would usually end up with the advice that our own boat had just been blown up! It would then be explained what mistakes we had made and what we should have done. Surprisingly, this training unit was not run by a highly experienced ex-Senior Officer of an MTB Flotilla but by a Wren Second Officer, whom, I concluded, knew more about fighting E-Boats than I could ever hope to.

This brings me to the part played by Wrens in supporting Coastal Forces generally. In effect, at Lowestoft they did virtually everything short of manning the MTBs. Apart from all the clerical and administrative work that one would expect, the girls completely manned the radio/telephone/teleprinter communication systems (and put us through our signalling exercises). They crewed several boats used in harbour, drove all the staff cars and lorries and manned the ordnance and torpedo depots. If one's torpedoes needed servicing, one took the boat to the torpedo depot (taken-over ice factory for the peacetime Lowestoft trawlers). A crane worked by a lovely Wren (named Rosemary Twigg) lifted out the 'fish' and placed each on a trolley. It would then be man (woman)-handled away to a workshop where the girls would take it to pieces and service it.

Each flotilla had allocated two Wrens (electrical and radio) who would be waiting on the jetty on one's return to harbour, ready for any odd jobs. They knew the names of every sailor and officer on each boat and had been known to darn MccGwire's socks (Mike would meet his sock-darning angel years later up at Cambridge). They were invaluable. No fighting units were ever better looked after than we were by these Wrens—we loved them all. Lowestoft was a fun place, even in mid-winter. Unlike the horrid Nissen huts at Arbroath, we were accommodated in the former four-star Royal Hotel on the promenade by the beach adjoining the Harbour. Four close friends were reunited for the first time since Mombasa nearly two years back. We were all honorary members of the Royal Norfolk and Suffolk Yacht Club close by, and any place with so many Wrens around had to be great. Sadly, this splendid state of affairs could not last and, after a few weeks, we were deemed trained. We crossed the North Sea, in the routine Fairmile D 'Despatch Boat' from Great Yarmouth, and joined our flotilla at Ostend.

MTB ACTIVITIES

Once at Ostend, the pattern of our operations soon became clear. The days of torpedo attacks on enemy shipping were over. Rather, all effort was to be concentrated on protecting shipping to and from Antwerp from E-Boats and any other surface forces the Germans could muster. Furthermore, this was to be strictly night-time work as, with almost complete air superiority, Allied aircraft could take care of any enemy surface craft by day. It was already clear that coastal forces in any form were virtually defenceless against air attack by day—as was to be seen off Suez in 1956 and, much later, in the Falkland Islands. However, at night in 1945 it was still hard to counter the elusive E-Boats—of greater speed than any of the Allied MTBs or MGBs. Nevertheless, reasonably effective tactics had been evolved, using frigates with good surface radar. Each controlled six MTBs, in pairs, and 'vectored' these to intercept approaching hostile craft—as for Fighter Direction.

The first line of this defence system each night comprised six MTBs of the 30th Flotilla, with a frigate controlling them. Behind these were formations of the larger, more heavily armed but slower, Fairmile Ds. This meant that our flotilla had six boats at sea and two in harbour each night, with the ninth boat refitting back at Lowestoft. Accordingly, one had three nights at sea and the fourth off-duty, unless for any reason a boat should be unserviceable, in which case two boats had to have four successive nights at sea. Naturally, therefore, great efforts were made to ensure all boats remained fit for sea.

Very occasionally, there would be a full gale in the North Sea, which meant that neither E-Boats nor MTBs could operate effectively. Once it had been ruled too rough to go to sea, a cheer would go up and all eight boats could have a night in harbour—and the crews go drinking together. No doubt, there would be similar rejoicing at the E-Boat bases of Ijmuiden and the Hook of Holland. Naturally, however, if operating conditions were even marginal, the boats had to be out there—and we experienced some rough nights at sea, when the weather deteriorated during the night. In fact, our stoutly-built boats could take almost any weather the crew could stand and could leap from wave to wave at 30 knots plus. Hitting each wave caused such a crash that one had to stand with knees bent, or the jarring to the body could cause injury. Obviously, however, the point would be reached at which this form of progress could not be maintained. It was then no use reducing speed slightly—the boat had to slow right down and wallow through the waves at 10 knots.

The other side of the picture was the tremendous exhilaration of planing over a smooth sea at 40 knots with the engines at full power. At the end of each night, the six boats would assemble, form line-abreast and the Senior Officer would radio 'Flag Yoke. Go Go Go,' which meant proceed at maximum speed. A race would be on to see which boat was fastest. In fact, this was less a test of how well the Packard 'Merlins' were tuned but rather how well the boats were maintained. For instance, any water in the bilges slowed the boat—so the bilges were kept spotlessly clean. Also, of course, no superfluous weight was allowed on board.

As might be imagined, there was great *esprit de corps* aboard each boat, but this meant that a high standard was expected of the CO and No.1 in everything we did. This applied to boat-handling expertise in harbour, to and from the fuelling depot, something always left to the No.1s. Sailors ashore had been known almost to come to blows over which of their respective 'skippers' was seen with the better-looking girl. Discipline was informal and virtually self-applied. For instance, there was an unwritten law whereby, if any sailor was even the slightest the worse for wear as the result of alcohol when a boat had to go to sea, it was a case of automatic banishment from Coastal Forces. Neither my CO nor I ever had a single 'defaulter' to see in all my time aboard 476.

Informality extended to occasional pre-arranged evenings when the two officers drank with the crew. But these never led to familiarity or loss of respect. The sailors all knew their officers' Christian names (and/or nick-names), which they used when talking amongst themselves about their officers—but never addressed the latter by anything but 'Sir'. There were no parades—other than inevitable funerals—and no 'spit and polish'. But each boat's engines, armament, communications, radar and all other equipment were meticulously maintained—and inspected by the CO or No.1. For instance, I knew where to find every one of the 114 grease nipples on the power-operated six-pounder mounting and, as already mentioned, the bilges had to be kept spotless. Uniform was not inspected; the sailors wore Service Issue clothing, including 'Submarine Sweaters', because there was nothing more practical. The officers, however, were reluctant to wear their expensive Gieves uniforms at sea, preferring to wear baggy old grey flannel trousers, Harlequin (or whatever) football jerseys and woollen scarves, knitted by loved ones. The only identifiable item of uniform was usually an officer's cap (with tarnished cap badge) as experience showed that no other headgear was as comfortable whilst keeping the spray out of the eyes. The Germans, as I later personally observed, never went to sea with one scrap of non-uniform clothing and even wore any Iron Crosses they had won. It was reported that, on one occasion, an MTB was sunk by the Germans who picked up survivors, including officers in motley garb. Their reaction was that they must be winning the war as the British were reduced to manning their boats with civilians.

So much for the general picture—now for some specific incidents. We had been warned by our predecessors to expect quite a lot of action with the E-Boats. I made some ingenuous enquiry as to what it was like to have a stream of tracer shells coming at one. Mike MccGwire assured me with confidence, 'Nothing to worry about at all—the enemy fire always passes overhead.' It was not in MccGwire's nature to worry about such things. I was briefly reminded of the silly story of the big-game hunter who had been twice startled by a huge ferocious lion leaping right over his head. On proceeding very gingerly he came to a clearing and—lo and behold—there was a huge lion, practising short leaps! Anyway, I decided there was nothing to be gained by pondering the matter. The fact was that on the relatively few occasions when my boat was under fire from E-Boats, every single round did pass overhead.

The E-Boats were still active, laying mines in the convoy channels. This was now the only tactic left to the enemy as the ships could transit the Scheldt Estuary by day, during which E-Boats dared not show themselves. However, their mine-laying brought them considerable rewards in tonnage sunk.

With the North Sea quite shallow, medium sized ships would often sink only to deck level, leaving masts and superstructure showing. There was one grotesque wreck of a Liberty ship, with after part flooded and stern sitting on the bottom but the forward third of the ship out of the water at 45 degrees, remaining so for weeks. It was possible to navigate all the way back to the Thames estuary from one wreck to another. A particularly

eerie wreck had some metal object—door, perhaps—that banged rhyth-
mically in the current, emitting Hydrophone signals that could be picked
up from a mile away.

On several occasions, our controlling frigates achieved interceptions
between our boats and the enemy. None of the ensuing actions were
decisive nor of long duration. The E-Boats were not there to fight and
once we found them, they would fire a few bursts—over our heads—and
make off at 50 knots under cover of smoke. On one occasion, we engaged
two and my CO thought we had hit one of them (below, plotting in the
charthouse, I saw nothing). Subsequently seeing only one echo on our
radar instead two, we claimed a 'possible' kill—but this is very dubious
as we saw no explosion nor any debris in the water.

There was another period of two or three nights, during which the
Germans made some determined sorties with radio-controlled explosive
motorboats. Two had their hulls packed with high explosive and a third,
unarmed, directed the other two and picked up the single crewman from
the other craft. This was a brave but completely fruitless venture by the
Germans. On each occasion all three boats were sunk or blown up. My
boat was involved in one of these actions—sinking the recovery boat.
Subsequently, we spotted two flashing orange lights in the water. These
proved to be the lights on the lifejackets of the two men who were on
board—an Ober Leutnant with an Iron Cross and a Petty Officer, as it
turned out. We hailed them as we approached but received no response.
It was hard to evaluate the position in the total darkness but both men
were found to be dead when brought aboard.

We had one night of considerable confusion. The frigate which directed
us was nearly always either the *Stayner* or the *Ekins*. We would never see
these vessels but had come to rely on them completely. We would find
our own way out to our pre-arranged patrol stations—two boats to
each—and report our arrival to the frigate, which would vector us back
on station if we drifted too far away. If ordered off to investigate a
suspicious radar echo, one would usually be too busy to keep track of
where the boat had got to. But this was not necessary as one only had to
ask the frigate 'Interrogative my "Uncle"' (Uncle being the phonetic word
for 'U') to be told one's bearing and distance from one of our standard
reference points.

On this particular night, there was much activity with the pairs of boats
ordered hither and thither and a number of so-called COFOX W/T
messages coming in. These required decoding but, with all the activity on
board, I had not had a chance to decipher these signals. At this point,
our consort, Freddie Shore's boat, asked us if we had the picture as to
what was happening. My CO, Paul Watkins, asked me if I knew anything
and I had to tell him I did not, and could not 'raise' *Ekins*—our controlling

Rotterdam Lloyd liner Willem Ruys, *laid down at Flushing, 1939. Completed late 1947. Seen by author in rusted state on stocks at Flushing in 1945. Sold to Flotta Lauro Line in 1964 and renamed* Achille Lauro. *Sadly was burned out and sank off Somalia, 1994.*

frigate that night. By this time Shore had taken off at high speed to the north without explanation. Paul asked me what did I think we were supposed to do now? I could only suggest that as the other boat had gone 'that-a-way' we should do the same. We did so at high speed but, a few minutes later, had to stop abruptly to avoid running into a completely darkened ship stopped in the water. Who should this be but the unfortunate *Ekins* which had herself been mined. The vessel appeared in no danger of sinking, and did in fact manage to return to her base in due course, but now had no engine power or electrics and was therefore unable to use her radio, let alone radar, any signal lamp or even her loud-hailer. Communication, therefore, had to be by megaphone. *Ekins* told us they did not need any assistance from us and we were left to find our own way home. Fortunately, it was now almost dawn and I was soon able to pick up one of our familiar wrecks and set a course for Ostend. I felt considerably chastened. I realised that I should have been quicker off the mark, decoding the COFOX messages and should not have come to rely so completely on our controlling frigate with regard to navigation. I resolved at once to smarten up on both these matters before I was told to do so by someone else.

There was one other night that we were again in company with Freddie Shore. We learnt that a patrolling aircraft had detected two craft proceeding down the coast off Walcheren. By the light of flares they had been identified as probable R-Boats. It so happened that Paul and Freddie had been together in action shortly after D-Day when their two boats had had to take on four R-Boats. These craft were heavily armed and easily out-gunned a Short Boat MTB. Yet in a determined attack, the two British boats had thrown themselves at the Germans and had managed to repel them from attacking the convoy lanes—but not without damage and casualties to both MTBs. I had no enthusiasm for taking on any R-Boats but found the two COs spoiling for a fight and relishing the fact that it would only be two against two this time. I well remember the smooth tones of Lieutenant The Hon. Frederick Shore drawling over the radio, 'Why don't we go and meet these gentleman half-way?' Damn you, Freddie, I thought to myself, I'm too young to die! Happily the R-Boats—if that was what they were—having been found by the aircraft, decided to abandon whatever operation they had in mind, to my very considerable relief.

We had one more adventure in the very last few weeks of the war (in Europe). A chain of improbable circumstances resulted in MTB 476 and myself facing the greatest danger we had encountered in all my time in the boat. Manoeuvring in harbour after fuelling one morning with an exceptionally low spring tide, I had felt one of our propellers foul some underwater obstruction. When I reported this to my CO, he declared that we could take no chances. Everything might seem well at low speed but, at full power, the slightest imbalance in a propeller would cause tremendous vibration. The Base Engineer agreed and arrangements were made to slip the boat on the next low tide and change all three propellers as a precaution. This was done without incident and that night happened to be one we were scheduled to spend in harbour anyway. The next requirement was to test the new propellers. Accordingly we put to sea next morning to carry out a full-power trial. This was expected to be little more than a formality—and an excuse to take the boat out on a non-operational run. Paul Watkins even invited a young Army officer he had met the previous evening to come along for the ride. His guest could have had no idea what he was in for. We cleared harbour on a beautiful late spring morning with a flat calm sea. We idly noted that a large eastbound convoy was passing about five miles ahead of us. All at once there was a large explosion and, through binoculars, we could see a heavily laden tanker had been torpedoed or (more likely) mined and was starting to burn fiercely. Paul at once gave the engines full throttle and headed for the stricken ship at 40 knots.

In under ten minutes, we were close to the burning tanker. By now, two-thirds of the ship was engulfed in flame and smoke, rising hundreds of feet in the air. Furthermore, the fuel (we were unsure whether it was diesel, petrol or fuel oil) now gushing out of the ruptured tanks, was ablaze on the surface of the sea for a quarter of a mile astern and outwards for 100 yards on each side of the stern. Yet the ship's engines were still turning and the tanker making an estimated 8 knots through the water. It was to be hoped that personnel in the midships and stern section had been able to get clear in the special flame-proof tanker lifeboats in the first minute after the explosion.

The rest of the convoy naturally gave this floating inferno a wide berth. Meanwhile, as we drew closer we could see that there were still about ten men trapped on the fo'c'sle. They could not jump overboard into the flaming sea and literally had nowhere to go—but were shouting for help. Paul Watkins was keen to do anything possible to rescue these men. But with our 100-octane petrol, the harrowing vision of the twelve MTBs recently blown up at Ostend, and the searing heat felt from 100 yards, how much risk should he take, hazarding his own craft and fifteen lives?

We were now joined by two other small craft—a small so-called HD ML (smaller version of the famous Fairmile Bs) and a high speed RAF rescue launch. A brief discussion by loud-hailer followed. Paul, not unreasonably, suggested that the ML would be at least risk in trying to get under the bows of the tanker and recover survivors, as their fuel was diesel as opposed to our 100-octane. This was met by a plaintive plea from that craft that they might only run on diesel but we had very much more power to 'get the hell out of it' if things went wrong. The RAF boat hung around to see what would happen next. All this time, we could hear the screams for help coming from the tanker's fo'c'sle. At this point, Paul made up his mind—time was being lost while the boats argued the situation. He declared, 'We're going in.' I had fire hoses playing on our deck and our men were covered as much as was possible against the heat. The tanker crewmen already had hawsers over the side of the fo'c'sle to climb down. In we went alongside the bows of the ship, still doing about 8 knots—with the whole sea on fire just a hundred feet astern of us. Two men slithered down the heavy ropes, one landing on our deck, the other holding the rope for dear life, being pulled through the water between boat and ship—until strong arms pulled him aboard our craft. As there was no one else on the ropes now, Paul hit the throttles and pulled clear. We had only saved two men (the team on the fo'c'sle were all Chinese deckhands) but Paul had set the example of bravery required, so that first the ML and then the RAF boat each made a run in and collected more men. There were still two or three men left on the fo'c'sle and Paul ordered, 'Stand-by for another run,' and we were soon under the overhanging fo'c'sle once more.

Unfortunately, things did not go so well this time. Two more crewmen were recovered but a third man was unable to hold on long enough for us to grab him and lift him inboard. He fell into the water and, moments later, was lost in the blazing fuel on the sea. The MTB itself was now in trouble. In watching the heroic efforts to save the third man, the Coxswain had somehow allowed the boat to get across the bows of the tanker—mercifully, at last, only moving slowly through the water. However, for agonising seconds, our craft was stuck squarely across the bow and being tipped further and further over. The situation was made worse as ammunition was exploding and tracers flying in every direction as successive Oerlikon AA gun positions aboard the tanker were engulfed in flames. In a trice, Paul flung himself at the throttles and 'gunned' all three engines. The MTB moved forward but, as the ships bows scraped off our stern, our boat was spun so that it was facing nearly aft down the tanker's side and, because the latter had now slowed so much, the flaming sea was only about fifty feet away. The Coxswain spun the helm to

Lieutenant Paul Watkins RNVR—CO of author's MTB. A brave man, a fine officer and a good friend.

hard-a-starboard, our Packard Merlins roared, the boat turned tightly and the wave of our wash and bow-wave threw up a wall of water that literally pushed the flaming sea away as we turned and got clear.

I am not sure whether all this was worse than a shower of 4″ shells from half a dozen Elbings; at least it was over quickly. As all surviving crewmen had now been picked up, we returned to Ostend. Our Army guest, no doubt, decided to think twice before accepting any more speed-boat trip invitations to sea with the Royal Navy.

Paul Watkins, an incredibly modest man, reported that the Full Power Trial had been completed satisfactorily but we had picked up some survivors, to be taken to hospital and cared for. No more might have been heard of the incident had not the RAF Rescue Launch put in a full report of proceedings, including high praise for the example and actions of MTB 476. Paul received another well-earned Mention in Despatches. I feel a DSC was deserved—George Crosses have been awarded for heroism of this order. I counted myself lucky to have had such a competent, level-headed, as well as brave, Commanding Officer.

A word or two should be given about Paul Watkins and my relationship with him. He was now aged twenty-five and had been fighting the

Germans in Coastal Forces for five years. By the age of twenty-three and as a Lieutenant RNVR he was judged sufficiently experienced to be given a command in the International Gunboat Flotilla, with MGBs manned by French, Polish and Dutch officers and men. This assignment must have called for a man of competence, diplomacy and leadership qualities. Paul was a quiet-spoken man who exercised leadership without emotional rhetoric but rather example and precept. He was the sort of person for whom one instinctively felt that anything less than one's best performance would be letting him down. I cannot recall his ever reproving me for a shortcoming—although I am sure such occurred—but he would give a word of encouragement when appropriate.

There was no intimate friendship between us as we saw little of each other. At sea, we each had a job to do and there was little chance for social conversation. Ashore, we lived in different quarters and, by a tradition that had developed for social drinking before lunch, the COs would foregather aboard one boat and the No.1s on another. The fact was the two groups were on quite different planes. I have told how, at HMS *Royal Arthur*, we regarded ourselves as on a higher plane than the newly joined Reserve Officers. In Coastal Forces, we were very definitely the new boys and our Commanding Officers all had many years of exacting war experience behind them. We did not have to be reminded of this—we simply recognised their superior status and respected them. If one's CO happened to have the personal qualities of Paul Watkins one's respect was that much the greater and a man such as our Senior Officer, Peter Magnus, was a demigod. I could not conceive that, in years to come in Australia, I would socialise with him and he would treat me as a more-or-less equal. In due course, I would learn that Paul was also a warm-hearted person with a well developed sense of fun—as will be indicated shortly.

CHAPTER 14

MTBs, Ostend

THE LIGHTER SIDE

REGRESSING TO THE DAY WHEN, with my four Term-mates, I arrived in Ostend by the Despatch Boat from Yarmouth; apart from the excitement of taking up our duties in the 30th Flotilla, there was also the novelty of finding ourselves quartered in a foreign country. Furthermore, this was one which, until recently, had been under German occupation, as was quite clearly evident.

Pre-war, Ostend was not only the Belgian end of the Dover-Ostend ferry and the principal fishing port of the country but also a major seaside resort. It had a promenade backed by large hotels, rather like Brighton but on a slightly smaller scale. However, the Germans had tried to fortify the entire north coast of Europe as their West Wall against invasion. This meant mining the beaches, covering the promenades with tank obstacles and barbed wire, sealing off and fortifying the sea-front hotels with gun emplacements and placing many booby-traps. Thus we never got to walking along the promenade and could only look at the backs of the former five-star hotels over barbed wire entanglements. The harbour was also something of a shambles. The Germans had sunk a dredger in the entrance as a blockship and, until this was removed, nothing bigger than an MTB could squeeze past it. Furthermore, the end of the Gare-Maritime had been severely damaged when the MTBs blew up. Finally, the Germans had demolished many of the bridges over the canals that ran through the town. Despite all these problems, the populace was cheerful and happy to be free of the hated Bosche at last, even though food was short and, of course, the place had to be blacked out at night.

On arrival, accommodation had to be found for the crews of the Short Boats—the Fairmile D MTBs' crews were able to live onboard. The ratings of the Short MTBs were put up in an old Belgian Army barracks but the COs and No.1s did not fancy the officers' quarters of these. Someone enquired where the *Schnellboote* officers had lived. The answer proved to be a small hotel in the Boulevard Van Isseghan, one block back from the promenade. This place looked better than the barracks and its management seemed keen to take the British Naval Officers. Accordingly, the No.1s moved into this establishment and the COs into a slightly superior looking building next door. So it was into the quarters assigned to the First Lieutenants that we moved on arrival and found ourselves being served lunch. Our first meal there was not remarkable as regards the food. However, it did not escape my notice that the girls serving us all seemed young and attractive. The meal over, these girls came and sat beside us and, without warning, I found my neighbour was kissing me. This was a confusing experience for an impressionable nineteen-year-old Sub Lieutenant.

The story, it turned out, was that when the Germans were organising themselves, with their Teutonic regard for order and discipline, they had decided that it would be undesirable for their officers to be found haunting the same bordellos as their men. Accordingly, they had their quarters listed on the official Belgian Register of Brothels (prostitution was legal and regulated in Belgium). Doubtless, a junior officer—judged appropriately qualified—was detailed to recruit suitable personnel to staff this establishment. Needless to say, the girls selected were regarded as *collaboratrices* and suitably punished by having their heads shaved, when Ostend was liberated. We had wondered why they all had rather short hair, but this looked quite attractive—like Ingrid Bergman, in the film *For Whom The Bell Tolls*. However, we knew none of this when we moved in. Wholly unbeknown to My Lords Commissioners for executing the Office of Lord High Admiral, British naval officers were now billeted in a functioning brothel.

Before proceeding further, I must assure the reader that the author did not avail himself of the services offered. I regarded myself as a reasonably broad-minded person and took the view that what other people do is their business. However, perhaps as the result of my Dartmouth training, I felt that in one's own mess, there is a code! It has to be stated that not all the No.1s felt the same constraints as myself. Furthermore, the 'services' were only too available. Each of us had our own bedroom and one had to do little more than smile at any of the girls for there to be a knock on one's door ten minutes after retiring. The main problem was that, as indicated earlier, we had to spend three nights out of four at sea—notionally, fighting the foe. Accordingly, the fourth night, in harbour, really was needed for sleep, but officers routinely engaging in other activities on those nights would eventually show signs of fatigue. At this point, the odd officer decided he had no alternative but to bunk down aboard his MTB. Unfortunately, the crews knew very well what the set-up was, and that any officer electing to sleep on board clearly showed that he could not stand the pace ashore.

This brings me to an improbable story that the reader may find hard to believe although it was later confirmed in every detail by the other member of our team who witnessed the event. As further background, it needs to be explained that although our quarters in the Boulevard Van Isseghan did constitute our mess, the place was also open to the public. We merely used one long table at the rear of the room, occupying the whole ground floor, for our meals, and had a bedroom each above. One night, with the No.1 of the only other boat left in harbour, my very old friend Joe Lungley, I had an evening out, around some of our favourite night-spots. We returned to our quarters, not intoxicated but in a more-than-happy state of mind. We ascended several flights of stairs (there was no lift) and were bidding each other 'good night' before going to our respective bedrooms, when events took an unexpected turn. Blanche, a genial middle-aged woman who was the manageress—the 'Madame'—of the establishment, arrived on our landing, out of breath from racing upstairs. She was in a great state of agitation and spouting French at a pace I could not hope to understand. Quite clearly something was wrong—perhaps the house was on fire.

Joe and I returned to the ground floor, where we were greeted by an extraordinary scene. Around the foot of the stairs, in a half circle, stood all the women of the house with worried looks on their faces. In the centre of this gathering stood two very young and callow looking officers of the Royal Air Force with the thinnest possible stripe of a Pilot Officer on their sleeves. As these presumably spoke English, I asked them what was happening. It took little time for me to realise that they were considerably more inebriated than we were. The story, it seemed, was that they were passing through Ostend on their way to a forward base—doubtless fresh from their Training Establishment. No doubt they had heard from their forerunners that Ostend was a good place for entertainment on their one-night stopover *en route* to the front and presented an opportunity not to be missed.

They had chanced to visit our establishment where they had set out to make the most of the night. Soon they were buying champagne for themselves and the girls, not at our ridiculously low price but the 'going rate' of about a pound a bottle. Paid no more than we had been as Midshipmen, their funds were soon exhausted—just when they were ready to head upstairs with the girls. Sadly, for them, however, they now had no money—but Blanche had been at pains to explain that the women had to be paid for separately. Drunk, fed-up and frustrated, they appeared to be about to create an ugly scene and seemed keen to break the place up. Hence Blanche's plea to us for help.

This situation, although now clear to me, suggested no obvious course of action. One look at Joe told me that he had lost interest in proceedings and he expected me to take charge. I reflected that Dartmouth had not instructed me on how to handle such situations—nor could I think of anything in King's Regulations and Admiralty Instructions to guide me.

Nevertheless all eyes were now on me and I was obviously expected to do something. I was encouraged by a (quite unreasonable) feeling of superiority over these airmen on six counts, namely: We were obviously older than them by at least a year; we were 'veterans'—they were rookies; we clearly out-ranked them, by dint of our one solid gold stripe as opposed to their very thin blue one; we represented the Senior Service, they the Junior; we were less drunk than them and at 6' 1", I was bigger than them. 'Right,' I said to myself, 'Here goes.' I drew myself up to my full height and, with the strongest note of authority I could muster, let fly at them.

'Look here. Do you realise you are in a Naval Officer's Mess and you cannot behave in this hooligan manner. If you have any complaints to make about the prices of our wines OR our women you should speak to the President of the Mess in the normal Service Manner,' (notwithstanding the fact that we had no such officer). Totally dumbfounded, the two turned and meekly walked out of the house; they are possibly still trying to work all that out to this day. Needless to say, all the women, who had not understood a word I had said, were unbelievably impressed.

This narrative opened with an exploit of Mike MccGwire, who preceded me as No.1 of MTB 476. Normally, the take-over should have taken no more than a week. In the event, MccGwire was so enjoying himself in MTBs and Ostend that he kept finding reasons to delay his departure, so that we overlapped by nearly four weeks. It was early in this time that the Baby Duck was acquired. Once painted grey, it was given the bogus number plate of RN 478 (the one missing boat number of our flotilla). Petrol was no problem as each boat, in addition to its 100-octane-consuming 'Merlins', had a Morris lorry motor as an auxiliary for electricity generation. We now had the chance to get around and see some of the country. I recall visiting the beautiful old mediaeval town of Bruges, happily untouched by the war. A more adventurous outing was to drive west along the coast to go and have a look at 'how the war was going'— getting as close to the front as we could and trying to see if we could spot any of the 20,000 Germans holed up in Dunkirk. I recall one poignant aspect was that near the village of Dixmuide there were some trenches, dugouts and barbed wire from World War I as a museum exhibit—somewhat irrelevant—within half a mile of the current front line around Dunkirk.

As already stated, we normally only went to sea for night patrols. However, for some reason unknown to me, on one occasion the six boats which had completed their night's work were ordered to Flushing (Vlissingen) on the Island of Walcheren at the entrance to the Scheldt. The scene was one of the worst devastation that I had seen to date, and the town was still under intermittent long range artillery fire. The harbour was so filled with blockships that our six boats could only just get in. At first sight, the town appeared to have no buildings left standing above the first floor. The streets had largely been cleared of rubble but I cannot recall any traffic on them. Incongruously, towering over the whole town was a large liner that was being built there pre-war and was nearly ready for launching. Work on this ship had stopped in 1940 and five years later she appeared to be little more than a rusty hulk with a few shell holes in the topsides. Amazingly, amidst this desolation there were evidently some 30,000 civilians still somehow living in the town. Furthermore, once the war ended, the Dutch managed to complete the liner, laid down nearly eight years back, and she entered service as the *Willem Ruys*, proud flagship of Rotterdam Lloyd. Remarkably, in 1994, this fine old vessel (of 23,000 tons) was still ranging the oceans of the world as the now Italian-owned cruise liner *Achille Lauro*—fifty-six years after her keel was laid. Sadly, she was burnt out at sea in December 1994.

Back to Flushing in 1945. Whatever the reason for our visit, after only about three hours we received an emergency signal to go at once to a ship that had been sunk in the estuary less than twenty miles away and pick up survivors. We were on the scene half an hour later but all survivors had been recovered—probably with few if any casualties because, as usual, the ship had settled with superstructure above water. Therefore, there appeared nothing for us to do. However, at this point it was noticed that tea-chests of cargo were beginning to float out of the hold. As we approached some of these, MccGwire, still with us, whipped his jacket off and plunged into the cold (late winter) North Sea and was soon paddling floating boxes towards the MTB. Three were recovered (with contents unknown) before the Senior Officer present decided it was time to head back to Ostend. The boxes were quickly opened to see what they contained. We were in luck—the wreck happened to have been a Canteen Supply Ship. The contents of all three boxes were undamaged, in watertight tins. One contained 100 tins of 50 cigarettes, one six large tins of 24 bars of chocolate and the third, sixty tins of cocoa. Mike soon found some dry clothes and, with a rum inside him, was well pleased with his salvage venture. The next question was what to do with our booty. It was decided the crew could use the chocolate bars. We did not need the cigarettes (having ample supplies of our own at the duty-free price of 6d. for 20). Nor had we any use for the cocoa. Mike, however, was well aware of the black market value of both these items and immediately made plans to sell these ashore, receipts to go towards a massive crew party.

Back at Ostend, I wondered how our spoils could be turned into cash through the black market. The latter was rife in Ostend at the time— almost as accessible as legitimate trading. Nevertheless, disposal of duty-free cigarettes (or liquor) was an offence punishable by court martial—and

I doubted if such court would be much moved by an assertion that the 5,000 cigarettes had 'fallen off the back of a ship'. However, MccGwire was not worried. He reckoned our sailors would know how to dispose of the cigarettes and could be trusted to bring the proceeds back for the boat's Canteen Fund. Getting our contraband past the Military Police at the entrance to the docks was the only problem. Again, Mike had a simple solution. The Duck was loaded with the goods and the driver armed with an 'authorisation' by the First Lieutenant of MTB 478 (illegibly signed) to take these to the shore barracks used by the sailors, for distribution to MTB crewmen. There was no problem—and enough money brought back to buy all the beer our sailors could drink. For the cocoa, things did not go quite as smoothly. It was judged that there was so much black market in Ostend that we would get a better price for the stuff if we took it to another town.

Accordingly, the Duck was loaded once again and four of us including MccGwire and myself (having the direct interest in the merchandise) and two of the other Sub Lieutenants went along for the ride. I now have no record as to who they were and feel I should not now ask the possible ones to incriminate themselves as accessories to our nefarious venture that day. We arrived in a small town some twenty miles from Ostend and decided this would be as good as anywhere. We pulled up in the *place* in the centre of the town. There seemed to be hundreds of people milling around and the unexpected sight of this strange vehicle, with four young British naval officers, attracted considerable interest amongst the locals. Meanwhile Mike MccGwire had set off on his own to seek out a buyer. In his absence the other three of us became increasingly worried by the attention we were attracting. Our embarrassment was increased when we discovered that we had chanced to park immediately outside the local Prefecture or police station. A beaming MccGwire returned shortly to report that he had found a good buyer and asked us to hand him down the large cardboard carton now holding our cargo. Regrettably, as we did so, the bottom fell out of the carton and sixty tins of cocoa fell into the road and rolled in every direction. Our business was quite obvious to the small crowd now gathered round us, who laughed uproariously as four faces turned scarlet. At this point, we decided we had had enough. We hopped aboard, sounded the horn and drove away, leaving half the population to have a free hot chocolate drink—perhaps their first in years. We did not grudge them this although none of them had had to plunge into the cold North Sea to acquire the goods. If asked how the cocoa had been acquired any English-speaking Belgian with a good grasp of American vernacular could reply, 'It fell off the back of a Duck.'

The end of the war was in sight and the last big push was on to link up with the Russians coming from the East. The final collapse could only be days away. But even when the armies from East and West met to signify the impending end of the war, the Allied ground armies would still be a hundred miles short of Denmark. Yet surely the peoples of these countries would be keen to welcome their victorious liberators. With this thought in mind and without reference to the Allied Supreme Command—or any other 'higher authority'—a master plan was quickly devised by CFMU. Three flotillas of MTBs under this command would race ahead and be the first Allied Forces to arrive in Copenhagen. There was no question of risking lives to arrive, perhaps a day earlier, by fighting our way there. It was simply a matter of getting to Copenhagen first, once the Germans had capitulated. The problem was that none of our boats had enough fuel to cover the hundreds of miles from Ostend, along the coasts and down through the Kattegat to Copenhagen. The journey could, however, be made with one refuelling stop *en route*. Furthermore, it was hoped that once the enemy had surrendered the three flotillas would have free passage through the Kiel Canal which would save many hours at full speed.

The selected staging point was Wilhemshaven, because it seemed likely that, being far to the west of Berlin, it would be in Allied hands a day or so before the final capitulation. Also, it was known to be a major German naval and air base and so should have plenty of 100-octane fuel and, hopefully, some petrol tankers. If fuel supplies could be organised as soon as the Army had occupied the base, the MTBs could come in and be refuelled in a couple of hours.

We would then be off to sea again, ready for the dash for Copenhagen. Obviously, we could not expect the Army to worry about lining up petrol supplies for us. This was something the Navy would have to do itself. To this end, a lorry with the No.1 (second in command) of the base and four sailors, including a radio operator, was fitted out, provisioned and told to head for Wilhemshaven, hard on the heels of the advancing Army, now well on the move.

All went well for two days, by which time the naval lorry was right up with the vanguard of the ground forces. They were across the Rhine and setting their own course for Wilhelmshaven; it would soon be time for the MTBs to move. Unfortunately, we were still required to carry out our night patrols and even the Officer Commanding of CFMU did not dare order these abandoned without higher authority. In any case, it was anticipated that it would be at least another two days before we would be able to get into Wilhemshaven.

Notwithstanding the constraints on the Ostend MTBs, to this point the whole operation was going according to plan. As far as the party in the lorry were concerned, their part was running perfectly. They had not communicated with Ostend by radio since they departed but were now so far advanced that the CO of the unit felt he just had to report their progress to CFMU. This proved a blunder. The lorry had been given a special call-sign but that of CFMU remained unchanged. The lorry called up base and made a very brief signal reporting 'position, course and speed'.

The news was heartening back at Ostend but nobody had realised just how completely British Intelligence now had mastery of the air waves. Every message sent by anybody was intercepted, decrypted if necessary, and passed to the appropriate High Command. (I'm sure that MSJ at Bletchley had nothing to do with this.) The upshot was CFMU's call sign was immediately identified and a Staff Officer at Admiralty was asking if this organisation had acquired another MTB with a new call-sign. The Captain of the base tried to be evasive, but it was all to no avail. The order came: 'Whatever this boat is, they seem to be in a muddle—they have just reported their position as in the middle of Germany! You had better recall this craft to Ostend at once,' and the monitoring organisation remained tuned to ensure the recall was issued. Sadly, the officer commanding the lorry was unable to emulate an illustrious predecessor of his—sailing into Copenhagen nearly 150 years before by holding a telescope to a blind eye and declaring he 'did not see the signal'. Regrettably, we did not 'liberate' Copenhagen nor have the chance to share with its citizens the remains of our captured stocks of French champagne.

THE FINAL CURTAIN

VE Day was not to find us in Copenhagen, but we would not celebrate victory in Ostend either. In the event, the eight boats were ordered to return to Lowestoft on VE Day itself. We had only our few personal possessions to pack up at our quarters and to say goodbye to Blanche and the girls—who looked genuinely sorry to see us go. Then it was into the lorries and down to the docks for the last time. The flotilla sailed at 1100 and headed down the swept channels past the familiar wrecks until we were in the open sea and headed for Lowestoft. This was the first and only time I would ever see eight of our boats at sea together, and on a beautiful late spring morning. We took up line abreast, simply because it is much easier to keep station that way than in line ahead. Also, close formation station-keeping was a procedure we had never practised and no one was in the mood for the intense concentration needed for this.

We set out in a spirit of exuberance, but the sense of jollification had a superficial quality to it. Paul Watkins, my CO, was unusually quiet and I began to realise something of the complex emotions he was feeling. Obviously he had to feel thankful that the war was over and he had come through all these years alive—but I do not doubt he thought of friends of his who had not. The war with Japan, of course, had still to be brought to a conclusion. Yet realistically Paul knew that there was not going to be any call for his services in the Pacific and that his war was definitely over. I had no such feelings. I assumed that I would soon be headed to the war in the Far East and, anyway, I was a regular officer and would still be seafaring. For Paul there must have been a sudden feeling of utter emptiness. For the moment, at least, we were content to stand together on the bridge on this beautiful calm day and enjoy the spectacle of eight MTBs in line abreast, roaring across the North Sea at 30 knots.

There was some desultory radio chatter between the COs but it was so inconsequential that one sensed that sentiments similar to those I have described must have been prevailing aboard the other boats. No doubt there would have been a deepening air of sombre gloom as we progressed towards Lowestoft, had there not been an unexpected turn of events. Our youngest CO, Bob Lang from Australia, broke in on the radio with an excited enquiry to the Senior Officer—Freddie Shore. (Peter Magnus and his boat were still at Lowestoft.) Had Shore received the latest W/T Signal from Admiralty? 'No. What was it?' The reply from Lang. 'A general signal to all ships "Splice the Main Brace"' (authorising an issue of an extra 'tot' of rum to all personnel). In fact, no such signal had been made—but if Bob Lang had received it, there could be no questioning its authenticity.

Throughout the eight boats, no further instructions were necessary. Our Coxswain was immediately sent below to fetch the rum jars from their locked stowage. Glasses appeared and the spirit was poured—not carefully measured, 1 gill per man, but freely into out-held tumblers. In a remarkably short time, any air of despond had vanished. I well recall sitting on the rear coaming of the bridge beside my skipper, each of us with a glass of rum in hand. Soon Paul was unburdening to me all the dark thoughts that he had pent up in him—and my heart warmed to him in a way it never had before, even though I thought the world of him as a Commanding Officer. Once the gloom had evaporated a sense of fun developed. Paul decided what to do. He summoned one of our older and more reliable seamen and gave him instructions. He handed him the microphone of the R/T and told him exactly what to say, using the correct R/T procedure to call up the Senior Officer: 'This is Able Seaman Mills of MTB 476. I am the only sober person on board. What shall I do?' Without a moment's hesitation the distinctive Mayfair drawl of Lt. Shore came back with, 'Hello Mills. Mills. This is Freddie—get drunk, obviously!'

It has to be admitted that, after a time, the line-abreast of eight boats was beginning to look somewhat ragged. However, things did not get out of hand even though I doubt that any of the COs would have been keen to undergo a modern police breathaliser test by the end of the three and a half hour journey. But at last Lowestoft hove in sight, whereupon the whole flotilla 'got their act together', formed line-ahead and powered majestically into harbour. We were greeted by base staff, including many Wrens, welcoming the only flotilla from that port that had been based away from UK on active service, back home after a job well done. The Captain of the base and our own well-loved Senior Officer, Peter Magnus, were on the dockside to greet us. Nobody had been expecting a heroes' welcome as, by Coastal Forces standards, the achievements of the flotilla over the last three months had not been particularly spectacular—but it was pleasant to be so warmly welcomed home.

From my personal viewpoint, although the time had gone quickly, we had been in another world in Belgium. I felt amazed that it was only three months since we had finished our training at Lowestoft and headed across the North Sea to join our flotilla.

With the boats secured and tidied up, the officers were soon back in the Royal Hotel and greeting old friends. We found that a lively party was already under way. Amongst those present was the stout and jovial Mayor of Lowestoft who, I recalled, had been quite a common visitor to our mess, before we went away. When darkness fell, once more the blackout screens and blinds were placed in position. The Home Secretary had decreed that East Coast towns were to maintain the blackout for one more night just in case there were any U-Boats or other German craft that had not heard the war had ended. This was an absurd proposition, not worth examining here, but the Naval Base and the Town of Lowestoft dutifully obeyed orders. That was until half a dozen gins later for the Mayor, who suddenly declared, 'This is a load of hogwash. I'm the Mayor—cancel the blackout.' Without more ado, the blackout material of the Royal Hotel was torn down so that this building alone stood out as a blaze of light. Bit by bit, the rest of the town followed suit. Meanwhile, most of the blackout frames from the hotel had been taken to the beach across the promenade and a large bonfire lit. Soon half the population of Lowestoft was on the beach, dancing, singing and drinking until the small hours, in a totally spontaneous celebration. But then a war (that had lasted five and a half years—and involved blackouts all that time) did not end every day. The Final Curtain had not come down. It had gone up—IN FLAMES.

Next morning everyone asked 'What now?' Clearly, there were no more anti-E-Boat patrols to be made. Nor were any further training exercises called for. In fact we realised that there was now no more justification for sending us to sea at all. With the nation practically bankrupt, notwithstanding victory, there was no justification for using any more expensive 100-octane petrol. It was now obvious that the three Lowestoft flotillas must soon pay off and the whole base close down, so that the trawlers could return to this ancient fishing port and resume their lawful 'business in great waters'. All this could not happen overnight and the question arose how to keep crews and base staff occupied until the wind-down plans could be implemented. It was decided that there should be a final inspection of the base and the boats by the Admiral Commanding Coastal Forces and preparing for this would keep everyone busy. The next two weeks were spent smartening up our boats as for a Spithead review. Every trace of rust was scoured and repainted, all brass was stripped of paint and polished until gleaming, while the boats inside were scrubbed until spotless. All this was a rather pointless exercise as the boats were all about to be scrapped but the personnel of a proud flotilla had nothing else to do and entered into the smartening up activities with enthusiasm.

The base, the boats and the crews were duly inspected and speeches of congratulations made. We were then told, in effect: 'OK. That's it. Now strip the boats of everything movable and prepare to throw them away.' In the following week, the MTBs were not only destored and deammunitioned but off came the guns, radar, most radio equipment, smoke-making gear, etc. The boats were little more than shells with engines, fuel tanks and basic radio. The final day came and in groups of four boats, with the two officers and skeleton crews only, we headed out of Lowestoft for the last time. In fact, this was the first time I had ever headed for sea from our base, just as our arrival on VE Day was the first and last time I ever sailed into the port. We headed through the Straits of Dover and on to Poole. The journey was unremarkable except that, with the boats now stripped and a foot higher out of the water than usual, our full speed proved to be in excess of 50 knots. We reached Poole that evening and turned our backs on the boats (which were to have their engines removed and then simply be placed in mud berths—to rot). After an evening meal and a bed overnight, I said my farewells to Paul and the last members of the crew and was on a train for my home, three weeks leave and then, I knew not what. I would not see Paul Watkins again for forty-nine years. I reopened correspondence with him in 1993 and was hospitably entertained by Paul and his wife at their Suffolk home in 1994.

CHAPTER 15

OFF EAST—ONCE MORE

BACK HOME ON LEAVE with the war ended in Europe, I found life in Britain starting slowly to return to normal. For the first time since 1939, there was no blackout. A million or so servicemen and women who had been fighting the Germans were no longer at risk of being killed in the European war. Families with a member held as a POW looked forward to an early reunion. Finally, the Home Guard and the Civil Defence (ARP) organisations were disbanded. Nevertheless, the nation was still at war. Servicemen were not being demobilised and reports of warship movements remained classified. Rationing of food, clothing and petrol, along with general austerity, would prevail for some years, as would conservation of electricity regarding neon signs and advertising. Nevertheless, each relaxation was a matter for satisfaction.

For the Navy in general, and for the author in particular, the next year would be one of turmoil and confusion. Whilst victory over Japan was now certain, it was assumed that this would take another year. The enemy were expected to fight for every mile of territory and every occupied island. Any pragmatic Japanese should have been aware, since the Battle of Midway, that their war could not be won. The forces opposing them would daily grow stronger, whilst their strategic position grew weaker. But it was assumed that, despite no prospect of winning, the Japanese nation as a whole would fight to the bitter end rather than surrender. In fact, until the last two weeks of the war, there was every indication that this would be the case. In the event, all this changed with the dropping of two atomic bombs.

This first use of mass destruction weapons has been the subject of bitter controversy ever since. The loss of human life at Hiroshima and Nagasaki was horrendous—with most of the victims civilians, women and children. Nevertheless, the loss of life was of a similar order to that inflicted by Allied bombers at Hamburg, yet few voices have been raised against that onslaught. On the other hand, how many Allied lives were spared by the early ending of the war—men attacking Japanese defences and starving POWs in Burma, Thailand, and elsewhere? How many Chinese were saved by the ending of daily atrocities in mainland China, as the result of the early Japanese surrender—directly resulting from the atom bombs?

Finally, who can say how many hundreds of thousands of Japanese would have died and how much more of their country would have been devastated? Should all their main cities have been subjected to the Hamburg treatment with 'conventional' weapons? Would such have been more acceptable from the humanitarian viewpoint? Or should the Allies not have persevered with the war until the Japanese were prepared to surrender? I recognise the right of individuals to hold their own opinions, but suggest the foregoing factors merit consideration by well-meaning anti-nuclear protesters.

Without further discussion about atomic bombs, the fact is that the war with Japan ended three and a half months after VE Day. There must have been very few servicemen who saw out the war in Europe and reached the Far East, or Pacific, in time to fight against Japan. Certainly, contrary to my own expectations, I did not.

I received my next appointment in the first week of July—to the Hunt Class (small escort type) destroyer *Lauderdale*, for operational service in the Far East. This was not the sort of ship I expected at all. Hitherto, Hunt Class had scarcely been seen outside the North Sea and their range was so limited that they were not even used on Atlantic convoys.

What use could they be in the Indian Ocean or the Pacific? The ship was to be given a major refit in South Africa, including the removal of the stabiliser gear, thereby making an extra fuel tank. But I wonder if this would have made much difference. Furthermore, taking the stabilisers out was worrying, as the class was notorious for lack of stability. Nevertheless, it was 'mine not to reason why'. Significant, however, was the evident anticipated duration of the conflict with Japan. The authorities clearly felt it worth having a minor warship take a month to steam to Durban, another three refitting, then work-up, to be ready for active service in five months' time. As it was, the ship's limited range necessitated no fewer than eight fuelling stops, *en route* to Durban—and I thought the endurance of *Revenge* was low! Happily, the River Congo was not to be one of the stops.

My actually joining *Lauderdale* was inauspicious. I still had my Dartmouth-instilled image of the formalities of taking up a new appointment, but had yet to experience such. I arrived at Portsmouth in the evening, took a taxi to the dockyard and asked the Naval Police where *Lauderdale* was berthed. They had not even heard of the ship. 'Never mind,' I said, 'We'll find her.' After half an hour's fruitless search for any ship faintly resembling a Hunt Class destroyer, I learnt that *Lauderdale* was on a mooring some way away.

I paid off my taxi and found a boat to deliver me. A recognisable dark shape was located—with no light, except a mooring light on the jack-staff. There was no boarding ladder but I was able to scramble aboard. I persuaded the boat to wait while I investigated, leaving my luggage (my usual trunk, suitcase and duffel bag) behind, whilst I did so. At length, I found an elderly night-watchman seated in an upper-deck compartment, with oil lamp and primus stove, cooking himself some sausages. 'You can't join now, Sir. Everything is locked up and the ship has no electric light or water.' I felt he was right, and it was no use my 'repairing on board' at that time. Accordingly, it was back to the dockyard, thankful I had not let the boat go as I would have had no means of summoning another to pick me up. I took a taxi to the Royal Naval Barracks and demanded a cabin—at least overnight.

Next morning, I learnt that a small working party from the barracks had started to prepare the ship for sea but I was the first officer on the scene. At least I was able to make some sort of inspection of this warship and ponder what adventures she might have for me. I was dismayed to find that the ship was crawling with cockroaches and there was ample evidence of rats. 'Don't worry about them,' said the Leading Seaman in charge of the working party, 'The ship's being fumigated tomorrow.' Indeed, the men were busy, papering over every port, weather-deck door, ventilator inlet and bridge voice-pipe—prior to filling the ship with hydrogen cyanide gas. I was glad I had not 'moved in'.

During the next week, the vermin and insects were killed and their remains swept up. A diesel generator and the ventilation system were activated, to blow out the hydrogen cyanide and make the ship habitable. Other officers and the ship's company arrived, *Lauderdale* was declared commissioned, and the ship sailed for South Africa. There was neither work-up nor functioning trials, and scarcely time for the crew to find their way round their new ship. It had been judged that, as long as the engines and essential radio equipment worked, the rest could wait until the refit in South Africa was completed. This was a day which neither myself, nor anyone else on board, would see. Not only would I not see a gun fired in anger, I would never even see if our impressive main armament of six 4″ guns would go bang.

I felt some concern on learning that I was to be the Navigating Officer. I hated navigation, because I found working sights from 'celestial obser-vations' far from easy. I should not have done, as we had been well tutored in these things at Dartmouth and had had to complete a dozen sun/moon/star sights, as Midshipmen. It was not that I found the subject difficult to understand. In fact, I was fascinated by the concept of 'celestial navigation'. Science and maths had been my best subjects. I had mastered plane trigonometry at thirteen, knew how to resolve any triangle, given the length of two sides and one angle and had no difficulty 'proving' the relevant formulae. Subsequently, I took to spherical trigonometry as a simple extension of plane trigonometry. I was proud of the fact that I was one of the few of my contemporaries who could actually 'prove' the

Haversine theorem. This was the basis of spherical trigonometry. Why then should I have a problem with astro-navigation? Strange though it may seem, with a brain that was clearly 'good at maths', I was remarkably weak at simple arithmetic. I was able to add and subtract figures but, given sets of logarithmic haversines, each of six digits, all too often I would subtract one from the other and get the answer wrong. One always knew—half a dozen steps later—that one had made an error. But this would involve the tedious task of reworking the calculation to find just where one had omitted to 'carry one', or whatever. I would get it right eventually but working a sight would often take me twice as long as the average competent navigator, despite my clear grasp of spherical trigonometry. It would be an overstatement to say that I lacked basic numeracy but, at least, I have every sympathy for those who do. I believe this should not be taken a measure of intellect—or lack of it. After all, I had passed out tenth out of forty-four (against some keen competition) at the RNC.

I will return to my difficulties with navigation later—but, at least, no HM Ship was lost or imperiled as the result of my weakness in this subject. Notwithstanding my problems with navigation, I made one shrewd move at Portsmouth which was to pay off six weeks later, thousands of miles away. I ingratiated myself with one of the staff at the Portsmouth Chart Depot, who sent his salaams to a mate of his at the Chart Depot at Simonstown. So, with slight misgivings as to my ability to find my way there, I set out in late July, round Africa towards my old 'stamping ground' of Durban.

I found that I had an interesting and congenial bunch of fellow officers and my Captain was an experienced destroyer CO—Lt. Cdr. Benians, whom I held in high regard. The voyage to South Africa started with few worries for a nervous navigator. I took my departure from Ushant, from which, once again, shone out the most powerful lighthouse in the world—and I no longer had to worry about those formidable Brest destroyers which I had held in such awe only eighteen months back. A dead-reckoning run overnight brought up the Cape Finisterre corner of Spain right on schedule at first light. I then enjoyed taking the ship on courses of my choosing—closer than the normal shipping route, but a safe distance off-shore (I had no problems over pilotage and coastal navigation). Accordingly, we passed inside the Berlenga Isles, some five miles off the coast of Portugal.

I well recall viewing, through binoculars, the Palace of Mafra, which stood on high ground some five miles inland. This imposing building which looked twice the size of Buckingham Palace had been the royal Portuguese summer palace until the country became a republic in 1911. I mention this only because of a thread of history, of which I was to become conscious more than twenty years later. Having left the RN, I settled and married in Australia. My wife had (and still has) an interest in a sheep grazing property in the Monaro district of southern NSW. This property is named Maffra and has been owned by connections of my wife's family for many generations. It was said that the land had originally been acquired by an early settler who had served under Sir Arthur Wellesley (later Duke of Wellington) in the Iberian Peninsula in the early 1800s. He was believed to have named the property after a place in Portugal. It will be recalled that the British and their Portuguese allies had withdrawn behind the lines of Torres Vedras. These protected the city of Lisbon and the southern end of the Estremadura—being the last tip of Europe not occupied by Napoleon's armies. From this base, Wellesley's army struck back and drove the French right out of Portugal and Spain. The Palace of Mafra (with one f) is located only a few miles south of Torres Vedras. It seems likely that several thousand troops were billeted there through the winter of 1810/11. It is therefore probable that this Napoleonic War veteran, settling in New South Wales, had himself been quartered in the Palace of Mafra.

In 1970, with our small son, my wife and I made a combined business and holiday world tour which included a day in Lisbon from the liner *Canberra*. We took a car and drove out to inspect the Palace of Mafra. We were the first people associated with Maffra Station in the Monaro to visit the place after which the property had been named 160 years before.

Lauderdale went to Gibraltar without incident, staying overnight. The 'Rock' was as popular as ever with the sailors. For me, it revived memories of *Revenge* there just two years earlier—and my childhood visit, at the age of seven.

Our next call was Casablanca, which looked an attractive city, un-damaged by war, but we gave no shore leave as the place was suffering a minor epidemic of bubonic plague. This last was well contained but the mere mention of the name of the disease was enough to send a shudder through me. I paid close attention to the rat guards on the mooring lines. The only other point of interest was the battleship *Jean Bart* which had lain there disabled by a British MTB attack since 1940. Eleven years later I would find myself in a ship on the same side as *Jean Bart*—in the Suez operations of 1956.

To report on every place visited would be tedious. The ship went on to Dakar—with Richelieu associations, Freetown—no more attractive than on previous calls, Takoradi—in what is now Ghana, and Pointe Noire. This last was across the Gulf of Guinea in what was then French Congo, only a hundred miles north of the mouth of the River Congo.

The Takoradi-Pointe Noire leg involved more than a thousand miles and two days steaming out of sight of land. This was to put me on my mettle as a navigator. My confidence was growing but I was still slow working my sights. I struggled through Morning Stars, Meridianal

Passage-run—Afternoon Sun and finally Evening Stars the night before the ETA at Pointe Noire at 0800. I had my collection of sextant altitudes and associated Greenwich Mean Times (to the second) and was departing for the charthouse to work my calculations, when disaster struck. As the result of extraordinary clumsiness, I managed to drop the wooden box containing the Deck Watch chronometer on to the steel deck of the bridge—in full view of my Captain. Had this been St John Cronyn, the air would have been blue. As it was, Lt. Cdr. Benians's wrath was considerable and he made some subdued, but fairly acid, remarks. I wished the deck would open and swallow me. It should be explained that, for the previous hundred years, ships' chronometers had been by far the most scientific items of equipment aboard warships and were handled like the Holy Grail. To drop a chronometer, if not constituting actual criminal negligence, could only be regarded as gross incompetence.

I still had the ship's main chronometer but this was for checking the Deck Watch and not allowed out of the charthouse. I had worked my previous evening's star sights and obtained an accurate 'fix'. However, I was not now equipped to take the vital morning stars, prior to our landfall. I was not too worried, as I knew where we were at dusk the evening before. The sea was flat calm (in the Doldrums—right on the Equator); there were no ocean currents indicated. I therefore felt I could safely head for Pointe Noire, on dead-reckoning. However, out of proper concern for the safety of his ship and his annoyance with me, my Captain ordered me to take soundings with the Kelvin Sounding Machine. I had to do this hourly, through the night, involving rigging the sounding boom and the assistance of two seamen.

I had the morning watch (0400-0800) anyway and, as the light grew stronger, I started to search for the land through binoculars. There was a cloudless sky above but just a trace of haze low on the horizon, particularly to the east. At 0730 there was no sign of land whatsoever. I started to feel nervous—it would not matter too much if we were, say, a quarter of an hour late arriving, but a more worrying thought occurred to me. Suppose the land should suddenly appear as an unbroken line of palm trees—would Pointe Noire be to the north or south of us? I even recalled being told at Dartmouth that there was no disgrace in 'aiming off', say, thirty miles one way or the other when in doubt about a landfall. Once could then be twenty or more miles out but still know which way to turn for one's destination. I had taken no such precaution and had aimed straight for Pointe Noire.

At 0745, my Captain, in exasperation, said, 'You gave me an ETA of 0800. It is now 0745—WHERE THE HELL IS AFRICA?' I could hardly reply, 'Good question!' although I wished 'to hell' I knew. Mercifully, on the point of despair, after a long hard look through my binoculars, I was able to answer my skipper with, 'Pointe Noire breakwater dead ahead—estimated distance five miles.' My spot-on landfall was, of course, sheer luck but what had happened was that the land along this coast was low-lying and absolutely flat, as I remembered the Congo. The town and port were insignificant with no buildings of more than two storeys and everything had been cloaked by the low-lying haze, which was scarcely noticeable. What I had seen through my binoculars was one solitary crane, of the harbour construction type, just appearing through the top of the haze. I realised that there would not be cranes every mile or so along the coast of darkest Equatorial Africa, so—Bingo—this had to be Pointe Noire.

Now it was on to Walvis Bay, part of Namibia today and, presumably, its chief port. I have never seen such a desolate looking country. I did not dare go within ten miles of the coast, which had not been properly surveyed. The shore line was ill-defined on the chart and there was a general warning that there were numerous off-shore reefs and rocks. Inland were spectacular peaks rising to 8,000 ft. and which I was eager to take bearings on. Sadly, however, not one was identified on the maps. There was just a statement: 'Here are mountains.' Closely examining the chart, in several hundred miles of coast I found one tiny improbable mark—a small circle of about 2 mm diameter drawn near the coast with the one word 'Post'. This was the more remarkable as there was no sign of human habitation or road for a hundred miles.

I drew my Captain's attention to this marking on the chart (I was not game to go close enough to the coast to see if it could be spotted). Surprisingly, my CO told me he happened to know all about this post. It seemed that survivors of a torpedoed ship had landed on this barren coast and, after great hardships, been rescued, one of them writing a book on the adventure. Evidently, not far from where they came ashore, they spotted a smooth round pole sticking up about fifteen feet out of the ground. It proved to be the mast of a long since wrecked ship of totally unknown identity, presumably now some 40 ft. below the sands. One of the survivors had noted its position as carefully as possible and reported it to the hydrographer. Having no other identifiable feature to chart on several hundred miles of coast, its location had been incorporated in a Notice to Mariners for updating charts. But what help it could possibly be to any mariner is hard to imagine.

Walvis Bay proved to be a really 'nothing place' without a single blade of grass or trace of green of any sort. There was, however, enough oil there to refuel us. We had been roughly retracing the steps of Bartholomew Diaz and the great Portuguese explorers of the fifteenth century (who had no chronometers or harbour cranes to aid them). Meanwhile, modern science had led to some of the most terrible—and momentous—events of the twentieth century. These were the dropping of atom bombs on Japan on 6 and 9 of August—whilst *Lauderdale* was off West Africa. It must have been evident then that our ship would never fight the Japanese. Emperor Hirohito broadcast on 15 August that Japan was accepting defeat and, on 2 September, the surrender was signed on the quarterdeck of USS *Missouri* in Tokyo Bay. Hirohito was agreeing to capitulation as *Lauderdale* left Pointe Noire. At this moment, the question for everyone on board was, 'What now?' We wondered if there was any point in giving the ship a long and expensive refit in Durban if she was never to go on East. Surely this mass-produced cut-price mini-destroyer could not be intended to be a unit of Britain's post-war Navy? These were valid questions. However, the Admiralty obviously had many more pressing decisions to make, concerning whole fleets and wartime bases, to worry about *Lauderdale* somewhere off southern Africa. Indeed, I doubt the Admiralty even got to considering the future of our ship until she was well into her refit in Durban.

Two days were spent in Capetown, to give some reasonable shore leave to the crew for the first time since leaving England and to take on fresh provisions. The ship then left on the final leg, to Durban. This led to one more spot of bother for myself as the navigator. Before leaving Capetown, the Chief Engineer Officer asked me, 'How far is it from Capetown to Durban?' I imagined this was an idle question, out of curiosity. Accordingly, I did not say, 'I will go and measure on the chart and let you know,' but rather, '1,300 miles, as I recall.' This was about right, give-or-take fifty (nautical) miles. What I did not know was that our 'Chief' planned to arrive in Durban, where we would enter dry dock, with as little fuel as possible. Had he told me the reason for his question, I would have measured the distance for him and advised that allowance should be made for the Agulhas Current. This ran at about 2 knots against us which, in practical terms, would put about another 120 miles on the trip, at economical speed. I was not aware of any problem until 3½ days later—perhaps twenty miles from The Bluff at the entrance to Durban harbour. A worried Chief Engineer appeared on the bridge and said, 'You told me it was 1,300 miles to Durban—we have logged 1,420 and Durban is not in sight.'

'Not far, Chief—what's the problem?'

'The problem is I only allowed for fuel for 1,300 miles and a 10% margin and the tanks are all but dry.'

Needless to say, fingers were crossed and the Captain clearly viewed this as another sign of my incompetence. He signalled for a tug to stand-by, in case we did not quite make it. The tug was not needed.

Once in Durban and in 'Dockyard Hands', I found I had no more duties to perform before I left the ship nearly three months later. I scored one of the few unfavourable CO's reports of my career. It was fair comment but disappointing: 'He should persevere in those branches of professional knowledge in which he is at present weak.' My regret was that Navigation was the only 'branch of my professional knowledge' that I had had a chance to display. No one knew how fast I could send and read Morse after MTBs, my knowledge of torpedoes from *Enterprise* or gunnery from *Revenge* and *Orwell*. I had to content myself with the reflection: 'You can't win 'em all.' I have to say my Captain also concluded that I had a somewhat slap-happy approach to my duties—with possible elements of justification. He showed me my Confidential Report—which a CO is bound to do if it contains adverse remarks. He had written, 'This officer should realise that the Navy in peacetime is a lot more serious than the Navy in war.' I can only ask: 'What officer would not have to learn this lesson after Happy Hooligan days in Coastal Forces?'

Shortly after the refit started, almost our entire crew left the ship, not to temporary shore accommodation but drafted elsewhere—mostly on to the Eastern Fleet to make up numbers in other ships. Retained were only a handful of cooks and stewards to keep the wardroom going. This was an extraordinary state—a ship with officers but no men. Even the officers had nothing to do—no duty officer, nor preparations for active service, as in the case of *Enterprise*. It was soon clear there would be no commissioning. The CO and No.1 moved ashore and lived in the Durban Club or such accommodation and those still on board only got in the way. As the navigator, I might have been busy correcting my charts from Notices to Mariners. I did not fancy this as the seaman assigned as 'Navigator's Yeoman' to assist me had gone. Accordingly, I played my trump card—I telexed my contact at Simonstown chart depot. After an exchange of pleasantries, he agreed to take my entire outfit of chart folios and look after them for the period of our refit. I now had nothing to do at all for the next two months.

This might have seemed a happy state of affairs but, in reality, I was soon almost at my wit's end. The ship was uninhabitable by day, with workmen making a fearful noise with pneumatic tools and generally tearing the inside of the ship apart. With nothing to keep me on board, I would try to flee ashore after breakfast. Unfortunately, apart from lying in the sun on the surf beach, there was little one could do that did not cost money—of which I had little. I contacted my old hosts, the Curries, who again kindly asked me to stay with them in Zululand—but now at Empangeni. This made a break from Durban and the Curries were good to me—but it was not the same without my mate Vaughan, with whom to ride off to the pub at Gingingdlovu.

Back at Durban, I found myself drawn into a smarter and older (than me) social set. This involved my attendance at either Clarewood or Greyville Racecourses most week-ends, at cocktail parties and even night clubs. Needless to say, a month or so of this life left me penniless. I had met one or two attractive girls and had taken a fancy to one—the daughter of a Norwegian shipping magnate. However, I had sufficient conscience to be unable to 'sponge' on other people completely. Aboard later ships, I could return hospitality by inviting my shoreside hosts aboard for cocktail parties, etc. This was out of the question now.

In the light of the foregoing, it is hardly surprising that I felt relieved when word came at short notice that, together with most of the other officers, I was being reappointed to '*Lanka*—for disposal'. This 'for disposal' was a standard Admiralty term but somehow suggested being got rid of. A few days later, I stood on the flight deck of the escort carrier *Khedive*, being used as a troopship. We waved goodbye to a few girls who had come down to the jetty to see us off. My emotions were confused, but I was bound for Colombo and waiting to see just how I was to be 'disposed of'. *Lauderdale* was handed over to the Greek Navy and became His Hellenic Majesty's Ship *Kriti*.

CHAPTER 16

COLOMBO AND POINTS EAST

MY ARRIVAL IN COLOMBO evoked a curious sense of *déjà vu*. It could not be said that I knew the place, although I had some recollection of a day spent there when I was seven years old *en route* to boarding school in England (as yet to be identified as 'Bigshotte'). I well remembered the busy harbour and had learned since that visiting ships always tied up between head-and stern buoys—bows north in the North-West Monsoon and west for the South-West. I was able to remember being taken to lunch at the Galle Face Hotel, by the sea south of the main city. This was one of the truly 'grand' hotels of the old days of the 'British Raj', which, I was happy to find, was still there in scarcely reduced splendour.

There was, however, a great deal more than my own meagre memories of Colombo to excite me. My father had served in the Ceylon Civil Service from 1905 until 1926 (with a break of four years for the War, 1914–18). My home in England contained quantities of memorabilia and photo albums my father had brought from Ceylon. My own birth certificate showed that I had been born in a residence named Lansdowne, in Maitland Crescent in the 'Slave Island & Kollupitiya–2A' Division of Colombo—twenty years before, in 1925. It had evidently given my father satisfaction to have entered under 'Rank or Profession of Father', 'Registrar General'—one of his appointments at the time. My family had moved away from Ceylon the year after I was born. Not surprisingly, even if subliminally, I felt some ability to identify with Ceylon in general and Colombo in particular. Both were of great beauty and enchantment even in 1945, peopled by gentle and cultured Sinhalese and Tamils who appeared to live contented lives. Sadly, forty-five years on, Sri Lanka is now bedeviled by civil war, poverty and general decay, making it one of the poorest nations in the world. I am in no position to make further observations on the state of that nation today but will be commenting on how I found the place in 1945 and 1946.

On arrival, with the handful of other ex-*Lauderdale* officers, I was advised that we were to be housed at an improbable establishment named *Lanka II*, rather than at HMS *Lanka* itself, a large naval depot and transit camp out in the jungle. The RN liked such arrangements, signifying that these outstations were under the administration of the parent establishment. Sometimes, the latter would be a purely nominal organisation. For instance, all officers serving at Admiralty in London were on the books of HMS *President*—even, say, an equerry at Buckingham Palace. I have no idea why this arrangement was made for us in Colombo, but had no complaints. *Lanka II*, it seemed, mainly existed to house relatively junior naval officers who had duties in Colombo itself, related to the port, etc. It was housed in a comfortable residence right on the sea, in the area known as The Fort, in which were situated the main Government Offices and official residences. The house even had its own narrow section of beach in a diminutive cove between outcrops of rock and sea wall of stone blocks. Generally it was considered unsafe to bathe anywhere in the sea near Colombo in the South-West Monsoon which was now at full strength. Nevertheless, it was refreshing and stimulating to bathe from our own tiny beach, onto which thundered mighty breakers from the Indian Ocean.

I was required to report daily to the naval authorities to enquire whether any decision had yet been taken regarding my 'disposal'. But, after a few days, I was virtually told, 'Don't call us. We'll call you.' I was thus able to do some exploring, and looking for traces of my 'roots' (albeit of no great depth), such as seeking out Lansdowne, Maitland Crescent. I also found that there was an overnight courier service by rail to take confidential despatches to the naval base of Trincomalee on the other side of Ceylon. I volunteered for this run, involving my own First Class sleeper compartment and costing me nothing. I particularly wanted to see Trincomalee as this had been one of the magic names of which I had heard so much, my father having been the one-time Government Agent there. Later, I would find myself in a ship briefly stationed there. But, at this point, I had no idea what the future held for me. Suffice it to say, that after becoming bored with Durban, I found no end of excitement and interest in Ceylon. I had yet to find any trace of my father's time in Ceylon but soon would.

My father had sent me a list of names of people he suggested I should contact, together with the precise protocol for doing so. I have since come to understand the merit of protocol—that it is not simply to establish individuals' status in society, but rather an elaborate organisation to minimise embarrassment and smooth the interaction between people, both officially and informally. This might be manifested in the time-honoured butler's advice that he would 'see if Madam was in'; only the most boorish caller would ask, 'Don't you know?' It could be argued that, for the Germans, protocol precluded their officers attending the same bordellos as their men in Ostend. In this instance, it turned out that the Governor (and, later, first Governor General) of Ceylon had been an old friend of my father. They had shared the same 'chummery' (whatever that meant) as young men.

Following instructions, I walked round to Queen's House, close to

Lanka II, and signed the visitor's book—adding the notation 'Son of A. W. Scymour, late of Ceylon Civil Service'. I found myself wondering how 'late' one could get. It was just under twenty years. The next day, I received a telephone call from the ADC advising that His Excellency (Sir Henry Monk-Mason Moore KCMG, etc.) asked if I might 'call in for a drink' at six that evening. Notwithstanding the evident informality of the invitation, I felt I had better present myself as smartly as possible. I therefore donned my 'No. 10' uniform (starched white trousers and tunic buttoned to the throat and wearing medal ribbons). I was, in fact, rather proud that I now boasted four ribbons: Defence Medal for Civil Defence duties during the Blitz in England; Atlantic Star with clasp for 'France and Germany' service, resulting from being based in wartime Europe, at Ostend; 1939–1945 Star; and the Victory Medal—all of which I felt I had earned.

At Queen's House, I was shown into a small sitting room and introduced to the Governor and his wife. The former was casually dressed in khaki shorts and open-neck shirt. A turbaned 'bearer' appeared and quietly asked what I would like to drink and the ADC retired. Sir Henry solicitously enquired after the health of my father and reminisced about their time together in Anuradhapura (I think) in about 1920. This was before I was born, or my father married. He then mentioned that he usually had a game of snooker at that time of day—did I play snooker? I replied that I did (in fact, rather fancying myself at the game), so we played and I was comprehensively beaten—but then H.E. did have rather more chance to practise.

Naturally, I was asked what I was doing in Colombo. I replied that I was awaiting disposal, that I had been living very comfortably in the small officers' quarters close by but, sadly, had been told I was to move to *Lanka* in two days time. At this point, Lady Moore declared, 'I don't see why you need do that. Why don't you come and stay here with us at Queen's House?' After mere token demurral on my part, it was arranged that a car would call round for me and my luggage—the trunk, suitcase and duffel-bag, with which I had left England—next day.

I lived the next two weeks in not only splendour but also delightful company. I was not wholly unaccustomed to the vice-regal atmosphere, as I had lived with my parents in residence at Government Houses, both in Suva, Fiji and in Port of Spain, Trinidad. But I had been only six and seven in the former and ten in the latter. In those times, with my sister and brother, I had only glimpsed the pomp and circumstance of 'The Raj', having been kept very much behind the scenes in the care of a nanny or governess. Our early family life had been largely along the lines of the splendid Mrs Beeton's *Handbook of Household Management*. This august writer strongly urged parents to try very hard to find at least half an hour a day to spend with their children. Strangely, I never felt deprived but only became really devoted and attached to my father and mother after they retired and we all lived together as a family in England.

I am not sure what family the Moores had, but a daughter named Deirdre in her early twenties was living with them at Queen's House. The menage comprised Sir Henry and Lady Moore, Deirdre and the ADC—a young and capable army officer whose name I cannot now recall—and, briefly, myself. Not only were the senior Moores kind and considerate but Deirdre and the ADC were healthy, outgoing and fun-loving young people. Needless to say, there were a great many dignitaries and VIPs coming and going, to most of whom I would be introduced. However, no demands were made to assist in any way at official functions. Each morning, I would be called with a cup of tea, slice of paw-paw and fresh orange juice. The housekeeper would send in a book in which I was invited to signify which meals I would be attending that day. If I should live to stay in the Presidential Suite at the Waldorf Astoria, I would not expect to be more pampered. I had a devoted Sinhalese servant assigned to meet my every need. The bath was run to the precise depth and temperature whilst I took my tea and paw-paw and my day uniform was laid out for me to put on when I emerged from the bathroom. White tropical mess kit with wing-collar and bow tie was the dress for dinner each night. I only had one white mess jacket but this—and indeed every other garment I ever wore—would be washed, starched and ironed for me after every wearing.

The life at Queen's House was not so demanding that there was no time for leisure activities. Deirdre would only have to suggest that it would be nice to go for a swim next day and it would be arranged. A vice-regal car and driver would convey a party of perhaps Deirdre, a friend of hers, the ADC and myself to Mount Lavinia for the day. I also recall someone saying that a film showing in Colombo would be fun. When the parents said they would also like to see it, arrangements were made with the cinema. Two shiny black cars conveyed us there, the cinema manager greeted the party and led us to the Governor's Box and the show commenced.

It can be imagined that this life was not hard to take. I had done nothing to deserve this splendid treatment but life is all about taking the good with the bad—as well as vice-versa. Memories of this happy time would sustain me through a period of squalor and misery that lay just ahead.

After two weeks, the Naval Authorities did finally 'call me' and told me to join the destroyer HMS *Cavendish*, sailing in two days time, for passage to Singapore. The appointment was HMS *Terror*—the Singapore Base—'for disposal'. So I still did not know my future.

Meanwhile, I had a pleasant enough voyage across the Bay of Bengal. *Cavendish* was a modern destroyer and a 'proper' warship, recently commissioned for the peacetime Navy. Whilst many of the crew were conscripts (National Service would continue for another ten years), the officers were nearly all regulars and the ship had a smart and purposeful air. In other words, she was just the sort of ship I hoped I would be joining.

Cavendish did not proceed directly to Singapore, but called at Port Swettenham (now Pelabohan Kelang). Unexpectedly, this brought me nearer ending my life than any wartime action I had seen. The ship was only in port for the day, but the Naval-Officer-In-Charge there happened to be an old friend of the captain of *Cavendish* (another example of the RN as a world-wide club—and perhaps the reason we had called at P.S.). As a result, the Port Captain offered his friend his newly acquired powerful American Lincoln Zephyr staff car (ex-local Japanese Commander's car). He also offered the services of one of his staff to drive to Kuala Lumpur, directly inland from Port Swettenham.

There was a spare seat in the car, which I was happy to accept. In my considerable travels, this was my first visit to South-East Asia and I was always keen to see new places. It was only an hour's drive to Kuala Lumpur which we inspected and found interesting, although far smaller than the modern capital of Malaysia with its skyscrapers and smart hotels. In the afternoon, we headed back to the port and *Cavendish*, just as it started to rain—as it only can rain in the monsoon season in South-East Asia.

Today, the road from Kuala Lumpur to the coast is doubtless a concreted dual-carriage freeway. In 1945, it was only a two-lane narrow sealed road running straight and flat through plantations of tall rubber trees. Unable to see clearly through the tropical downpour, our driver, going too fast, accidentally allowed the near side wheels to move off the sealed road. The 'soft shoulder' of the road was softer than usual, in the torrential rain. A shower of red-brown mud came through the side windows, which the clammy heat had forced us to keep open, and spattered the clean white 'No.10' uniforms of both the Captain and myself. More importantly, the driver lost control of the vehicle as the near-side wheels ploughed into the soft mud. In his struggle to get back on the road, our driver over-corrected and crossed the road at 45 degrees with the car still moving at high speed. This meant we were now headed for standing rubber trees of some eighteen inches diameter—and more solid than a telegraph pole.

Whilst events moved too fast for me to assess the situation, I sensed that our car was about to wrap itself around one of these trees and we must surely be killed. This was, indeed, a reasonable expectation—but it did not happen. There was a mighty thump, throwing four occupants forward (long before the advent of seat belts) and the car—or wreck thereof—came to rest in some six feet, with a fraction of the number of 'g's deceleration than would have occurred from the impact with a standing rubber tree. We got out of the car, bruised and covered with mud but otherwise unharmed.

Some Divine Protector of unworthy naval officers had placed a sawn 8 ft. length of tree exactly in our path at 45 degrees to the road—to act as a near-perfect crash barrier for our careering monster of a car. The Captain, of course, was not best pleased at having to stand at the roadside in sodden uniform and hitch a lift in the next passing lorry headed for the coast. Nevertheless, like me, I am sure he felt extremely lucky—and thankful—to be alive. There were no other felled trees on either side of the road to be seen within miles. Only later would I lament that I no longer had a faithful personal valet to have my one-and-only 'No.10' white uniform washed, starched and ironed in time for me to report on board such warship as I would be joining next day in Singapore.

LANDING SHIPS (TANK)—LSTs

On arrival, there was a signal to tell me I was appointed as the Navigating Officer of LST 164, at Singapore Naval Base. The dockyard itself was a sorry sight. Singapore Island had been overrun so fast by the Japanese in 1941 that no demolitions had been done by the British. This dockyard had been carefully planned, including a graving dock large enough to take the biggest ship in the world, and was completed not long before the war with all the facilities a refitting warship might require. The place had remained in this condition for most of the war, although it appears that the Japanese made little use of the dockyard. Then, sadly, just a few months before the war ended, the Americans decided to hit the base with a raid by two hundred Flying Fortresses. No one would deny the effectiveness of their bombing—the dockyard was a shambles. Both Portsmouth and Devonport had been severely bombed, but as most of the buildings were over a hundred years old and brick-built, they were simply reduced to rubble, and relatively easily cleared away. At Singapore, every building was of reinforced concrete and, after bombing, remained as twisted and battered fabrications, requiring much oxy-cutting before the site could be cleared. The power station had been wrecked and the only electrical supply available was from a submarine tied up alongside with its diesel engines running.

Offshore, in the Johore Straits, were two Japanese cruisers, painted a weird green colour, doubtless in the belief that this would render them less conspicuous against the jungle of Johore beyond them. These ships had been disabled by British X Craft (midget submarines) with which

Sub Lt. Joe Brooks was still serving. The cruisers' immobilisation at Singapore may well have saved them for destruction in the battle of Leyte Gulf.

I found LST 164, 'repaired on board' and reported for duty. As I boarded, I noted the ship looked rusty and dirty. The sailors were scruffy and the Captain did not seem to be expecting me. All the officers were reservists and the CO a tugmaster from the Pool of London. I have no doubt (but had no chance to observe) that he was a competent mariner, but sadly he showed little talent for running a 'taut ship' and maintaining smartness and discipline amongst a demoralised ship's company. This was hardly surprising as the Captain, officers and crew had all lost interest in everything except being returned to UK and demobbed. When asked what I had come for I replied, 'As the navigator—when do we sail?' I was greeted with a hollow laugh. 'That's a joke. This ship isn't going anywhere—except in tow to the ship-breakers.'

LST 164 was one of dozens of such Landing Ships, supplied by the Americans under 'Lease-Lend', for the duration of the war. The war had ended and so had the Lease-lend Agreement—hence, no spare parts with which to repair the broken-down main (diesel) engines were forthcoming. It was therefore hardly surprising morale should be low, as the ship rotted in the stinking heat of Singapore, with no prospect of performing any further useful role. My own natural reaction was: 'Under the circumstances, why do they need a Navigating Officer?'

I found I had little in common with any of the other officers, whose only interest now seemed to be getting drunk and picking up Dutch/Indonesian half-caste women who had fled from Java and Sumatra and now lived in a refugee camp in Singapore. My mess-mates appeared even less attractive as they all had a deathly greenish-yellow pallor about them as the result of compulsory daily dosing with Mepacryn. This drug had proved an effective prophylactic against malaria—then endemic in Singapore.

Three weeks after I joined the ship, it was Christmas Day (1945). Sadly, there was no Christmas conviviality and 'Goodwill toward Men' evident aboard LST 164. I found myself Duty Officer—not by roster, but because I was the only officer capable of performing any duties on board. The Captain and other officers decided to celebrate Christmas by simply drinking until they passed out. Foolishly, the Captain considered that the easiest way to keep the sailors happy was virtually to tell the Chief Boatswain's Mate to issue the men with as much rum as they wanted. Under the circumstances, I was powerless to prevent pandemonium on board. By about 1300, however, I realised that I had to do something, as most of the forty-odd crew were now either reeling about the decks or had passed out where they stood, many on the hot steel upper-deck under a fiercely blazing sun. I managed to find one level-headed Leading Seaman who was not drunk and begged him for help, promising him he would be well rewarded if he kept off the liquor for the next hour and helped me sort things out (memories of level-headed Leading Seaman Frampton who had got me out of trouble aboard *Enterprise* when *I* had been drunk). He assured me no special reward would be needed and he would help in any way he could. The two of us then went round and picked up unconscious bodies, one by one, and carried them, by fireman's lift, out of the sun to the nearest empty bunks below. After an hour, we had cleared the upper deck, bundled the last staggering, but still conscious, drunk below and even hosed the vomit off the upper deck. I then took my helper into the now-deserted wardroom, where I made sandwiches for the two of us, from contents of the fridge, gave him a cold beer, thanked him profusely and, at last, we wished each other 'Happy Christmas'. It was, in fact, the worst Christmas I have experienced—before or since; worse than two years earlier in the Bay of Biscay, when I had witnessed my first gun 'fired in anger'.

There had been some happier moments during that December, but precious few. I found that I could indulge my enjoyment of sailing by visiting the Barracks adjoining the dockyard (HMS *Terror*), happily left untouched by the American bombers. Recreational facilities there included a boatshed with half a dozen naval 14 ft. sailing dinghies under the charge of a Japanese POW Petty Officer and a few Japanese sailors. All that was necessary was to obtain an authorisation from the Duty Officer at *Terror* and, following a phone call to the boatshed, one merely went there to find a dinghy rigged and ready to step into and sail away. Likewise, on return, one handed the boat over at the jetty and the Japanese did all necessary unrigging and stowing away. This was my first contact with Japanese prisoners of war but the officer at *Terror* assured me that, once their Emperor had ordered surrender these former enemies could not be more docile or co-operative. As he put it, their attitude was one of 'Velly solly—all big mistake. We want help you.'

Few operational warships came to the dockyard as there was nothing for them there. But I would check up what ships might be in the roads south of the Island of Singapore and was delighted to find that aboard one of the British-built so-called Mk. 3 LSTs was my old friend Mike Vaughan. The two of us had sailed together through an Atlantic gale aboard *Antenor*, frolicked with Wrens aboard *Christian Huygens* in the Indian Ocean, served in *Revenge* at Mombasa and round Africa back to UK, fought the Germans aboard *Enterprise* in Biscay, spent four months in the same Home Fleet Destroyer Flotilla, and shared another five of improbable adventures in MTBs. We both now found ourselves in LSTs on the other side of the world. There was, however, a big difference. His ship worked and went to sea, while mine was broken down and rotted in harbour. Needless to say, we had a convivial evening together, but his ship moved on and we only saw each other once. Our next meeting would be two years later, in the Mediterranean.

There were now a few hundred Wrens in Singapore, but there were tens of thousands of servicemen and I had no such advantage as having arrived aboard the same ship as them, as with the *Christian Huygens* at Mombasa. I somehow managed to strike up an acquaintance with an attractive 3rd Officer Wren and started to plan a date. Alas, however, I found that, without one's own staff car—or jeep, at least—and if not a member of the smart Tanglin Club, or wealthy enough to dine at Raffles Hotel, one was 'not in the hunt'.

After Christmas, I saw my Captain and asked if I could be transferred to some ship where I would have some more active employment. This only evoked, 'How would I get on without a navigating officer?' I might have replied, 'You could look out of your cabin port each morning to ensure the dockside was still there.' However, with no likelihood of support forthcoming from my CO, I went over his head (or behind his back) and saw Senior Officer, LSTs at his headquarters. This man gave me a sympathetic hearing but told me that there were a number of junior regular officers looking for ships and, anyway, he had no power to appoint me to any ship other than another LST. This seemed unpromising and I returned to my ship crestfallen. A few days later, after another unpleasant run-in with my Captain, who had returned aboard drunk having smashed the car he had acquired, I began to feel desperate.

Next morning, I had a jeep run me to Sembewang Naval Air Station. I asked to see the Commander (Flying), whom I respectfully asked if I might be accepted for training as a Fleet Air Arm pilot. After my unhappy time at Arbroath this showed that I felt I would do anything to escape the 'hell-ship' I seemed sentenced to for life. In fact, the idea of flying rapidly grew on me and the smart and orderly appearance of this Naval Air Station was itself attractive. Unfortunately, this improbable request appeared to throw the Commander (Air) off balance. He was pleased that a young regular officer wanted to become a pilot, but did not know what could be done about this. They had two operational squadrons and a few transport planes, but no facilities for initial basic flying training. At least this officer said he would think about the matter and would be in touch with me in a few days' time. Regrettably, I wasted his time. On my return to my ship, there was a message for me from Senior Officer LSTs, telling me to transfer to LST 2 (presumably the second LST the Americans had ever built) that very afternoon. The ship was sailing (from Keppel Harbour) next morning and I was needed on board as the Navigating Officer.

I began to wonder if the RN had any employment for regular Sub Lieutenants other than as navigators. But this was a minor consideration compared with my joy at the prospect of escaping from 164 and getting to sea again. No. 2 was probably the last American-built Mk.2 LST still operating for the RN. The tank deck had been fitted with railway lines, so that with an elaborate system of pontoons and ramps at each port the ship could be used as a train ferry. Unlike the variety of railway gauges in Australia, the main line systems of India and Malaya had the same gauge, so that rolling stock from the former could be used with the latter, without modification. Many of the goods wagons (freight cars) of the Malayan Railways had been sabotaged, demolished or simply worn out by the Japanese, so that more were badly needed to reactivate the railway system of reoccupied Malaya. LST 2 was busy running a shuttle service of sixteen large 4-bogie (8-wheel) wagons and, perhaps, a hundred jeeps and 15-cwt. trucks on deck, from Madras to Singapore.

As expected, I found a totally different atmosphere aboard this ship, compared to my last. She looked smart and well maintained, the health and morale of the crew were good and I found the officers truly congenial. They were all reservists but the Captain was from one of the prestigious merchant shipping lines (British India, I think). Evidently the previous navigator, an RNVR Lieutenant, had fallen sick and had to be put ashore at Singapore—hence the opening I had been looking for. I gather he had been a pleasant enough fellow but had not been noted for his navigational skills. It seems that, on his last run, he had fallen into the trap that had worried me over my landfall at Pointe Noire. He had aimed for Madras but had arrived at a coast with an unbroken line of coconut palms, and no hills identifiable behind, as is characteristic of the Coromandel Coast. The Captain had asked him whether the ship should turn north or south. The navigator disappeared into the charthouse and flipped a coin, emerging to assert that, having just checked, Madras was, in fact, slightly to the north, in which direction the ship then turned. An hour later, there were as many palm trees—but no sign of a port. Fortunately, at this time, a merchant ship appeared, proceeding south. HMLST 2 then, rather officiously, challenged this vessel: 'What Ship—Where Bound?', not to establish that she was not a disguised Japanese commerce raider, unaware the war had ended, but under a procedure designed to keep Merchant Navy officers in practice with their Morse signalling. Back came the reply, 'SS ——, bound Calcutta to Madras'. LST 2 left a discreet pause before executing a U-turn and heading south for Madras. By now I felt sufficiently confident about my navigation to aim straight for Madras, despite the misfortune of my predecessor.

The ship had quite a rough passage on the tail-end of the monsoon. The waves were not high enough to worry most ships, but unladen LSTs had problems in a seaway. Whilst Hunt Class destroyers like *Lauderdale* were built with marginally acceptable stability, an LST, in ballast, had too much. Without going into technicalities, the fact is that the greater the stability factor (measured as the Metacentric Height), the more the ship tended to 'bob like a cork', the more violent the motion and the greater the actual angles of roll. For the benefit of mariners familiar with these things, a cruiser's Metacentric Height was measured in inches, making the ship a reasonably steady gun platform, whereas an unladen LST had an MH of 12 ft. On that passage, I recall rolls of up to 30 degrees being registered. I had now been at sea long enough not to suffer seasickness—but found taking accurate sextant altitudes under such conditions was far from easy.

I am happy to say the ship arrived spot on my ETA with no problems. Madras proved an enjoyable stopover. The city had been untouched by the war, had seen few visiting warships and the 'Raj' Establishment was particularly hospitable to us. We were well entertained at the beautiful Gymkhana Club—similar to the Mombasa Sports Club but on a rather grander scale. Loading our rolling stock and vehicles took two days and proved an interesting exercise in seamanship. We then had an uneventful trip back to Singapore. I enjoyed this appointment and felt happy at the prospect of more such trips, which seemed to be as meaningful an activity as I could expect at that time. However, we were no sooner back in Keppel Harbour, unloading our trains, etc., than a signal arrived appointing me to a third LST—No 11—as the First Lieutenant. During my short stay aboard No.2, the Captain had evidently formed such a favourable opinion of me that he not only awarded me my Watch-Keeping Certificate (required before one could become a Lieutenant) but went so far as to recommend me for 'accelerated promotion'. No doubt this arose from the joy he felt at having a navigator actually able to find Madras for him.

I wondered what LST 11 had in store for me. I found her in Singapore Dockyard not actually broken down—although the Engineer Officer reported the engines were pretty shaky. The ship herself and her crew were not nearly so run down as 164, but no one knew what further sea-going the vessel might be doing. I was in an unusual position as, at twenty, I was the youngest officer on board yet was the ship's Executive Officer, responsible to the Captain for good order and discipline and the proper maintenance of the ship and its equipment (other than engine-room machinery). I was, of course, also second in command. I had evidently been so appointed as I was RN and not a reservist. The appointment, however, was irregular and anomalous. Theoretically, the second senior officer should have been the No.1, whether RN, RNVR or RNR. A tricky situation would arise if I had to discipline an officer older, and of greater seniority, than me. Happily, no such event occurred and the others did not resent me, having no desire for added responsibilities. I did my best to smarten the ship up, even finding that for the asking a party of Japanese POWs could be had to red-lead and repaint topsides, etc. Morale on board was reasonably good and I had no serious disciplinary cases to deal with.

However, once again I found my appointment was to be quite short-lived. No operations of any sort were planned for the ship. We were advised that in two weeks time all the LSTs that were capable of making the voyage were to form a convoy and proceed to Subic Bay in the Philippines, where the ships would be handed back to the Americans. Thereafter, I forgot about smartening the ship up and concentrated on sea-going gear and life-saving equipment.

On schedule, a dozen LSTs set sail for the Philippines. Station-keeping was difficult, because few officers were practised in this and because the engines in all ships were unreliable—not to put too fine a point on it. This was the more worrying as we were coming into the China Sea typhoon season. Indeed, as we reached the northern end of the Palawan Passage and were a day short of our ETA, word was received of not one but two typhoons joining together as they moved across the Pacific. It was at this point that the Engineer Officer reported that the starboard engine was running very rough and might have to be stopped. The Captain urged him to 'nurse' the engine but, if humanly possible, to keep it running as far as Subic Bay—before the typhoon arrived. We could no longer maintain convoy speed and dropped astern to join a couple of other stragglers; at least there were no U-Boats such as had been wont to hang around the tails of convoys just to pick off such stragglers, representing easy pickings. We limped into Subic Bay next afternoon as our engineer reported that the flywheel of the starboard engine had actually fallen off when this diesel was finally stopped.

Subic Bay is a large anchorage and was crowded with every type of US Navy ship. The LSTs were put on heavy moorings, two to a buoy. We heaved a sigh of relief at reaching this haven in one piece. However, our problems were not over. The double typhoon was now approaching Luzon, with the added hazard of a sixty-foot tidal wave that had started with a volcanic eruption in the Aleutians and swept right across the Pacific, causing great havoc in Hawaii *en route*. We were now under the orders of the US ComCincPac. who decided to order all ships to sea to ride out the typhoons and tidal wave. I knew this was standard typhoon drill for Hong Kong so assumed the same precautions were sound for the Philippines. However, I did not relish being tossed about in an empty LST in a typhoon—a moderate monsoon in the Indian Ocean had been bad enough. Now, with one engine written off and the other suspect, we were in no shape to go to sea at all. But I knew that in Hong Kong, for one typhoon just before the war, ships had elected to stay in port on new so-called typhoon-proof moorings. Next day the shores had been littered with stranded ships, from ocean liners down. We tried to find out what the US naval authorities wanted us to do. Unfortunately, the R/T discipline of the USN was poor. I was in our Wireless Office for some time but we just could not get a word in edgeways because of operators calling out, 'We're leaving Manila, folks—good-bye. We'll be seeing you soon— we hope—good-bye.' Under the circumstances, our own Senior Officer signalled us and three other lame-duck LSTs to remain where we were.

It was a spectacle to watch some fifty miscellaneous warships proceed to sea—leaving us feeling abandoned. For me, however, the coming tempest presented a challenge requiring most of the seamanship I had ever learnt. We still had about twelve hours to the expected arrival time of the typhoon and this was put to good use. Without going into too much detail, I had the anchor cables securing us to the buoy doubled up, our own anchor on a further length of chain and our heaviest steel wire rope ready to let go should the mooring buoy's cable part, and used up almost all cordage remaining to lash us to the ship alongside. All watertight doors were then secured and hatches battened down. Emergency lighting was rigged, a system of 'action messing' organised, with food for the next twenty-four hours—and finally, the Petty Officer Sick Berth Attendant was told to lay out his surgery gear and emergency dressings. I felt I had taken every possible action to prepare for the worst, and then waited (with some excitement) to see what would happen.

In the event, it all proved an anticlimax. The wind briefly reached gale force but we never looked like dragging our moorings. By dawn, the storm had blown itself out and the great armada of ships steamed past us back to their moorings. I wished we had some way to convey our smugness and ask the returning ships what they had got so excited about. However, things might have been different and it had been a good exercise for me personally.

THE *ROCKSAND* MUTINY

As far as I know, there is no official record of a mutiny aboard HMS *Rocksand* (Landing Ship, Infantry—LSI) in 1946. Nor will it appear, from what follows, that there were violent scenes, necessitating Courts Martial and mutineers to be hung from the yard-arms. Indeed, it is hard to identify who, if anybody, might have been blamed. Nevertheless, a mutinous act did occur, and although I was not directly involved, I witnessed every act of the drama—*from the viewpoint of the mutineers*.

We spent the next two weeks aboard the LSTs in Subic Bay, with little shore leave and no chance to make the short run to Manila, while the ships were destored. In due course, the Landing Ship Infantry (LSI) HMS *Rocksand*—an American-built 'Victory' ship converted to transport five hundred combat troops and equipped with a dozen landing craft slung on davits—appeared in the bay. Doubtless, this ship would soon, herself, be handed back to the USN under the Terms of Lease-Lend. But now she had a last job to do, namely, to collect and take away the British crews of other ships handed back.

This organisation was fine except that, a week after our arrival, ten ocean-going salvage tugs (all Lease-Lend ships, being returned) turned up. These craft were quickly handed over and the crews ready to leave at the same time as those of the LSTs. Someone had asked the Captain of *Rocksand* if the tug crews could hitch a lift back aboard his ship. Knowing that there was spare room in the troopdecks of the LSI, the CO readily agreed.

What had not been considered was available officer accommodation, or the fact that these tugs had quite so many officers. The latter resulted from an anomalous situation, whereby they were manned by Merchant Navy crews, under naval control and wearing naval uniforms, but organised like merchant ships. This arrangement went by the improbable name of the T124X Agreement. The primary difference between Navy and Merchant ship crew structures was that even Fleet destroyers had but one Engine-room Officer, usually known as 'Chief', whilst the watchkeeper in charge in the engine-room was an Engine Room Artificer—with the status and uniform of a Chief Petty Officer. Under T124X, such personnel were classed as Engineer Officers. I make no comments on the rights or wrongs of this system—this was simply the way things were. Consequently, each of these tugs carried eight or nine officers, as opposed to the usual five aboard the LSTs. The unforeseen result of the *Rocksand* Captain's helpful agreement to lift the tug crews was that, with six-to-a-cabin accommodation for forty officers, the ship found itself lumbered with 150 officers to transport.

I had wind of this situation in advance and foresaw that all Sub Lieutenants and below (Midshipmen and Warrant Officers) would be in the troop decks (holds) in multi-tier pipe cots. Being an 'old campaigner' by now, I decided to make my own arrangements. I took a boat to *Rocksand* on the morning before the afternoon of our scheduled embarkation and departure. I reconnoitred the small boat-deck amidships and marked with chalk an area 6′ × 3′, alongside the Captain's quarters, 'Reserved for Sub Lt. Seymour RN'. I then instructed the Captain's steward not to let any one else lay claim to this space. It was earmarked for my stretcher camp bed, in a spot, I had judged, which would be sheltered from any strong winds but protected by an awning from the blazing sun.

In the afternoon everybody embarked and the ship sailed. With 150 officers to feed in a wardroom that could seat fifty at a pinch, it was necessary to have three sittings for every meal. Furthermore, nobody could sit around the wardroom between meals as these were being served there all day and half the night. The sailors were reasonably well off as they had quite spacious well decks forward and aft, well covered by awnings. The officers, however, whilst not eating, had only the short boat deck of the midships island superstructure on which to spend their day. There was nothing to sit on and if four squatted on the deck to play a game of cards they would be occupying more than their share of deck space. Anywhere not under an awning with no breeze—with the gentle following wind at the same speed as the ship—was unbearable under a vertical (mid-day) sun in the China Sea.

Suffice it to say that life was pretty good hell on board, although I, at least, had managed to retain my reserved camp bed space at night. Furthermore, I soon found that, for a small inducement, the Captain's steward would bring me a bucket of fresh water to wash with each morning. This saved me from having to queue with a hundred sweating bodies for the limited ablution facilities down in the holds. Unpleasant though things were, I had long ago learnt that people will endure great discomfort, provided the 'Law of Equal Misery' is seen to be applied. Failure to follow this principle was the cause of the trouble that followed. The Lieutenant Commanders and Lieutenants, numbering about forty, found their (third sitting) meals were getting later and later despite the best endeavours of the overworked cooks and stewards. Their Senior Officer complained to the Captain who agreed that the only solution was for all the other (junior) officers to take their cafeteria-style meals in the sailors' mess deck. This caused widespread indignation amongst the junior officers, particularly the T124X officers, mostly designated as Sub Lieutenants who insisted that their terms of service clearly specified that they were entitled to be treated as officers.

There was much muttering amongst the officers during our first cafeteria (evening) meal. This became more voluble after the tables had been cleared. Successive 'stirrers' stood on tables and started rabble-rousing, speakers became more and more heated as indignation rose. This was a fascinating experience for me as it gave me a good insight as to how a mutiny—or industrial strike—gets started. The grievance, I felt, was justified, but the rhetoric became more and more inflamed until common sense and reason looked like being abandoned. At last, a relatively moderate resolution was passed on a show of hands, so overwhelmingly that there was no need for me to cast a dissenting vote or even be seen to be abstaining. The resolution was that signatures of officers of former ships should be placed on a demand that the former messing arrangements be restored. This was to be presented to each former Commanding Officer by the First Lieutenant involved.

This placed me in a spot as I was aware that the presentation of such a 'demand' to one's senior officer would be judged as an act of mutiny. This did not worry all the other 'No.1s' who were reservists headed home for demobilisation. I had a career to think about. I was soon approached by my former shipmates and asked what I was doing about the matter. I had to use all the diplomacy I could muster. I declared that I fully supported the outcry against the new arrangements but presentation of 'demands' was not the best way to get things changed. I promised personally to represent the complaint to our ex-CO in the strongest terms and my former messmates reluctantly agreed to leaving the matter to me to handle. Meanwhile, all other (LST and tug) officers hastily prepared their demands and the ex-No 1 s rushed off to present them—while I hastened slowly. Next day, the *Rocksand* Captain acknowledged the inequity of the changed messing system. The *status quo ante* was restored, menus were simplified and the rest of the voyage completed without further trouble. Two days later, my own ex-CO sent for me and expressed his pleasure that his ex-officers were the only ones who had not presented a demand—amounting to a mutinous act. He felt his officers had shown great loyalty and I was asked to pass on his appreciation. I refrained from saying, 'Don't kid yourself—it wasn't your officers' loyalty that brought this about—merely Sub Lt. Seymour's concern for his career.' I felt something of a snake in the grass—especially as I scored a particularly glowing Commanding Officer's Report as the result of the incident.

When I had boarded *Rocksand*, I was told I would be disembarking at Trincomalee—yes—'For Disposal'. I seemed to be proving particularly hard to dispose of! I had served in four ships in nine months and taken passage in three others. *Rocksand* was scheduled to stop at Singapore *en route* for Trincomalee. However, once again, things did not turn out as expected. On arrival at Singapore, another signal required me to make a 'pier-head jump' there to join an operational Mk.3 (Steam) LST leaving next day for Java. I was now to join HMS *Loch Eck* (frigate) as the navigator. This gave me one more problem aboard *Rocksand*. All luggage for Trincomalee was in No.1 hold and that for Singapore in No.2. I was told I would have to find my trunk and duffel-bag in No.1 (I had my battered suitcase with me). I found the trunk but had to abandon the search for the duffel bag. I was not too upset as it contained only my cold weather gear—sweaters, seaboots, seaboot stockings, etc. In due course, I made a claim against the Navy for my lost gear—only to receive the missing bag, six months later, serving in the Mediterranean. It had turned up in the Clyde and been rerouted to me!

LOCH ECK

The next morning, I found myself travelling in comfort, in a cabin once again. I do not know the purpose of this voyage—probably taking supplies to the forces that had been re-occupying the Dutch East Indies. In fact, the sudden and unexpected capitulation of the Japanese had created a power vacuum in the Indies. Mountbatten, Supreme Commander South-East Asia, with one army re-occupying Burma and another Malaya, was struggling to find any more troops to occupy the Indies. The Dutch could not be expected to do much, with their own homeland only liberated a few months earlier, and most British conscripts felt that, with the war over, they should be repatriated and demobbed as quickly as possible. When Japan capitulated, there were about 160,000 Japanese in Java, Sumatra, Borneo, Celebes and Moluccas. They were hard put to it to find anyone to accept their surrender, or to whom they could hand over their arms. It was in this power vacuum that Sukarno was able to seize power and declare Indonesia independent. There followed a difficult and painful struggle to restore Dutch authority over their former empire—even temporarily until an orderly transition to a constitutional national government could be arranged.

Mountbatten managed to find two Indian Army divisions for the task but realised that these could not be deployed there for long. Not only were most Indians eager to return to India, but they could hardly be expected to enthuse about being required to suppress an Asian 'National Liberation' movement, for the sake of Dutch Imperialists—when the Indians were looking forward to their own independence. South-East Asia Command had problems but, fresh from other turmoils and starved of news of political developments in the region, I had little idea of the complexity of the problems of the High Command. Indeed, for weeks, our only radio service had been KZ(Zee)FN in Manila, which treated us to the on-going saga of Buckskin Frank Lester ('that six-shooting killer from Tombstone, Arizona'), political news from Washington and the music of Tommy Dorsey ('Take it away, Tommy').

I was simply headed for more interesting places which I had not seen before. The first of these was Palembang—an oil-field town fifty miles up the river of the same name in Southern Sumatra, where the LST which I was aboard, called *en route* to Java. In total contrast to the arid mountainous country I had viewed in South-West Africa, the terrain on either side of the Palembang River, as far as the eye could see, was mangrove swamp or rain-forest, with no hills of any sort. Indeed the jungle appeared to be both impenetrable and uninhabited. The map of Sumatra shows no roads east of Palembang and only a few native villages on some of the rivers, only accessible by canoe. The many tight loops of the river were naturally deepest on the outside of each bend. Accordingly, at times, the wing of the bridge was almost brushing the branches of the trees. The jungle was so dense that the ship's siren echoed and re-echoed from one bank to the other, giving an eerie effect.

After five hours in the river, we reached Palembang. The port had an unreal air about it. The ship secured at a wharf but there were few people, either European or Asian. Neither the town nor the oil refinery appeared large. The latter comprised a few acres of storage tanks and the usual conglomeration of tall pipes, columns, retorts or whatever, silvery painted. It looked as though the Japanese had not worked this oil-field, which is surprising as lack of oil supplies was the main reason that Japan had gone to war. However, it seems possible that the Dutch technicians had either fled or been killed and that the Japanese simply had too few engineers to operate all the oil-fields they had acquired in their conquests. Be this as it may, Palembang certainly had an abandoned look. In the steamy tropical environment, the whole place looked like being reclaimed by the jungle. Even the massive refinery installation was being rapidly covered with giant lantana vines and one sensed that, in another few years, it would have been like one of the lost cities of the Mayas in Central America. Palembang had a ghostly air and looked like something from an H. G. Wells novel. I felt no urge to go ashore there.

When we left, the ship had some trouble at the bar of the river. It is unlikely that any survey work or dredging had been done since the Dutch left. The chart showed a depth of 15 ft. over the bar and our ship drew 12 ft., so there was not going to be much margin. But we had got in without grounding and tried to take the same track out. However, mud was boiling up on both sides of the ship showing the vessel was now pushing its way through soft mud, at ever decreasing speed, until it had to be acknowledged the ship was stuck. Shortly, a cargo ship, looking to draw more water than us, appeared approaching the river mouth. This should be worth watching, as she steered to pass us inside one cable. To our amazement, she steamed straight past without even slowing. 'One-Nil' to the Red Ensign over the White! Our LST finally got clear after much 'backing and filling' and made Tanjong Priok (Port of Batavia) next day.

I located HMS *Loch Eck* and reported for duty around mid-day. But yet again, there was no Dartmouth-taught joining ritual. I was conducted round to the port side of the fo'c'sle (away from the dockside) where a number of officers without shirts on were seated under an awning sipping iced pink gins. I was cordially greeted and asked what drink I would like. Minutes later the Captain appeared. He was a man of ample build with an impressive red beard and clad only in a bath towel around his waist. He greeted me as warmly as had the others—and I was deemed to have joined HMS *Loch Eck*. I enjoyed the four months I spent aboard this ship, which I regarded as a proper warship, proving an efficient and a happy one. The captain was Lt. Cdr. Peter Hoare and the No.1, Lt. Jack Maidwell, to both of whom I found myself well attuned. As things turned out, I was to serve with both these officers again—Maidwell three years later, in 1949 and Hoare, by then a Commander, eleven years later in 1957. I would remain aboard *Loch Eck* until she paid off in Plymouth in August 1946. Whilst

Loch Eck was a proper warship in my eyes, she was strictly an anti-submarine frigate with modern Asdics, the latest A/S weapons—two triple 'Squid' A/S Mortars—but only one little 4″ gun. As the Allies now had no enemies left with any submarines, and it was hard to see just how our one 4″ gun was going to help subdue Sukarno, the ship was scarcely a valuable fleet unit. In fact, the 'fleet' was irrelevant as we were only briefly in company with two other warships returning to UK.

The ship remained in Tanjong Priok for another two weeks, during which I had a strange experience. In 1946 Batavia had a population of 600,000 although it is now just a small part of the City of Jakarta, of nearly ten million inhabitants and beset with intractable urban blight and terrible squalor. Tanjong Priok is also now a suburb of Jakarta but, in 1946, there were several miles of virtual jungle between the two. As Sukarno's rebels/Freedom Fighters controlled all but the major cities and towns, one was liable to be ambushed, or at least sniped at, *en route* to and from Batavia. One day, I had to go to the HQ in that city to collect despatches. Such army personnel as there were were too thin on the ground to provide armed escorts for such journeys. The answer lay in utilising the only other disciplined armed forces around who could be depended on to obey orders—namely some of the tens of thousands of Japanese POWs in the area, who were reissued weapons with which to defend their former enemies against attack—from a completely new enemy.

Loch Eck moved on to Sourabaya, where we heard of brutal massacres that had been carried out by Sukarno's guerillas. The place seemed calm and pleasant enough but I was not unhappy to leave for Singapore, the High Command having evidently established that Sukarno had no submarines for us to sink.

After only a short stop for fuelling and provisioning, it was on to Colombo, where I had had such a happy time six months back. I could not expect to be further entertained at Queen's House, but again felt I should write my name in the visitor's book, to register the fact that I was re-visiting Ceylon. This led to an invitation to lunch, attended by a number of VIPs. Sub Lt. Seymour felt a little uncomfortable seated next to Commander in Chief, Eastern Fleet, Vice Admiral Power (I suspect this may have been a little bit of devilment on the part of Deirdre and the ADC). However, it proved a pleasant enough occasion. One trivial matter had me intrigued. Before arriving at Colombo, the officers of *Loch Eck* had seriously discussed the proposition of getting tattooed whilst in Ceylon and I was quite taken with the idea. Seated alongside Admiral Power, I noted he had a small dove tattooed on the back of each hand, perhaps done twenty-odd years before when he had been a Sub Lieutenant. I was itching to ask him if he had regretted this but prudently decided that was not the sort of personal question a Sub Lieutenant asks his Commander in Chief. Happily, in retrospect, I overcame the urge to look more like an 'old salt' and remained untattooed.

With two weeks' local leave, I was able to do some more exploring of my 'roots'. I was invited to spend a week with a charming couple—'Kit' Owen and his wife—on a tea plantation, west of Nuwara Eliya and close to the spectacular Ragalla rocks (which I unsuccessfully tried to climb) Mrs Owen was a connection of my mother's by marriage and the couple had been close friends of both my parents twenty-five years back. The Owens were true builders of Empire of the best sort. Kit had lost a leg fighting at Gallipoli but managed quite well with his wooden one. I enjoyed walking and talking amongst the Tamil tea pickers. A visit to the tea factory at Bandarawella was interesting and the aroma of the drying tea could be smelt half a mile away. My most impressive day was one spent at Nuwara Eliya (summer residence of the Governor), nestling under the mighty peak of Pidurutalagala of 2518 m. (8,250 ft.—or slightly higher than Kosciusko, the highest mountain in Australia). The houses and gardens were beautiful but most memorable was the Hill Club which, I am told, is still a delightful establishment with one of the finest golf courses in Asia and a members' library that will draw gasps of amazement from any bibliophile. The climate at the elevation of Nuwara Eliya is superb and, in winter, there would be great log fires in the reception rooms.

An improbable outcome of my 'roots search' arose out of a Sunday afternoon visit to the Udapussalawa Gymkhana Club for tennis. In the changing room there were fading photos of early groups of people. Examining one of the Founder Members in 1910, I identified my father. When I drew my host's attention to this, he examined the photo closely and said, 'Do you see those two young girls there? Would you believe they are both in the club this afternoon—I must introduce you to them.'

On doing so, one of these ladies remarked, 'Yes, of course I remember Wally Seymour well—he has been gone some time now. What would it be—five years?'

I had to say, 'I am afraid it is twenty years.'

'Goodness Gracious Me!' Such was the way time stood still in Up-Country Ceylon in those days.

I had one other glimpse of my father's time in Ceylon. He had often spoken of Diyatalawa in the hill country. Built originally as a POW camp for prisoners taken in the Boer War, it was subsequently used as the headquarters and training ground for the Ceylon Planters Rifle Corps, a unit for which my father had great affection. This was a Volunteer, or Yeomanry, organisation, in which he served for many years as an 'other rank' but just not long enough for his OR Volunteer Medal, before being promoted to Officer—rising to Lieutenant Colonel before leaving Ceylon.

He was able to qualify for his Officer's Volunteer Medal (counting his World War I service) and had the satisfaction of qualifying for his OR medal years later after three years as a Sergeant in the Home Guard. By 1946, Diyatalawa was a popular Leave Camp for officers and men of all three services, and together with several mates from the wardroom of *Loch Eck*, I spent a week there. Doubtless, a full search through framed group photos would have revealed one or more containing my father. However, I recall finding only one trace of him in some Honour Roll for rifle shooting. Importantly, we all thoroughly enjoyed our week's R & R at Diyatalawa.

The ship then moved to Trincomalee for two weeks. Most of the warships that had recently been based there had moved on but there was still plenty of activity and evidence of what had been an important naval base. Despite my father's earlier presence there, I failed to find any trace of him. However, 'Trinco' proved an attractive place with dazzling white beaches for bathing. I do not recall any Wrens—they must have moved to Singapore.

By mid-July, it was judged that, with no hostile submarines—nor even any friendly ones to practise sinking—*Loch Eck* might as well return to UK. The voyage home was unremarkable. Stops were made at Aden (last seen by me aged seven), Port Said, after transiting the Suez canal, and Gibraltar. The night spent at Port Said was significant to me personally. An old friend of our Captain was a Canal pilot who lived with his wife in a pleasant house at Port Tewfik, opposite Port Said. This hospitable couple invited our officers to drinks. When it was revealed that this happened to be my twenty-first birthday, they turned the evening into a real party. Sadly, my £50 p.a. private means was over.

In the Mediterranean, we joined HMS *Venerable* and watched her push her American-built Lease-Lend fighters overboard into the Atlantic Ocean after we had cleared Gibraltar.

Two days later, we were in Plymouth and were paid off in another three weeks. I had been away from UK for a year, served or taken passage in nine ships, revisited South Africa, seen many ports of South-East Asia and explored the land of my birth. But I fear very little of my year's service had been of much value to my King and Country—other than conducting one train across the Indian Ocean. But I had been able to note, at first hand, how ships should (and should not) be run, seen the emotional factors involved in mutiny and could, at last, be described as a competent navigator.

CHAPTER 17

MEDITERRANEAN—HMS *OCEAN*

I WAS HOME AGAIN, for six weeks of enjoyable Foreign Service leave at home in Torquay. I was not asked what type of ship, or which fleet, I now fancied. My appointment was to the light fleet carrier *Ocean* in the Mediterranean Fleet, based on Malta. Both the type of vessel and the station would be a whole new experience to me.

I took passage aboard the large fleet carrier *Formidable*, transporting personnel back from the Far East, with few outward passengers. I therefore had a far more pleasant passage than aboard the unhappy *Rocksand*.

Formidable had been with the British Pacific Fleet and had been in the Okinawa landings, where the enemy had launched *kamikaze* attacks against Allied warships—particularly aircraft carriers. This inhuman form of warfare achieved some success against the American carriers, crippling several by disastrous fires amongst planes in the hangars below, with heavy loss of life. This was because USN aircraft carrier design philosophy had been to have wooden flight decks, sacrificing armour for larger hangars and more aircraft. The two sides to this argument are: More armour to help a ship survive punishment or maximum offensive capacity?

Possibly attributable to losses of lightly-armoured battle-cruisers at Jutland, the RN tended to favour protection rather than hitting power. The Americans, on the other hand, felt that the more combat aircraft a carrier could throw at the enemy, the greater the chance of success. Certainly, the USN needed every plane it could muster to win the decisive Battle of Midway. They could not have expected attacks by suicide *kamikaze* bombers. But, when these occurred, they were effective. The RN fleet carriers, notably the five *Illustrious* Class (of which none was lost during the war), had 2½" thick armoured flight decks.

When *Formidable* took a *kamikaze* on the flight deck, two or three planes were destroyed and a dozen lives lost, but the carrier was operating aircraft again within half an hour. These were indeed fine ships but, as noted earlier, for most of the war the planes carried were definitely inferior to those aboard American carriers. The only evidence of the *kamikaze* hit I saw was slight denting of the armoured deck. Sadly, *Formidable*'s days of operational service were nearly over. Such ships were too expensive to maintain and run in peace-time. This vessel would soon be headed for the ship-breakers.

Arrival in Grand Harbour Valetta was exciting, but I was appalled at the battering Malta had sustained during the war. There were half a dozen sunken vessels still to be raised and every other building in the dockyard appeared to have been destroyed or damaged. The large floating dock (to lift a battleship) was sitting on the bottom of the harbour and the fleet oiler *Plumleaf* was lying with decks awash alongside Parlatorio wharf. The sunken hull had been reinforced and HMS *Ocean* was berthed alongside the wreck.

From recollection, the fleet comprised two carriers—*Triumph* and *Ocean*—with Flag Officer Air, Med (FOAM) flying his flag aboard the former. There was a cruiser squadron of five ships under Rear-Admiral Lord Louis Mountbatten, who had stepped down from Supreme Commander South-East Asia and who was then Viceroy of India. Resuming his 'normal' naval career, Mountbatten was now only Second-in-Command Med. Fleet. The Commander-in-Chief was Admiral Sir Algernon Usborne Willis. His detractors would (unfairly) say his greatest claim to fame was that his wife was the sister of Clement Attlee, the Prime Minister. His flagship was *Liverpool* (sister to *Enterprise*'s old consort, *Glasgow*). There were two flotillas of destroyers—the 'CA's (leader *Caesar*) and the 'V's whose leader had been *Saumarez*. The fleet included a flotilla of frigates, Destroyer Depot Ship (*Tyne*), Submarine Depot Ship (*Forth*), with submarines, together with fleet minesweepers and other small craft.

Regrettably, *Saumarez* and *Volage* (of the same flotilla) had just been knocked out in the 'Corfu Channel Incident' of 1946. One might have supposed that, with the war over, ship losses would have ended. However, conditions were anything but settled around the Mediterranean. Yugoslavia and all the Balkans had turned Communist and the Greeks had just come back from the brink of Communism. Corfu was (and is) a Greek island, but closer to the mainland of Albania than Greece. Notionally, the channel between the island and the mainland was an international waterway, open to free passage by ships of all nations.

The Albanians, keen to show their contempt for the West, perhaps, had had the temerity to fire on a British warship transiting the channel. This was seen as an attempt to 'twist the Lion's tail'—something not to be tolerated—and Albania must be taught a lesson. Unfortunately, things did not go as planned. The entire Med. Fleet formed up close to Corfu. The plan was for the destroyers to steam through the Straits followed by the cruisers—asserting their right to pass through this channel. However, all crews were at action stations and guns loaded—although trained fore-and-aft—but with the 'directors' of all ships pointing towards Albania, picking out possible targets. Furthermore, the two carriers, off-shore, had launched four squadrons of aircraft armed with live rockets, ready to unleash when the word was given. This procedure was known as 'trailing a coat'. The concept was that, should a single hot-headed Albanian be rash enough to fire even a rifle at the warships, the latter would be entitled to return the fire in self defence. There would be a deluge of 6″ and 4.5″ HE shells and 5″ aircraft-launched rockets. Such was the plan—but not what happened. The outcome was the loss of two British fleet destroyers and a number of lives. No shot was fired by an Albanian so no retaliation was in order. Instead, the two leading destroyers hit mines that could have been laid by anyone. The *Saumarez* was so badly damaged she had to be sunk and *Volage* broke in two. The forward half sank but the after half was towed back to Malta.

Subsequently, British minesweepers swept the remaining mines laid and the matter was referred to the Allied Mediterranean Mine Clearance Board in Rome. This organisation proved remarkably ineffective, unable even to decide what type of mines they were or where made. I believe the final consensus was that they were German mines, probably laid by the Yugoslavs. As my friend Gavin Wemyss would have said, 'All torpedoes missed astern—useful lessons were learnt.' On my arrival in Malta, I found the surviving half of *Volage* was berthed immediately astern of *Ocean*. This half-destroyer was of no use and so was taken to sea and sunk as a gunnery target.

I was to spend nearly two years aboard *Ocean* in the Mediterranean, until the ship returned to Plymouth to pay-off. During this time, I would visit many interesting ports and participate in one historic event. Life was seldom dull but it cannot be said that I greatly enjoyed *Ocean*. There was nothing wrong with the ship nor the way she was run. It was simply that, after four years of greater or lesser excitement, my duties involved little responsibility and life on board was often boring. By now, I was a Lieutenant with two gold stripes on my sleeve. I would have some responsibility as the Officer of the Watch at sea, nominally taking care of the safe handling and station-keeping of a 17,000 ton ship but, with many watch-keeping officers and relatively short periods at sea, watches on the bridge were infrequent. Furthermore, during these watches, flying operations would often be taking place with the Captain, Commander (Air) and Navigating Officer on the bridge with me.

I felt I was now competent in a number of professional skills—Gunnery, Torpedo, Signals, Anti Submarine Warfare and Navigation. I was, however, to have no opportunity to exercise any of these. More importantly to me, I was to have little chance to show any leadership of men. I was only the Second Divisional Officer of seamen of the Quarterdeck Division so that I had no men to command, or even look after. Rather, I was bogged down in the paperwork of Service Certificates, etc.

Life was the more discouraging because of the gulf that still remained between Fleet Air Arm officers and Executive (or Seamen) Officers, but

I tried to make friends amongst the airmen. Sadly also, aboard this ship, before the advent of the Angled Deck and the Mirror Deck-Landing system, a distressing number of aircrew officers were dying in flying accidents. As a junior Lieutenant, all too often it became my lot to conduct naval funerals at Bighi Cemetery. Such were always moving services even if I did not know the officer being buried. Much later, on this subject, Mike MccGwire wrote to me, (regarding Fish-heads and Fly boys):

> As long as we didn't run across the enemy, our lives were pretty safe. Theirs were inherently dangerous—not just lousy combat aircraft—but aircraft un-suitable for flying from those flight decks. Besides the dangers of take-off and landing (the number I saw plop into the sea on landing and take off—or plough into other aircraft on deck), there was always the navigational problem of finding the carrier again, before the plane ran out of fuel. On the August '42 Malta convoy, I saw *Eagle* go down and *Formidable* take a hit. I visited the latter and saw the squadron log, with something like 25 deaths through misadventure and only 5 in action.

I soon began to understand why officers I had told I was joining an aircraft carrier had tended to say 'Bad luck!' Ten years later, aboard another carrier, I would find life much happier, but a lot would have changed in that time. So much for the 'down' side.

Shortly after I joined the fleet, I had a somewhat eerie—almost bi-zarre—experience. I feel I can write freely about this, as there was no sinister outcome and the other person concerned took it all in good part. Nevertheless the circumstances were strange to the point of being weird. For a year or two, a number of officers had asked me if my name was Emerson. When I said it was not, people would say something like, 'You bear a striking resemblance to Charles Emerson.' Enough colleagues had said this to me for the name to stick in my mind. Someone did so again in Malta but this time added, 'You really must meet Emerson—he is a Lieutenant Commander on C-in-C's staff aboard *Liverpool*.' No special meeting was arranged but we chanced to run into each other at a cocktail party aboard *Ocean*.

I must say that I could not imagine how anyone saw a likeness between us. This officer was at least ten years older than myself and had a handsome red beard. In fact, I thought him so good-looking and possessed of such charm and good humour, I felt flattered that people should see a resemblance to him in me. I introduced myself and told him what others had said. Emerson thought this was great fun and suggested we told people we were brothers; then changed this to half-brothers, as we had different names. He went further and, there and then, invited me to the next cocktail party to be held aboard the flagship. In due course, aboard HMS *Liverpool*, the Commander-in-Chief, Admiral Willis, addressed me as Emerson and said, 'You must be the brother I have heard about, of Charles Emerson—my Staff Torpedo Officer.' This put me in a spot as I could hardly tell my C-in-C that we were pulling his—and everyone else's—leg. Fortunately, Lt. Cdr. Emerson himself appeared at that moment and talked himself, and myself, out of the situation—along the lines that we were not actually brothers, just related. But the myth persisted that we were half-brothers, as we took pains to greet each other warmly each time we chanced to meet.

We got to know each other quite well despite the substantial difference in age and seniority between us. We soon learnt that we had both been born in Ceylon and agreed to ask our respective parents (I believe his mother only was still alive) whether they had chanced to have met. This was a reasonable probability as every British person there over time seemed to have met all the others. To neither of my parents did the name Emerson mean anything. My mother, however, had only had two years in Ceylon. My father could have met Mrs Emerson before she was married but I could not tell him her maiden name. Charles Emerson said that when he asked his mother whether she had ever met an A. W. Seymour in Ceylon, she came straight out with, 'Ah yes, that would have been Wally Seymour. As a matter of fact, he was an old flame of mine.'

At this point, the implications crossed my mind and I had to say, jokingly, to Emerson, 'Well if that means anything, this is clearly your worry—not mine.' In fact, even if, when unmarried, she had been another founder member of the Udapussalawa Gymkhana Club in 1910, I am certain there was no hidden significance in his mother happening to have met my father. Anyone who knew my father saw him as a model of rectitude and propriety—a man who insisted on dressing with 'black tie' to dine by himself at the Residency in the jungle in Mulataive and drink a Loyal Toast each night. He could have conceivably been someone's 'old flame'—but anything else defies credibility. Furthermore, if there had been any serious relationship between our respective parents, one would have expected Mrs Emerson to have been rather more coy on the subject. At any rate, neither of us felt embarrassed by the latest information and we remained on good terms. At least the impression that I had good connections on the Admiral's staff did my image no harm.

We did have sundry sporting and recreational activities ashore. One sailing expedition made by six of us in the whaler over a week-end was memorable. From Grand Harbour, with an overnight stop at St Paul's Bay, we sailed this boat through the Comino Channel to the south side of Gozo, the second largest island of Malta. Our exploration objective was a tiny inlet on the south coast, which the chart suggested should offer a safe boat haven. By the time we reached the entrance, the wind was blowing at 25 knots from the north. This had afforded us a fast sail with a beam-wind blowing off-shore, giving us relatively smooth water. However, the quarter mile long inlet was much too narrow to sail into, against the wind that was funneling down it at over 30 knots. We dropped the sails, put out the oars and started rowing. We had not realised just how hard it would be to row a boat against a gale of wind and, after ten minutes, had only made about a hundred yards. Nevertheless, we were gaining ground, even if slowly. Accordingly, we would row for five minutes, with all our 'might and main', then move one thwart aft until, in turn, each had a rest as the coxswain. After an hour of hard work we reached the beach at the head of the inlet, now perfectly sheltered. We were able to camp there and cook up a splendid evening meal over a Primus stove.

We might have been an exploring boat party from Captain Cook's *Endeavour* except that there was a tiny café by the beach, able to provide us with further comforts. Next morning, we made the four-mile walk to Victoria to inspect the main town of Gozo. This was very like similar sized towns on the main island but without British servicemen or other foreigners, very few of either ever getting to pay a visit to Gozo. The sail back was uneventful but we felt we had had an enterprising and adventurous week-end.

I had always enjoyed racing and sailing whalers even around Scapa Flow in winter. I was also able to race Star Class yachts at the Royal Malta Yacht Club. These craft had been taken from the Italian Navy as war reparations, even though Italy ended the war theoretically as one of the victorious Allies. Perhaps they were taken in Sicily, before Italy changed sides.

I am not sure of all the ports the ship visited but they included: Toulon, Genoa, Rapallo, Leghorn, Taranto, Nauplia, Istanbul, Beirut, Haifa, Port Said, Tripoli, Algiers and Gibraltar. Each proved interesting in different ways but I can only touch on some of them.

At Genoa, I recall a Grande Ballo at a magnificent *palazzo* reminding me of the ball setting of the operetta *Die Fledermaus*, with freely-flowing champagne. I could not get over the incongruity of this opulence in defeated Italy, compared with the harsh austerity still in place in victorious Britain. Also the grandeur of our *ballo* contrasted starkly with the evident poverty of the mass of the Italian populace, amongst whom the Communist Party flourished.

From Leghorn, with other officers, I was lucky enough to work in a two-day visit to Florence and absorb some of the wondrous art of this fabulous city, including the Pitti, Uffizi, Duomo, Michelangelo's David and much more.

From Nauplia (in Greece), I visited ruins allegedly of Agamemnon's castle, from which he went off to fight the Trojan War. Regrettably, there were only a few stones that conceivably did not get on top of each other by accident. The guide's assertion that a flat slab of rock was the exact spot where Agamemnon's wife, Clytemnestra, stabbed the hero to death in his bath, defied my credulity. I begrudged the cost of the trip in an uncomfortable wooden-seated bus with all the dust, heat and flies. Perhaps I was a Philistine, but I would later be enthralled, viewing the Acropolis at Athens.

The fleet visit (by two carriers, three cruisers and two destroyer flotillas) to Istanbul was memorable. This was the first post-war visit by any British ships, and possibly the first full fleet visit since the 'troubles' in 1922. The passage through the Dardanelles, with a running commentary of the events of 1915 by the Commander Operations, was fascinating. At one point he stated that, as near as could be judged, the ship was now passing over the spot where the battleship HMS *Ocean* had sunk—a sobering thought.

At Istanbul, the Turks were determined to show us a warm welcome. On our arrival, they made gifts of a fine carpet for every Commanding Officer; crates of red and white wine for every wardroom; and a packet of 25 cigarettes—in a special presentation box with crossed Turkish Flag and White Ensign—for every man in the fleet. There followed a lavish programme of hospitality and entertainment. I recall a cocktail party aboard the flagship of the Turkish navy, the *Yavuz*. This was of historic interest because this vessel was none other than the old German battle-cruiser *Goeben* of World War I. This ship had led the Mediterranean Fleet of 1914 a merry dance before fleeing up the Dardenelles to the Bosphorous, where she remained for the rest of the war. Why the Turks, as allies of the defeated Germans, were allowed to retain this ship is unclear. However, no such reflections marred the conviviality of the occasion.

The British Embassy gave a reception, at which I fell in with a lively and glamorous international group of young people including the son of the Turkish Foreign Minister. They pressed me to join them the following day for a visit to the Princes Islands (Kizil Adalar). Sight-seeing included a visit to old Istanbul (Constantinople), the St Sophia museum and the Blue Mosque. We took a launch through the Bosphorous to the Black Sea, and inspected Kemal Ataturk's Presidential Yacht, that was probably the largest and most luxurious pleasure yacht ever built.

The grandest function of all was a ball given for the officers by the Vali of Istanbul at the Taksim Casino. This was a party on a scale I never saw before or since. Present were the Diplomatic Corps and Turkish Government Ministers, resplendent in court dress and impressive uniforms. Also present was what must have been the cream of the glamorous cosmopolitan women of this historic city where East meets West. A sumptuous buffet dinner was provided and all the champagne anyone could drink. There were bands and dancing on three levels, including the roof garden, and the carousing continued until the dawn rose over the Bosphorous at 6 a.m. The occasion brought to my mind Fitzgerald's lines:

> Awake! for Morning in the Bowl of Night
> Has flung the Stone that put the Stars to Flight:
> And Lo! the Hunter of the East has caught
> The Sultan's Turret in a Noose of Light.

The officers struggled back aboard their ships, and the Fleet sailed at eight. Lt. Seymour did his best to stand erect on the flight deck with other officers and sailors 'manning ship' as our vessel steamed slowly out to sea. Later, surveying an officer 'out to the world' in a wardroom armchair, another Omar Khayyám verse came to mind:

> They say the Lion and the Lizard keep
> The Courts where Jamshyd gloried and drank deep:
> And Bahram, that great Hunter—the Wild Ass
> Stamps o'er his Head, and he lies fast asleep.

Beirut, in those days, was an enjoyable and stimulating city. For me, however, the highlight of that visit was a day trip to Damascus. The route passed through mountains to 11,000 ft., with some fine ski resorts. The road afforded spectacular views down the other side, across the Plain of Baalbek with a descent of 5,000 ft. in five miles. Damascus had a modern quarter as the capital of former French—now independent—Syria. But the old city was something of a time warp, back to Biblical times. We spent hours walking around the ancient bazaars, which included St Paul's 'Street that is called Straight' in the Acts of the Apostles.

All the 'streets' were incredibly narrow, with barely room for donkey carts to cross, and were, of course, seething with humanity. Today, wandering alone around such areas, one might well end up as another 'Western hostage' of Muslim Fundamentalists. In 1947, I felt perfectly safe. All around was a hive of activity amongst craft workshops of every description—silversmiths, leather-workers, wood-carvers, etc. The welcome by every trader was elaborate. Before any purchase, there was a ritual of cups of green tea and endless haggling. One felt the seller would have felt 'robbed' if he had not had a good half hour's haggle. The goods offered were of high quality and, in one establishment, we were shown a bolt of magnificent blue and silver brocade said to be a wedding present from the people of Syria to Princess Elizabeth, soon to marry Prince Philip.

The visit to Port Said was to escort the two Italian battleships *Littorio* and *Vitorio Venito* from the Suez Canal back to Italy for breaking up. They had been at anchor in the Bitter Lakes since the surrender of the Italian Fleet in 1943. These looked the most impressive battleships I had seen and felt it was extraordinary how ineffective the Italian fleet had been during the war.

Ocean had several days at Port Said giving an opportunity for a visit to Cairo. With some fellow officers, I made the standard tourist trip for the previous fifty years. We visited the old part of the city, with a bazaar, characterised by Arab hubbub, cups of green tea and lengthy haggling, just like Damascus. We were shown round the Mahomet Ali Mosque, politely removing our shoes before entering. We also took in the Pyramids of Giza and the Sphinx. At the latter we duly paid a few piastres to sit on camels and have the traditional photo taken. Doubtless, in bygone years, this signified that one was an ardent Egyptologist and had travelled by camel to view the wonders of the Pyramids and the Sphinx.

The Great Pyramid proved more impressive than I expected. There was no question of climbing up the outside as each layer of stone had slab faces about nine feet high. The tunnel to the interior burial chamber seemed endless. At the Sphinx, however, my friend and I were less respectful. Having paid our money to mount our camels we were determined to ride them and set them off at a lolloping trot, despite screaming *felaheen* in hot pursuit. I cannot say I enjoyed the ride, having been highly uncomfortable and fearful I would be pitched forward over the beast's head at every stride. However, we had had our few minutes devilment and were happily on our way, after giving the camel owner a few more piastres.

Another obligatory item of the traditional trip to Cairo was lunch at the famous Shepherd's Hotel. This was a few years before this magnificent hotel was burnt to the ground, so ending the era of one of the truly Grand hotels set up by the British in the late nineteenth century when Britain was at its peak of world-wide power and influence. Such hotels included: The Peninsular in Hong Kong; Raffles in Singapore; Eastern and Oriental in Penang; Grand Pacific in Suva Fiji; Grand Oriental and Galle Face in Colombo; Taj Mahal in Bombay; The Rock in Gibraltar; Banff Springs and Chateau Frontenac in Canada, to name a few. Around Europe there were—and still are—many British-built and run hotels, with names like the Bristol, Grand, Majestic, Metropole, etc. Napoleon called Britain a 'Nation of Shopkeepers'. A hundred years on, he might have said a 'Nation of Hoteliers'. I imagine this came about as wealthy Britons were the principal travellers of the world. Now Americans have largely taken their place, the world is dotted with Hilton, Sheraton, and Hyatt hotels. Some older hotels have lost their former splendour, whilst others like the Goring in London (still owned and run by the Goring family) have quietly modernised, without losing their calculated understated elegance and ambience.

Algiers was lively. The place was still very French and the show-place of French North Africa. I visited the famous Casbah, which appeared to me to show little evidence of the romance reputed to it. But an evening spent at the Casino, losing only a modest sum, was my first encounter with a grand gambling house.

Our most historic visit was that to Haifa from 12 to 15 April 1948. For the previous year, the RN had struggled to control an increasingly difficult political situation in the Middle East. Irreconcilable pledges had been made to the Arabs and the Jews by British Governments, in the form of the McMahon Letters and the Balfour Declaration. The latter had promised that Britain would terminate her Mandate of Palestine and allow the formation of an independent Israeli Nation. The year 1948 had been set for this, before which a fixed quota of Jewish immigrants was to be allowed in monthly.

Unfortunately, with Jewish refugees streaming out of Europe and Russia, many were keen to jump the queue, to the anger of the Palestinian Arabs. Despite passionate later condemnation of the British by Israel, the former were doing their level best to walk the fine line of fairness to both Arabs and Israelis. In those days, all the terrorism and vilification were coming from the Jews. They had a number of underground Resistance/terrorist organisations, such as the Sterne Gang, specifically to harass the British and to murder any British servicemen found in a Jewish area. The British eventually countered these organisations with their own undercover agents charged with the assassination of selected terrorist leaders.

Meanwhile, a steady stream of small ships, mostly from Black Sea ports, tried to bring illegal immigrants into Palestine. The Navy had the task of intercepting these vessels and escorting them to Cyprus where the refugees/illegal immigrants were placed in internment camps. Initially, this was a straightforward process. All ships were intercepted by the specially assigned force of fleet minesweepers and escorted to Famagusta.

Soon, however, the migrants, perhaps three hundred to each craft, felt they should be able to repel the small boarding parties from the minesweepers. The whole exercise then started to get nasty. HMS *Welfare*, prominent in the Palestine Patrol, decided the only way to protect their own men in the boarding parties was to neutralise the would-be boarder-repellers. For this purpose, tear-gas canisters were fitted to the ends of poles thrust out sideways and ignited as the warship came alongside the immigrant ship. These devices were given the somewhat bizarre name of 'Welfare Grenades'. The Jews responded with welded inclined steel spikes on the upper deck to impale the feet of boarders jumping onboard.

The climax came with the interception of *Exodus 47*, an old American ferry, once named *President Garfield*, with several thousand migrants aboard. The ship was eventually captured, but only after fierce resistance with lives lost on both sides. The Jews' next move was to fit out two large freighters, *Pan York* and *Pan Crescent*, and prepare to mount even fiercer resistance than with the *Exodus 47*. This was, however, a game they simply could not win. All along, only the very minimum force had been used to enforce the exclusion of these ships but, if necessary, the entire Mediterranean Fleet could be deployed against them.

Accordingly, the sailing and progress of the two *Pan* ships were monitored and two cruisers and four destroyers were waiting for them. Fortunately, radio contact was established with the so-called Hagganah Commander, who was asked, in effect, 'Are you going to come quietly—or do you really want bloodshed?' Happily, the Jewish Commander saw he could not win and the ships were quietly turned and escorted to Cyprus. This long drawn-out operation had been distasteful to the RN but had not been of their making.

The curtain came down on the last act, with the ending of the British (League of Nations) Mandate. HMS *Ocean* played a role in the grand finale. The ship was at Haifa (the British base) for four days, going to sea each night from dusk to dawn to avoid sabotage by Jewish terrorists using limpet mines. Ashore, there was increasing chaos as the rearguard of British troops were embarked for evacuation, and sporadic bursts of small-arms fire could be heard.

Despite all this turmoil, the British were determined not to be seen as being bundled out of Palestine by hot-headed terrorists. Accordingly, a ceremony was arranged that would mean nothing to either Jews or Arabs but would be satisfying to the British. The Mandate officially ended at midnight on 15 May. It was decided *Ocean* would not go to sea that night. But anti-limpeteer patrols of motor boats—one under the command of Lt. Seymour—would circle the ship, dropping a series of 1¼ lb. TNT charges in the water. Meanwhile, our Admiral, Rear Admiral Sir Thomas Troubridge KCB DSO*, formally invited the High Commissioner, Lieutenant General Sir Alan Cunningham, to dinner aboard *Ocean*. After dinner, the Admiral led his guests up to the flood-lit flight-deck, where the party settled in armchairs with their cigars. A display was then presented by the marching and counter-marching Pipe Band of the Irish Guards—notwithstanding occasional bursts of small arms fire ashore. At 2300, the High Commissioner transferred to the cruiser *Euryalus* and the barge was hoisted. These two ships and four destroyers, also present, already darkened, weighed anchor. The naval force quietly slipped out of harbour to leave territorial waters on the stroke of midnight, Britain's League of Nations Mandate having been finally discharged. However, Admiral Troubridge was not going to let the moment pass without ceremony.

Ocean was steaming slowly with two destroyers on each side in a tight formation with no lights. In the dark, five hundred men including Royal Marine Guard and Band fell in on the flight-deck. Up the port side of

Ocean, between the carrier and the two destroyers on that side, steamed the darkened cruiser *Euryalus*. A single spotlight shone on the lone figure of General Cunningham atop the bridge superstructure. As the cruiser drew level, searchlights from the four destroyers made a pyramid over *Ocean*, the flight deck of which was simultaneously flood-lit. The Band played as the Marines presented arms for the General Salute and then played 'God Save The King'. This was followed by Troubridge's voice, over the PA system, 'Three Cheers for His Excellency the High Commissioner of Palestine, General Sir Alan Cunningham . . . Hip hip Hurrah,' etc. This was followed by 'And a "tiger" for his brother!' (Admiral of the Fleet Andrew Cunningham—now Viscount Cunningham of Hyndhope whom, I recalled, my old maths teacher had assured me 'had been a GOOD BOY'). *Euryalus* steamed off into the night as the band played 'Auld Lang Syne', with the refrain taken up by the voices of the men on the flight-deck. This was all good Edinburgh Tattoo stuff—a bit of nonsense, perhaps, but Britain had not quit Palestine with her tail between her legs.

Returning to my own service aboard *Ocean*, the Commander did try to find one interesting task for me. He put me in charge of the ship's Motor Fishing Vessel (MFV), which would accompany the carrier, or proceed ahead, to ports to be visited. If *Ocean* had to anchor off-shore, the MFV would ferry the libertymen to and from the landing. This looked like being fun—taking my own little Command independently around the Med. My crew enthusiastically set about repainting the craft, polishing its brasswork and trying to make it the smartest MFV in the fleet. Unfortunately, the engine was old and unreliable. Starting it each morning involved removing four spark plugs, heating these on the coke stove in the after mess, pouring half a cup of neat petrol into each cylinder, replacing the plugs and cranking the engine round by hand as vigorously as possible. With luck, two of the four cylinders would fire, giving just enough momentum to switch it over to diesel. This could take half an hour but the engine would then be kept running all day.

My excitement mounted with the prospect of the first sortie away from Malta for the Spring Cruise to the South of France (my second such with *Ocean*). Sadly, shortly before departure, my MFV was nearly wrecked. She was alongside in the little harbour in the bay of Marsaxlokk in the south-east corner of Malta, with the carrier at anchor in the bay. Normally this was a safe haven in both the winter *gregale* and summer *sirocco* gales, from the north and south respectively. On this occasion, there was a rare gale from the south-east straight into the bay. I was called from my bunk aboard *Ocean* at 0200 and told to get to the MFV and try to salvage the craft before it was wrecked. I found the vessel in a sorry state with waves washing right over the mole to which she was moored and breaking in the little harbour, dashing the bows on to the bottom, whilst successive ropes holding the craft were parting. Under the circumstances, there was no hope of starting the engine. After two hours of heroic exertions by the crew and seamen from the ship—all of us soaked to the skin—the MFV was saved. My battered little command was repaired—but, to my dismay, too late for the Spring Cruise.

Perhaps this was as well, as the fleet encountered the worst weather I had seen in the Med. in the Gulf of Lyons. Even with speed reduced to 10 knots, *Ocean* was taking seas over the flight-deck forward. On return to Malta, she had to be docked for repairs to the plating at the bows. This storm also involved me in a slight mishap. I had always been fascinated by ships in rough weather. Clearly, I could not look at the sea from the flight-deck, so went on to the quarterdeck, only to be bowled over by a quartering wave coming in through the 'shell openings'. I fell, striking my head on the solid steel towing clench in the deck, splitting the back of my head and having to have it stitched up. Although this occurred around 1800, I was still expected to stand my watch on the bridge at 2000.

There was one other incident worth mentioning, on a different cruise in the Western Mediterranean. After exercising in the general Gulf of Lyons, the fleet had dispersed to various French and Italian ports. One of our jobs was to act as the Post Office for the fleet. This meant that, having collected mail for a dozen ships, we would distribute this by means of our Sea Otter. This aircraft was the successor to the famous old biplane Walrus flying-boat, but had a 'puller' engine and propeller, as opposed to 'pusher' on the Walrus. I had always hoped for a flight in one of the ship's planes but the Seafires (of 805 Squadron) were single-seater fighters and our Fireflies (of 816 Squadron) only flew with their own observers. But I was now offered a seat aboard the Sea Otter for the Riviera Mail Run— which sounded great fun.

The plane was hoisted out on to an oily-calm sea outside Genoa and we attempted to take off. Unfortunately, with five people aboard, many bags of mail and a few sacks of potatoes that had been requested, the plane was simply over-loaded. After a two mile run without lift-off, the pilot throttled back and the engine cut. This happened twice more before the mission was abandoned. What I had not expected was that it would fall to me to restart the engine after each stall. This involved climbing out and standing alongside the motor and slowly winding up a heavy fly-wheel inertia starter. Each restart involved several tries—the engine would cough and splutter before stopping—for the whole exercise to be repeated. I did not mind, but this was somewhat pioneer aviation, this 'Would you mind just hopping out and restarting the engine'. I was sorry to miss the Riviera Mail run.

Where had all my old mates gone? It might well be asked. Initially,

Gavin Wemyss, Dartmouth Term-mate, friend since 1939, Fellow Sub Lieutenant in the 30th MTB Flotilla.

there seemed to be none of my particular buddies around Malta though there were many people I knew. However, towards the end of my time in *Ocean* the V Destroyers were relieved by the CHs. Aboard these ships, I found Mike Vaughan in *Chieftain* and Gavin (now stuck with the nickname 'Whisky') Wemyss in *Chivalrous*. Happy reunions followed.

Mike MccGwire in *Whitsand Bay* and Mike Kersey also turned up in due course. Not surprisingly, meeting with MccGwire once more meant trouble. With these two, I had a lively evening ashore, involving considerable drinking. We missed the last lift that took one down the cliff-face to the landing place in Grand Harbour. 'Don't worry,' said MccGwire, 'I know a short cut, through Lascaris.' This was an ancient battlement which constituted Naval Headquarters. As such, it was guarded by Royal Marine sentries—slap into one of which we ran. The sentry could see that we were not terrorist saboteurs, only slightly inebriated naval officers. Accordingly, he shouted at us to stop but did not fire. MccGwire and Kersey ran off down one corridor in the rock, with the sentry in pursuit. Meanwhile, I was able to make my escape by another, emerging at the landing stage and catching a boat back to my ship.

Unfortunately for them, the two Michaels were apprehended and brought before the Duty Staff Officer, a senior Commander who was far from amused. As for MccGwire, his ship happened to be Duty Destroyer and perhaps he should not have been ashore at all. Furthermore, *Whitsand Bay* had just been ordered to sea. To miss his ship on sailing would have meant real trouble for MccGwire. But with his fast-talking manner he told this senior officer that he therefore had no time to lose and must rush off and catch a boat at once. This enabled the two of them to make a rapid exit before the Staff Officer could decide what to do with them. Half an hour later MccGwire was on the bridge conning the ship out of harbour in the dark.

So we did have some fun ashore, but our social lives were strictly limited—mainly by on-going shortage of funds. I worked out that my monthly pay came to £24. From this, I was obliged to pay Gieves £5, leaving £19. Having so little to spend ashore I tended to entertain more on board. This led to higher Mess Bills—about £15 a month—leaving me only £4 for all shore-going expenses. This was in stark contrast to grand balls in Genoa and Istanbul. My commission in *Ocean* had not been dull but I would have preferred a smaller ship. I would be back in the Med. Fleet within eighteen months in a destroyer for the happiest commission of my naval career. *Ocean* returned to Plymouth and paid off in early July 1948.

CHAPTER 18

1948–9—A Year in and around UK

THE NEXT SIX WEEKS of Foreign Service Leave, from mid-July to late-August, had little to do with my naval career or the general subject of this narrative but a few words on this time will indicate how life in UK had changed in the two years I had been away.

In 1948, the Olympic Games were held in England and the nation was trying hard to 'put its best foot forward'. The aim was to give a good impression to the rest of the world and allow the people to live it up a little, after so many years of wartime hardship and post-war austerity. There were still shortages and restrictions but many of these were lifted in the locations where Olympic Games events were being held. The Sailing Olympics were held in Torbay, on my doorstep. Accordingly, before the Olympic races, British selection trials were conducted.

I secured a place in the crew of one of the contending six metre yachts. We failed to gain selection but were not disgraced, being placed fourth out of sixteen entrants. In the process, I met many top British yachtsmen and, later, some of the visiting Olympic sailors from the USA, Australia and the Argentine. My family hosted several parties for local and overseas crews, with some of whom I would catch up much later. Julian Roosevelt kindly took me cruising aboard his Ocean Racer in Long Island Sound, twenty years on. I also again met Jock Sturrock of Australia, after settling in that country in the sixties.

Unlike the austerity of 1946, Torquay now had a gala air. Neon signs and coloured lights blazed for the first time since 1939 and there was a hectic round of social activity. The harbour and adjoining corner of Torbay held a large fleet of yachts. These included the Norwegian Royal Yacht *Norge*, which had been T. Sopwith's *Philante* (nearly as grand as Attaturk's Presidential Yacht). There were visiting foreign warships and the RN tried to impress with the battleships *Anson* and *Howe* and the fleet carrier *Indefatigable*. These ships were not operational. They were virtually in a state of care-and-maintenance as non-seagoing training ships, normally permanently moored in Portland Harbour, and had only made the forty mile trip across Lyme Bay to put on this notional display of naval might. However, *Anson* flew an Admiral's flag and the ships certainly added to the general spectacle.

On a personal note, I found myself—together with half the young swains of Torquay—chasing after the glamorous daughter of a British aviation magnate. The father was racing a six-metre in the Olympic Trials. I found myself vying with a man several years older, of great sophistication and charm, but who had the misfortune to have lost a leg and arm in the RAF. Sunbaking on the private bathing beach of the Imperial Hotel with this wounded war hero and glamorous young thing, I listened to the former airman's story. He had been badly smashed as a test pilot, flying Manchester Bombers—the disastrous twin-engined forerunners of the famous Lancaster bombers. Most of these aircraft had crashed, their aircrew becoming known as the Manchester Martyrs. Our blonde put on a sweet smile and declared, 'Yes, I know, Daddy's aeroplanes never were any good.'

I assessed my chances against the rest of the 'field' and decided the only trump card I could play would be an invitation for this girl to dine aboard one of the warships. I found an old shipmate—not a close friend but one happy to help—on the promise of one or two introductions to girls in Torquay. Thus a private dinner was arranged in the Officer's Guest Room of HMS *Howe*. It was arranged that I would collect the girl from her family's suite at the Imperial at a certain time. I had been at pains to explain that she would have to be ready, as the routine officers' boat would not wait. I presented myself on time, hopefully cutting quite a dash in my mess kit, with starched shirt, wing collar, bow tie and decorations.

Regrettably, my partner was not ready. I looked dismayed, whereupon Daddy pressed me to a glass of champagne. Needless to say, by the time we reached the jetty, the boat had gone. There was, however, a group of important looking people standing around. My blonde, recognising one, exclaimed, 'Hello Peter. What are you doing here?' He was Peter Scott, son of Captain Robert Falcon Scott of Antarctic fame, noted ornithologist, painter, recent Coastal Forces war hero and on the International Olympic Yachting Committee. I understood from his reply that, with other VIPs, he had been invited to dinner by the Admiral.

'Will the Admiral be sending a boat for you?' my guest asked.

'Yes, he will.'

'Oh good, then it could drop us off at our ship.' By now, as a junior Lieutenant, my acute embarrassment was intensified when the Admiral himself appeared aboard his barge, having come ashore to greet his guests. At this point, the charmer shot an irresistible glance at Peter Scott who felt obliged to explain to the Admiral that we needed a lift to *Howe*. After only a moment's hesitation, the latter said, 'Very well then, jump in.' Feeling more uncomfortable by the second, I tried to escort my guest to the after cockpit of the barge. This was a more gilded and chrome-plated version of the picket boat I had smashed up in the River Congo.

I wished to keep my distance from the Admiral, although I was appreciative of the lift to *Howe*. But this time, the Admiral was given a pathetic look—as if to say, 'I cannot believe you want ME to travel "steerage".' The Flag Officer could but respond with, 'All right then, jump in amidships, here.'

The boat went first to *Howe* and must have caused the Officer of the Watch concern to see the Admiral's barge approaching with the Admiral himself aboard. He must have felt relieved to hear 'Aye Aye' (meaning 'Officers coming') as opposed to 'Flag' ('Admiral coming aboard'), in response to the hail of 'Boat Ahoy'.

I suspect there may have been a few chuckles amongst the VIPs after our departure. The Admiral could well have remarked, 'That young man seems to have got himself more of a handful in that girl than he had bargained for.' Perhaps Peter Scott, who had already met her socially, may have said, 'You can say that again—but you have to admit that she's Some Girl.'

I saw a little more of this delectable—if maddening—creature and her family did take me out for a day cruise, in a chartered motor boat. This was round to Dartmouth, up the River Dart I knew so well, and past the Naval College. Papa opened successive bottles of champagne as a steward produced picnic hampers. Meanwhile, his daughter sunned herself alongside me in the most daring two-piece swimsuit I had ever seen—straight from the South of France and virtually a bikini. This was a year before such attire became generally worn.

The whirlwind of sailing and socialising came to an end with my appointment to the corvette *Flint Castle* of the Portland Local Flotilla. From Torquay to Portland was a mere forty miles as the seagull flies. However, by rail, it meant an all-day journey changing at Exeter, Dorchester and Weymouth—with my luggage. Happily, my one-legged, one-armed friendly rival had the answer. This man, staying at the Imperial, seemed to have met almost 'everyone who was anyone' in Torquay at that time and the previous evening had been drinking in the cocktail bar with Bernard Mills. The latter was son of, and successor to, Bertram Mills, founder of the most famous circus in Britain in those days. This would perform at Olympia every Christmas and tour the seaside resorts in summer. It was Bernard's practice to move from one such venue to the next aboard his luxury motor yacht, accompanied by lady-friend. It happened that the circus was moving to Weymouth and he was headed there with his yacht next day anyway. A word from my friend provided me with a lift, enabling me to take up my next appointment by water even though the ship was berthed alongside. Again, this was not the prescribed Dartmouth method—but far more convenient for me.

Lock Eck *in Mediterranean 1946, bound for UK.*
(Photo by aircraft from Venerable.*)*

Flint Castle, *Portland Local Flotilla, 1949.*

FLINT CASTLE

I spent the next nine months in *Flint Castle* but did not greatly enjoy the time. The reader might conclude that I was hard to please. *Ocean* had been too big, with not enough work or responsibility for me. *Flint Castle*, on the other hand, was too small and I felt I was grossly overworked. *Ocean* had at least visited all sorts of exciting places; *Flint Castle* was a 'Home Sea Service' ship that never went anywhere. This was fine for most of the crew—home to their families each night—but not for young unmarrieds.

Initially, all was fine on board. Fellow officers included my old shipmate, Jack Maidwell, who had been First Lieutenant of *Loch Eck*. Good appointments were already becoming harder to come by in the RN. After two years successful commission aboard a Loch Class frigate from UK to the Far East and back, Maidwell now only rated the same job in a corvette. And this ship only made day trips to sea from Portland. For myself, being third-in-command of such a vessel was hardly a big excitement. Nevertheless, Jack Maidwell was good company and I was happy to find him as No.1. Also present was another Lieutenant, David Heap, who had been one Term behind me and in the same House, at Dartmouth. He was someone I already knew and liked. With a Sub Lieutenant, fresh from his Sub's Courses, it could be said that this ship had considerable talent and experience amongst the executive officers. Our 'Chief' was a competent Warrant Engineer Officer. The only one for whom I felt limited enthusiasm was the Captain. He was what was known as an Upper-Yard Man— promoted from the lower deck. I held no prejudice against such officers (my enormous respect for Lt. Foord of *Enterprise* will be recalled). Regrettably, in this case, we seldom saw eye-to-eye. I suffered no injustice under this Captain, but it cannot be said that he did much to endear himself to his officers. I subsequently learned that he had various financial and domestic problems and was still suffering from the effects of ghastly war experiences. To give this man his due, he took a personal interest in his sailors and got on well with them. He was also a reasonably competent ship-handler, except that on one occasion he ran the ship into a wooden jetty under construction in Portland Harbour. This was exactly the same mistake as had been made by (or under the supervision of) Captain Grant aboard *Enterprise*—omitting to order Half Astern before increasing revolutions, an error many officers have made in their time.

Notwithstanding the foregoing, I am happy to report that another officer, whom I respect, served with this man aboard a cruiser (his next appointment) and found him congenial, popular and great fun. It seems that he had remarried and overcome such personality problems as he had appeared to exhibit aboard *Flint Castle*.

The role of this flotilla was the training of officers and key ratings in practical anti-submarine tactics and procedures. This was in cooperation with HMS *Osprey*, the shore-based Anti-Submarine School at Portland, and the locally-based flotilla of submarines. We were at least doing something useful and our officers became skilled at hunting and attacking submarines. However, with our Asdic (Sonar) equipment and the relatively slow (compared with the German's final Type 21 U-Boats) T Class submarines, this was relatively simple. Accordingly, every exercise ended in a notional 'kill'—so the training programme became somewhat tedious. Some diversion arose when, about once a month, we carried out live firing of our 'Squid' A/S Mortar for demonstration purposes. With our own skilled Asdic team we would pick up an echo that was, in fact, a wreck on the bottom, which we knew exactly where to find, about ten miles offshore. A 'copy-book' attack would be carried out and the (triple) mortar fired. Each of the projectiles had several hundred pounds of high explosive which invariably went off right in, or on, the wreck. Our engine would be stopped and the whaler and skiff would be lowered for eager hands to scoop up hundreds of pounds weight of dead or stunned fish. These ranged from whiting to large conger eels which were never dead and could be quite alarming, slithering around the boat's bilges. We would be able to keep the whole flotilla in fish for a week. Such was the limit of the professional skills we were ever required to display. There would be no life-and-death action with German destroyers, no rescues from blazing tankers, no anxious landfalls on African shores—we practically never went out of sight of land. No precautions had to be taken against approaching typhoons or gauntlet-running jeep-rides to Batavia. My former Captain may well have been right about the Navy in Peace being a more serious business than the Navy in War. It was, however, beginning to be seen to be a very much duller one.

Notwithstanding all this, we did what we could to make life interesting. David Heap, the Sub Lieutenant (whose name escapes me) and I each acquired a motorcycle. Mine was a pre-war BSA 350 cc machine which broke down frequently, until I had taken it to pieces so many times, it had no more tricks to pull. This bike was to be part of my life for the next three and a half years, accompanying me back to the Mediterranean. I landed it in many countries and rode it home across France back to UK. Around Portland, I was able to explore all sorts of places I could not otherwise have visited. I recall one Sunday afternoon venture by the Sub and myself to take a close look at a prominent tower we had often taken bearings on from the sea. It was simply shown on the chart as 'Hardy's Mo', and this was how we always referred to it. We learnt the 'Mo' stood for Monument and somehow assumed that it was honouring Thomas Hardy, the writer, this part of Dorset being known as 'Hardy's

Country'. We managed to find this rather gaunt tower—perhaps 40 ft. high—standing, unfenced, in a field with no notice to enlighten visitors. We saw there was a lichen-covered inscription over the high opening that might once have had a door, but the wording was quite illegible from the ground. However, the Sub, with his feet on my shoulders and penknife in hand, was able to scrape out the inscription. He was able to decipher: 'Thomas Masterman Hardy . . . Flag Captain, HMS *Victory* . . . Trafalgar 1805. On this spot . . . by public subscription . . . .' So, at least, we had established to which Hardy this was a memorial. I felt any other country with a monument to such a distinguished man would have ensured that it was not neglected. Perhaps the National Trust has now remedied this situation. If not, and the inscription has now weathered away altogether, the reader may take my word for it that this tower is a memorial to Nelson's famous Flag Captain.

My motorbike also enabled me to ride back to Torquay for an occasional short week-end. Alas, however, towards the end of my time aboard that ship, I could spare little time off, even at week-ends. At the end of 1948, David Heap left the ship and the Sub was promoted to Lieutenant and appointed elsewhere. Before his departure, David made one long-standing impact on my life. In a careless moment, he said to me, 'Let's give up smoking—I mean it and suggest we have a five pound bet as to which of us lasts the longer.' We both smoked heavily—at around forty a day—but cigarettes still only cost us 10d. a packet and we had yet to hear the dreaded words Lung Cancer. I accepted his challenge and assumed it would not last long. But he went on to say, 'We are bound to attend the odd party when we will weaken, and so I feel that we should then be allowed a cigar.' Five pounds was a lot of money, representing about a month's disposable income, and neither of us could afford to lose. The cigar 'let-out clause' was never spelt out in detail. So, three years later, serving with the Royal Australian Navy, I had still not touched a cigarette but did enjoy one good-sized Ritmeester cigar every night after dinner. By this time, Heap was serving with the Royal Canadian Navy and had not been seen to smoke a cigarette. But 'my spies' told me that he was now practically chain-smoking cigars—and was not expected to keep off cigarettes much longer. In due course, I challenged him and he admitted he had succumbed and would pay up. I made him pay five pounds to the 'King George V Fund For Sailors'.

I confess that I subsequently became a rather heavier cigar smoker myself. I developed a distinct liking for a good Havana even on an enclosed bridge in the morning watch—around 0600—which must have been nauseating for others around. Aboard *Bulwark*, the last ship I served in, fortunately for me, my Captain was also a heavy cigar smoker. I only 'kicked' the smoking habit altogether some years after leaving the Navy, but have not had a smoke now for seventeen years. I never ran into David Heap again—I would be interested to know how he is getting on today and, if still alive, whether he ever finally gave up smoking.

Aboard *Flint Castle*, after the departure of Heap and the Sub, we only had an occasional RNVR Sub Lieutenant for training, leaving me a big work-load to carry. On a typical week-day, I would have to be on deck by 0700 as Forecastle Officer, to oversee unshackling from the buoy. I then stood, to look decorative, at the tip of the fo'c'sle for leaving harbour—although goodness knows who ever saw me. I then had to go to the bridge and, as the Navigating Officer, to order the courses to our exercise area. Special Sea Dutymen would fall out (usually the point where the navigator hands over to the Officer of the Watch). But apart from the No.1, I was the only watch-keeper so I would 'hand over' to myself and keep the forenoon watch until noon. At this point, the First Lieutenant—successor to Jack Maidwell, who had also gone—would relieve me while I had lunch, before taking over again for the afternoon watch. We would then head back for Portland, and I would again assume the duties of navigator, before taking charge on the fo'c'sle for securing to the buoy. Then, and only then, from 1700 onwards, could I start on the mounting pile of paper-work awaiting me. This included sailors' Service Certificates and other documentation, keeping the books for the Wardroom Messing—getting out the other officers' mess bills and wine bills. There was all the ship's office correspondence—endless compulsory monthly returns with no 'writer' to punch the typewriter for me. I would have to amend my chart folios, even though I knew that we would never need any of the charts except for those of our exercise area. I knew the latter so well I could practically navigate the ship around them blind-fold. There would be occasional defaulters and requestmen and a hundred and one other little matters to attend to. They say no one is indispensable. However, it is hard to imagine what would have happened if I had fallen sick. As it was, when I finally left the ship, no fewer than four officers arrived to take my place.

The reader will find it hardly surprising that I was delighted when my request was approved to be sent on a Destroyer Gunnery Officer's course.

CHAPTER 19

DESTROYER GUNNERY OFFICER—

GRAVELINES 1949–50

I LEFT *FLINT CASTLE* in May 1949 and, the following month, reported to Whale Island—HMS *Excellent*, the Gunnery School at Portsmouth. It was here I had lived aboard the old Royal Yacht *V. & A.* on Subs Courses back in '44. The course was over three months, after which (assuming successful completion), I was to join a ship commissioning for service in the Mediterranean. In the event, we only reached Malta shortly before Christmas. My time on this course might have been included in the last chapter as '1948–9—A YEAR IN AND AROUND UK'. But as the course was specifically to prepare me for my service aboard HMS *Gravelines*, I have included the course in the chapter on that ship.

I was determined to specialise in Torpedo Anti/Submarine, with a 'Long Course' (14 months). I had, however, decided that I ought to know a little more about gunnery first, having not seen any gun fired since my Midshipman days (apart from Coastal Forces). Furthermore, qualifying as a Destroyer Gunnery Officer guaranteed appointment to a modern Fleet destroyer—representing my ideal type of warship.

I went to Whale Island with certain long-held prejudices about the Gunnery Branch. I felt great emphasis was placed on something called 'Power of Command', assessed on how loud one could shout at a squad on a parade ground. Clearly, this had little to do with the more subtle quality of Leadership. I was to find that Gunnery Officers were quite human after all, and had similar traits of sensitivity and humour as other officers. But I concede they exhibited perhaps a shade more enthusiasm and heartiness than their fellows in other branches. This was exemplified in the nature of guest night dinners routinely held in the Wardroom, usually involving some unlikely after-dinner entertainment. There was to be such an evening in mid-July, with some visiting French Officers, following a NATO exercise. The Dinner Night happened to fall on the 'Quatorze Juillet'—a very meaningful day for all Frenchmen. The Commander determined that we should fittingly salute our French guests. Accordingly, a grand spectacle was organised. Many sailors spent the afternoon building a 'Bastille' out of portable cricket-watching stands on the lawns in front of the Wardroom. All officers present were given roles—Sub Lieutenants on course there were designated as *Prisoniers*, dressed in sacks and rags. Our course and the 'Long G' officers (in a variety of contrived theatrical uniforms) were the defenders of the Bastille. The Commander, in an imaginative get-up and huge wooden sword, was *Le Commandant*. All other officers, in any garb they could devise, were *Les Sans-culottes*, attacking the Bastille. Following the after-dinner port and cigars, everyone quickly donned their costumes and the French visitors were escorted out to spectator arm-chairs. All stood for the band to play the 'Marseillaise' and 'God Save the King' and the show started. There was little attempt at historic realism—simply a good 'rag' was held, with fire hoses, 'thunder-flashes', smoke canisters and other fireworks. In due course, amid bugle calls for 'Cease Fire' and trumpet fanfare, a huge Tricolore was hoisted over the smoking Bastille. Some of the French may have felt this simply confirmed that the English were all crazy—or that we treated their National Day with insufficient solemnity. Britain is one of the few countries without a National Day as such. However, they were able to enter into the spirit of things and the entertainment was enjoyed by all.

The course itself proved absorbing and was specifically tailored for the Gunnery Systems of Battle Class destroyers, to which we were all being sent. These were the latest fleet destroyers—although the first of them had appeared four years back. Most of the course was held at Portsmouth, but we had one week at Wembury Firing Range, just east of Plymouth Sound, close to the entrance of the River Yealm—one of the loveliest beauty spots in Devon. The rustic atmosphere in the local villages was in sharp contrast to the city atmosphere of Portsmouth. In the local pubs the main beverage sold was not beer but 'Scrumpy' (rough cider). This break was the more fun, as three of us were able to travel on our motor-bikes.

Following a brief leave after the course, I found myself joining HMS *Gravelines* at Plymouth. It was strange that practically every ship I served in was Devonport-manned, namely: *Revenge, Enterprise, Loch Eck, Ocean* and now *Gravelines*.

The Battle Class were mostly named after naval battles but, with forty ships planned, even the glorious history of the Royal Navy could not provide so many victories. Accordingly, quite a few land battles were included—*Agincourt, Aisne, Alamein, Corunna* and others. Even for the sea battles, a good knowledge of naval history was required. The naval actions included *Hogue, Sluys, Barfleur* and our own Leader *Saintes* (derived from the 'Battle of the Saintes', after the Isles des Saintes between Guadaloupe and Dominica in the West Indies).

Gravelines meant nothing to most of our sailors, who had great difficulty with the name. They were prepared to accept that it was not 'Grave Lines' but few got beyond 'Gravlines'—unable to come to terms with the 'i' pronounced 'ee' or the silent French 's' on the end. The correct pronunciation, of course, was 'Gravleen'. The battle, so I discovered—having had to look it up myself—was the decisive action of the defeat of the Spanish Armada. It was decisive in that, after an all-day battle, with about 130 ships-a-side, The Spanish had lost one ship and the English none—One-nil to England! I was at pains to point out to Scottish shipmates that this was an English victory—Scotland was neutral, and allowed some Spanish ships to revictual in Scottish ports. With so many ships, one might argue that, losing one of them, the Armada could hardly be said to have been decisively defeated off the little Flemish port of Gravelines. But the Spanish had failed to secure command of the Narrow Seas and had to abandon their plan to transport the army under the Duke of Parma to invade England.

The ship's coat of arms intrigued me—being a combination of the arms of the Duke of Medina Sidonia and those of Lord Howard of Effingham. The former were 'Crossed Saltires, Argent' (if one was familiar with 'saltires'), while the latter were a 'Lion, Gules' [wait for it] not 'Rampant', 'Passant' or even 'Couchant' but 'Statant Gardant With Tail Extendant' (sic). I felt our sailors could be forgiven for being unable to manage the French pronunciation of Gravelines, as the College of Heralds gave up trying to master French four hundred years ago!

Returning to 1949, I soon sensed that this was going to be a splendid commission—and I was not disappointed. *Gravelines* proved the most efficient, happiest and most enjoyable of all the ships I served in. Some sixth sense also told ratings that this was going to be a good ship to be sent to. A month before commissioning, men from Chief Petty Officer downwards were scheming with the Drafting Office of the Depot to get their names put down for *Gravelines*. The ship herself had been completed three years before but, on trials, had somehow 'blown up' (or wrecked, in some way) the astern turbine on one shaft. Repairs were going to take months and, with many destroyers completing as the war ended, the ship was put on one side and the ship's company sent elsewhere. Accordingly, although not brand new, the ship was practically 'unused'. This did not mean that, with the astern turbine replaced, the ship was in mint condition. In many ways, she was; but much of her equipment—particularly radar—would not work as the result of being out of use for three years.

The ship had more than her fair share of teething troubles. For instance, we went to sea one day for some trials unrelated to the engine-room, with no requirement for full power. With 24 knots obtainable from only one of the two boilers, one only had been 'flashed up' and steam raised from it. Unpredictably, however, the firebricks of the furnace caved in. This extremely rare occurrence would normally necessitate immediate shutting down of that boiler and steaming on the other. But it was going to take an hour to raise any steam on the shut-down boiler. Furthermore, at this time, all three of the ship's diesel generators were unserviceable and all electric power was coming from steam generators. If the No.1 boiler was shut down, all electric power would be lost. It would not even be possible to pump oil fuel to raise steam on the other boiler, so that the ship would become completely 'dead in the water'. With a fine degree of judgement—and, no doubt, crossed fingers—our Chief, Lt. Cdr. (E) Bryant, kept a minimum number of burners going—with main engines stopped. This was to maintain turbo-generated electric supplies long enough to let No.2 boiler take over. It was an anxious time, as the furnace casing became white-hot and could have caused an oil fire in that boiler room, with no power for fire pumps. However, we just made it and returned to harbour.

Our Captain, Lt. Cdr. 'Bill' Shaw, agreed with the Chief that we could not risk proceeding with any more trials until: a) the firebricks in No.1 boiler were replaced and b) we had at least one diesel generator working. This resulted in an Engineer Lieutenant from the dockyard working, heroically, on one of the diesels until 2200. He appeared at the wardroom, with his white overalls covered with grease and oil, but with a happy grin, to tell the CO that one diesel was now operational. I mention this minor incident because, I feel, it said a great deal about Bill Shaw. Unable to do anything personally about the vital generator, he had decided he could remain on aboard and make encouraging noises to the one man who could. His wife was waiting for him ashore—but clearly understood that the demands of the 'other wife' had to be met. Once the engineer had cleaned up as best he could, and been provided with something to eat, my captain gave our visitor a stiff whisky and expressed his sincere appreciation for the efforts of the latter. I was the only other officer left in the wardroom as drink followed drink and the atmosphere became relaxed. They invited me to join in the spirit (in more senses than one) of the occasion. The other two left by taxi around midnight. Not only had the ship taken an important step to becoming operational but I had noted what a fine and caring CO we had.

Commissioning trials were completed without further troubles. The ship had to carry out Gun Functioning Trials. I had charge of four 4.5″ guns in two fully enclosed and highly automated turrets, as well as no fewer than ten 40 mm Bofors AA guns. Four of these were in sophisticated twin Stabilised Tachymetric Anti Aircraft Gun (STAAG) mountings—each incorporating its own 'lock-on' radar system for fully automated 'blind fire'. We had yet to prove how accurate all these guns were but functioning trials were required just to prove they would fire when the trigger was pressed. Regarding the 4.5″, these guns would normally be fired by remote control, through an elaborate fire-control system, but could be fired locally. The 'captain of the turret' had a small thick glass dome in the roof of the turret. He had visual sights, high-speed handle-bar controls—for training and elevating—and a trigger to fire the guns. I decided to conduct these trials myself. With the two guns of the turret loaded with solid practice shells, I checked with the bridge, by headphone, that the 'range was clear' in a predetermined direction. I slewed the guns round, elevated them to a nominal 15 degrees, and fired. It is hard to imagine the sense of power this gave—perhaps an unhealthy sense of power—but these were 'my guns' and their proper functioning was my responsibility. I have never been a personal firearm enthusiast, even though I briefly owned a 12-bore shot-gun and a 'double-barrelled 500 Express' rifle, inherited from my father. But firing my 'double-barrelled 4,500 Express' guns gave me an insight as to why some people develop a passion for guns for their own sake.

Gravelines, in her day, was a fine ship—2,500 tons displacement, 50,000 hp engines (c.f. 40,000 for *Revenge*) with a top speed of over 34 knots. She was armed with eight torpedo tubes and depth charges, in addition to the guns already described, and had a Ship's Company of 285. At last, I felt I was getting somewhere. As the next senior Lieutenant after the 'No.1', I was third in command of this powerful warship. This was a good step up from being 3rd i/c of a little 900 ton corvette of the Portland Local Flotilla.

GRAVELINES IN THE MED

The ship finally sailed from Plymouth six weeks late, as the result of teething troubles, in no case attributable to incompetence by anyone on board. We joined our consorts of the Third Destroyer Squadron in Malta. By 1949, with many Captains and not enough Commands, instead of flotillas of eight destroyers, there were now 'squadrons' of only four ships. Our Leader, as I have mentioned, was *Saintes* and the other two *Vigo* and *Armada*. Indicative of the ship-naming problems, they 'cheated' by having *Armada* as well as *Gravelines*. The Naming Committee at Admiralty had long been somewhat perverse. In 1949, four special destroyers came out—the Weapon Class, with the names *Broadsword*, *Crossbow*, *Battleaxe* and (of all things) *Scorpion*. They were ready to field the inevitable question: 'Why?' The answer was: 'See II Kings—Old Testament—"My father chastised you with rods; I will chastise you with Scorpions".'

At any rate, our four ships made a fine sight steaming at high speed in line ahead. The work-up in and around Malta went smoothly and *Gravelines* quickly made a name for herself as one of the smartest and most efficient ships of the fleet. I had volunteered for the job of Sports Officer and, with the morale of any unit soon evident in the way the ship performed in competitive sport, I am happy to say that *Gravelines* was soon winning competitions, with strong spectator support from the crew. Somewhat later, the Arbuthnott Trophy Cross Country running race was held. This event always attracted more attention than Cross Country merited, simply because it was one of the few sports all ships could compete in simultaneously and so all the Admirals and COs would be present and winning brought much kudos.

Gravelines won the small ships event. This did not take much doing—the trick was to find out the best runners in the ship and train them up as a team. Simply asking who would like to enter seldom produces many takers but hold a series of internal representative races, and one has half the ship's company running. Thus we had several athletes entered who had no idea they would excel at cross-country running. By the end, we had so many enthusiasts that we were able to enter two teams. Two of my fellow officers were in the A Team with another and myself in the B. This was despite my declared lack of enthusiasm for this particular form of masochism, as a Midshipman back in *Revenge* at Mombasa. Ours was the only 'small ship' to enter two teams. The A team won comfortably and the B team was not disgraced. We did not tell people the secret, just letting them assume *Gravelines* would excel!

In fact, our chief rival in many sports was the destroyer *Chequers*, of which Prince Philip was the No.1. He threw himself so whole-heartedly into every sporting endeavour by his ship (the Leader of the 'CH' destroyers) that *Chequers* was hard to beat at anything. But, as we shall see shortly, the officers of *Gravelines* had a satisfying win over the officers of *Chequers* in the Fleet Regatta (rowing).

Not only was our ship making her mark as an efficient warship but she was also a great success socially in Malta. As background, I should first introduce the other officers. The Captain, Lt. Cdr. Shaw, had been commanding destroyers during the war as a Lieutenant, yet, ironically, *Gravelines*, his third destroyer Command, was finally taken from him, he being judged *too junior* to command a destroyer. The No.1 was Lt. Paul Newton—married, four years older than the other Lieutenants and soon to become a Lieutenant Commander—competent, energetic and a thoroughly 'nice guy'. Strangely, he had also been born in Ceylon and our respective fathers had known each other, twenty-five years back. His had been Colonel to mine in the Ceylon Planters Rifle Corps, both Paul and my father telling me that Paul's had the nickname of 'Mouldy' Newton. (There was nothing 'mouldy' about Paul any more than, I suspect, there had been about his father.) After myself, as the No. 2 and Gunnery Officer, came Lt. Nigel Fawcett ('ex-Dart', a year behind me) as the Navigator. Lt. Mike Wilson was another watchkeeper and my assistant as the Gunnery Director Control Officer, later to follow me into the T A/S Branch.

The most junior executive officer was Sub. Lt. David Brown, showing early signs that he would go a long way. In fact, after also specialising in T A/S, he went on to become Vice Admiral Sir David Brown KCB. There was Doug Honey—Gunner (TA/S), the gunner(G) and the Commissioned Electric Officer. These three, formerly classified as Warrant Officers, would soon be known as Sub Lieutenants SD (for Special Duties). Our 50,000 hp engines and a great deal of auxiliary machinery were under the control of Lt. Cdr. (E) Paul Bryant. In addition, we would often have one of the Squadron Staff Officers, and, from time to time, a Midshipman for his small ship time—a total of between ten and twelve.

What made the ship interesting, from the social point of view, was having four young unmarried Executive Officers, and the fact that Paul Newton, although himself married, took on the role of Social Secretary of the wardroom, coming up with some imaginative initiatives. It was agreed that we should try to burst onto the Malta social scene with panache. Normally, a newly-arrived ship would give a Wardroom cocktail party. However, when you have seen one Wardroom cocktail party, 'you've seen 'em all'.

It was decided that *Gravelines* would herald our arrival with a DANCE. Nobody had regarded a destroyer's Wardroom as large enough to have a dance in before. But, by unbolting the mess table and moving out all armchairs and coffee tables, a surprising space was made. The Captain generously allowed his day cabin, next door, to be used as an ante-room and the setting was fine. The party included a buffet dinner, but with the numbers involved, Paul Newton felt the Maltese stewards would take too long serving the meal. Accordingly, he had us all practising serving salads, etc. with serving spoon and fork in one hand like professional waiters— something we did on all future occasions. We could not manage a band, but with a good radiogram and latest records from England, the evening was a huge success. Furthermore, the word soon got around the smart younger set that, rather than a stuffy official reception aboard the Flagship, an invitation aboard *Gravelines* promised far more fun.

In a very short time, our regular guests included many of the most eligible—and glamorous—daughters of the local Establishment. Amongst these were the daughters of our own Flag Officer, Destroyers—Rear Admiral McCall; the daughter of the General Officer Commanding; the daughter of Flag Officer, Air Med., Rear Admiral Norman, whose son David had been one of MccGwire's team who preceded us in the 30th MTB Flotilla. Sadly, we soon lost the delightful daughter, who became engaged to another officer whilst we were away on the Spring Cruise. There were Margaret and Elizabeth DeTrafford—daughters of the most prominent Anglo-Maltese family and, finally, the charming PA to the Governor of Malta. To the last, I confess, I lost my heart—and kept in touch with her after my return to UK. But I was over-ambitious, being too immature for this most talented and attractive young woman.

To illustrate the degree of enterprise shown by our Social Secretary, we were designated Host Ship for a visiting French warship. Normally, one would organise some sporting activities—which I did—and have a cocktail party for the officers. We officers asked ourselves, 'What would we like, if visiting a French Naval Port?' Answer: 'To meet the girls, of course!' 'What would the girls we knew like'? 'To meet some dashing young French officers!' We thought we could risk allowing such liaisons for a few hours. Accordingly, after drinks and lunch aboard *Gravelines*, teams were made up of the girls (who provided the cars) and the British and French officers for a round-Malta 'Treasure Hunt'. After a swim at St Pauls Bay, the final rendezvous was the magnificent Villa Bologna. This was the home of the DeTraffords (next door to the Governor's San Anton Palace) where a sumptuous afternoon tea was provided. I am happy to say all parties agreed this had been a highly successful occasion, and all thanked us—although we had done no more than plan the operation. One could say that we soon got to know some delightful girls. I would like to hope they look back with fond memories of HMS *Gravelines*—even though no true romances materialised.

My meeting the PA to the Governor resulted from my being invited to lunch at San Anton Palace, through the good offices of the (naval) ADC. This event was almost a disaster for me as, unable to afford a taxi, I had elected to ride my motorbike out to San Anton. This was a questionable proposition anyway, dressed in my starched white buttoned-to-the-throat 'No.10' outfit. Unfortunately, my veteran old bike chose that day to have a puncture—always a problem on a motorcycle, with no spare wheel. I thought I was in luck as this occurred close to a garage, into which I pushed the machine and told the mechanic to fix the thing. Regrettably, whatever other qualities the Maltese may have, they are not renowned as skilled mechanics. After a few minutes' prevarication, this man said, 'Ow Senor' (I never discovered what the 'Ow' meant but the Maltese always seemed to open any statement in this way), 'I do not know how to take the (rear) wheel off.' I had no alternative but to remove my tunic—with only a singlet underneath—put on an apron to protect my white trousers and do it myself.

I arrived at Government House half an hour late, and nothing like as immaculate as I had set out. Before joining the Navy, I had never envisaged what problems those smart white uniforms would cause. Happily, there were no other guests for lunch that day and my host and hostess were forgiving. My father had not given me the name of this Governor, who, nevertheless, had known my father, whom he had succeeded as Governor of Fiji and High Commissioner for the Western Pacific.

The young officers of *Gravelines* were not actually moving in the top social circles of Malta—but could be said to be involved with some of their daughters. In fact, the Top People in Malta were of really high standing. The Flag Officers in Malta included now Vice Admiral Lord Louis Mountbatten who, once more, excelled himself in his job. This could still not be compared with his earlier assignments as Supreme Allied Commander, South-East Asia and then, Viceroy of India. As a born leader, he got through to the lowliest Ordinary Seaman and raised the morale and pride of every man in the fleet. Amongst innovations he later instituted was the Mediterranean Fleet, Outward Bound Association, known as 'MedFOBA'. Groups of officers and sailors were encouraged to undertake all sorts of expeditions. Such included boat trips from one port to another independently of their ship, climbing a nearby mountain or canoeing down some river. I was to lead quite an ambitious expedition in the Med. four years later.

A few years later Mountbatten would demonstrate just how effective a man of action he was in an emergency. There was a disastrous earthquake in the Greek Ionian Islands, centred on the town of Argostoli. There were hundreds dead, thousands more injured or homeless, and water and electricity services were cut off. No contingency plans for such an event existed and no rehearsals had been carried out. However, within forty-eight hours, Mountbatten had most of the Med. Fleet steaming to the rescue at high speed, with large quantities of relief supplies of all sorts. Mountbatten's wife, Lady Edwina—long the Superintendant-in-Chief of the Nursing Division of St John's Ambulance—recruited all women in Malta with nursing experience and took them to Greece. Food supplies, tents, field kitchens, emergency hospitals, portable generators, etc. poured ashore from the fleet and the dazed populace were able to start rebuilding their lives. This sort of thing is expected following natural disasters these days. But the scale of the operation mounted by Mountbatten and the speed of its execution left onlookers gasping. This man had not been the wartime Allied Chief of Combined Operations, Europe, for nothing.

As already mentioned, the Med. Fleet was also lucky enough to have Prince Philip amongst its officers, with his wife, the future Queen of England. Princess Elizabeth lived very much as any other Naval Officer's wife although not in a naval married quarter but in Mountbatten's residence, the Villa Guadamangia.

To sum up, I regarded myself a very fortunate young man. I had a responsible job aboard what I regarded as the best ship of the best destroyer squadron in the best and most prestigious fleet of the RN. The fleet was commanded by some of the finest naval officers of the century, and belonged to the finest—if no longer the biggest—Navy in the world. My work and play were full of interest, I had the best Commanding

Officer I had served under and a truly congenial group of fellow officers. Added to all this, several of my old mates were also in this fleet, Mike Vaughan—still in *Chieftain*—amongst them.

Life was not all play and we took our training and special assignments seriously. For instance, there had been 'industrial troubles' and near-riots in the dockyard, through scaling down employment for the fewer ships to be refitted. To prepare for possible violence, in Malta or elsewhere, all ships were told to train up landing parties specifically for 'Aid to Civil Power'. As the Gunnery Officer, I was to command our landing party and attended a series of lectures. These covered crowd control, the legal requirement of a Magistrate reading the Riot Act and exhorting the crowd to disperse, and the use of MINIMUM force to restore order. In theory, a well disciplined platoon of thirty men, properly led, should be able to control a crowd of a thousand or more excited demonstrators.

But if the worst came to the worst, the landing party had to be ready to fight. To this end, I took my thirty men on a special Commando Course run by the Royal Marines at Ghajn Tuffieha in the north-east corner of Malta. I need hardly say that any commando course run by the Royal Marines was going to extend us to the limits of our mental and physical endurance. There was an obstacle course around, and over, the Agility House, which involved leaping over a six foot gap filled with barbed wire and climbing a rope up two storeys (with pack). Stronger team members hauled up weaker ones—and everyone jumped off the roof, all against the stop-watch. The finale was a rigorous inspection (in full marching order) then: 'Right Turn. Quick March'—for the fourteen mile route-march back to the ship, under the blazing sun.

Morale was high and we had been praised by the Marines. We set off in good spirits, determined to break the unofficial record for the return march. For the first half hour, the men sang as they marched, then they simply talked, until the strain got to them and muttering started. Finally the men were too exhausted even to complain. I made things worse by trying to take a short cut—only to lose our way. Malta is a labyrinth of sunken lanes and successive shallow valleys, with no landmarks except the hundred-odd churches, which all looked alike to me. The upshot was that we marched and climbed over a number of stone walls for at least two more miles more than we need have. The platoon reached the dockyard looking like the bedraggled remnants of a defeated army. However, the men had enough spirit to halt for a few minutes to smarten themselves and march round the corner to the ship like Guardsmen.

Before proceeding to recount some of the ship's activities, away from our base at Malta, there was one incident that is worth reporting. As already indicated, we thought the world of our CO Bill Shaw, who was an experienced and competent destroyer captain as well as being a fine officer. But he was involved in one seamanship error of judgement which might well have ruined his reputation, yet, fortunately, succeeded in enhancing it. I am sure though Bill Shaw would be the first to acknowledge that it was a 'close run thing'—that could have gone either way. There was always quite unreasonable drama associated with any mishap involving running aground. Even if no damage was sustained, should the ship so much as touch the bottom, a 'Collision or Grounding Report' had to go in, followed by a Court of Enquiry. In this case, the ship must have come within a whisker of touching the bottom, with the inevitable consequences. Happily, this did not occur and the Captain was praised for his actions to avoid 'hazarding his ship'. In fact, with hindsight, I am sure Bill would agree he should never have let the potentially hazardous situation arise in the first place.

The ship was scheduled to carry out a practice surface gunnery 'shoot' on a towed Battle Practice Target. With a near-gale force *gregale* (north wind) blowing, conditions were marginal for going ahead with the exercise. But *Gravelines* put to sea anyway, only to be informed that the fleet tug could not control the target. The practice firing was abandoned and the ship ordered to return to her berth in Sliema Creek, which was where the destroyers and frigates moored. Sliema Creek was long and narrow with enough room for two lines of ships on head-and-stern buoys but there was no room to turn round once in the creek, which ran east-west with entrance from the north. The procedure was to enter harbour, bows first, turn 90 degrees to port and then go astern (in other words 'back in') to the allotted berth.

This sounds simple enough, and with our 50,000 hp of engines, one would imagine there would be no problem making the ship go where required. In practice, however, it is almost impossible to steam a destroyer straight astern in a strong cross-wind. This is because, when 'making a sternboard' ('backing' to landsmen), a ship pivots on a point a third of its length from the stern. A destroyer, with raised fo'c'sle, bridge and funnel well forward of this point, will always head up into wind when moving astern. This problem with Sliema Creek was recognised and so a tug was made available to assist berthing. But with our unscheduled return to harbour, we were advised that if we wanted a tug we would have to wait for two hours. With his years of handling destroyers and complete faith in our powerful engines, Bill Shaw felt he could manage without the tug. This proved the error of judgement—the wind was so strong that the ship simply refused to 'back' straight up the creek. This was even with the port engine on 'Half Astern' with a lot of power 'rung on' and the starboard on 'Slow Ahead'. We tried three times, even dropping and weighing an anchor on one occasion, to swing the stern. But each time, the ship went astern, the stern headed up-wind, against the rudder (hard-a-starboard) and the opposite torque exerted by the two propellers.

It was a fine clear day, despite the strong wind, and all other ships were at their moorings. The officers of the other destroyers evidently had nothing better to do than observe the 'watch-them-they're-supposed-to-be-good' *Gravelines* team make a muck-up of picking up their moorings. Indeed, this promised a splendid unexpected morning's entertainment—but an act in which Bill Shaw now had no wish to play the leading role.

To make matters worse, our Captain D from *Saintes* had taken to his motor boat to watch from close quarters. Worse still, Flag Office, Destroyers, Rear Admiral McCall, appeared on the jetty just fifty yards to leeward of us on Manoel Island to watch the drama. One of his finest ships was drifting on to the rocky bottom off the island. I was in charge on the fo'c'sle with men ready to secure to any buoy we got near, and to drop and pull up anchors, as required. By this time, I was almost eyeball-to-eyeball with both Captain D and Flag Officer Destroyers, and felt as uncomfortable as, I am sure, did Bill Shaw. I had a good team but there seemed to be nothing we could do.

At last, our chance came. The ship drifted sideways on to an unoccupied buoy near the after end of the fo'c'sle on the starboard (leeward) side, fifty yards from our Admiral. The Captain leaned over the side of the bridge and called to me, 'Quick—Grab that buoy.' In a flash, a man was over the side on a rope's end and on the buoy, with the (steel wire) picking-up rope. He had about ten seconds to snap the hook on to the ring of the buoy. The latter then submerged, as the ship drifted over it, leaving the heroic 'buoy-jumper' to swim ashore. This line just saved the day, stopping the ship going on to Manoel Island. Meanwhile, our motor boat quickly passed a line from the stern to another buoy and it was then only a matter of tidying up.

It was to the credit of the ship that her crew responded effectively when required, thereby getting *Gravelines* out of a tricky situation—which she should never have got into.

The improbable sequel to this incident came six months later back in England, when I was on my Long T A/S Course. I had been invited by his daughters to a tennis party at the home of now Vice Admiral McCall. Their father had also invited the now-retired war hero, Admiral Sir Philip Vian. I did not expect McCall to remember me personally but I mentioned I had been serving aboard one of his destroyers in the Med.—the *Gravelines*. 'Ah yes,' said the Admiral, 'Lt. Cdr. Shaw was your Captain—I remember watching him berthing his ship under difficult conditions, in Sliema Creek in a strong wind. I was particularly impressed by the way he handled his ship.' 'Yes, Sir,' I said, 'We all thought he was a very good CO', but privately reflected that he had also been a very lucky one.

My ship's visits around the Mediterranean were nearly as extensive as had been those of *Ocean* a year and more back, although over a period of one year instead of two. One visit was made with Wilson and two other mates on our own initiative over a long week-end, while the ship was having a brief overhaul. We chartered a small 25 ft. yacht belonging to the Navy (being an ex-German Navy craft, taken as war reparations and known as 'Windfall' yachts). We sailed through the Friday night, in unpleasant weather, headed for Syracuse in Sicily. Next morning found us off the coast of Sicily but some way from Syracuse. The wind had gone down and the sun had come out but we were cold, wet and weary, after a sleepless night, with bedding, etc. below, soaking wet. We anchored off the little fishing village of Pozzallo just round the corner of Cape Passaro, on the south coast, to sleep and dry out wet gear. After a time, a small boat came out to us with boatman and an official in an impressive uniform. We never discovered the purpose of the visit as this man spoke no English and we knew very few words of Italian. However, after these two had been given several glasses of wine, they returned to the shore quite satisfied. Regarding Italian, we soon found one could guess the meaning of many words. One could ask the *direzione* to the *stazione*, go to the *plafformo* and finally board the *treno* (pronounced 'traino'). Accordingly, we found it worth trying to add a selected vowel to the English noun we wanted to use and 'Italianise' the pronunciation.

We made Syracuse that afternoon, secured, stern-to-the-wall among some other yachts and pressed on with our plan—*treno* to Catania and bus to the 'Grande Albergo Etna'. This proved a luxury hotel—so much so that, having checked how much bill we had run up next morning, we could not even afford breakfast and cleared out. Our goal was to climb Mount Etna—10,900 ft. We bought some bread rolls, salami and a bottle of *vino* and made the summit by mid-afternoon (having started from the Albergo at 5,000 ft.). So at last, I had ascended one mountain—as opposed to admiring Mont aux Sources in the Drackensbergs, from a distance. The view from the top was magnificent and looking down into the smoking sulphurous crater of this active volcano was quite an experience. The descent took little more than two hours and, with limited remaining cash, we decided we had better bus and train straight back to our boat at Syracuse. We were happy to find everything in order, having entrusted the yacht with a swarthy Sicilian with practically no English, who had seemed keen to act as caretaker. He could have made off with binoculars, compass, etc., but seemed entirely happy with a few spare tins of baked beans and about 5 shillings worth of lire. We sailed back to Malta—about 120 nautical miles—next day, without further incident. Later (after I had left the ship) Nigel Fawcett and David Brown emulated our venture and also sailed to Sicily and climbed Etna.

The reader may have noted that I had become a sailing enthusiast. In fact, I was keen on sport generally but, having poor eye-to-hand co-ordination, was never good at ball games. Accordingly, my principal sports were rugby (where, as a second-row forward, precision ball-handling was of minor importance), sailing racing and, later, skiing. The last was not to high competition level, but in 1958 I was offered the position of non-playing captain of the RN's Inter-Services Ski Team.

As for sailing, I was disappointed in 1950 at not winning the Med. Fleet Sailing Dinghy Trophy in the regatta held at Aranci Bay, Sardinia. With Nigel Fawcett crewing, we reached the first weather mark a quarter of a mile ahead of anyone else but on the opposite tack to most other competitors. The race official sitting in the anchored boat being the mark, declared, 'You still have to go round a mark over there'—pointing to other boats approaching. I doubted this but sailed back towards the rest of the fleet, letting several boats pass me before realising I had been right all the time. I still finished third but sailed over to the Flagship to notify a protest at being ordered round a non-existent mark by a race official. I was told my protest could only be accepted if submitted in writing. I returned to my ship, had the boat hoisted, dressed and headed back to the Flagship—with written protest. It was dismissed on the grounds that it had not been lodged within one hour of completion of the race. I was sad but 'it was only a game'.

Our Spring Cruise of 1950 was memorable. The RN had returned to annual 'Combined Fleet Manoeuvres' of the Home and Med. Fleets in the Western Mediterranean. Ships of both fleets then had their 'reward' of a week in a French or Italian Riviera port or bay. We called at Toulon and visited St Tropez by motorbike. St Tropez was a delightful spot, before it was glamorised—and spoilt—by Brigitte Bardot.

All ships then rendezvoused at Gibraltar, where the results of exercises were analysed—and all possible lessons learnt. There would also be inter-fleet sporting fixtures and, of course, much inter-ship entertaining as one met up with old friends, perhaps not seen for several years. There were no fewer than twenty-five destroyers in the 'Pens' along the North Mole of the harbour, all within a few minutes walk. I suppose I must have met up with nearly half of our original Term from Dartmouth. I feared this was not going to be healthy.

Also perceiving this, our Admiral sent a signal that it might be good for us to take some exercise and climb to the top of The Rock. After considerable drinking aboard several destroyers at lunch time, someone called out, 'Come on fellows, that's enough drinking—it's time to head off up The Rock'—and so we did. We took a bus up to the place where tourists feed the celebrated Gibraltar apes and followed a rough track from there. We reached the knife-edge ridge from which there was a near-vertical drop of

1,200 ft. of the concrete water catchment on the eastern side. Such can be off-putting for anyone without a head for heights—but happily this was something that had never worried me. It was hard to tell which of three humps was the highest. However, we followed the ridge until we came upon a stone engraved 'Highest point of Rock of Gibraltar 1395 ft. Surveyed by . . . ' with a long-past date. I suspect few tourists ever view this spot. It is a pity I cannot recall the surveyor's name, but it is immortalised in stone for those prepared to climb up and view his inscription. I challenge any younger reader to do this—it is not a hard climb. Unlike that to Thomas Masterman Hardy in Dorset, this inscription, on the exposed pinnacle, is unlikely ever to be obscured by lichen.

The Gibraltar get-together normally concluded the Spring Fun and Games. But *Gravelines* would not return to Malta for another month. The Duke of Gloucester was due to fly back to UK from Kenya. Strange though it may seem today, it was thought a destroyer should be waiting, just in case HRH's plane should come down in the sea. C-in-C told Flag Officer Destroyers to see to it. FO, D nominated the 3rd Squadron and our Captain D—for reasons unknown—designated *Gravelines*. We were told to proceed to Cannes and wait for the Royal aircraft to fly over—involving a whole week at this delectable resort. Cannes today has a harbour with every foot of space seemingly occupied by marinas or yacht moorings. But in 1950 our 2,500 ton destroyer was able to actually moor, stern-to-the-wall, right inside the harbour. It must be admitted, however, that when we came to weigh anchor, we did pull up half a dozen yacht moorings, which took considerable disentangling.

For many years, Cannes had been a meeting place for the rich and the famous, so much so that, if neither, one went quite unnoticed. In fact, everyone we met seemed just that much larger than life. The officers and ratings were well looked after although the locals might have imagined they had seen the last of the Royal Navy for another year. I was hospitably entertained aboard a number of luxury yachts including one owned by a British Air Marshal. His wife's dress plunged to the navel—in Cannes, women were expected to dress strikingly. Sir Bernard and Lady Docker's yacht *Shemara* was the largest in the harbour—not to mention their enormous green custom-built Daimler. Docker was perhaps the wealthiest man in England at that time. We did not visit *Shemara* at Cannes but our Captain and Nigel Fawcett subsequently dined on board at Monte Carlo.

An English couple whom I found fascinating were Commander and Mrs Marten. He was currently an equerry at Buckingham Palace, and his wealthy wife had inherited the magnificent estates of Crichel Down in Dorset. Part of this land had been taken over for the war for a fighter aerodrome, as happened in a hundred or more places in England. This was fair enough but the deal was that, once the war ended, the land should be returned to the owners. Here, however, the Labour Government in England were keen to retain this prime stretch of farmland for a state-owned agricultural research centre. The Martens fought this act through successive courts, with the Prime Minister throwing his full weight into the case. Happily, Commander Marten and his wife won the suit in their final appeal to the Privy Council. I had followed this case with great interest and regarded the Privy Council's finding for the Martens as the greatest triumph for British jurisprudence since Magna Carta. This was, perhaps, an overstatement. It was also sad that the case was only able to be fought to the bitter end because the plaintiffs were wealthy enough to do so. Regrettably, today throughout the Western World, litigation is increasingly only for large corporations, the very rich or the very poor on Legal Aid. However, those of us who got to know them found the Martens a delightful couple. The Commander's stand has remained an inspiration to me to resist bureaucratic tyranny, as far as I am able.

After our week at Cannes, we did not return at once to Malta. Before we had left Gibraltar, Monaco asked for a British warship to attend the celebrations surrounding the Accession of His Serene Highness Prince Rainier III. This was to be for seven days starting a week after our departure from Cannes. As *Gravelines* was going to be in that area anyway, we were assigned this further role. The Captain was told that the intervening week could be spent at any place of his choosing. He picked the Bay of Villefranche, only five miles east of Nice and about two hours steaming from Cannes. My Captain kindly allowed me to go ahead by road to collect mail awaiting us and make contact with the local authorities. Subsequently, I was allowed to do the same thing, preceding the ship into Monte Carlo. These journeys were, of course, on my venerable motorbike and took me along the scenic route, with majestic views over the brilliant Mediterranean, from the famous Corniche d'Or. I should mention that Mike Wilson and David Brown also had motorcycles on board and so we could explore the hinterland of many ports in company—often with Nigel Fawcett as a pillion passenger for one of us.

Villefranche proved a fascinating little port and close enough for us to visit Antibes, Nice and Cap Ferat. The intriguing thing about Villefranche at that time was that it was the established base of a large fleet of smugglers and their high-speed motor boats. Everything seemed quite open. I asked the Harbour Master which boats were the smugglers—there must have been twenty craft stern-to-the-mole. His answer was, 'You see those three yachts at the end there. Well, those ones are NOT smugglers (*contrabandiers* to the French).' Furthermore, one could find oneself having a drink with a young Englishman in a Villefranche bar. On asking what he did for a living, one might be given the un-embarrassed reply '*Contrabandier*, old boy'. It was not that the French condoned or turned a blind eye to these activities—they simply could not catch the smugglers. It seemed the 'bread and butter' came from running American cigarettes out of Italy, where the duty on them was low, into France, where it was high. The *contrabandiers* could outrun any French police launches and delivery was effected by placing the goods, in watertight wrappings, in lobster pots for local fishermen to collect. There was more money in running sophisticated machinery into Spain and duty-free cameras, watches, etc. back from Tangiers. However, I was told that one hit the jackpot, assisting the escape of a wanted political activist or a fugitive from justice. This would be effected from a secret inshore rendezvous by small boat, rather than directly from Villefranche.

At this point, I have to relate the story of a certain member of my Term. He was invalided from the Service after being stricken by meningitis, but recovered, worked hard for a law degree and was called to the Bar. But finding briefs hard to come by, he is said to have decided that life was not meant to be that hard. With a friend, he allegedly bought a surplus naval MTB and headed for the Mediterranean—and the *contrabandier* trade. This man was said to have been last seen, living in a luxury penthouse in Rome, surrounded by glamorous women, some twenty years ago. I have no verification of all this. The last positive word from him was a polite note, declining the invitation to attend the Term's 35th Year Reunion, from an address in Rome—because of pressure of business.

From Villefranche, several of us spent an afternoon watching a 'Concours d'Elegance', a parade of classic cars—Delahayes, Hispano Suizas, Alfa Romeos, etc., and even more elegant women—a show that only the French could put on. One evening we went on to Antibes, where my friend Mike Vaughan back in Malta had told me I had simply got to go and see 'Monsieur L'Amiral'. This turned out to be Vice Admiral Cumberlidge RN Retired whom the Navy List showed had the seniority of Vice Admiral as of 1925 and who was now aged eighty-two. It seemed he had had Mike Vaughan to dinner, during which a nine-year-old girl—without a stitch of clothes on—burst in. She was chased out by the Admiral with, 'How many times have I told you not to interrupt us at dinner time?' The old boy apologised and explained that was his youngest daughter, who was a bit wild. Whilst his current wife (he had been twice a widower) was much younger than him, a quick calculation showed that the Admiral was still doing well in his seventies. Nobody who knew the old man doubted for a second that he was truly the father. He had not been keen to talk about the Navy, considering that the Service had never been the same since 'they invented Wireless Telegraphy'. There was, however, plenty of life in the old boy. He and his wife contrived to run a night club in Antibes. There was no flashing neon sign outside—you simply had to know the place. We entered alongside a greengrocer's shop and went downstairs to a cellar and along a dimly lit corridor. However, at the end of this was a cheerful room with an ensemble, tables and chairs and a small dance floor. At one of the tables with several glamorous women, sat the beaming *Amiral*. It appeared that his personality, a good little band and an adequate supply of champagne were all that was needed to make this place a roaring success. Every now and then another beautiful creature would appear and give the Admiral a kiss; he would pour another glass of champagne and beam a little more. Clearly, the old boy was enjoying his declining years—if, in fact, they were declining.

One day, I was Officer of the Day and all other officers were ashore but the ship was open to visitors. I was greeting the populace generally and sailors were showing people around. Amongst the visitors were two youngish smartly dressed English couples. I decided to take them on a conducted tour myself, for which they appeared remarkably appreciative, but, before leaving, both men said they would like to leave their cards for the Captain. I took these, to comply with their request, and, glancing at them, read the names of Lord Bearstead and another peer, two well-known Captains of British Industry at that time. The former said before leaving, 'I would be delighted if you and a friend would drop in at my villa (at Cap Juan St Ferat) if you have time. It is possible we may be out but, should you call when we are not there, I will leave word for you to be looked after.'

Two days later, Mike Wilson and I decided to call round, having failed to get through on the telephone. Our would-be host and hostess were out but a polished English butler said he had been told to expect us. He suggested we came through to the lounge room, opening on to a terrace with a magnificent view out over the sparkling sea. He then wheeled in a well-equipped drinks trolley and asked what cocktail or other drink we would like. We felt a little uncomfortable but thought we should have one drink. We were shown round the grounds, which descended steeply to the water. I believe the house next door belonged to Somerset Maugham. It had been a kind gesture to two impecunious young naval officers.

Whilst at Villefranche, I had been training up the Guard of Honour we would be parading at Monaco. This was not the kind of duty our sailors were often required to perform. Morale in the ship was at its usual high, so I called for volunteers, with no rewards or incentives offered. Nearly half the crew offered, allowing me to hand-pick thirty smart men, all of around six feet. They were told to put their best boots aside but polish them hard every day, until they really gleamed. All other gear was also smartened up—rifles, bayonets, webbing, gaiters, etc.—and the squad drilled and inspected for an hour each day. In truth, the person needing most practice was myself, doing the old elaborate drill of saluting with drawn sword whilst marching past, and other procedures. By the end of the week, I judged we were ready.

The ship moved on to Monte Carlo, arriving two hours after me. Even before *Gravelines* was moored, I found myself involved in tortuous international negotiations. The arrangements for the Accession ceremonial activities were bound to be complicated. Four nations—Monaco, France, Britain and the USA—each had their own ideas as to how such an event should be staged. Whilst the show was to be a Monegasque presentation, such an event needs to have a parade to have any impact at all. This, however, presupposes a reasonable number of men in uniform. Monaco alone could only muster their thirty-man 'Army' (albeit in splendid sky-blue uniforms and silver-plated helmets). Even throwing in the Fire Brigade and the Boy Scouts, there would still be insufficient bodies for a parade worthy of the Accession of His Serene Highness. Hence the request for visiting warships.

The show would have the elements of a Gilbert and Sullivan operetta regardless, but with goodwill and everyone doing his best, it was hoped a reasonable display could be mounted. But each nation had its own ideas how to conduct the parade. I sensed the French had limited enthusiasm for the whole exercise, tending to feel Monaco should be part of France anyway. Britain might feel similarly about independent celebrations in the Isle of Man. The French Services tend to spend their lives having ceremonial parades and so the deal had nothing like the novelty appeal it had for the bluejackets of *Gravelines*. The Americans appeared somewhat perplexed as to what was expected of them anyway. The Yanks felt they could make the most colourful contribution by parading a huge banner of 'Old Glory' on a 15 ft. staff. I mentioned this to my Captain who seemed to know his international protocol. He declared one should only parade national colours in a foreign country if one had just conquered it or for international sporting events, such as the Olympic Games. Furthermore, after consulting some improbable NATO reference book, he informed me that the CO of the French ship (*La Fantasque*) was the senior officer present and I should see what he had to say.

I was ceremonially piped aboard *La Fantasque* (as a visiting foreign naval officer) and shown in to see the French Captain. I outlined the problem and he advised me that they had a routine for such occasions (as I sensed they would). This was to have a handkerchief-size silk and fringed tricolore, embroidered with the ship's name, attached to the bayonet of the rifle of the man in the centre of the front rank. But he agreed that parading national colours, as such, would be inappropriate. I then went aboard the American ship (USS *Larsen*) and put the position to their Captain. 'OK then,' said the American, 'In that case, it's no Old Glory—but we'll parade the United States Naval Infantry Flag.' This proved to be just as big a banner—blue with arrows-clutching eagle, etc. 'What flag will you have?' 'No flag,' I said, 'There will just be two officers in front

Gravelines *at Monte Carlo, 1950.* USS Larsen *closer to camera.*
(Photo courtesy Principality of Monaco.)

Parade, Palace Square, Monaco for Accession of His Serene Highness, Prince Rainier.
Author in front of RN Guard (furthest away).

with their swords.' Soon afterwards I learnt that the Americans felt the British would steal the show with their swords if their own officers had none. Three Ensigns from their ship had been designated to stand in front of their guard. They had no swords on board and the Ensigns had never heard of sword drill. The young officers were told to 'go, get themselves some swords'. They did so—from a theatrical costumes rental shop, returning with a variety of weapons: cavalry sabre, Scottish claymore, Turkish scimitar. I had to tell them that none of these were suitable for a naval Guard of Honour. They were so crestfallen that I offered to provide three Royal Navy officers' swords from *Gravelines*—for which they were inordinately grateful.

The big day and the parade all passed off smoothly. To avoid favouritism, the organisers arranged for the guards from the three visiting ships to be inspected by Prince Rainier in the sequence: British, French, American. But the march-past was to be in the reverse order. This suited us fine. The inspection went well—after biting my tongue to resist the temptation to order 'Serene Salute . . .' as opposed to 'Royal Salute . . .' for His Serene Highness.

The march-past, however, was where our sailors shone. I do not know why they appeared smarter than the men from the other ships, but the crowd certainly thought they did. The onlookers, from many nations, clapped politely as first the Americans and then the French marched past, but burst into whole-hearted cheering as the *Gravelines* guard passed by. They did look smart in their white belts and leggings and their rifles 'at the slope' in line at the same angle. I like to feel that I did not let the men down, in my black patent leather gaiters, wielding my gleaming sword in salute as we marched past HSH. The men knew they looked good and the cheering crowd made them stick their chests out just that little bit more. They were really pleased with themselves—you could call it vanity, but they were only human. On completion of the march-past in the square in front of the palace and on to the Cathedral, my Petty Officer approached me. A little sheepishly, he said that the men were asking if, instead of taking the bus back to the landing stage, they could march back to the ship. They marched—and drew more cheers.

For all this Bill Shaw was made a 'Chevalier of the Order of Albert (2nd Class)'. Paul Newton, who, with the Captain, had been invited to attend the service inside the Cathedral, scored 'Companion' of the same order (Third Class). For my performance, I received a nice little gilded medallion with Rainier's head on it, none being more than pleasant little souvenirs.

The air of comic opera and unreality lasted through the week. There was a glittering reception at the palace, with the high officials and Ministers of State—being a third of all Monegasque nationals and every conceivable European Pretender. An important looking man with blue sash of some noble order and a collection of diamond-studded stars on his chest assisted me. Seeing that I was having a little trouble reaching the flunkie bearing the glasses of champagne, he gave an imperious order to the man, who thereafter plied me with 'bubbly'. My benefactor, I learnt, was His Highness (Royal or Serene), Le Duc de Bourbon-Parma. All the while, a section of the Monte Carlo Symphony Orchestra played popular classics.

We had other pleasurable activities, including a visit to the famous Casino, from which, to my amazement, I emerged with a small profit from the (low stakes) roulette tables. The actual gambling meant little to me but the ambience of the establishment was fascinating, I can still recall the repetitive call of the croupiers: '*Eh bien, Mesdames et Messieurs . . . Faites vos jeux, s'il vous plaît . . . Les jeux sont fait . . . Rien ne va plus,*' etc. Naturally we were playing for the smallest stakes possible but getting excited over each spin of the wheel. However, in the top rooms small groups of seven or eight in evening dress were playing baccarat and chemin-de-fer, betting thousands (of pounds) on each deal. Fortunes seemed to be being won or lost by the minute, but good form dictated that not an eyelid should be batted for either. I watched entranced and wondered how long some of these people could maintain this *sang-froid*. I felt that if I watched long enough some elegantly dressed woman might unobtrusively take a small pistol from her handbag and, without a word, blow her brains out.

So much for the glitter and unreality of Monte Carlo. For *Gravelines*, it was back to Malta, renewed intensive training, and seeing the girls we had left behind, one of them, to our dismay, having become engaged during our absence. It has to be confessed that, with many distractions since leaving Malta two months before, we had not spent every minute thinking of the girls back in Valetta. Nevertheless, we were soon back in the swing of life in Malta—but not for long. After a few weeks, the ship was ordered off on one of the few operational stints we put in that year.

Ever since the establishment of the State of Israel some two years before, there had been an uneasy truce between Israel and her Arab neighbours. One of the potential flash-points was the northern end of the Gulf of Aqaba in the Red Sea. If a ship anchored five miles short of the tip of the Gulf, it would be within gun range of Egypt, Israel, Jordan and Saudi Arabia.

Despite being hemmed in by three potentially hostile neighbours, the seemingly invincible Israelis appeared to pose the biggest threat to peace in the area. It was considered that they could seize Aqaba, eliminating Jordan's only port, any time they chose. To counter this threat a British garrison at battalion strength, with tanks and artillery, was stationed there for several years. A warship also was anchored off-shore to provide fire support. Militarily, as I understood it, the situation was impossible, with the HQs of the Israelis and the Jordanians/British only five miles apart. Neither side could be on full alert round the clock for year after year. In a surprise attack either side could overrun the other's defences in min-utes—before the officers had time to get back from the beach and get their uniforms on. There was an elaborate system of bunkers and minefi-elds to a depth of a few hundred yards only and a barbed wire fence at the actual frontier—but only for five miles inland into the desert. Even if such would stop a tank (which it would not), one could drive round the end of it in a quarter of an hour. On the other hand, Israel, for all its new-found confidence, would think twice about an act of war against British forces.

Against this background, *Gravelines* dropped anchor off Aqaba one morning. In accordance with earlier briefing, we immediately fired a seven-gun salute to the Bey of Aqaba (to which he was not entitled—but it was judged good diplomacy). The Bey would be welcomed aboard with full ceremonial and a Guard of Honour. After an elaborate exchange of greetings, the Bey would return ashore, change out of his flowing robes and come back in his bum-boat to collect the ship's washing!

The next caller was the adjutant of the Sussex Regiment, currently stationed at Aqaba, to deliver an invitation to a regimental dinner at their officers' mess that evening. One felt a little dubious as to the sort of evening in prospect, viewing the collection of mud huts constituting the Arab town of Aqaba and the Army's rows of tents. Accordingly we asked, 'What rig do we wear?' 'Full Mess Kit with decorations, of course. We will have transport waiting for you at the jetty.' So we gratefully accepted but were still unsure what to expect. We should have known—with a famous County Regiment like the Sussexes. There to meet us outside a primitive but well-furnished hut stood the CO and other officers in their scarlet jacket mess kit, miniature medals, etc. The Regimental Band was playing and mess waiters appeared with a variety of drinks in silver goblets. A first class dinner followed, Loyal Toast, some witty speeches and the usual port and cigars. As one of their officers said, if they had to spend six months in the desert, they might as well make the best of it. Morale seemed high amongst both the officers and the troops and we had some inter-service sporting activities. We also carried out practice indirect bom-bardment (of targets that we could not see)—the spotting being done for us by RA observers. When there was nothing else to do one could always hold a fishing line. The fish were so prolific that making a big haul required neither skill nor even patience. Altogether, we enjoyed our visit to Aqaba and we took off our hats to the Sussex Regiment.

After only a few weeks back at Malta it was time to set off for the annual Med. Fleet Summer Cruise to the Eastern Mediterranean. Our squadron alone, this time, visited Istanbul. We could hardly expect the same treatment the fleet had been given two years before but we still had a most enjoyable stay. Indeed, the whole squadron was particularly well looked after as David Brown's father was the Naval Attaché there. I was lucky enough to be entertained by one of the long-time British Levant trading families, notably by a Canadian cousin, in her last year at McGill University. We had a delightful evening of dining and dancing at the beautiful Kadikoy Yacht Club. The open-air dance floor was at the edge of the smooth waters of the yacht harbour, under a brilliant moon. I was beginning to feel the trouble with Navy life was that one never stayed in one place long enough. But it should not be supposed that any of us spent too many evenings wining and dining at Istanbul. The fact was our next port of call was Athens before the gulf of Marmaris on the south-west corner of Asia Minor, for the Fleet Regatta. This was something every ship took very seriously indeed.

The next stop was for the whole fleet at Piraeus—the port of Athens. The usual four of us made some explorations inland on motorbikes, including one to look at Mount Parnassus—which someone felt we should see, although I cannot remember why. Also, Mike Wilson and I felt the urge to go up and view the Acropolis by moonlight, only to find the area around locked and barred by night. But we did take in some of the wonders of this ancient city during our short visit.

There was, I fear, one 'black mark' for *Gravelines*. Our Captain was required to 'render his reasons in writing' as to why the officers from our ship had arrived aboard the Flagship fifteen minutes late. We arrived for the official cocktail party after the King of the Hellenes. These functions were planned like a military operation, with no illusion that the officers were there to enjoy themselves, but with every effort made to ensure official guests did.

The regatta was organised as two series of races—one for the 'Big Ships' (carriers, cruisers, etc.) and the other for twenty-seven 'Small Ships' (destroyers and frigates). The racing was in standard naval 27 ft. 'whalers', with five oarsmen and a coxswain. Each event, of which there were about twelve, was for representative crews from each ship. There would be Junior Seamen, Junior Engine-room Personel, Supply and Secretariat Branch, Communications Ratings, etc. There would be a Petty Officers Crew, an Officers Crew and finally the 'Racing Whaler', the crew for which was to be the best from the whole Ship's Company. There was, of course nothing like the same technique as for rowing an Eight for example. But skill still counted, with the striking rate set by the stroke oar and the cox picking a line and knowing when to call for a supreme effort. However, the key factors were really strength, fitness and endurance—even 'guts'. Understandably, therefore, for weeks in advance the whaler would be out with training for some crew all day, every day, the ship was in port. The locals of Istanbul might well have wondered why, from our four ships, whalers would be out under oars all day.

The races were spectacular with twenty-seven whalers in each event for the Small Ships regatta. Even for those not rowing there was excitement and cheering for the crew from each man's ship. An official Tote was run from the Flagship and anyone could bet on every race. This was all done by radio, as was race call.

On the day, the results were surprising. The fleet included two New Zealand frigates, *Hawea* and *Taupo*—working-up with the RN—and these two ships appeared to be winning every single race. I have the greatest respect for the sporting prowess of the Kiwis. However, one could not believe that every one of their crews would be superior to all the twenty-five other crews from the RN ships. It might be 'sour grapes' but the explanation may have lain in the fact that the NZ whalers had been built in New Zealand of that superb boat-building wood, kauri. This made them appreciably lighter than the RN's mahogany-built whalers. Be that as it may, I would not wish to deny the Kiwis the glory with which they covered themselves that day. However, as can be imagined, towards the end of the racing, the Tote was taking very few bets on any starter other than *Hawea* or *Taupo*. But there was always a chance that one of the races might just be won by a non-Kiwi crew.

When it came to the Officers race, everyone knew that Prince Philip, as stroke oar of *Chequers* Officers' crew, had trained his team really hard. The punters still made the two New Zealand crews favourites—as they had yet to be beaten—but some of the 'smart money' was on *Chequers*. *Gravelines*'s Officers crew comprised Nigel Fawcett (stroke), myself, Mike Wilson, Midshipmen Glennie and Mathews (a Reservist who later rowed for his College at Cambridge), and the relatively lightly-built Doug Honey as cox. We had trained hard but I cannot say I fancied our chances against the seemingly invincible Kiwis or Prince Philip's crew—nor did many others. Accordingly, long odds were available and many of our own ship's company felt we could be worth a bet. Perhaps this was out of loyalty and a sense that the ship's officers made up a good team and could well pull something out of the hat. To cut the story short, by really rowing our guts out, we won the race—out of a field of twenty-seven. This was the only race that day not won by a New Zealand crew; *Hawea* was second and *Chequers* third.

I do not think I have ever savoured so sweet a sporting victory. There was a tremendous welcome for us when we returned to the ship. I would like to think this was because we had earned some glory for *Gravelines*. More realistically, no doubt, it was because many of our people were substantially richer for backing us. But even this, of course, enhanced our personal standing with the ship's company.

With the races over, the whole fleet let its hair down. A huge marquee had been set up as a 'Wet Canteen' for the sailors in which they could

Winning Officers' Whaler Crew—Med. Fleet Regatta, Marmaris, Turkey, 1950.
Back row (l. to r.) Lt. (later Cdr.) Nigel Fawcett, Lt. (later Cdr.) Mike Wilson,
Midshipman J. Glennie, author.
Front row (l. to r.) Gunner (TAS) Doug Honey, Midn. (RNVR) G. Mathews.

Prince Philip's Officers' Crew from Chequers *placed 3rd, behind* Gravelines.
(Photo courtesy Longman—Philip by Basil Boothroyd.)

celebrate their wins—or drown their sorrows. Tests for drunkenness were none too strict when the men returned on board, as long as there was no 'trouble'. The officers set about calling on, or 'raiding', other ships and demanding drinks. The normal motor boats' crews were dispensed with and the officers ran their boats themselves. I cannot remember which ships we visited but know I got to bed that night 'feeling no pain'—not even from aching muscles and joints.

There is one story of that night that may never have been told but I really feel it can be now. It concerned Prince Philip, for whom I, like every other officer or sailor who served in his company, had the greatest admiration. He was as ready as anyone to let his hair down after weeks of strict training. Philip, with his officers from *Chequers*, decided they would 'raid' the *Vigo* (of our Squadron, and whose No.1—George Shaw—was an old mate of his). However, all the officers of *Vigo* except the Officer of the Day were off raiding some other ship. George Shaw had left orders that if any officer raiding party tried to come aboard whilst his officers were 'out', they were to be repelled by force. As the *Chequers* motor-boat approached the *Vigo* gangway, Prince Philip at the helm, it was met by fire hoses and a barrage of potatoes. The Prince was not one to be deterred so easily and led the rush up the ladder. He was grappled by the Leading Seaman quartermaster (i/c the Gangway Staff) and the two were soon wrestling it out on the deck. However, as Philip was no weakling, this brief tussle ended with the Leading Seaman being pitched overboard. The former would not have complained if he had been the one ending in the water. Having established themselves on board, the *Chequers* officers claimed a drink on the Wardroom of *Vigo* before leaving. No doubt that Leading Seaman has told his grandchildren how he wrestled with Prince Philip.

The only immediate consequence was a signal, next day, from the First Lieutenant of *Chequers* to the No.1 of *Vigo*. This congratulated him on the spirited resistance put up by his Gangway Staff. Needless to say, I did not witness the incident and so cannot swear to the accuracy of the foregoing, but that was the way we heard it from *Vigo*.

Shortly after the Regatta, we received orders to proceed back through the Suez Canal for another stretch at Aqaba. It should not have been our turn for six months but the ship designated had broken down or was otherwise unavailable and a replacement had to be sent. *Gravelines* may have been nominated to teach us a lesson after our misdemeanour at Athens, or because we had reported enjoying our previous visit there. Perhaps it was because *Gravelines* had fewer officers than most ships with wives in Malta awaiting our return (with no allowance for our girl friends!). In any case we were delighted to get away from all the ceremonial and wearing of No. 10 uniforms.

I looked forward, once again, to sitting with bare legs dangled over the ship's side, without a shirt, but a straw hat on my head, holding a fishing line. In the event, our visit was not like that for me. In fact, I very nearly did not return from Aqaba at all.

I do not know how it came about but, after only two days there, a spot appeared on the inside of my right elbow and started to fester. Whether or not I had been bitten by something, and if so, what, I had no idea. I reported to Sick Bay where our Sick Berth Attendant Petty Officer dressed it but said he did not like the look of it. Next day, my whole arm had started to swell up like a football and I clearly had a bad case of blood poisoning. The SBA declared I must be got ashore to see an Army Medical Officer. By now I had a temperature and high fever. To make matters worse, a hot wind was blowing in from the east (the *khamseen*). The mercury rose to 115°F—the highest I had seen it anywhere in the world—and the ensuing sand storm reduced visibility to a hundred yards.

They got me to the Field Hospital somehow, feeling like death. In truth, in another twenty-four hours, I would have been dead. Were it not for the discovery of penicillin by the commendable Dr Fleming, I would not be writing this story. The Acting Gunnery Officer of *Gravelines*, Mike Wilson, no doubt, would have had to take charge of the funeral firing party to fire a volley as they lowered my coffin into a hole in the sands of the Arabian Desert, far from home. Their main problem would have been to preserve me until the *khamseen* stopped. Otherwise, the grave would fill with sand before they had a chance to pop my coffin into it. I can imagine the comments—that I had chosen a damned unreasonable time and place to die—but then someone might have had the charity to say, 'At least he was good enough to wait until after the regatta to snuff it.' Needless to say, these were not my thoughts at the time. Rather, I was plain fed-up at being in solitary confinement in a small wooden hut. This was open on all sides, but encased in fine wire mesh to keep the flies out. It was like the little outhouses they have on sheep stations for hanging animals that have been slaughtered. It was stinking hot and, once my fever broke, the perspiration ran off me in pints.

Happily, I only had to spend two days in my 'meat safe'. The penicillin did its stuff and I recovered enough to be allowed to return to my comfortable cabin on board. I would have been much better off there all along—but I could hardly expect the doctor to come all the way out to the ship in the *khamseen*. In fact, the reader may have noted that throughout this narrative, I have made scant mention of ill-health. That is, apart from self-induced—aboard *Napier* and again *Enterprise*, and a sore head after hitting it on the quarterdeck towing clench aboard *Ocean*. I had been truly fortunate with my health over the last seven years, but the next twelve months would see me in hospital for two more periods, each of three weeks. For the moment, however, within four days, I was right as rain.

Vice Admiral Sir David Brown KCB—Sub Lieutenant aboard Gravelines. *Not in Officers' Crew in 1950, but was the following year.*

We were back in Malta within three weeks. The ship made other visits, notably to Tripoli (Libya), and Philippeville (now Shikda), where our Squadron team was thrashed at rugby by the Chasseurs Paratroop. This avenged the defeat our team from *Enterprise* had inflicted on *Richelieu* back in 1943. From Philippeville we visited the amazing city of Constantine, going back to Roman times and reached by a suspension bridge two hundred feet over the gorge below. On to Arzew, where we carried out a demonstration bombardment for the French Army, and finally Oran. The last was the second city of Algeria and I found myself in charge of the Shore Patrol, to see our crew behaved themselves ashore. The French Military Police felt I should be taken to see some of the brothels so that I would know they were properly run. I had no enthusiasm for this, and could hardly say that I knew all about brothels, from days in Belgium. What was interesting was the usual four of us, on our motorbikes, winding our way up and over a high hill to have a look at Mers-el-Kebir. Here the British had inflicted crushing losses on the French fleet just ten years before.

On a historical note, we made very brief visits to Benghazi, Tobruk and Suda Bay (Crete). At this last, one could still see the wreck of the 8″ gun cruiser, HMS *York*, bombed and sunk there during the German attack on Crete in 1941. As the water was shallow, the ship had only settled a few feet to rest on the bottom, with its back broken. As a warship, she was, of course, finished. But superficially she had evidently appeared intact. No latter-day Sir Richard Grenville had been able to order, 'Sink me the ship, Master Gunner', being already on the bottom. However, the enemy had the dubious satisfaction of hoisting the German Naval Ensign at her stern. I believe HMS *York* was the only British warship ever to have the ignominy of having jack-booted Nazis pace her quarterdeck. By 1950, the ship was reduced to a rusting hull just showing above the water—but still provided food for thought.

One other incident is worthy of mention. *Gravelines*, as Duty Destroyer in Malta one night, was ordered to sea in a full gale to assist a British merchant ship driven onto the rocks of Sicily. We were there within four hours, only to find there was nothing we could do, being unable to get near the stranded vessel for outlying rocks. However, the ship signalled that they were in no danger of breaking up and all their upper deck lighting was shining brilliantly. Accordingly we left them for professional salvage teams to deal with. I only mention the incident because the journey to Sicily at 30 knots in a full gale was the roughest passage I ever made. I had seen bigger waves, but never had to steam through them at 30 knots. One could not move aboard the ship without holding

Commander Nigel Fawcett—Lieutenant aboard Gravelines—*rowed in winning whaler, 1950.*

on to rails or lifelines. In the wardroom, the armchairs were not just sliding across the deck; they were being flung from one bulkhead to another, until lashed to steel pillars.

A few other places were visited but this book is not intended to be an out-of-date travelogue. It was now time for me to return to UK. Most people can remember an outstanding year of their lives—an *Anno Mirabilis*. It may not have been the most memorable of my whole life but 1950 was the most notable of my twenty years with the RN and I had had one flirtation with death.

BACK TO ENGLAND—HOME BY CHRISTMAS ?

In early December 1950, I was advised I was to be on the 1951 Long T A/S Course, starting on 9 January. I was to take passage for UK aboard a troopship, leaving Malta on 10 December. Unfortunately, I had so many duties aboard *Gravelines* (including Boys Divisional Officer), that I found it impossible to complete my turn-over in just over one week. Accordingly, the 10th came and went and the trooper sailed without me. I was then told the next available passage for me would reach UK on 8 January, the day before my course started. I therefore asked to make my own way back to England with the nominal £30 the Navy calculated they would be saved not having to transport me.

It may have been noted that my life in the Navy had involved considerable 'swings and roundabouts'—taking the rough with the smooth. But my last year had been almost unbroken 'roundabouts', one could say 'a great big bowl of cherries'.

I was finally able to leave on 19 December. I aimed to reach UK as directly as possible and be at my home in Torquay for Christmas. The journey proved far more eventful than I had expected and I underwent a bewildering succession of 'swings' and 'roundabouts', ending in a touch-and-go race for Torquay by the 25th. The events are best told in diary form:

Dec. 19: Flew (BEA Viking) to Rome—my first-ever commercial flight, at a time when anyone flying was assumed to be a millionaire—whisked into the luxury Hotel Quirinale overnight—excessively 'roundabout' and already exceeding my budget to this point.

Dec. 20: A.m. train (2nd Class) Rome—Ventimiglia (French frontier)—Nice (change trains)—Marseilles. On arrival (still on schedule, timewise), found HMS *Armada* of my late Squadron stern-to-wall in the Vieux Port as planned, with my battered old motorbike on board, again as previously arranged. Convivial evening with old mates and a comfortable cabin overnight.

Dec. 21: At crack of dawn, off on the bike headed for Lyons but taking the one small detour I had allowed for sightseeing. Having long admired Cézanne's paintings, I detoured through Aix-en-Provence in order to view the subject the great artist had so often painted—the Mont St Victoire. This bore no resemblance to Cézanne's landscapes, as painted in summer—now snow-covered. On towards Avignon—to pick up Grande Route Nationale No. 7 for Lyons. Five miles out of Aix, the dynamo fell off the bike and was broken.

I cursed the person who had stolen the previous dynamo and the other who had failed to fit the replacement properly just before I left. I pushed the bike back to Aix and found a garage where I was told I would have to go back to Marseilles to the Lucas depot for a replacement. A bus was leaving within minutes; I was on it and headed for Marseilles. Timing and money now became critical. I had budgeted for neither the expensive Hotel Quirinale nor for a replacement dynamo—not to mention one more night's accommodation or garage bill. I judged I could beg, borrow or steal some money—or cash a cheque aboard *Armada*. The trouble was that that ship, I knew, was timed to depart at 1200. This was the exact time my bus was due to reach the Vieux Port at the end of the Main Street of Marseilles, La Canabière. I leapt off the bus and dashed across the road to find the ladder just being lowered from the stern of *Armada* but managed to scramble aboard. At this point, I realised I had left the broken dynamo aboard the bus. With no word of explanation I was over the gangway again and running like fury to catch the bus at its next stop— which I just did and recovered the dynamo. Dashing back to *Armada* I found the gangway now gone altogether and the last line to the shore about to be let go.

The longshoreman undoing it saw I was keen to get aboard. He let the line go, but beckoned me to jump into his put-put boat and brought me alongside. This must have been entertaining for the locals seeing the ship off. A strange figure in motorcycle overalls and French beret was scrambling up over the side of this British warship with rows of smart sailors neatly fallen-in for leaving harbour. I quickly found the Sub Lieutenant, whom I knew was the Mess Secretary and said, 'Quick—cash me a cheque on the Wardroom Funds.'

He said, 'I can't leave my men here.'

'Yes, you damned well can and for Heaven's sake be quick about it!'

We hurried forward to his cabin where he cashed me a cheque for 20 Maltese pounds (which subsequently proved useless ashore). All this time, I could hear the engine revolutions picking up as the ship headed out of the Vieux Port *en route* for Malta. I rushed aft again, to find my faithful Frenchman just keeping up with the ship. I tumbled over the side and dropped in a heap into his boat, waved farewell to *Armada* and was soon ashore again. There followed visits to the British Consulate General, Lucas depot, etc., and bus back to Aix where I turned in at a cheap pension— after a hectic day.

Dec. 22: With my bike repaired, I was quickly on the road again, through Avignon (sad not to have time to explore this ancient town dating back to Roman times with its famous *Pont*). I pressed on to Lyons which I reached after dark, in bitter cold. But I was able to have a luxurious hot bath and a hearty, if not gourmet, meal at the relatively cheap hotel I selected.

Dec. 23: (with two days to reach Torquay) I was on the GRN No 7 before daybreak with a cry of 'Paris or bust!' If it had been cold the previous night it was now well below freezing. I was soon hitting patches of black ice on the road—extremely dangerous for motorcyclists. By 9 a.m. after two hours on the road but only fifty miles north of Lyons, I reached the little town of Tournus, where I decided I could cycle no further. I found the railway station with a train standing in it. I asked when the next train left for Paris and was told the train in the station was for Paris but was about to depart. Before I could organise myself and bike aboard, the guard blew his whistle and the train chugged out. 'The next train?' I asked. 'Midnight.' However, I was told that if I could get myself to Chalon-sur-Saône, some fifteen miles away, there would be a train leaving for Paris from there at noon. So off I went, on the fresh snow on the grass on the roadside to avoid the icebound highway, covering the fifteen miles in two hours. I made Chalon station with an hour to spare and time to thaw out sitting on a radiator in the waiting room, having almost died of cold *en route*. I could now only afford 3rd Class—the legendary *Huit Chevaux/Quarante Hommes* of French railways.

Actually, it was not as bad as that. The compartments had wooden seats but, two days before Christmas, the train was packed to capacity. I could only secure standing room in the crowded corridor—for the five-hour journey to Paris. But it was WARM—it could hardly be otherwise with all the bodies on board. In fact, although this part of the journey was definitely 'swings', not 'roundabouts', my five-hour journey proved highly entertaining. My immediate travelling companions had all told me their life stories and what they thought of the Bosche, Americans and the world in general by the time we reached Paris. An old fellow (veteran sergeant of the French Army) handed round a bottle of cheap cognac. I could only respond by giving out some of my cigars—to make the air even fouler than it already was, but, thereby, enhance the general bonhomie.

The train pulled into the Gare de Lyons at five p.m. It was already dark and I had never been to Paris before but, mercifully, the streets were not covered with ice, nor was it snowing. I had a contact in Paris—the wealthy M. Jacques Dupont, the head of the French equivalent of the National Trust.* He had a chateau at Eaubonne but was now at his penthouse apartment in the Rue de Rivoli, close to the Tuilleries, where he awaited my arrival. In so prominent a location, the abode of my host was not hard to find. He had kindly delayed his departure for skiing at Chamonix, whither he had packed off his family that day. I was royally entertained—back on the 'roundabouts' again. After a luxurious hot bath, a superb dinner, and my host's finest 'Napoleon' brandy, I slept well in a feather bed—after another event-filled day.

Dec. 24: (Christmas Eve and still some way from Torquay.) It was cold next morning, but not as cold as at Lyons the previous morning. The sky was overcast but there was no snow on the ground and, with luck, I should make my destination of Dieppe in just over two hours. Having set off early (with my flask filled, at my host's insistence, with his magnificent brandy), I felt confident I could easily make Dieppe by 1 p.m., the departure time for my ferry to Newhaven. Alas, luck was not what I was

---

* Director General of Historic Monuments—Introduction furnished by MSJ.

going to have. In under an hour it had started to snow and I was soon driving through a blizzard. Furthermore, it had turned colder than at any time on my journey to date. I was forced to stop at each village, fortify myself with the brandy and make sure I was still on course for Dieppe.

Eventually the brandy ran out, visibility was reduced to yards and I became hopelessly lost in the snowy wastes of Normandy as well as freezing cold, as the 1 p.m. deadline came and went. The weather improved slightly and I regained my route, staggering into Dieppe around 4 p.m. I was now definitely back in the 'swings'—cold and miserable with the prospect of spending Christmas Day in the cheapest pension I could find in Dieppe.

But one never knows what miracle may be round the corner. There, at the jetty, was a cross-Channel steamer—the SS *Falaise*. No, it couldn't be. It had to be the ferry just arrived from Newhaven. But I went round and enquired and, 'Glory Be!' the *Falaise* was waiting to sail for Newhaven. It seems it had been so cold that the points had frozen, derailing the boat-train from Paris and the ship had had to wait for the passengers to be brought in by bus.

They were embarking now. I joined them, having put my bike on board and, half an hour later, was at sea headed for 'England Home and Beauty'. It was 'roundabouts' once again! The ship made Newhaven by seven (where the Customs Authorities told me the papers for my bike were not in order. I told them they could do what they liked with the thing—I never wanted to see it again!). I was in London by nine thirty and, by eleven, was on the night train for Torquay. I arrived home, in the 'bosom of my family', at 6 a.m. on Christmas morning. I had won—against all odds—with help from Jacques Dupont and his superb cognac. The distillers could have had my story for any advertising they liked.

CHAPTER 20

TORPEDO ANTI-SUBMARINE COURSE

1951–2

ON 9 JANUARY 1951, a completely new sort of Navy started to open up for me. Except for four months of war-time Sub Lieutenant Courses and three becoming a Destroyer Gunnery Officer, my whole career since Dartmouth had been service afloat. I was now to embark on fourteen months of in-depth training to qualify as a Specialist Torpedo/Anti-Submarine Officer. From now on the Branch and the Course will be simply referred to as TAS (this being the spoken acronym, pronounced as in Tasmania). One was not obliged to take a specialist course, nor was there supposed to be any advantage, in terms of promotion prospects, in so doing. Many of my friends, including Gavin Wemyss and Mike Kersey, had already qualified as TAS Officers and more friends would follow. There was an element of self-perpetuating type-casting in the choice one made of a specialist branch. If like-thinking officers to oneself—and ones who happened to be friends—picked a certain branch one tended to follow suit. I will not explain the perceived characteristics of the different specialisations. But naval officers themselves could usually pick to which one of their fellows belonged, within minutes of small-talk at a cocktail party. Needless to say, TAS officers were quite the most balanced and well-adjusted of the lot!

On the other hand, several of my friends, including Joe Lungley, Mike Vaughan and Mike MccGwire, chose not to specialise at all. But Vaughan and MccGwire qualified respectively as German and Russian interpreters.

It was in the nature of the various 'Long Courses' that one would become involved in much more technology than hitherto. We had received a good science and maths grounding at Dartmouth, but the authorities, rightly, assumed that after eight years we would have forgotten most of the theory involved. Accordingly, we had to start our course at RN College Greenwich, sometimes called the Naval University of the Commonwealth. This was because of high-level Staff Courses conducted there. For us, however, there was nothing 'tertiary' about our tuition. It was simply a matter of recalling for us a mass of learning we had acquired years before—in four short months. We went right back to basics with maths, starting with one apple plus one apple makes two apples, through to advanced forms of calculus in a matter of weeks. Likewise, in physics we practically started with Ohm's Law and raced through to nuclear fission. Other subjects taught included applied mechanics, metallurgy and chemistry. Naturally one had to cudgel the brain, but most of it was simply recalling knowledge believed lost. In later years, I was to feel grateful for the revision of quite rudimentary geometry. For instance, without this I would not have known how to calculate the area of paper of given calliper on a mill-reel of known width and given outside and core diameters. I reflected that it is sad how much education individuals receive but later forget. This applies to languages, history and many other subjects. Fortunately for some of us, we had been able to brush up our French in Ostend—beyond the legendary '*Monsieur, je regrette . . .*'!

Whilst I welcomed the return to an educational background, it was astonishing to realise that, for the first time in years, I had practically no responsibilities. There was no need to worry whether the ship was dragging her anchor or being navigated safely, if explosives were being properly handled or even Greek royalty properly entertained! Accordingly, there was a tremendous urge to let one's hair down and act like schoolboys. On the other hand, one could not but be awed by the naval heritage all around. Space only permits me to take the reader on the briefest guided tour of RNC Greenwich and its environs. But any overseas visitor with a feeling for history is strongly urged to visit Greenwich. For its architecture alone it is worth seeing, with work by Vanburgh and Wren, including the magnificent chapel and the famous Painted Hall—the finest banqueting hall in Britain. There is much more than the Naval College to see at Greenwich. Laid-up there, but lovingly preserved, is the clipper ship *Cutty Sark* and Sir Francis Chichester's yacht *Gypsy Moth IV* in which he made the first solo circumnavigation of the world.

More importantly, there are other landmarks, built in harmony with the College, which fronts onto the Thames. A quarter of a mile south, and on the same axis—between the twin domed towers of the Chapel and the Painted Hall—lies Queens House. This is a long low Palladian building, the home of the National Maritime Museum—a veritable treasure-house of naval memorabilia. Exhibits include the dress uniform Nelson wore at Trafalgar, with the hole where the fatal bullet passed through his epaulette. Fascinating for me was Harrison's prize-winning chronometer—the first timepiece accurate enough for navigation. It had been hand-made over two hundred years ago but still kept near-perfect time—I shuddered at the memory of my clumsiness aboard *Lauderdale*. What I found most poignant was the stern-sheets back-board, engraved HOOD, found weeks after that ship went down with the loss of 2,500 lives.

Continuing up the same axis through Greenwich Park, one arrived at what was then still the Royal Observatory. This unmarked line, extended to both North and South Poles, constitutes Longitude zero. However much British influence may decline, it is now certain that the world will still begin and end at Greenwich. Time kept aboard all international airliners and even by astronauts out in space is Greenwich Mean Time.

I was therefore in a mentally stimulating environment and one steeped in Britain's maritime heritage. I had fifteen congenial companions including four known to me at Dartmouth, three Australians and one New Zealander. All of these I would get to know well during the fourteen month course. In charge of us was Lt. Cdr. John ('Horse') Lewis, whom we came to like and respect more and more as the course progressed, assisted by a genial Gunner (TAS). The sporting facilities were excellent, and glittering Mess Dinners, with silver candelabra, gold and black liveried waiters and a Marine band playing throughout, were memorable.

Unfortunately the sporting activities proved my undoing. Playing rugby for the College I sustained an injury to my shoulder. At first I thought it was minor and tried to carry on, only to feel my arm slip out of the shoulder socket and back at the next line-out. So I left the field and headed for the Sick Bay. This was the start of a saga of mismanaged treatment.

I was not allowed to see any of the Medical Officers (doctors) and had to be content with having the Warrant Wardmaster declare, 'Ah yes, another routine football injury. Put your arm in a sling and come for infra-red treatment twice a day.' Ten days later, no improvement was evident and I asked to see the MO. He told me that it was not getting better as I was obviously using my arm too much, despite my vehement denials of this. After another week, they reluctantly agreed to my request for an X-ray. This showed that the muscle that raises the arm had torn a flap of bone away from the humerus.

I was sent to Chatham Naval Hospital to see the Surgical Specialist—a pompous individual who would not look at my X-rays, declaring his equipment far superior. So, after more X-rays, he said, 'The injury stems from a flake of bone to which the [technical term] muscle is attached being torn away from the humerus bone.' As a junior Lieutenant, I was not game to tell a Surgeon Commander: 'That is exactly what the Greenwich PMO found and what I was trying to tell you'! He went on to tell me that, notwithstanding the raised flap of bone, this would heal—but only if I stopped trying to wave my arm about. Further protest seemed pointless. Another ten days elapsed and I was back at Chatham.

This time, the Surgical Specialist said to me, 'Of course, you should not have come to me—you should have seen the Orthopaedic Specialist'! The latter examined my shoulder and declared, 'This will heal up without surgery. The reason you cannot move your arm is that you have not done so for a month and the muscles have wasted away.' The upshot for me was three weeks in Chatham Hospital with my arm in an 'aeroplane splint'. Thereafter, with daily physiotherapy, I slowly got better—but not before my opinion on the whole naval medical service reached rock bottom.

Routinely, all patients admitted had to undergo blood tests, to ensure they had not got venereal disease. I could not argue with this, but was unhappy about the methods for conducting the tests. A sensitive young sister made two unsuccessful attempts to draw a blood sample. Upset at her failure, she apologised and sent for the senior—battleaxe—ward sister. 'Where's this man with no blood?' demanded the dragon, 'I'll soon fix him.' After really 'belting' my arm about, she tried—not once, but twice, both unsuccessfully. Naturally my enthusiasm for this began to wane, but the battleaxe declared, 'Don't think you are going to get away with this—I am sending for the House Surgeon.' This man finally succeeded in obtaining a small sample, declared sufficient under the circumstances—I did not have VD!

I had a problem with clothing as every shirt I wore had to be slit right up the side. I asked if I could have one of those comfortable-looking floppy hospital blue coats, made of flannel. 'Certainly not,' was the answer. 'Those are for ratings—not officers.' Yet another problem arose over washing. I would have had no difficulty stepping gingerly into a shallow bath, but this was forbidden—I might slip on a bar of soap with only one arm to steady myself. In vain, I asked the battleaxe how often she had fallen, treading on soap on the floor, when not taking extra care. She judged me to be a 'difficult' patient, although I could tie my tie, do up shoe laces single-handed and even write letters—with unaccustomed left hand. Initially, wearing this contraption, particularly in bed at night, was uncomfortable, but I soon got used to it.

Notwithstanding my problems, I was allowed generous 'shore leave'— every afternoon until late at night. I would take the train to London, being embarrassed by women offering me a seat, assuming I was a wounded hero back from Korea, to spend an evening with MSJ. She was living a 'swings and roundabouts' existence like myself. Since her discharge from Naval Intelligence, she had taken her degree in History of Art at the Courtauld and now worked for the National Buildings Record. She had 'come out', as a belated debutante, been 'presented at court' and a portrait of her had been hung at the Royal Academy of Portrait Painters. Nevertheless, her life was now more akin to that of Mimi in *La Bohème*— except that, happily, she was not 'consumptive'. I would visit her in her Hampstead basement bed-sitter and we would cook sausages on a gas-ring—somewhat 'swings' for me also after banqueting in the Painted Hall. The big plus for me though was that she had a bath!

I recovered and resumed my studies at Greenwich, although I was never able to catch up on the chemistry I had missed. (I also tell my well-educated son, appalled by my ignorance, that I had measles for a crucial period of the teaching of this subject at Dartmouth. For other gaps in my knowledge, he may cheekily ask, 'Was that during measles, Dad?').

Regarding my injury, the Navy issued me with a Hurt or Wound Certificate, which I thought absurd at the time. But, forty years on, X-Rays still show that flap of bone, my shoulder remains permanently weakened and I have twice more dislocated it. One of these days, I will present HM Government with my certificate and ask for compensation—not for the injury but for the mismanagement of it.

Things got better—as they usually do—and I retrieved my venerable motorbike, which the Customs had refused to dump. I patched it up once more and got another thousand or so miles out of it, including a tour of France and Belgium. Spring came and we moved to HMS *Vernon* at Portsmouth. Sadly, however, I was soon to face further health problems.

In April, during a return to wintry weather, I accepted an invitation for a long week-end with a cousin, Wallace Seymour, who farmed in Oxfordshire. I fell sick the evening of my arrival and soon had an unaccountable temperature of 104°F. The doctor called but could not identify the trouble. Two days later, after many aspirins, I appeared to have recovered and—somewhat prematurely—took to the road, back to Portsmouth. Unfortunately, the day proved cold and wet and, in my weakened state, I started to feel the cold. I remembered my ride through Normandy and, being back in Hampshire with only fifty miles to go, I resorted to fortifying myself with a double brandy in a pub *en route*. This was my second mistake.

As I approached the village of Bishop's Waltham, I was faced with a right-angle turn in the road, with a stone wall ahead of me. I realised I had no hope of making this turn and 'stood on' the brakes. I am unsure what happened next but found myself spreadeagled in the road with my bike vertically upside down, some feet away, with the engine still running. I gingerly checked and found I was unhurt except for slightly grazed hands and knees. Accordingly, I got to my feet, turned off the motor, put the bike the right way up and pushed it off the road. Only then did delayed shock catch up with me and my knees gave out under me. I was soon up again but judged that it would be unwise to resume my ride to Portsmouth until I had taken a break and pulled myself together. It seemed prudent to knock on the nearest front door, say what had happened and ask if I might sit down for a few minutes, perhaps with a cup of tea. A slightly formidable-looking woman answered my knock. I learnt she was the housekeeper and that the master and mistress were out. However, she beckoned me into a small study, where I sat with my head between my knees, in the approved fainting recovery posture, whilst she made a cup of tea. After a minute I sat up and took stock of the situation. The room seemed familiar and the walls were almost covered by signed photographs of allied War Leaders. I suddenly knew where I was, having recently read the autobiography of Andrew Cunningham—*A Sailor's Odyssey*. I recognised his study, of which there had been a photo in his book. I realised that I had asked myself into the home of the illustrious Viscount Cunningham of Hyndhope. My old maths teacher may have assured me that young Cunningham had been a GOOD BOY, but this realisation revived me faster than any cup of tea. I resumed my journey and made *Vernon* without further mishap.

I carried on with the course as if nothing had happened, but two months later, at *Vernon*, I had a nearly identical attack—only worse. I was whisked into Haslar Naval Hospital, where they decided my appendix had to come out. I was, in fact, 'prepped' for an appendectomy for the first operation next morning. Happily, the surgeon had second thoughts before operating and they decided to keep me under observation for another day or so. During this time, no symptoms related to my appendix developed and I seemed to be recovering. By the end of the week, I appeared to be fully fit once again. This time, however, the doctors decided they had to get to the bottom of my recurring attacks, yet could not justify keeping me in a hospital bed all day. We reached a compromise, whereby I would sleep at Haslar and undergo a series of pathology and other tests each morning but have the rest of each day off.

During the ensuing week I had an afternoon racing a Royal Naval Sailing Association dinghy, attended the *Vernon* Summer Ball, and the previously-reported tennis party at Admiral McCall's. By the following Monday, this Cinderella's ball was over. The hospital had found my problem and were now about to start treating it. After all the criticism I levelled at Chatham NH, I have to say that I could not speak too highly of Haslar. It turned out that I had one infected kidney that played up from time to time. Fortunately, this was something easily rectified with antibiotics, but I was back in bed on three-times-daily injections for another week.

I have already said that one never stopped meeting old friends in the Navy. Who should I find in hospital with me, recovering from major surgery, but George Shaw, previously No.1 of *Vigo* of my old squadron in the Med. He was the officer congratulated by Prince Philip on the spirited resistance put up by his Gangway Staff at Marmaris. Poor George had had a problem not wholly dissimilar to mine—kidney trouble—but far worse. Antibiotics could not cure him as one kidney was dead and had probably been so since being nearly frozen when Shaw had survived being sunk on a Russian convoy during the war. Fortunately, one can manage on one kidney and George's condition had not prevented him captaining our Rugby XV against the Chasseurs Paratroop at Philippeville the previous year. It seems, however, that any dead organ inside the body will not remain preserved for ever and the time was up for his useless and decaying kidney. This case history caused my doctor to speculate whether I might have suffered damage to a kidney in sub-zero temperatures motorcycling across France a few months back. I doubted this, reckoning my old French Army veteran's cheap brandy and Jacques Dupont's superb cognac would have taken care of any such problem! So much for stories of ill-health—no more will occur in the remainder of this narrative.

Back at *Vernon*, we had been learning all about torpedoes. I say 'all' because the Navy had only one type of torpedo, the 21″ Mk.9** and its two variants—the Mk.8** used by submarines and the 18″ version for aircraft and MTBs. This basic 'fish' had been introduced in World War I and was still in service in the Falklands War—sinking the *General Belgrano*.

By 1951, the old hands at *Vernon* knew every inch of these torpedoes and expected us to acquire the same knowledge. In pairs, we took on one torpedo to strip to the last nut and bolt and then reassemble, it being continually impressed on us that these things cost £4,000 each—half a million Mars Bars. The final test was for two of the torpedoes, picked at random, to be taken to sea and fired—with 'Blowing Heads' to make them resurface for recovery. Recorders showed whether the torpedoes had run correctly, and Heaven help us if the torpedo did not resurface. The torpedo prepared by my mate and myself drew one of the 'short straws' but happily performed correctly, to our immense relief.

The whole course took us to many places other than *Vernon*—all over Britain, in fact. We spent several months at the Anti Submarine School, HMS *Osprey*, and with the A/S Training Flotilla (including *Flint Castle*) at Portland. We had a week flying far out over the Atlantic with RAF Coastal Command in Lancaster and Shackleton aircraft. At last I was getting in some time aloft. My previous flying was limited to fifteen minutes in a Sunderland Flying Boat at Plymouth as a Midshipman, my hated Flying Course at Arbroath and my airline flight from Malta to Rome.

The conclusion of that week provided some fun. We were given week-end leave and some of us had a lift to London in the base's utility aircraft, an ancient Airspeed Oxford, with only the pilot as aircrew. The weather was poor, with about seven-tenths cloud, and the pilot was too busy to pay much heed to navigation. Air Traffic Control must have been primitive in those days and navigational aids rudimentary. The pilot tossed us some maps and said, 'See if any of you can figure out where we are. The easiest way is to spot an airfield and read the number on the main runway.' We didn't see an airfield but, in due course, I was able to call out, 'That has to be Newbury Race-course' (an area I knew well). 'Oh good,' said the pilot, 'Then we are nearly there.' Minutes later we landed at Black-bushe, where I had managed to leave my bike.

As a slight diversion from this narrative, and my movements at that time, I found I was only five miles from my old Prep School, Bigshotte. I had not been back since leaving twelve years before and felt I had to call in. Little seemed to have changed, except that everything appeared so much smaller than I had remembered, as a little thirteen-year-old. My old Headmaster had gone but several staff of my time were still there as was an old friend and contemporary, now a teacher. I gladly accepted an invitation to stay for supper. No one seemed surprised at my dropping in, and none from my time needed telling who I was. One remarked, 'We now have supper at six-thirty—I believe it was at six in your day.' Apart from some new staff, this seemed the biggest change in twelve years and six of World War!

Other periods were spent at Port Edgar, Scotland for practical mine-sweeping and minehunting, and at *Defiance*, Devonport on Seaward Defence. We visited several naval and commercial research and development establishments and ended back at *Vernon*, on Practical Diving and Mine and Bomb Disposal. An improbable element of the course was on Instructional Technique, including use of instructional aids. The exam consisted of presenting a lecture on a subject of one's own choice on any matter unconnected with the Navy. Attendance at these lectures was compulsory for teaching staff at *Vernon* and the Captain and Director of Studies. I fear these were not taken too seriously by many of the course—otherwise I would not have scored the top mark with my talk. This was on Post-Impressionist Painting (for which I did feel an affinity—my detour to view Cézanne's mountain will be recalled—and had put in some effort). However, these lectures said much about the course-member in question.

The unquestioned wag (but also bright) member of our course was one Peter Mylchreest, who decided he would bamboozle everyone with an involved discourse on philosophy. His main worry was handling the mandatory twenty minutes of question time—in case someone had actually studied philosophy. His ploy consisted of devising a series of 'Dorothy Dix' planted questions. As a mate of his, I agreed to ask the first one, rehearsed as, 'In your address you spoke of — Perhaps you could tell us what you meant by —' Without batting an eyelid, Peter came back with: 'That's a very good question. I am very glad someone asked me that . . .'

Quite the most memorable lecture was given by John Barratt, who had become a close buddy of mine—and of practically everyone else. John, at twenty-three, was the youngest member of the course, but unquestionably the brightest. There was a great deal for us to learn and most of us had to do many hours of 'home work' or private study. Barratt, however, was one of those maddening people who never had to do a moment's work 'out of school' yet almost invariably got 90% or more in each exam. He would have done so as usual for Instructional Technique, had he taken this test seriously—which he did not. His selected lecture subject was 'The Party Spirit', and he kicked off with, 'Now in England, we have the Conservative Party, the Labour Party . . . but that was not the kind of party I am going to talk about tonight.'

There followed a forty-minute dissertation on the finer points of making and presenting cocktails—with a fine array of 'instructional aids' in the form of cocktail shakers, mixers and ingredient spirits and liqueurs. He carefully prepared a concoction that he said he had devised in the West Indies and was pleased to call a 'Rosy Dawn'. All this was being done with a happy grin on John's face but the teaching staff were unsure how they were expected to react. They looked to the Director of Studies, who now wore a decided frown. Undeterred, the lecturer picked up a cocktail glass, carefully polished it and held it up to the light. After some accomplished cocktail-shaking over one shoulder then the other with fine panache, he neatly filled the glass. Stepping down from the stage, he approached the Captain with, 'Would you care to try this, Sir?' After only a moment's hesitation the Captain took a sip and declared, 'Good!', proceeding to quaff the rest of the glass. After that, there was no looking back and Barratt dispensed Rosy Dawns to the entire audience. The mandatory question time was entirely occupied with answering the Captain's questions about pre-chilling the ingredients and suitable garnishes. The officers of the staff, who normally regarded their compulsory attendance at Long Course test lectures a tedious duty, voted this the best such session they had been to. Regrettably, the Director of Studies remained not amused and awarded a low mark. This cost Barratt the Ogilvy Medal (for topping the class) by one mark, but John was not one to lose sleep over this.

With Tony Woolley—one of the brighter lights of the course—Peter Mylchreest, the course 'wag' (and incomparable mimic), and John Barratt, I made up a bridge-playing 'school' as well as combining for other social activities. On completion of the course, Woolley, Barratt and I all headed for Australia for two years of Exchange Service.

Peter left the Navy at the same time as myself. I met him three years later, on a business trip I made to UK. He was clearly flourishing as a public relations consultant. He had landed an assignment to mastermind the opening of a large oil refinery for Shell near Copenhagen. I asked him how one set about such a task. He assured me it was all quite easy really. 'First, you line up the Danish King to open the plant, then simply write out operational orders as for naval staffwork. You specify a formation fly-past by two squadrons of jets of the Danish Air Force. They will come to the party; they have nothing else to do. You organise a good band and find a suitable caterer to provide the usual caviar and champagne. The total cost will be peanuts for Shell and come out of petty cash from the promotions account—there really is nothing to it.' Obviously not, I reflected—if you happen to be Peter Mylchreest!

I must also mention another good friend I made on the TAS Course—Harry Hawkins. We would opt to share a room at sundry establishments visited. Harry had a great sense of humour and his wife and family were good to me both then and after we had both left the Navy.

All this time in UK had allowed me to indulge my enjoyment of sailing. Back during my time in *Flint Castle*, I had joined Mike Kersey and two others of the Long TAS Course he was then doing, for a week's cruise to Cherbourg and the Channel Islands. That was in *Vernon*'s 'Windfall' yacht *See Otter* (sic—German spelling). This had been the first sailing venture for any of us out of sight of land and was a big excitement. Our cruise went smoothly to Cherbourg, Guernsey and Jersey. At this last, our presence coincided with the annual regatta of the Royal Channel Islands Yacht Club. We entered one race and, with help from a local pilot who knew the treacherous tides there (rising and falling through 35 ft.), we won our race easily with 'line honours' and on handicap.

Returning to Portsmouth had provided some excitement. We lost our main halyard up the mast but screamed through the Alderney Race at nine knots with wind and tide behind us and only the Genoa set. We put into Cherbourg again, just long enough to get up the mast and recover the halyard, before sailing through the night in a fresh gale back to the Solent. Sadly, our two mates, who had been most genial cruising companions, succumbed to seasickness, leaving Mike Kersey and me to sail the boat home. This meant one only on watch at a time, with no chance to reduce sail or gybe in an emergency. I had one close shave with a coaster that refused me any right of way and I had to pull under its stern at the last moment.

There were other gentler sails at Cowes and elsewhere locally. On one of these aboard a larger yacht belonging to *Dolphin*, the Submarine base, we had Joe Brooks, of *Bismarck* and midget submarine memories, on board. In an easy quartering wind sailing over to Cowes, I made a rash remark that I enjoyed going aloft on yachts to see the view. 'Okay, then,' said someone, 'Up you go to the upper crosstrees!' I had no option but to struggle up the halyards to this point about 45 ft. above the deck. Upon my return, Joe Brooks piped up with, 'I agree with Philip—I like going aloft myself.' He then performed a feat of strength I would not have believed possible. He ascended to the same upper crosstrees, up the windward 'runner'—a wire of under ½″ diameter, hand-over-hand, without touching it with his feet. If this was not remarkable anyway, I should mention that Joe, wearing no shirt, had his chest tightly bandaged in Elastoplast at the time.

The time has come to regress a little and take a closer look at Joe

Brooks. He had himself taken the TAS Course (as had so many other worthy fellows!) and been appointed Staff TAS Officer to a squadron of Battle Class destroyers (like *Gravelines*). The four ships were visiting Setubal, near Lisbon in Portugal. Joe was one of a group of officers invited to some glittering reception and was headed there in his mess kit—miniature medals, etc.—the company being in two cars, one driven by the British Naval Attaché. I do not know how the accident occurred but one car failed to take a turn and went over the dockside, into forty feet of water, with the occupants trapped inside. The other car in which Joe and his Captain were riding stopped at once. Without a word, Joe pulled off his mess jacket and plunged into the dirty oily water and fought his way down to the sunken car. He stayed long enough to struggle with a door handle but could not open it before having to surface for air. He made several more dives in an heroic attempt to save his fellow officers from drowning. However, after the third dive Joe came up coughing blood. His Captain felt further effort was useless. He had clearly lost four officers and saw no point in losing Brooks as well. This, however, was not how Joe saw things. He had nearly succeeded and knew that if any could be got out within minutes—assuming some air had been trapped in the car—lives could be saved. Brooks therefore decided to defy his Captain's orders—until the latter literally arrested him and had him placed under guard in his cabin on board. Even this did not stop Joe. In a flash, he was out of the port of his cabin and again diving for the stricken car load of officers. It was all of no avail and Joe himself had to be hospitalised.

As can be imagined, this 'iron man' quickly recovered and it was whilst under convalescence that I found myself sailing with him and watching him seemingly effortlessly streaking up the rigging. I indicated earlier that Brooks was tough—men did not come tougher than Joe! Yet he was a modest and quiet-spoken man.

I cannot vouch for the absolute veracity of the next story about Joe Brooks and I have avoided upsetting his—or anyone else's—sensitivities by researching the matter in detail. But I was around *Vernon* at the time and what follows is how the story was being told there, and I believe it is substantially true. Joe was due for reappointment and had set his heart on taking a highly specialised Clearance Diving course. This was an area for which his physique, not to mention his iron nerve, fitted him well and the probability was that he would quickly advance naval diving technology generally. Naturally, he told the Appointments Officer at *Vernon* of his aspirations. Sadly, however, this senior Lieutenant Commander said he was sorry but a TAS Officer needed to be appointed to HMS *Warrior* (I think)—a light fleet carrier about to commission. In vain did Joe plead in terms of 'anything but an aircraft carrier'. In fact, knowing Joe, I suspect he was more outspoken and told the Appointments Officer what he could do with the *Warrior*! Days of confrontation followed with neither side budging, until the issue was brought to a head with the formal appointment of Brooks to *Warrior*. This was the time-honoured: 'I am directed by my Lords Commissioners for executing the Office of Lord High Admiral in the United Kingdom, etc. to appoint you . . .' Joe was totally unmoved and took this paper round to the Appointments Officer and said, 'It's no good sending me bits of crap like this—I've told you I'm not joining any carrier!'

The Captain of *Vernon* was now in a spot. Brooks had been an outstanding officer, had great potential and was clearly well loved. On the other hand, he could not be allowed to disobey a direct order like this and blatantly flout authority (whether or not Dartmouth had made him this sort of person). After some deliberation, the Captain decided that no one (at least not since Nelson at Copenhagen) in his right mind, had so defied authority. Therefore, perhaps Joe had a psychiatric problem—he had been through much strain recently. Brooks was therefore sent to RN Hospital Haslar for three weeks of psychiatric observation. This at least gave everyone some breathing space and time to consider the matter calmly. This was probably the best thing that could have been done as people's attention was diverted to other matters. Nevertheless, at the end of the observation period, the Specialist's report is reputed to have stated: 'We can find nothing clinically wrong with Lt. Brooks—it would appear that this officer simply does not wish to serve aboard HMS *Warrior*.' By now, *Vernon* probably just wanted to see the back of Joe Brooks. Almost unbelievably, his appointment to *Warrior* was cancelled and he was sent on a Clearance Diving Course! This was not the end of the Joe Brooks story but that is enough for the time being.

Returning to my own activities, and sailing, I had one adventure worth recounting. We were at Osprey (Portland), it was October and winter was coming on. Nevertheless, four of us (under my leadership) took a short week-end sailing Osprey's Windfall yacht *Nimrod* round to Swanage and back. This craft, unlike most of the ex-German Windfalls, had been built for inland sailing and was of shallow draught with a drop keel. She did not sail well in a seaway, but would have been fine on the Norfolk Broads. More significantly—and not realised by me—the yacht was poorly maintained and ill-equipped; that was as far as essentials were concerned although it was lavishly fitted for living aboard. The total sail wardrobe comprised main, Genoa and storm tri-sail and, sadly, all these sails were cotton (not Dacron) and at least eight years old. The proper upkeep of *Nimrod* appeared to be nobody's responsibility.

We sailed to Swanage through Friday night without incident, although worried by radio reports of an approaching south-west gale. Once at Swanage, with the wind already rising, we had a hurried lunch and decided we had better head for home while the going was good. Anyone who has sailed the coastal waters of southern England will know that compared to the dreaded Portland Race, the race off Durlston Head is almost as dangerous. We accepted that *Nimrod* had no chance of rounding Durlston against both wind and tide-race. Yet sailing with the race, but against the rising gale, could involve a dangerously steep seaway. The remaining option was to make the transit at slack water, and this is what we planned to do, at around 1600.

Accordingly, we sailed at 1500 and should have made the headland comfortably as planned. Before we got there, however, a 6″ length of stitching came away on a seam in the (triple-reefed) mainsail near the peak. This could not be ignored. We bore away and came to anchor in the sheltered cove right under the cliffs of Durlston Head. With sailmaker's palm and needle (unfortunately, our only one), I feverishly stitched many feet of dubious-looking seams in the upper mainsail. An hour later, we weighed and headed on our way. Sadly, however, we had now missed our slack water, but with the strong tide up our stern, there was no turning back. The chart suggested that one might be able to dodge the worst of the race by sailing as close inshore as we dared, around Anvil Point. Meanwhile, we braced ourselves for trouble. All hatches were firmly secured and the four of us, on deck, bent on rope lifelines. Dodging the race by going close inshore looked a doubtful proposition as we watched the yacht being drawn into the maelstrom ahead.

It was now darkening, but we could make out the silhouette of the Anvil Point lighthouse-keeper who had come to the edge of the 400 ft. cliffs to look down on us. He might well have been the last other human we saw, or who saw us. As we entered the race, one wave broke right over the yacht, drenching us to the skin (in our less-than-Fastnet-type wet weather gear). But then, as quickly as we had entered, we were out of the race on the other side, in comparatively smooth water.

Just as we were congratulating ourselves, more trouble appeared. A torch revealed that another rent had opened, near the peak of the main—it was now touch-and-go. Would enough of this sail hold together to let us work another ten miles to windward (with the tide behind us) into the lee of Portland Bill? We kept watching this split, with a light on it, as it lengthened inch by inch, and kept our fingers crossed. Alas, this last measure (not given in the *Seamanship Manual*) proved ineffective! All in the space of a minute, the sail 'blew out', leaving no more than tattered shreds on mast and boom. We now had to set the storm tri-sail. None of us had set such a sail before and the time to learn is not when beating into a full gale in total darkness. Our problems were increased by the fact that one of our number had succumbed to seasickness and had retired below to quietly await his end. We were therefore reduced to three effective crew and one had to remain at the tiller. Nevertheless, half an hour later, the tri-sail was set and the yacht manageable once more, although only making very slow progress to windward.

We had but brief respite before more woes beset us. Well might Hamlet have said that we were 'taking up arms against a sea of troubles'. The storm tri-sail was no sooner drawing than the main sheet block disintegrated without warning and then our one headsail blew into tatters. At length, a jury main sheet was rigged, but with the tri-sail now our only sail, it became clear that we were not going to sail anywhere, except perhaps down-wind. We had few options—none of them attractive. We could remain hove to where we were. We might run for shelter in Lulworth Cove, which had to be somewhere close to the north of us—but how would we find its unlit entrance? If we could find Lulworth, would the entrance be navigable in a south-westerly gale by a yacht under tri-sail only? It was now 2300 and the tide had turned against us, thwarting our chances of making the lee of Portland Bill. But we were past the point of no return and the long run back round Durlston meant going through the race again. There was even worse news for us. Until now we could at least ride out the gale and hope things would be better next morning. Now, even the option of doing nothing disappeared—a call from our ailing shipmate below told us the yacht was making water fast. Regrettably, practically nothing on this craft worked. We had tinkered unsuccessfully with the engine for an hour or so at Swanage. The two-way radio was dead and now, to our dismay, we found that the main bilge pump was unserviceable. We seemed to be 'suffering the slings and arrows of outrageous fortune'!

We failed utterly to reactivate the bilge pump, the water level was now sloshing a foot above the cabin sole and, in another few hours, we would sink. A chain of buckets seemed our only hope and our seasick crewman did his best to help, but only three could bail as one still had to steer. We worked hard on this for half an hour, rotating the helmsman until we were exhausted—but the water level had not dropped. Under such circumstances, one puts the best face on things possible, out of an instinctive refusal to accept that things are becoming desperate. I was under greater pressure to keep up morale as I was in command and could therefore be said to have got us all into this mess. I finally had to conclude that we were now 'in distress'—but what could we do to call for help? The radio was out so we could not make a 'Mayday' call. Fortunately, the yacht's electrics were still serviceable and we had lights, even an Aldis signal lamp. But who would we try to call on a dark stormy night with no sign of any shipping around? The naval signal station at East Weare on the top of Portland Bill was our only hope. But would they see a weak blinking light nine miles away on such a wet and windy night? We would have to attract attention first with a Very's light.

The Very's pistol box with ammunition was found. It had come with the boat and neither pistol nor cartridges had probably been tested in seven years, so we just had to hope. The pistol was a curious double-barrelled firearm, such as was not used in the RN. I loaded both barrels, held the thing at arm's length, prayed it would not explode and pulled one trigger. Precisely nothing happened and so I pulled the other. This time there was a stream of sparks as the cartridge was fired—but it failed to light up. I reloaded both barrels and, to our enormous relief, the third try produced a brilliant red flare in the sky. I had the Aldis at the ready and the moment the flare died started making the 'general call' towards East Weare. To our even greater relief an answering light started blinking back. There was no question of my demonstrating how efficient a signaller I had become in MTBs as I could only pass a word or two at a time as we reached the crest of successive waves. However, some perverse pride stopped me signalling 'Help—come and save us' but, rather, identifying the yacht, advising our sails were torn, the craft was making water and we 'required assistance'. A tug was sent and towed us into Portland like drowned rats as the murky dawn was breaking. We were none the worse for wear but not a little shaken and one could say some useful lessons had been learnt!

I can think of no other items of special interest before our course ended except that on the date we were to hold the *Vernon* Spring Ball, sad news came. King George VI had died and our new Queen and Prince Philip were on their way home from Kenya for the former to ascend the throne. Philip's happy days of Fleet Regattas and 'raiding' other ship's wardrooms were over for ever. Meanwhile *Vernon*'s Ball was cancelled.

SOME REFLECTIONS

Our fourteen month course was over. We had learnt a great deal but, in retrospect, I am not sure we had been taught all we should have been. The Navy was in danger of reverting into a peacetime rut, with only the Cold War and the perceived threat of Russia's huge submarine fleet to keep people on their toes. I referred to the unchanging Mk.9 ** torpedoes, which made all the Old Guard at *Vernon* feel comfortable. This was unhealthy. I felt that one could earn a pat on the head if, when asked to identify a ¾″ rubber ring held up in forceps, one could call out, 'Easy, that is the Inlet O Ring on the second main reducer on the HP airline of the Mk.9 **.' On the other hand, a student who replied, 'I have no idea—but do know that if the torpedo motor could run on oxygen released from High Test peroxide, performance could be almost doubled and the cost of machining precision high-pressure air vessels could be greatly reduced,' would be in trouble. He would be marked as a dangerous radical who should be watched.

Likewise the teaching of Asdics (soon to be called Sonar) was not much more imaginative. The Battle of the Atlantic had been won with the Type 144 Asdic set and variants and one had to know the ins and outs of this quite primitive equipment to the last detail—virtually where every electron went from cathode to anode in the simple amplifier unit with its five little thermionic valves. In fact, the days of radio valves were already numbered and we should have been concentrating on transistors. Occasionally, magic phrases like Twin Germanium Crystal Modulators were breathed but we were not taught about them. Microchips and the world of silicon were still decades away but thermionic valves were—or should have been—history. The fact was that new Asdic equipment such as the Type 170 of three hundred times the power of the 144 was already entering service, but the lion's share of our training was on the World War II equipment. This was partly accounted for by the respect, rightly, shown to the Battle of the Atlantic heroes. Through years of experience these men had developed an uncanny instinct as to how a submarine in an Asdic beam was manoeuvring, through the minutest change of echo pitch (doppler). The Navy and the nation owed a tremendous debt to these veterans, and their DSCs for sinking submarines had been well earned. However, by 1951 these people should have no longer been setting the agenda. More of our Dartmouth-instilled irreverence should have surfaced.

The more fundamental point was that people generally were not yet geared to a world of technical change—and some people are still not. Yet we were young and eager, in our early twenties, and with fertile brains ready to absorb technology, which, alas, we did not have teachers to impart to us.

I recall in the sixties it being said that mankind's total scientific knowledge over all previous millenia doubled between 1900 and 1950 and would redouble in the next fifteen years (This obviously did not include the Mk.9** Torpedo!). Since then, the acceleration has risen exponentially and can no longer be measured. This is illustrated by the fact that computers of (then) mind-blowing power and occupying whole specially-constructed buildings in the sixties could be matched by 'desk-top' equipment by the mid-eighties. This was largely attributable to silicon chips—but this was only a beginning. By the late eighties an IBM PC handling two million instructions per second (m.i.p.s) was regarded as a powerful tool but was already about to be left behind by the next generation of hardware utilising so-called transputers working at not two, but two hundred, m.i.p.s.! At the age of seventy, I am unable to keep abreast of developing technology—but, at least I am aware that it is all happening and have no time for people who simply have no desire to know about any of this.

On a much more personal and human level, I have already written much about 'swings' and 'roundabouts'. Now, at last, I was beginning to perceive that, although the contrasts had enriched my life, there was more to be appreciated amongst the 'swings' than some of the more glamorous 'roundabouts'.

I had been enthralled by the life stories of my 3rd Class travelling companions *en route* to Paris. My sister and I were never closer than during evenings eating a meal from her gas-ring and sharing a cheap bottle of wine. Well do I remember the pleasure we had from listening to the (Bakelite, thermionic valve) radio—without tweeters, woofers or graphic-equalisers. On Saturday nights we would have 'Jack Jackson and his Record Round-up'. He would play absurd songs like one, sung with a lugubrious air, 'The sun is shining—Oh happy dayee' and renditions by Yma Sumac, allegedly an Inca Princess and whose voice spanned four octaves—'her top notes are so high, only a dog can hear them!'

I also came to appreciate occasional solitude—particularly alone up top at night, sailing in a gentle breeze under a cloudless and moonless sky, contemplating, in Banjo Patterson's words, 'The wondrous glory of the everlasting stars'.

CHAPTER 21

AUSTRALIA

WHEN THE LONG TAS COURSE ENDED everyone was told their next appointment and sent off on leave. At least, everyone but myself—I had no idea where I would be headed. A curious set of circumstances led to this situation. I had assumed that I would be sent to Australia for two years of Exchange Service with the RAN. I had volunteered for this and was looking forward to it. The system was that the Australian Navy would send such officers as they wanted trained in the various specialisations to UK for Long Courses. However, in order to get their money's worth out of the return fares involved, such officers would remain with the RN for a further two-year commission. This would enable them to gain experience in a larger fleet and take part in exercises on a bigger scale than was possible back in Australia. In our case, there had been three Aussies and it was assumed that three of us would be needed to replace them in the RAN. Tony Woolley, John Barratt and myself had volunteered so the situation seemed uncomplicated. At the last moment, however, the RAN decided that only two exchange TAS officers were needed.

With three volunteers but only two appointments offering, what should be done? Tony Woolley was the most organised of the three of us and the only married one, with two small children. He knew all about the exchange system and had applied for appointment to Australia before the course started. Accordingly, apart from having the strongest claim, he had been promised he would go and had made all arrangements for his family. So it was down to John Barratt and myself. Neither of us had any special consideration for priority—indeed one of the attractions of the appointment for me was the prospect of going with two good mates I had made during the course. Our Course Officer, 'Horse' Lewis, was told to adjudicate and decided the only fair way to resolve the matter was to cut a pack of cards. We both agreed this was reasonable and a pack was produced. John cut first and, to my dismay, cut the Ace of Hearts. I cannot make this a good story by reporting that I then cut the Ace of Spades! In fact I lost, Barratt was told to make plans for two years in Australia and I went on leave while *Vernon* thought about what to do with me. I accepted all this as fair and above board. Later, I reflected that few are faced with: the Antipodes or not for the next two years, on a cut of cards—at two weeks notice!

At the time, I was disappointed and concerned to know just what appointment they would dream up for me, as I was now clearly surplus to planned requirements. I hoped a TAS Officer had been found for *Warrior*! However, since leaving Dartmouth, I had really had no say as to where the Navy might send me, except that opting for a Destroyer Gunnery Officer's Course had ensured I was sent to a destroyer some-where. I was not a single-minded person like Tony Woolley who knew what he wanted, or strong-willed like Joe Brooks who knew exactly what he did not want. I had simply been content to drift with the tide, wherever the Service sent me. In the event, after two weeks on leave a telegram came telling me the RAN had changed its mind and wanted three officers after all. I was to take passage aboard the P&O liner *Strathmore* leaving Tilbury in one week's time.

I have written at some length over the circumstances surrounding my appointment to serve with the RAN. This is because it would affect not only my next two years, but the whole pattern of my future life. It would indirectly lead to my eventual migration to Australia, spending the last thirty-five years in that country and assuming Australian Nationality (albeit retaining a UK Passport). This all eventuated, if not from cutting cards, then from a minor change in perception of manning requirements—or just whim—of someone in Navy Office, Melbourne. My view remains a simple one of '*Que sera, sera*'. I still had options but made my choice—which I have not regretted.

My next two years would largely comprise an on-going great big 'bowl of cherries'. There would be minor disappointments and a couple of officers with whom I did not have a good rapport. But these were greatly outnumbered by happy memories and officers I served under, or with, for whom I developed great respect and affection and who treated me well.

The fun ('roundabouts') started with the voyage and all the prospects looked auspicious. For the first time, I was no longer scratching to make ends meet. With help from my parents, I kitted myself out with a full range of civilian clothes, beyond the grey flannel trousers, tweed jacket, shirts and tie. I now sported a lightweight tropical suit, a Panama hat, dinner jacket and trousers—even a white sharkskin jacket. My father had told me I should wear this last for dinner as of the date the ship's officers went into white uniforms. Clearly there were standards set by the British Raj that had to be upheld!

I had enjoyed myself on leave. Each time I had returned home, the country seemed more prosperous as the war became more of a distant memory. The year 1951 had been the Festival of Britain and the whole nation still felt like celebrating. Spring had come early and England did seem an attractive place. But my imminent sailing for Australia was uppermost in my mind.

No one came to see me off but my excitement rose as I boarded the boat train at Liverpool Street Station. This was mainly due to distant memories of the luxury and glamour of Australia-Britain travel eighteen years back in 1933. My mother had brought MSJ and myself, aged eight and nine, to school in England from Fiji via Sydney aboard the Orient Liner *Otranto*. *Strathmore* and her later sister, *Stratheden*, were the last two pre-war P&O liners, representing the ultimate elegance in general first class sea travel. This was never matched by the post-war successors of these ships. (I subsequently made voyages aboard *Oronsay*, *Orcades*, *Orsova*, *Oriana* and *Canberra*.) Importantly, in 1952, ships still represented the only practical way of travelling between UK and Australia, mass air travel still being at least a decade away. Accordingly, the passenger lists comprised individuals and families relocating between the two countries with all their luggage and often household effects as well. My father had moved out of Fiji accompanied by forty crates and tea chests containing everything from a grand piano down!

I do not know the average age of the passengers but guess it would have been early thirties. Today, passenger ships still roaming the world carry passengers who are on board purely 'for the ride' and their average age is over seventy. In fact, even though we were travelling to get somewhere, there was a great deal more fun in the 'ride' than aboard most luxury cruise liners today. The naval contingent of a dozen Lieutenants aged between 23 and 26 were virtually treated to five weeks of 5-Star Hotel accommodation with full board and entertainment all gratis. My cabin-mate and I had a stateroom with two proper beds (not bunks), two portholes and an entertainment area large enough for six to take cocktails before dinner. For such, stewards would bring trays of canapés on request—at no charge. I need hardly allude to the contrast between this sort of travel and the poor old *Antenor*, not to mention the *Rocksand*. Perhaps some of my colleagues did not realise how lucky they were. I was fully conscious of this, even before boarding at Tilbury, and ready to make the most of our voyage. I had taken a certain amount of rough in my time and was now prepared to revel in the smooth. For five weeks we lived as only millionaires could today.

There was plenty of lively company on board—glamorous young women, Australian and British officers, government officials and captains of industry. Stops were made at Algiers, Port Said, Bombay and Colombo before Australia. All these ports except Bombay were known to me and so we were able to conduct young women passengers on shore visits. Others in our party had good connections at Bombay and we had a splendid time ashore there including a visit to the Breach Kandy Swimming Club.

Regrettably, there were three minor incidents which brought down the

Captain's wrath on me. For one, I was entirely blameless and the other two were the result of wholly unforeseen circumstances. First, only two days out from UK, one of our number (a slightly wild submariner) after an evening of carousing, felt compelled to climb the funnel, up a guy. Unfortunately, this man was no Joe Brooks and fell off, breaking his ankle. I agreed with the Captain that this was a very foolish act but could not see what it had to do with me, having been asleep in my cabin at the time. Perhaps the Captain had noted I was the senior member of our group. If I was, I was unaware of the fact and certainly had never been told I was responsible for the behaviour of the other officers.

The next contretemps occurred in the Indian Ocean, between Colombo and Fremantle. No land or other ship had been seen for days, when HMS *Loch Quoich* (sister to *Loch Eck* aboard which I had sailed these same Indian Ocean waters) appeared, steaming in the opposite direction. *Strathmore* did not change course and the frigate steered to pass safely—but close—down the port side. This was doubtless to give the officers on the bridge a look at our female passengers through their binoculars. I could understand this. Nine years earlier, a group of very young naval officers had waved furiously at attractive girls lining the guard rail of another *Strath*! Naturally, signals were exchanged and, standing directly below the wing of the bridge, I had no difficulty reading the warship's signals—but could only hear the clicking of the *Strathmore*'s signal lamp above me. As the ships passed, *Loch Quoich* signalled 'Your passengers look charming.' I called up to the 3rd Officer, who was on watch and whom I had come to know, 'What was the reply to that one?' In a discreet aside the mate called down to me, 'The Old Man made back, "You should be with them for a day or two".' I laughed and would have thought no more of it, but a fellow passenger standing beside me asked, 'What was that all about?' and, unthinkingly I told him. This story spread rapidly through the 1st Class passengers and two old ducks officially complained to the Purser about insulting signals being made about the passengers. Again, the Captain summoned me and asked, 'How dare you read and relay my private signals?' I felt this was an overreaction but the Captain had already decided Lt. Seymour was 'Bad News'!

The third occasion did amount to an understandable, although un-intended, provocation for the Captain. Steaming through Bass Strait the night after leaving Melbourne, *Strathmore* had engine trouble. For all the ship's luxury and elegance, her main engines were now eighteen years old and had done a great deal of steaming. In the small hours, an ominous noise was heard coming from the engine room and, on rising, passengers noted that our speed—previously 18 knots—was considerably reduced. Around 1100, the solemn and sonorous voice of the Captain came over the PA system. He announced that trouble had been experienced with one of the main engines but the ship's engineers had taken care of the defect, and the ship was resuming full power. He hoped that the ship would still make Sydney in time for New Zealand passengers to tranship to the *Monowai*.

Sadly, the Captain had scarcely finished his announcement before the ship was shaken by the noise of major mechanical trouble in the engine-room. It seems that the rotor of the low pressure turbine of the starboard engine had now fallen apart—putting this engine completely out of action. I was infinitely less worried than when the engines of *Antenor* had failed— another day aboard our five star hotel upset me not at all. Not surprisingly, this was not the way the Captain saw matters. It happened that my mate Tony Woolley and I had been invited to the Wardroom for a drink by Tom Winyeates, the Second Officer at whose table we dined. Around 1200, after a couple of gins, Woolley and I were in a friendly argument as to what speed the ship was now making. Our only guide was our seaman's eye as to visible movement through the water, but we took a bet for: above or below ten knots. Tom broke in with, 'Young Penny [the standing forenoon watchkeeper, who had told me the Captain's signal] is on watch. If you nip onto the bridge [just above us], he will tell you our speed'. I stepped onto the bridge, saw Penny and called out, 'Hey, we've got a bet on. What speed is the ship doing?' I then saw the Captain, dividers in hand poring over the chart. He glowered at me with a look that said, 'Not Seymour again!' and icily called out, 'We haven't got time for bets here—I must ask you to leave my bridge.' Rapidly, exit Seymour with mumbled apology! We never learned who had won the bet.

There was one other incident which happily never came to the Captain's attention. The rule was that the bars no longer sold liquor at duty-free prices around the Australian coast, after reaching Fremantle. Our ETA there was 0730 one morning but everyone had to undergo a medical inspection before the ship could berth. This was rudimentary—a quick look at the inside forearm for tell-tale smallpox (or whatever) spots— but there were dire penalties for non attendance at 0630. There was bound to be a big last duty-free night party the night before. My other TAS buddy, John Barratt—of Rosy Dawn fame—always keen for a party, declared it was quite unrealistic to go to bed before the medical inspection. Accordingly, we 'partied' through the night and about twenty young people presented themselves for inspection still in evening dress. Not amongst these, however, were the author and an attractive New Zealand girl, both of us having been thrown into the swimming pool around 0400. I had been in black tie attire and the girl in her glamorous turquoise strapless evening gown. I headed for my cabin and some dry clothes but not before seeing this gorgeous NZ lass reappear from somewhere clad only in a Blue Ensign swathed around her!

Such proceedings would be unthinkable for the diamond-digited dowagers aboard the QE2 today. However, the writer has to admit to being much the same age as many of the latter who may well be trying to recall the carefree salad days of their youth. It is true we were now beyond the age of youth but were only beginning to enjoy our salad days—delayed by the grim realities of war and post-war turmoil in Britain and the Royal Navy.

AUSTRALIA AND DOWN TO WORK

We reached Sydney on a Saturday morning on a calm autumn day. After fond farewells to shipboard girl friends and promises to keep in touch (which, regrettably, were never honoured), we were collected by naval transport and distributed as required. I found myself appointed to HMAS *Rushcutter*, then the RAN's TAS School, where I was to be on the training staff. Tony Woolley was to be Staff TAS Officer to the First Frigate Flotilla and John Barratt the No.2 of the training minesweeper HMAS *Wagga*. This last really was an extraordinary appointment. The RAN now had about the most brilliant young TAS specialist officer fresh from UK with his brain crammed with all the latest anti-submarine technology and tactical doctrine as well as a multitude of other specialist TAS skills. Yet no one could think of any more useful employment for him than third in command of a ship smaller and less significant than *Flint Castle* had been for me. The ship carried out elementary minesweeping training during week-days and spasmodic basic seamanship training for reservists at weekends. In other words, the appointment in no way called for a Specialist TAS Officer—let alone a very bright one—any more than *Flint Castle* rated a so-qualified officer. However, the cheery John Barratt was not one to complain. His only request on arrival on board was that he be made the wardroom wine caterer, to ensure the right liqueurs were stocked for his cocktail mixing!

Woolley soon had his family installed in a rented house in Mosman (harbourside suburb of Sydney) and settled down happily in his sea-going appointment. Meanwhile, I moved into HMAS *Rushcutter* where I felt I was usefully employed passing on as much of my newly acquired TAS know-how as possible. However, as will have already been noted, one could not fail to run into old mates anywhere in the world where British or Commonwealth warships were to be found. Who should I find waiting to greet me for Saturday lunchtime drinks at *Rushcutter* but my old Termmate and close friend Mike Kersey and the one and only Happy Hooligan—Mike MccGwire! Neither were actually serving at *Rushcutter*. Kersey was with the frigates and would soon hand over to Woolley and of all jobs, what was MccGwire doing but No. 1 of the little *Wagga*! This was clearly another waste of talent. Happy Hooligan he might have been, but it will be recalled that MccGwire was also brilliant. He had been awarded the King's Dirk at Dartmouth, had an exceptional war record and other distinctions. Also he had already qualified as a Russian interpreter. However, like Barratt, he was not one to complain. The Aussie sailors loved him as much as the RN ones had, but with MccGwire and Barratt on board, *Wagga* soon had a name for entertaining and it was hard to leave that ship sober!

The authorities had not sent me to Australia simply to have a good time and I like to feel I did render worthwhile service. For the first time, at *Rushcutter*, I was teaching, lecturing or generally training both officers and ratings, and found I really enjoyed this. The classes were enthusiastic and eager to hear the 'good oil' on the latest anti-submarine warfare techniques as well as other TAS subjects. I found it a challenging exercise, holding a class's attention and sustaining their enthusiasm. I also had administrative duties, structuring and programming courses in my capacity as Senior Instructional Officer, as well as general personnel and disciplinary responsibilities.

Other duties included TAS Equipment Trials Officer. This involved carrying out functioning and calibration trials on all new TAS weapons and equipment fitted to RAN ships. Occasionally, I was seconded to one of the frigates for a few days for a major exercise, notionally so that the ship would have as capable an Anti Submarine Control Officer as possible. This was enjoyable as it was pleasant being at sea again. Also, if I could not get good results from the ship's old Type 144 Asdics, after all my time in *Flint Castle*, then I should be ashamed of myself. However, one had to avoid being too cocky and acquiring a 'watch-him-he's-supposed-to-be-good' image. Finally, I had to liaise with, and arrange studies for, reservists, both officers and ratings, who would attend for evening classes once or twice a week. An extra-curricular activity was Secretary of the Command Sailing Association and Committee Member of the RAN Sailing Association.

I was soon fully occupied with my work at *Rushcutter*. However, after only six weeks, I was temporarily transferred to Navy Office, Melbourne, as the Assistant Director of Underwater Weapons (2), the incumbent having been temporarily transferred elsewhere. I was to return to this job on a permanent basis some months on. Meanwhile I had an interesting and enjoyable month in Navy Office before returning to my previous job at Rushcutter.

The administrative/disciplinary duties at *Rushcutter* had some interesting sidelines. Generally, I found the Lower Deck ratings of the RAN were possibly somewhat smarter than their counter-parts in the RN—perhaps as the result of being paid rather more. On the other hand, problems arose through *Rushcutter*'s location so close to the heart of the city of Sydney and particularly to the entertainment and 'red light' area of King's Cross, less than a mile away. As a result, libertymen were rather more prone to return to their quarters drunk than was usual for shore establishments. Before my time, when Mike Kersey had the posting I now had, he had to cope with two or three inebriated sailors, returning 'on board'. We all knew how to handle such situations. One simply had a small 'fisting party' of sober on-duty ratings, who would be told to place the offenders in the lock-up overnight to be seen as defaulters next day. By then, the men would almost invariably be truly contrite, often declaring they could remember little of the night before and perhaps adding the rider, 'I would just like to say, Sir, that if I was any trouble, I am very sorry.' No other defence would be offered and the standard punishment of one day's pay and one day's leave would be docked. What we were taught was not to argue with a drunken man, who might easily hit the Duty Officer and risk the court martial offence of striking an officer. At Dartmouth, we learnt that, however degrading it might appear, the officer should run away, round and round 'Y' turret if necessary, until the drunk could be grabbed. On the occasion in question, Mike Kersey found himself cornered in the small office at the main gate. A really belligerent drunk made a rush at Kersey, who had no option but to stop him with a straight left. In fact this not only stopped the assailant but broke his jaw. The upshot was that Mike received a severe reprimand but the word soon got around the men that one should not make trouble on returning to barracks if Lt. Kersey was Duty Officer!

I had an improbable incident one night when it was my turn for duty. I was fast asleep in my cabin when there was a loud bang on the door and a sailor burst in with a baby in his arms. At such an hour one takes a minute or so to sort out a strange situation. Why should this man be in my cabin with a baby and a flood of verbal explanation heavily laced with Lower Deck vernacular, before I was ready to absorb it? Once fully awake, I was able to note a few details for myself. The sailor was a leading seaman, I knew, and I observed he was wearing belt and gaiters and must therefore be the quartermaster on duty at the gate. It turned out this man, a recent father, suspected his wife, who lived in the King's Cross area, was 'carrying on' with another sailor from *Rushcutter*. This other man knew the husband was on duty at the depot and therefore presumed he could safely spend the night with the wife. The on-duty Leading Seaman figured all this out, deserted his post at the gate and dashed to King's Cross to see if he could catch the other man in bed with his wife. I think it will be understood that all this was not immediately comprehensible in the first ten seconds after being violently awoken at 0200.

It seems our post-deserting quartermaster found things just as he expected. In blind rage, he rushed into the next room, collected their months-old baby and fled out of the house into his waiting taxi, with his wife (in dressing gown) in hot pursuit. Indeed, the pursuit was so hot that as he entered one door of the cab (baby in arms), his wife came in by another. They went at each other hammer and tongs as far as *Rushcutter* where the Leading Seaman fled inside, with baby. The Boatswain's Mate barred entry to the wife/mother, who was left screaming hysterically outside the gate. It was at this point that my intervention had been sought. I told the man to return to the gate-house, dressed quickly and headed there myself. I could hear the screaming woman from a hundred yards away but this only served to confuse me further as to what I should do next.

I confess to feeling sympathy for this man with his unfaithful wife and took the precaution of sending him and baby out of sight as I told the Boatswain's Mate to show the woman in. I also took care to have a large table between myself and this angry virago—I would not have even been able to resort to the Kersey behaviour if attacked! The moment the woman entered she subjected me to a positive torrent of abuse. As in the unusual incident at Ostend, there was clearly no guidance in any manual for dealing with this situation. I tried to be rational. In all humanity, it did not seem right to take the baby from the distraught father and return it to the drunken and hysterical mother. On the other hand, I could visualise no provision of Queen's Regulations that empowered me to enrol a three-month-old infant into the Ship's Company of HMAS *Rushcutter* at 0200.

Unable to get at me physically, the woman started issuing wild threats as to what she would do if she did not get her baby back at once. Fortunately, one of these struck a chord in my still not fully cerebrating mind. She would have me arrested and put in prison! 'Ah ha,' I thought, 'A civil matter—not the concern of the Navy.' 'Yes Madam,' I said, 'Allow me to call the Police for you,' and did so without more ado. Remarkably quickly, a fatherly Police Sergeant, clearly well versed in sorting out 'domestics', appeared on the scene and took charge. In no time he had 'sorted out' the mother until she had stopped screaming and was merely sobbing. He then ordered the return of the baby to the mother and advised the sailor what options under the law were open to him to seek redress. I thankfully returned to my bed.

As far as 'play' was concerned in Sydney, I was able further to indulge my sailing activities and was kindly invited to crew in the Montague Island Race—my first-ever offshore Ocean Race. The yacht was very small, the crew comprising the Skipper, his fiancée (whose family owned the boat), A. N. Other and myself. As so often happens with the Montague Island

Race, early in the season, the weather was foul, with a tearing southerly up the stern through the night once we had rounded the Island. We all suffered from seasickness, and only one of us was on watch at the time, to sail the boat in the gale through the night. This was a little daunting on one's first-ever Ocean Race. I would mention that my skipper was Gordon Ingate, who later would skipper one of Australia's challenges for the America's Cup. He put me up for the Royal Sydney Yacht Squadron on my return to Australia and become a lifelong friend.

The social scene in Sydney was never dull. There were the usual Navy ship parties, including one impromptu one aboard the dangerous HMAS *Wagga*. Back aboard *Napier* in Mombasa, I had formed the impression that all Australian naval officers drank like fishes. Now I was to find it was RN officers (notably MccGwire and Barratt) aboard RAN ships who represented the menace. On this particular night, after many hours drinking, MccGwire called out, 'Okay fellows—now we're off to the Glaciarium [which old-time Sydney-siders will remember as Sydney's only ice rink].' This seemed an entirely sensible suggestion at the time, and so off we went. I had attempted to skate once before, only to fall over every few yards. That night, however, feeling no pain, as they say, I was skating 'like a bird'!

I made many friends amongst the reservists who came to *Rushcutter*. A particularly enduring one, whom I claim as a close friend to this day (after forty years) was Marsden Hordern (now in his seventies and an acclaimed historical writer). In 1952, however, he was a gay young bachelor, who had half the glamorous young women of Sydney chasing him. He introduced me to some of them including the outstanding beauty of the time—and still a well known and attractive personality—June Dalley-Watkins. During the war, Marsden (as indicated in my chapter on Coastal Forces) had had interesting and distinguished service in MLs around Northern Australia, Papua New Guinea and 'The Islands'. In Sydney in 1952, however, I knew him as a 'social lion'. He offered to show me a real Sydney New Year's Eve (1952/3). Unfortunately his car was out of action, so my own beautiful little new Morris Minor Tourer had to be used. Happily it survived the night—Marsden having warned me not to expect to get back to *Rushcutter* before the following morning!

Marsden had the whole evening planned, so he assured me. He had found two girls who, with others, had taken a holiday cottage at Newport (northern beach suburb). He told me that he had invited these two out for an afternoon's sailing aboard his little yacht, which he had at The Spit, to encourage them to invite us to the New Year's Eve party he knew they were throwing. Having asked me to join him for the whole afternoon, evening and night, he went on to explain that the key to a successful New Year's Eve in Sydney and environs was a bath-tub in the boot of the car with crushed ice and a dozen bottles of champagne. Such constituted one's entree to any party one could find in progress between Sydney and Palm Beach! Marsden apologised that a necessary call had to be made at the home of his uncle, the great Sam Hordern, head of the whole Hordern Clan who always had a party on New Year's Eve. The implication was that this was a family duty but would be dull and to be escaped from as early as decently possible. As it happened, I found this entertainment far from dull with many attractive young women amongst the other (older) guests. It seems that Marsden was finding this party more lively than he expected. However, after an hour he felt it was time to move on, but declaring what the party at Newport would be like—with half a dozen girls and a swarm of young men. It would therefore be prudent for us to persuade two of the more attractive young women present to join us, something Marsden had no difficulty in doing. So, it was on to Newport.

On reaching the party, we were embarrassed to find it well under way but with at least a dozen girls and only two men. As can be imagined, we were not over-popular turning up with two more girls! Marsden said, in an aside to me, 'We've got to get out of here—but it is going to cost us.' With his glib tongue, he contrived some improbable story as to why we simply had to leave, but cost us it did—half our lockerful of champagne, left as ransom. The rest of the night remains something of a blur to me but I recall an hour or two of sleep on the floor of the beautiful new house at Palm Beach of one John Baynton. I came to know John better in future years. It happened he also knew my future wife and so attended our wedding.

In the first week of the New Year, I was given two weeks leave and found, to my amazement, I could now afford a First Class cruise ticket aboard the *Oronsay* to Fiji and New Zealand. This was only the second post-war cruise ship in the South Pacific (the *Orcades* was the first a month before). Accordingly, we had a celebrity-packed passenger list. My chief motivation was to do some more 'roots tracing', having not seen Fiji since leaving there at the age of seven in 1933. I thrilled to the sight of remembered scenes. I took a cab, past the Suva Boys Grammar School which I had attended for a year or so, past Albert Park, where Charles Kingsford-Smith had landed on his historic trans-Pacific flight, and the Grand Pacific Hotel. I carried on up Thakombau Road to the Colonial Secretary's Residence, which had once been my home (except the building I had known had burnt down and been replaced). I knocked on the door and asked if the Colonial Secretary was in. He was—having a late Sunday breakfast. His name was Mr Frederick R. Stoddart CMG. He greeted me cordially and, after a cup of coffee, took me on an interesting tour round Suva, Lautoka and environs, in his car.

In Fiji the Governor was someone my father *had* known and suggested

I call on. He was Sir Ronald Garvey and had been a 'Cadet' in the Fiji Civil Service under my father twenty years back. Accordingly, I 'signed the book' with the notation 'son of A.W. Seymour—late of Fiji Civil Service' (as per Colombo). The upshot was every bit as cordial. I was officially invited to a reception next day for VIPs from *Oronsay*, at Government House (which had also been my one-time home). I felt honoured but this was not really 'my scene'—being about twenty years younger than any other guest. Happily, Lady Garvey, who also remembered my parents, felt they could do more for me. Accordingly, she suggested that the following day the ADC should call for me and two girls, whom I should invite, and take the four of us off to the resort of Deumba for a swim and lunch. This seemed a splendid idea although, after only two days at sea from Sydney, I had yet to meet many girls aboard the ship. I asked two bright young things who dined at my table. They were unsure what they were in for but were as impressed as I was when, next morning, the vice-regal Daimler drew up alongside. Out stepped a handsome young Captain in his Rifle Brigade khaki uniform and greeted the two girls and myself (in sandals, shorts and Hawaian shirt) with a flourish of a military salute! Perhaps he thought he had been sent to pick up an off-duty admiral. Happily, we were able to persuade our escort that no protocol was involved and he could relax. We then had a pleasant day and only just got back to the ship before sailing time at 1700. The rest of the cruise, including Auckland, was enjoyable but not sufficiently eventful to merit comment.

I was scarcely back at *Rushcutter* before I was told I was to return to Melbourne and resume my position as ADUW(2) for the rest of my time with the RAN. I was sorry to leave Sydney, but would make a number of trips back, by air travel, as I remained TAS Equipment Trials Officer for the RAN and most of the trials seemed to be in Sydney. I had, however, made friends in Melbourne on my last visit and played rugby with the Victorian Harlequins, with whom I would soon start a full season of football.

The work was interesting and stimulating. I found myself taking decisions—or at least making recommendations—regarding weapons and material for new warships and shore training establishments, of much greater significance than I could have expected in the RN. Furthermore as most of this related to brand new technology there were few others in Navy Office qualified to question my recommendations. The system was I would make submissions which my boss, the Director of Underwater Weapons, would forward to the so-called Directorate of Training and Staff Requirements, whence, if agreed, it would be submitted to the Navy Board for approval. There was, in fact, a TAS Officer on the staff of DTSR who had to pass all matters related to TAS equipment. Fortunately this officer, Peter Wilson, was a buddy of mine—we played alongside each other as second row forwards for the Victorian Harlequins and shared various social activities. Accordingly, if at all doubtful about any submission, I would clear the matter informally with Peter before I put it up. The result was that decision-making and approval-acquiring reached a speed of execution that positively amazed the somewhat red-tape bound civil servants with whom we worked.

Occasional diversions would come through my being seconded for a few days to participate as the Naval Consultant or Liaison Officer for the annual War Games run by both the RAAF and the Army Staff Colleges at Point Cook and Queenscliff, respectively. Another function—not part of my job, but very satisfying—was being invited to a Levee and presented to the Governor of Victoria, Sir Dallas Brookes, a warm-hearted and dearly-loved State Governor.

I should now report the one matter that left me with a sad feeling about the RAN. It should be clear that I had made many friends amongst the Australian officers and was presumably quite well thought of by my superiors in Navy Office, judging by the favourable comments on the relevant Certificates of Service (known to us as 'Flimsies'). Also my re-appointment to Navy Office was specifically requested. Theoretically, Tony Woolley should have had the job and I should have relieved him in his sea-going appointment. In fact, Tony did not want the Navy Office post, having no wish to relocate his family from Sydney to Melbourne. However, there was one on-going matter related to the Department that left a bad taste with me. I will name no names—if any hat happens to fit, so be it.

I shared an office with another officer. Between us we were supposed to supply all necessary know-how for TAS-related technology. I was the junior of us but found myself responsible for all Asdic Equipment, A/S Weapons of all types, all Torpedoes and other elements whilst my colleague only looked after Diving and Mine Disposal. This last sounds important and dangerous but, in fact, was quite routine for any TAS officer. In other words, I felt I had about four-fifths of the load, simply because this man was not a qualified TAS officer.

He was a reservist who had done some diving during the war and was retained with a regular commission at the war's end. However, I do not believe he even had a Watch-Keeping Certificate and so was not technically qualified as an executive Lieutenant. Nevertheless, he had somehow built up an image around himself that he had been a war hero and had performed great feats of bravery as a diver. Conceivably he had, yet by the war-end he had been awarded no decorations or even been 'mentioned in despatches'. In fact there were one or two RAN divers who had made names for themselves in the field of diving during the war but who had never heard of this man. Nevertheless, he somehow built up this hero image so much that he was in great demand as a dinner guest and lecturer at Rotary Clubs etc. I would meet a Civil Servant in Navy Office who would say, 'I went to—'s lecture last night. What a great guy and what a magnificent war record he must have had. Also, the great thing about him is that he said so little about his own achievements—he was so modest—he always gave the credit to other people.' I would nearly choke but say nothing—although thinking of some of the COs of my MTB flotilla with Distinguished Service Crosses and bars, who would not dream of giving lectures to public meetings.

I might have felt scorn for this individual but would have lost no sleep over it. There was, however, another aspect to his conduct which was not only unethical but probably criminal and certainly in total contravention of Queen's Regulations and Admiralty Instructions.

Naturally, serving officers are not permitted to engage in commerce or any other activity for personal gain, unless granted permission to do so under special circumstances. Even Joe Brooks selling his sketches of the *Bismarck* survivors to the *Illustrated London News* was frowned upon. However, this officer set up a company, in which his own participation was only thinly disguised, to manufacture and sell a cheap version of Captain Jacques Cousteau's Aqualung. He probably infringed some Cousteau patents and almost certainly did not meet safety standards that would be applied today, but then he was notionally *the* Australian diving authority. To promote the sales of his equipment, he established (in his partner's name) an organisation called the Melbourne School of Underwater Swimming and Diving (or similar). Regular classes were held using his locally-made gear, which was sold to any trainees who could be persuaded to buy. The officer in question attended every class and gave the instruction—simply because he was such a great guy, keen to provide an activity for youth and dedicated to diving! All this was unethical but possibly not indictable.

However, I had to suffer sharing my office with this man whilst he spoke by the hour on the (Navy Office) phone to his business collaborator. During this time he would be doing no work for the Navy and putting me off work I might be trying to get on with. One whole morning he gave an interview to two sycophantic reporters who wrote a glowing article, virtually demanding to know why this modest hero had never been awarded public recognition. Almost unbelievably, he received an OBE in the next Honours List! The last straw for me was when he received a letter through the mail office drawing attention to the potential defence implications of having many young men trained as SCUBA divers, and requesting some official support for the Melbourne Diving School and suggesting some suitably qualified Navy Diving Officer should inspect the school. He had of course written the letter himself and it was naturally passed to him for action. He then drafted a reply—back to himself—stating that Lt. Cdr—, who was suitably qualified, would make the inspection and if his report was favourable, he would be appointed as the official RAN liaison officer to the school. This letter, of course, went out over the signature of the Secretary to the Naval Board (as did all correspondence). I need hardly spell out the final exchange of letters!

I could finally stand this no longer and told the man how disgusted I was with all his nefarious machinations. He tried pulling rank on me and asking how I dared speak in such terms to my superior officer. He would not have understood my telling him that Dartmouth bred non-respecters of persons. However, he changed his tack and told me (although I still do not believe it) that two members of the Naval Board were shareholders in his company—so I had better watch out. I discussed the whole story with my mate Peter Wilson who told me that he was well aware of the situation. But he said there was so much intrigue around that it was rash for any junior RAN officer to do too much stirring, unless he had concrete and irrefutable evidence of corruption—even then he would have to be brave. At this point, I lost my own nerve and decided not to be a 'whistle blower'. After all, it would be easy to paint me as the 'Pommie Ring-in', denigrating this brave Aussie war hero. However, I regret this and feel I did a grave disservice to the Royal Australian Navy, which I held in high regard. With hindsight, and more recent revelations of corruption in State Police Forces, it would not be unthinkable there should be an occasional 'rotten apple' even in the distinguished RAN.

Notwithstanding this unpleasant matter, I enjoyed working in Navy Office and retained both respect and affection for my real chief, Commander 'Tusky' Calder. His actual title, I believe, was Deputy Director of Ordnance and Underwater Weapons. On the questions of titles, I mentioned that I was named as Assistant Director of Underwater Weapons (Two)—ADUW(2) whilst my odious colleague was ADUW(1). My successor was Bryan Cleary who had been on my Long Course and had just been promoted to Lieutenant Commander (he retired as Commodore). Happily, Bryan was able to have the assignments redesignated as ADUW(TAS) and ADUW(D)—D for Diving. He was therefore no longer subordinate to this man.

On the social and play side of my life in Melbourne, I can only say that, in the slang of the time, I 'had a ball'. My social activities centred around the Victorian Harlequins, the Royal Yacht Club of Victoria (from which I regularly sailed aboard an 8-metre yacht in the summer), the English-Speaking Union (for which I was on the Younger Members Committee), the UK Officers' Club (which held weekly Scottish Dancing evenings), and friendships made (and in some cases still maintained) amongst my fellow residents at the pleasant Guest House 'Corrabert' in Orrong Rd, Toorak. I had a close association with The Little Theatre, through the good offices of a charming and talented young actress who prevailed on me to act as adviser for a naval play (Charles Morgan's *The Flashing Stream*). I was principally needed as a borrower of uniforms. But I had a lot of fun at The Little Theatre and this delightful girl was also a Younger Member of the English Speaking Union. At one stage the social whirl became altogether too much, when I found myself at five balls in two weeks!

I would get away from Melbourne from time to time. I have mentioned my occasional returns to Sydney on duty. I had a week's leave around Christmas 1953 in Adelaide, making my way there in an unusual way— aboard the liner *Orcades*. Adelaide proved a week of more social whirl as I was the guest of Walter Kidman and his family. Walter's father had been known as the Cattle King of South Australia. My introduction came from his sister who had married one Captain Nelson Clover RN Rtd. and who lived in my home town of Torquay, England. I also made an approach to Sir 'Tommy' Bar-Smith—head of a well-known South Aus-tralia family—with the unexpected advice that his mother had been my step-aunt (if one can have such a relative). His mother had been the younger sister of my mother's first husband, from whom she had been widowed before she met and married my father. Remarkably, Sir Tommy said he could recall meeting the young bride of his uncle way back in England just before World War I. At any rate, he kindly invited me to spend a day with his family at their holiday house at Victor Harbour. A charming girl named Natalie Barratt kindly undertook to accompany me for the day. She even suggested we called in on the way back to visit friends of hers at the homestead of one of the well-known South Australia wineries, where we were pressed to stay for dinner. This was most pleasant except that our host somehow assumed that I would have a cultivated palate for good wines and started asking my opinion about some of his finest vintages. I could not think how to tell him I could hardly tell the difference between a claret and a burgundy! Also whilst in Adelaide, I was taken to watch the South Australia Tennis Championships. Those were the halcyon days of Australian tennis—I had been privileged to watch Lew Hoad and Ken Rosewall win the Davis Cup tie against Seixas and Trabert of the USA at Kooyong, Melbourne.

My existence was not all big city glitter. A close friend was one Jim Grover, wartime subaltern in the Royal Marine Commandos, now a fellow member of the Victorian Harlequins and President of the English Speaking Union Younger Members. We had a mutual friend of Dutch extraction named Martyn Knottenbelt, who was a book reviewer and an intellectual. He had a very small 'hobby farm' in the beautiful Dandenong Mountains.

The three of us would often drive out there for a week-end and put in some strenuous work clearing scrub and landscaping the place. I was proud of a sizeable plot I cultivated and planted with sweet corn which came up and looked like yielding a good crop—until Martyn's one cow, Wilhelmena, got in and ate the lot! However, after hard work we could relax in front of a log fire, drink a tankard of mulled red wine, with cinnamon and lemon, eat a hearty dinner, listen to each other's tales of exploits in many countries and jointly sort out all the problems of the world!

I had several other ventures into the country as the guest of Doug Carnegie and his wife, on a large sheep station and Poll Hereford cattle stud named Kildrummie, at Holbrook, over the border in New South Wales. This acquaintance came about rather improbably through the governess the Carnegies had to help look after their youngest daughter, who had unfortunately suffered from polio. This governess had somehow tracked me down, having been the nanny/governess to my brother, sister and myself as children in Fiji twenty years back. It will be recalled that I reported earlier that we had been largely brought up by nannies as children. It must be assumed that this admirable person did a pretty good job as we did not grow up as uncontrollable monsters. Nevertheless, I cannot say that I had unbounded affection for our custodian. However, I am sure it was a kind thought on her part to ask the Carnegies if I could be invited to Kildrummie. I soon established a good rapport with Doug Carnegie and his wife but, unfortunately, found it difficult to think of anything to say to my old nanny.

Importantly for me, this provided a fascinating introduction to life on the land in Australia. I told my host that I would like to join in the work going on. He told me that I did not have to but could if I wished. This was country of lush green pastures but conducive to foot-rot for the sheep. I joined a team of four station hands, engaged in clipping sheep's feet for foot-rot. I will not inflict on my gentle readers the unpleasant details of this arduous work, beyond saying that it was smelly, messy and not for the squeamish. Initially, I did not fancy the clipping myself and so was assigned the job of 'catching'. This consisted of picking up a heavy sheep about every minute or so and dropping it, feet up, into a trough with hinged flap side, for release of the animal on the outside of a revolving turntable. I soon realised that this was far the hardest work job, quickly overcame my misgivings and took my turn at the clipping. The sheer number of sheep was daunting—as the charge-hand would say, 'The first ten thousand are the worst!' The satisfaction for me was getting to know these station hands who could not have been more friendly to me. I think I put in four days of that work but, one day, Doug invited me to come riding with him round the property. He was obviously a fine horseman and I felt I was a passable one, although I had not ridden since cantering through the canefields in Zululand with Mike Vaughan ten years back. The daughter of the house said, 'You'll be stiff tomorrow and unable to touch your toes.' I am happy to say I was not stiff and could still touch my toes! I would not ride a horse again until after leaving the Navy, when I would stay with Michael Kersey on his sheep grazing property in New South Wales.

On another visit, Doug told me a great deal about breeding poll Herefords and I was even allowed single-handedly to conduct the 'fostering' of six eleven-month-old stud bulls from a small herd of Jersey cows kept just for this. I found this fascinating as well as an extraordinary spectacle. Each young bull always went to the same foster 'mother' and looked almost absurd suckling from a cow only about two-thirds its own size. I soon knew all my young bulls and tried to evaluate from the breeding points Doug had told me, which had the best potential as a Royal Easter Show Champion. I was tickled pink when he said he was inclined to agree with my selection. Doug Carnegie's son, Rod, whom I only met once or twice, had recently returned from Oxford, where he had been a Rhodes Scholar. He was later to become a Captain of Australian Industry as Chairman of Conzinc Riotinto Australia (CRA)— Sir Rod Carnegie.

At length, my time in Australia came to an end. After a wonderful farewell party, with many friends collected from the various interlocking circles in which I moved, I sailed for UK aboard the *Orsova*. Is it surprising I would, one day, return—to stay?

CHAPTER 22

BULWARK

AFTER USUAL FOREIGN SERVICE LEAVE with my parents at Torquay, I put in two months at *Vernon*. TAS officers were expected to visit their base depot from time to time, no doubt to remind them they were TAS officers and let the TAS hierarchy view its adherents every now and then. I was delighted, as this enabled me to take in Cowes Week.

The next question now was where to send Messrs. Barratt, Woolley and Seymour. I had now completed my eight years as a Lieutenant and acquired an extra 'half stripe', as a Lieutenant Commander. Woolley and Barratt, slightly younger and of less seniority, would have to wait a little longer. I now hoped to be sent to a squadron of destroyers or frigates and start using the new hi-tech Sonar (as we now called Asdic) equipment and A/S weapons. But it was not to be. There were three new aircraft carriers commissioning, each requiring a TAS Officer. With three appearing out of the blue from Australia, the Appointments Officer's job was made easy. I said to myself, 'Not another carrier! When am I ever going to be able to put what I had learnt about A/S equipment, weapons and tactics to work?' Indeed, I finally left the Navy six years after qualifying in TAS, without ever serving in a warship with either a Sonar (Asdic) set or torpedoes! However, my name was not Joe Brooks (and I had no desire for three weeks under psychiatric observation at Haslar) and so I accepted my fate. In theory, as the senior one of our trio, I might have aspired to the biggest and most important of the three new carriers—the *Ark Royal*. But it was decided that as I had been ashore all my time in Australia, I should go to *Bulwark*—due to commission three months ahead of *Ark Royal*. Meanwhile, Barratt was appointed to *Albion*. In the event, *Ark Royal* and her sister *Eagle* would be the largest and most impressive ships in the Navy for the next fifteen years (twenty-two in the case of *Ark Royal*). But for me, contrary to my expectations, *Bulwark*'s first commission turned out to be stimulating and satisfying, even though involving negligible TAS activity.

Late September found me in Belfast for two weeks of 'standing-by' the nearly completed ship and familiarising myself with its layout. I selected a single cabin—outboard with port, on the starboard side, one deck below the hangar—which would remain mine for 2½ years.

During this time, I was happy to show Capt. Riddlesdell and his young son round the ship. He had been First Officer of *Oronsay* for my cruise to

Fiji. I would later see him as Staff Commander of *Oriana* (on her maiden voyage) when I migrated to Australia. Later still, he warmly greeted me aboard the *Canberra*, as senior Captain of P&O for an Atlantic crossing—from Miami to UK in 1971. Such was the comradeship of the sea. I also met up with Tom Winyeates when he had some time ashore at his home near Southampton. He would borrow my car while I was away from Portsmouth in *Bulwark*. Aboard *Oriana* he was the Chief Officer. One could say 'Small World' or 'Small Oceans'!

I was back in Portsmouth for the first three weeks of October, at the Royal Naval Barracks, where the main body of the ship's company were being assembled. My main assignment was to work through the list of several hundred seamen and, as far as possible, find round holes for round pegs, for a large number of special duties ranging from Ship's Office Writer, through Commander's Messenger to Chaplain's Yeoman. With the Chief Boatswain's mate (designate) I interviewed every seaman and we did what we could to meet all requirements. We also tried to arrange for friends—old shipmates, perhaps—to be in the same mess. Looking back, this would have been much simpler with a computer. However, we did our best and our efforts were appreciated. My final assignment at Portsmouth was to plan the accommodation for, and assume command of, the special Commissioning Train. This was to convey some seven hundred men all the way from the Barracks' own siding to Heysham in Lancashire, whence the overnight ferry would transport us to Belfast. This must have been one of the last such trains to move the main body of a new ship's company from Portsmouth Barracks to the commissioning point. The undertaking started well. I had the ten carriages manned by different branches of ratings, special coaches for Chief and Petty Officers and, in accordance with tradition, the dozen odd officers in the 'Wardroom' at the rear of the train. Also by tradition, dating from the mutinies at the Nore (nearly two hundred years back), the Marines were placed immediately forward of the 'Wardroom', notionally between mutinous sailors and the officers!

The Barracks gave us a good send-off. The Commodore farewelled us in person and the Command Band played on the platform. The route was interesting, in that the train managed to weave into London from the south-west and out again to the north-west, without stopping. We reached Heysham that evening without a hitch. Thereafter, I had had nothing to do with the planning—of which there had been none. It was a cold, wet and windy night and there was no planned sleeping accommodation for the men who were just expected to bed down in their uniforms anywhere they could in corridors or any nook or cranny they could find. I did what I could and appealed to the Captain to issue any spare blankets on board, but was told there were none. I could do no more than walk round and make encouraging noises to the huddled groups of men. I told them it was only one night and they would be aboard a fine new ship next day. Thank Heavens, I had previously talked the Commander out of his silly idea to form up the disembarked men and march them through the streets of Belfast.

As it was, the first day was one of confusion for the weary sailors, just trying to find their way around this strange big ship. Slowly things sorted themselves out and some sort of order emerged from chaos. But when we finally commissioned and sailed from Belfast under the White Ensign for the first time, morale was far from high. It was now midwinter and the weather was foul for our journey round the north of Scotland to our initial work-up base of Invergordon. The place looked much less inviting than when I had last been there aboard *Orwell* preparing for the Normandy operations ten years before. It was bitterly cold with practically nothing to do ashore. Perhaps I was feeling the contrast from sunny Australia. Unfortunately, the ship's company had yet to settle down and morale remained low. This was aggravated by our not over-imaginative Commander who was very keen on ceremonial (like marching through the streets of Belfast). He felt it important that there should be Sunset and Colours ceremonies night and morning. I am sure no one would have noticed from the shore and our own ship's company would not be up on the flight deck unless they simply had to be. In order to hoist and lower the ensign it took five men to rig and unrig the ensign staff at the after end of the flight deck. Yet the colours would no sooner be hoisted each morning than the whole thing would have to come down so that we could go to sea for trials.

After a few days of this, not altogether surprisingly, two or three sailors decided to put an end to this nonsense by tossing the ensign staff overboard. The Commander insisted on regarding this far more seriously than I did—as an open act of defiance, disloyalty to the flag, and tantamount to mutiny. He harangued the whole ship's company over the public address system and stopped all leave until the perpetrators of this shameful act came forward or were apprehended. This vaguely reminded me of the famous Dartmouth Ice Cream Robbery of '42. (I suspect our Commander was not a product of Dartmouth.) I am not sure whether the villains were found or owned up. Next day, shore leave was restored, but not before the gutter press had descended on Invergordon. The upshot was a headline right across the top of the Scottish edition of the *Daily Express*: TROUBLE IN CARRIER IN MUTINY PORT. At Invergordon, there had been a token fleet mutiny in 1919 (totally irrelevant as I imagine few of our ship's company had even heard of it).

This was to be my first 'baptism of fire' in the role for which I had volunteered, and received special instruction, namely the ship's Press

Bulwark—First Commission 1954–7. Bulwark *under full power.*
A solitary World War II 'Avenger' was our 'mail van'.

Liaison and Public Relations Officer. It is hard to see how I could have
headed off this incident. On the other hand, it opened my eyes to how
some sections of the media worked. Far from wishing to help this fine
new ship settle down and take her proud place with the fleet, there was
a ghoulish desire to do as much stirring as possible. No doubt there would
have been great joy in Fleet Street if they could have a follow-up story
reporting that the Captain and officers had been cast adrift at sea. Ideally
the ship would have steamed at high speed—with women collected *en
route*—to set up a utopian colony on Tristan da Cunha! Sadly—for the
press—their *agents provocateurs* achieved nothing. My own (TAS) Petty
Officer told me that one of these Gentlemen of the Press appeared in the
POs' 'wet canteen' ashore. I asked what happened and he simply told me,
'We passed him through the window'! Perhaps this made him a martyr
in the eyes of his employers—a zealous seeker of wisdom and truth,
suffering at the hands of barbaric thugs of a repressive system! For me
'useful lessons were learnt' and on nearly all occasions thereafter I either
had the media on my side—or was a jump ahead of them. Needless to
say, this particular incident was soon forgotten. Morale steadily improved
to the point that, by the end of the commission, any one of our sailors
would have 'knocked the block off' anybody saying a word against *Bulwark*.
There will be more tales of encounters with the media—some 'landmark',
such as the first-ever live TV broadcast from a ship at sea, and others
absurd, like the Cautionary Tale of Peaches Page (a stripper)!

Bulwark commissioned not as an operational carrier but as the so-called Trials and Training Carrier. Our role was to sea-test new-design carrier aircraft as they were developed and 'work-up' newly formed operational squadrons before they went to carriers in commission. Accordingly, we were not part of the Home Fleet but under the direct command of C-in-C Portsmouth. All our radar and equipment related to flying was operational but our anti-aircraft guns remained cocooned. Nevertheless, at least once a year, the ship would participate in a major NATO exercise and have operational aircraft flying from our deck. Such exercises would take us up to the Arctic Circle and into Norwegian fjords.

For the most part, however, we would operate in waters close to UK 'showing the flag' at a different port or anchorage each week-end. Some visits were paid to European ports and these proved highlights. They included Oslo, Stockholm, Copenhagen and Cherbourg. In all these ports both officers and ratings were treated most hospitably but I need not go into details. There were, however, unusual aspects regarding the visits to Oslo and Stockholm.

Bulwark went to Oslo so that Admiral of the Fleet Sir John Cunningham (not to be confused with Andrew—of Hyndhope), could present to King Olaf of Norway some relics of the cruiser *Devonshire*. The latter, under Cunningham's command, had evacuated the Norwegian Royal Family in 1940. Normally, an Admiral of the Fleet (comparable with Field Marshal) never serves at sea and is usually given this rank at the end of his active service. Exceptionally, the First Sea Lord could be an Admiral of the Fleet and, in 1955 Commander in Chief, Portsmouth was Admiral of the Fleet Sir George Creasy. (It was his brother, Sir Gerald, who was Governor of Malta, and to whose PA I had become so attached.) By tradition, C-in-C Portsmouth technically had a flagship, at the masthead of which he flew his flag. This flagship never went anywhere—and had not even been afloat for sixty years. She was, of course, HMS *Victory*—

Captain Villiers and C-in-C Home Fleet Admiral Sir Michael Denny, Stockholm 1955.

Nelson's flagship at Trafalgar. But as she 'wore' the flag of the highest ranking officer in the Royal Navy, outside Admiralty, every warship entering Portsmouth Dockyard saluted her. Big ships would sound off with a bugler and small ones with a boatswain's call and the ship's company, fallen in for entering harbour, would come to attention. The *Victory* must have been so saluted for a hundred years.

However, in theory, Admirals of the Fleet never retire—they are simply removed from the Active list (it is incorrect to add 'Rtd.' at the end of an Admiral of the Fleet's name on an envelope addressed to him). Thus, when we embarked Sir John Cunningham, although off the Active List for some years, he came aboard in full uniform, and we hoisted the Union Jack to the masthead. For perhaps the first time in history, HMS *Victory* had to sound off to a warship leaving harbour. This may be dismissed as an item of insignificant trivia—but such things are felt worth recording in the Royal Navy. We even refurbished our (never otherwise used) Admiral's bridge in case the great man felt like pacing it to give him a warm feeling of being at sea in command once again. The Oslo visit proceeded smoothly and uneventfully.

The Stockholm visit was intended as a major fleet visit under C-in-C Home Fleet. Sadly though, the Home Fleet seemed to have very few impressive-looking warships with which to 'show the flag'. Indeed, the Commander in Chief was reduced to flying his flag aboard the small cruiser/minelayer *Apollo* and was accompanied by four A/S frigates. This was puny compared with the two aircraft carriers, three cruisers and two flotillas of destroyers Admiral Willis had taken to Istanbul nine years earlier. The answer was to throw in *Bulwark*—a brand new 27,000 ton carrier—and hopefully no one would ask why the guns were cocooned. In the event, as the Press Liaison Officer charged with acting for the 'fleet', I had to field far more 'curly'—though seemingly innocuous—questions.

The climax of the visit was the inspection by HM King Gustav Adolf of not only *Bulwark*'s crew but contingents from all the other ships. As the King was elderly and frail, it would have been unrealistic for him to walk past and inspect over a thousand men. Accordingly, the ship's own Land Rover (for general purpose use in port) had been really worked on and was the most chromium-plated such vehicle in existence. The King was to be driven sedately around the serried ranks of sailors, in the manner of the Pontiff in the later 'Popemobile' but without bullet-proof glass. With augmented central band of the Royal Marines, brought specially, and the ship smartened to the utmost, an impressive display was planned. My own arrangements were extensive. I had a list naming every reporter, photographer and film cameraman coming. For all twenty-five of these, I had a personalised information kit, with details of the ships present and answers to all the questions I could conceive. Furthermore, I had all the sixteen

Midshipmen thoroughly briefed, and allocated them to look after no more than two media people each. I had permission for photographers to leap in front of the Royal Land Rover to get a good shot, regardless of how this might impair the overall spectacle. In other words, I felt the image presented to the Swedish nation was more important than that given to His Swedish Majesty. I had fallen over backwards to be helpful to the media. Was I rewarded? Was I hell!

The inspection went like clockwork and on completion, the Midshipmen duly marshalled their charges on the top of the island superstructure. I had planned this to give them the best view possible of the King's departure in the Royal Barge, while the sailors lined the edge of the flight deck giving three rousing cheers for HM. In the five-minute interval between the conclusion of the inspection and the King's departure, I did my affable best to answer a barrage of questions. None seemed unreasonable like, 'How many floggings have been held this week?' Accordingly, I really felt I was winning this time. Only one question seemed more earnestly asked than I expected. A group of reporters wanted to know all about the RN's time-honoured tradition of 'Splice the Mainbrace'—a double issue of rum to all sailors. Asked when this happened, I replied, 'Usually, when our Sovereign inspects a warship or the fleet' (and did not add 'or when a junior officer from Australia thinks it would be a good idea, after just winning a war'!). The reporters scribbled and asked, 'Will our King order "Splice the Mainbrace" today?' I replied that, although our men would be delighted, regrettably protocol did not provide for their King doing this aboard British warships. I was sure of my ground as it had been mooted that perhaps the Swedish King could do this, as an Honorary Admiral of the Fleet of the RN. I did not mention this last but the reporters still scribbled.

Next morning there was a magnificent photo of the King riding past inspecting the crews. But the story, as the most prominent item in that day's *Svenska Dagbladet*, went SPLICE THE MAINBRACE (in English), followed by a mass of Swedish which I could not understand. I rushed to the Swedish naval liaison officer assigned to us and asked him what was printed. He groaned and then smiled, saying, 'It's not your fault—I'll have to explain.' My heart sank. What could all this mean?

He read out, 'SPLICE THE MAINBRACE—the signal that was not made. All the sailors were waiting for the king to order this—to authorise an extra issue of rum . . .'

'Why on earth should they print that?' I asked.

For several reasons, he told me, namely: this paper was republican-slanted anyway, keen to report that the King had done the wrong thing; the Liquor Laws were a hot political issue in Sweden; and, finally, the King was personally a total abstainer!

I groaned, 'Talk about Traps for young Press Liaison Officers!' I instantly took a boat to *Apollo* to 'get my oar in' with the Admiral's Chief of Staff—before he sent for me. Apart from this, I had a wonderful time in Stockholm.

Before proceeding to other matters, I should recount some more of my involvement with the media, which proved almost my major preoccupation. In addition to incidents reported there would be press releases and handouts as well as occasional press conferences. In mid 1955, the Admiralty asked us to provide a press facility, mainly for Midland and Northern provincial newspapers. The thought was that many recruits came from such areas but their families saw little of the Navy and read less in their local papers. Journalists were invited to come and spend three days on board at sea observing life aboard a warship at first hand. Hopefully, they would also find a local lad from Wigan or Macclesfield to feature. About twenty reporters from local newspapers jumped at the invitation, had their few days aboard, wrote glowing articles and every one was happy. But such an invitation had to be made to the press in general. It was ignored by Fleet Street with the exception of one national daily (my mistrust of the Fourth Estate still cautions me against identifying the paper involved). Their naval reporter was the recognised doyen of Fleet Street naval journalists and turned up to my surprise with his own photographer (we had offered all photographic support needed). The invitation had stated that the exercising would include the historic first carrier landings of jet fighters by Reservist pilots. This man belonged to the 'Oh-for-a-train-smash' school and felt that, if he was lucky, one of the nervous inexperienced pilots might crash his plane and kill himself. This might well lead to the prize-winning press photo of the year! This became evident when the reporter drew me aside and said, 'Of course we all hope nothing will go wrong but, if it should, you realise that it is our duty to report all news—good or bad.' Under my breath I muttered, 'You hypocritical BASTARD!' Happily, for me, the pilots, and the Navy, everything went smoothly. Our guests left with profuse expressions of appreciation. For this one man, however, I could not resist saying with a smile, 'Bad Luck'—and was glowered at in reply. I scored this as a love-game win over the media, solely attributable to ace serves by the pilots!

The next encounter was an unqualified success, but the medium concerned (the BBC) did not come aboard for a 'blood-match'. Far from it; there was unlimited cooperation from the start. I cannot claim to have initiated the project, arranged at Admiralty level and largely masterminded on board by our Commander (Air). However, I had a significant coordinating role. The whole exercise was for two days' worth of mostly live TV camera coverage of life aboard an aircraft carrier at sea. The commentary was in the hands of some of the very top BBC TV personalities of the day, such as Richard Dimbleby. For the third day, with all the BBC equipment still aboard, there was to be a live telecast of a concert in harbour, in the hangar, with top entertainers. 'So what?' today's viewers might well ask. But in 1955, this was a great technical challenge. The first Russian Sputnik had yet to be launched, and it was years before the first communications satellite. Accordingly, TV transmissions were still limited to 'line-of-sight' range. Furthermore, the signal, of relatively low power and transmitted from the ship, had to be carried in a narrow beam to an amplifying and relaying station ashore. The tall radio towers at Ventnor, Isle of Wight, were used while the ship transmitted via a Close Range Blind Fire Director, gyro stabilised for roll and ship-head-

Members of the Tiller Girls chorus— Copenhagen 1955. This was before the days of women at sea in the Navy!

ing. Everything went remarkably well. But it was strange, hearing a helicopter doing a rescue demonstration visible through the wardroom port, whilst watching this live on our TV, via Ventnor and London.

The concert was a huge success, starring such notable performers as Jon Pertwee, Eric Barker, Fred Emney, Jill Day, Shirley Abicair, Shani Wallis, plus the Tiller Girls Chorus. Shani Wallis had such a clinging costume, permitting movement from the knees down only, that she had no hope of ascending our steep ladders. It was not an arduous duty for me to carry her as required! We would next see the Tiller Girls in Copenhagen when they came aboard in their mini-skirted sailor suits while the ship was open to visitors.

The final media episode was probably a drawn game, although at one stage I was down Love-Forty. As background, the forty strong RAF Staff Course was visiting Portsmouth to learn about the Navy. *Bulwark*, refitting, had spare cabins and accommodated ten officers. By mutual arrangement, on their first evening, they were entertained in various wardrooms. The Course Officers were then taken by the various hosts to see an unpretentious Revue at the Coliseum Theatre, Portsmouth. Unpretentious was probably a generous description but I felt it would be unkind to write 'rubbish'! One of the billed star performers was a stripper, known as Peaches Page, who had a new gimmick. The regulations for such shows were determined by the Lord Chamberlain,* who ruled that women could legitimately appear, totally undressed, in artistic poses—provided they did not move. They were not even permitted to sing in the nude. Peaches's gimmick was to pose while a recording was played of her singing. Sadly for Peaches, whilst performing her act in another seaside town, a mouse had run on to the stage. The artiste had fled in terror, with a shriek, while her recorded voice crooned on. She had broken the Lord Chamberlain's rules but as her crime was clearly not pre-meditated she escaped retribution by the law. Her enterprising agent, however, on the premise that any publicity was good, practically had her billed as the Mouse Girl by now.

Unexpected by me and the rest of the audience—including the RN and RAF officers—the four theatre boxes were filled by *Bulwark*'s Midshipmen. They were all wearing white collars back to front—like clergy—and looking as if butter wouldn't melt in their mouths. The appearance of so many young ministers at a low strip show caused surprise amongst the audience. However, the Midshipmen remained poker-faced until the moment of poor Peaches's act, whereupon, predictably, a dozen white mice on handkerchief parachutes descended to the stage. The curtain came down quickly and the show ended in uproar—but with Peaches melodious voice singing on! By now, the management, expecting trouble, had the police in attendance. The Midshipmen were arrested, 'questioned' and released. Everyone—except the unhappy Peaches Page—felt it had all been 'good clean fun'. My worries started next morning with a short three-inch column item in the *Daily Sketch*, reporting the incident quite factually—attributing it to 'a number of young men in clerical garb, believed to have been naval officers in disguise'. Not much harm—so far. But, next day, the alarm bells started to ring for me when the same paper had a follow-up story. This reported that the 'Middies' of HMS *Bulwark* had invited Miss 'Peaches' Page, and other members of the company playing at the Coliseum, aboard their ship for a drink, to apologise for the incident on Monday night, when white mice had descended onto the stage. This report took up about 6″ of column. My ship's name was cited, interest in the matter was growing, and this was not the publicity I sought.

My fears were confirmed that morning, when by 1000 I had received 'phone calls from the *News of the World* and half the national newspapers. Their requests were the same—could they please send a reporter and photographer to cover the 'Middies' and Miss Page. I had visions of Peaches doing a strip-tease act on the Gunroom table for the Midshipmen

---

* Other than making Rules for Strippers, I had no idea what else the Lord Chamberlain did! (See Appendix 2)

and having this all over the front pages of the more lurid national press. It was time for me to warn the Captain, who had been quite amused by the initial report, but now saw the dangers ahead. He declared, 'She is not coming aboard my ship.' I advised him to tread warily or we could have a headline 'CAPTAIN BANS PEACHES'. He said, 'They would not do that.' I had to advise that in my view this is just what they would do. Captain Villiers was a veteran officer and I feel sure had never flinched in the face of the enemy, but now he positively blenched. He said he would have taken the ship to sea, but we were in dry dock. What could we do? I suggested an immediate notice of a Harbour Damage Control Exercise at the time in question, when, of course, no visitors could possibly be allowed aboard. Such announcement was made—and cancelled as soon as it was safe to do so. The Midshipmen were given a metaphorical kick in the pants and told to entertain the 'damned woman' in the Keppel's Head saloon bar. The press was not told this until it would be too late for them to get there. Even this was not the end of the story. I still had to suffer a half page article in the local *Hampshire Telegraph and Post* by the RSPCA on the theme 'Unfair to White Mice'!

So much for the media. With negligible TAS responsibilities I had volunteered for several other jobs including Sports Officer. I would like to quote a few highlights from the chapter on the Commission's Sport from the ship's First Commission commemorative pamphlet—which I wrote myself forty years ago!

> One of the difficulties about the role of trials and training carrier is that the ship is so seldom with the Home Fleet that there is little chance to take part in fleet competitions. Thus most of our sport has been in the form of Inter-part Competitions and Ship matches arranged with any team that would play us. Furthermore the ship's programme was not favourable for sport. Most of the time the ship was at Portsmouth there would either be a watch away on leave or everybody would be working flat out getting the ship painted . . . Notwithstanding the above, I think that many people will remember *Bulwark* for the amount of sport they did get onboard.

Mention is made of several matches which were played and won against Home Fleet ships including defeating *Glasgow* at soccer and our eventual defeat at rugby by the mighty *Eagle* in the final of a competition for aircraft carriers. Regarding cross-country running, I am happy to be able to quote:

> *Bulwark* entered for the Arbuthnott Trophy H.F. event in September 1955 and somewhat humbled the Home Fleet by winning it with almost 100 points over the next contenders.

I continued:

During the commission the ship will have completed three inter-part Deck

Hockey Competitions, one Soccer, one Cricket and one Tug of War, apart from a multi-sport competition which was held in the Spring of 1956 for the magnificent Rosebowl presented by the B.I.A. [British Insurance Association], which had 'adopted' the ship . . . The B.I.A. Competition was a unique event in which six groups competed on a league basis in six sports—the trophy going to the highest aggregate scorers. The sports played were Soccer, Water Polo, Tug of War, Deck Hockey, .22 Rifle Shooting and a Whaler Race (pulling). Excitement became intense as different groups excelled at different sports. The final result was a tie for first place between the Junior Engine Room and the Chief and Petty Officers . . .

I thoroughly enjoyed running the ship's sport. I had a weekly 'spot' on the ship's Sound Reproduction Equipment (Entertainment Programme) called the *Bulwark* Sports Review, complete with its own signature tune— the opening bars of The Entry of the Boyards. I am happy to say this programme enjoyed 'top ratings' throughout the commission.

Another job for which I volunteered was Seaman Boys' Divisional Officer. This was something I had thoroughly enjoyed aboard *Gravelines*. I put a lot of effort into this duty and did my best both to enthuse and to educate these young sixteen- and seventeen-year-olds. I would try hard to persuade some officer to give the Boys a talk on a general knowledge subject once a week. I believe I managed to engender an *esprit de corps* amongst the Boys of both ships. The *Gravelines*'s Boys earned a commendation for having their tents erected and ready for occupation first at a camp for Boys of the Fleet at Marmaris, where, with my mates, I was 'rowing my guts out'. I would like to think some at least of these were commissioned. I know one of my *Gravelines* Boys, Tim Humphreys, reached Lieutenant Commander, and Bob Perry, Leading Seaman of the Boys' Division, became a Commander.

The only other activity that concerned me personally was the one element of TAS I had left, namely Diving. As the ship might conceivably be required for operational service I had to have a shallow-water diving team (using oxygen closed-circuit rebreathing lung, with CO_2 absorbent canister) capable of carrying out a methodical search of the whole of the underwater hull for limpet mines in a matter of minutes. Volunteers to train for this were accepted from all departments and we never lacked starters. I often dived myself with the team, on training exercises. Displays of all sorts of diving, including time-honoured Standard Diving in suit and brass helmet, would be staged at most ports we visited. At Torquay, our divers proved their usefulness by laying a whole line of new moorings in the outer harbour.

The Torbay visit was significant to me as it was the only time in my seventeen years after leaving Dartmouth that I had the pleasure of calling in at my home town. In fact, my Captain, perhaps feeling particularly benevolent, on a Thursday afternoon during Flying Training off the Channel Islands sent for me on the bridge. He said there were one or two arrangements he would like to check regarding our week-end in Torbay and would like me to 'go ashore' and fix things up. He told me he knew my home was at Torquay and so I could stop overnight and he would see me the following evening. This was my first introduction to a new concept of life at sea. Hitherto I had always considered that, once at sea, one stayed there until the ship returned to port and vice versa. The advent of helicopters changed all that. I was told to grab an overnight bag and a 'chopper' would be ready to take me in fifteen minutes. I took off on schedule and forty minutes later was alighting on the playing fields of RN College Dartmouth—right alongside the canteen, scene of the Great Ice Cream Robbery of '42. This time I was there under very different circumstances, greeted by the Officer of the Day and shown into a shiny black car, to be driven to my home at Torquay, fourteen miles away.

I have made scant reference to date of the ship's main role—operating aircraft. This is because as far as the flying was concerned I was only a member of the supporting cast, also because, having no squadrons of our own—merely ones embarked for a couple of weeks at a time—I had little chance to get to know many airmen. Nevertheless, the animosity between Fly-Boys and Fish-heads, evident aboard *Ocean*, was now a thing of the past or, at most, a matter of good-humoured banter. We had one fixed-wing plane of our own—a World War II Avenger for mail runs and general-purpose use. The pilot, Lt. Cdr. Carmichael (who also flew helicopters) became a good mate of mine and took me up for the odd flight in his Avenger. He was later to play an unkind practical joke on me, but I did not mind, and I feel he knew I would not mind—more on this anon. There is always some drama associated with flying, particularly jet aircraft from carriers, and some planes and aircrew were lost during the commission—but only a fraction of the losses I had known aboard *Ocean*.

There were a number of 'ditched' aircraft from which the aircrew were quickly winched to safety by our rescue helicopter. Such choppers could not operate at night when a 'plane-guard' destroyer would be required. During one session of flying training for a squadron of night-fighter Sea Venoms, a remarkable—almost miraculous—incident occurred. Through a partial failure of our starboard steam catapult, the Sea Venom of the Squadron CO and his observer was launched with insufficient airspeed to become airborne. The plane gently 'pancaked' into the sea, albeit at 50 knots, and immediately started to sink. The aircraft had ditched about four hundred yards ahead of the ship, which, in light winds, was bearing down on the plane at 30 knots. I suspect ninety-nine out of a hundred people placed as that pilot was would only have thought, 'Let me out of here!'

With incredible cool-headedness, the pilot sat tight until he heard the thrashing propellers of the carrier pass right over them. Only then did both aircrew eject, and bob to the surface, presumably from about fifty feet down. Their Mae-West lights were quickly spotted by the planeguard destroyer and they were back aboard *Bulwark* fifteen minutes later!

Finally, I was, of course, aboard *Bulwark* as a Seaman Officer and had my responsibilities as a bridge watch-keeping officer. Although I had been doing this for years, great concentration was needed to keep a 27,000 ton ship, manoeuvring at 30 knots, perhaps on rapidly changing courses, out of trouble. Furthermore, as with driving a car one must also allow for possible errors of the 'other driver'. I had a worrying moment one forenoon on the bridge during flying operations up near the Dover end of the English Channel. This is about the busiest shipping bottleneck in the world, with ships to and from the major ports of northern Europe *en route* from and to the rest of the world. We seldom carried out flying training in those waters and I cannot recall the reason for doing so this time. Be that as it may, we had tried to find some clear water, worked up to full power—to attain enough wind-speed over the deck, in light airs—and launched six Seahawk jets. We steamed back down-wind avoiding the shipping lanes as best we could until it was time to recover our aircraft. On the Captain's orders, I turned the ship into wind, the jets joined the landing circuit, International Flag F was hoisted and we prepared to receive the planes. At this point, I noted a large merchant ship about 30 degrees on our port bow approaching on a converging course. I took an accurate bearing and made a quick radar check of the distance—five miles—making a mental note to watch this one closely.

A minute or so later, when I checked again, the range was four miles and the bearing unchanged. If two ships remain on constant bearings they must collide, unless one alters course. I alerted the Captain who also started watching this ship closely—just as the first jet landed. *Bulwark* had right of way, on two counts. Flag F means 'Am operating aircraft—all ships keep clear' (apart from the fact that the planes could be seen landing). Secondly, as we were on the other ship's starboard bow, they were required to give way, aircraft or no aircraft. The Captain exclaimed, 'Surely they can see us,' being now only 2½ miles away, and the bearing still steady. He then called to Commander (Air), 'Hold it, Wings—you may have to stop the planes landing—we've got an idiot here who looks as if he is keen to run into us.' Commander (Air) mentioned that the planes had only a few minutes fuel left. 'Can't help it, Wings', as I reported, 'Range now one mile—bearing unchanged.'

'My God!' said the Captain, 'They are mad—stop the landings.'

Red flares were fired and the planes told by radio to remain aloft. The Captain shouted down the voice pipe, 'STOP BOTH. FULL ASTERN

BOTH ENGINES.' Engineroom telegraphs clanged and the ship juddered as the engines went from Full Ahead to Full Astern. Three short blasts (My Engines Are Going Astern) were sounded.

It was still going to take a mile to stop the ship but she started slowing immediately. The other ship, a 10,000 ton Swedish cargo/passenger liner, steamed across our bows with under a cable (200 yards) to spare without altering one degree. We could even see passengers waving cheerily at us. They never knew how close they were to scrambling for the lifeboats! My Captain was nearly apoplectic and called, 'Yeoman, call them and make . . . What's the use—they probably can't read Morse . . . Okay, Wings, get the other planes on.'

This incident never reached the newspapers but could so easily have proved a Roman Holiday for Fleet Street. I can see the headlines: DISASTER IN CHANNEL—RN CARRIER CUTS SWEDISH LINER IN TWO—HUNDREDS MISSING. This story illustrates the hazards ships at sea still face, nearly always through gross human incompetence or negligence. *Bulwark*'s Captain was almost placed in a 'No Win' situation. Had the Swedes woken up at the last moment, realised they were supposed to go astern of us and ordered 'Hard-a-Starboard', they would have hit us amidships. They might then have claimed they would have cleared our stern had *Bulwark* not gone 'Full Astern'. Something like this occurred with the collision between the Swedish liner *Stockholm* and the brand new 29,000 ton Italian *Andrea Doria*, sunk off New York. Somehow one expects negligence with Panamanian and Liberian-registered ships but not vessels from countries with centuries of maritime history behind them such as Sweden and Italy. I would have to add Britain to the list of unlikely, but actual, offenders. In fact it was in these very waters that Scrym and I had played ducks and drakes amongst the invasion convoys—but we had not been incompetent, although a tad foolhardy.

On a lighter note, there was one other item of seamanship that also occurred when the author was on watch one afternoon in the Irish Sea. Briefly, we found a 300-ton Dutch coaster (with a cargo of potatoes) which had broken down in a rough sea. Communication was difficult as we could not establish radio contact and they did not use signal lamps. We eventually resorted to sending over a 'chopper' which lowered a basket with a pad and pen! This enabled them to pass to us the two-word message: ENGINE KAPUT. *Bulwark* towed them to Milford Haven. The story is only of note because I doubt whether, in the Annals of the Sea, such a small ship had ever been salvaged by such a large one. *Bulwark* could only steer at 10 knots in the strong wind blowing, but this little ship had probably never travelled at more than 6 under her own power. They must have looked like a dinghy behind a large motor yacht. It was almost as though the *QEII* had stopped to salvage a fishing trawler.

Salvage in the RN earned one a share of established rewards for marine salvage. Benefits could be substantial but, ideally, one needed to be a crew member of a very small ship single-handedly salvaging an abandoned large one with a cargo of gold bullion. I received 7s. 6d. for my part in the salvage of m.v. *Rigel* and her cargo of spuds! My main concern was to exploit the potential publicity of this heroic saving of life at sea. I told my Captain we could have a film crew hovering over our charge, zooming in on the frantic face of the Captain's wife. We could have the film processed in half an hour and flown to London in time for the evening TV News bulletins. I had received so much 'stick' from the media they would have to give prominence to this drama of the sea. Alas, my Captain was of the Old School silent service all-in-the-days-work type and would not agree. Ah well, I tried!

This is about where the *Bulwark* section of this book should have ended. The ship was at the Isles of Scilly* for the weekend with one more week's flying programmed, and a last weekend at Penzance. It would then be back to Portsmouth to pay-off, refit, and recommission.

I had spent a happy day with my divers in the crystal clear waters amongst the rocks of an uninhabited island where we were able to exercise with underwater explosives. On return to the ship, the weather looked threatening. All boats were hoisted after libertymen had been brought off. As the wind rose, with the ship in a relatively open roadstead, the engineroom was brought to short notice for steam and an 'anchor watch' set. But those in the sky were not the only storm clouds gathering—there was trouble brewing in the Near East. Instead of a last week of flying training, a festive week-end at Penzance and then the end of the commission, a very different future lay ahead. In ten days, the ship would be in the Mediterranean, at war not long afterwards and not back at Portsmouth to pay off for another four and a half months.

BULWARK PREPARES FOR WAR

By midnight on 28 July 1956, a signal arrived, ordering *Bulwark* to leave the Isles of Scilly, return to Portsmouth forthwith, prepare for active service, and proceed to the Mediterranean with all despatch. I do not know whether this rather archaic terminology is used in the Navy today. But in the fifties, 'forthwith' meant 'at once', not as soon as is convenient, and no 'ifs' or 'buts'. 'With all despatch' meant as quickly as you can, giving the matter absolute priority, with no shore leave or other

---

* The Locals tend to get upset by the term 'The Scilly Isles'

constraints. At anchor off St Mary's, Isles of Scilly, on receipt of this signal, the Captain would simply say to the Commander something like, 'Okay, let's go.' The Engineer Commander would be told to raise steam for Full Power as quickly as possible, Special Sea Dutymen would 'close up' (assume their stations) and the Cable Party would head for the fo'c'sle. The Bridge would order 'Weigh anchor' and, within fifteen minutes, the ship would be under way and working up to full speed.

On this occasion, however, immediate departure would have been far too hazardous—in the dark, in the teeth of a gale, now blowing Force 10, through a tortuous rock-strewn entrance to the roadstead. I had the morning (anchor) watch on the bridge and was soon being handed numerous Mayday distress signals from yachts in trouble. These were in a major Ocean Race and had been caught unawares by the gale which had got up without warning.

At first light, the Captain and Navigator were on the bridge, the ship weighed and we were soon headed up-Channel at full speed. Without slowing the ship, our helicopter was busy rescuing injured yachtsmen and crews from craft that had been lost.

The late afternoon of 29 July found *Bulwark* alongside in Portsmouth at the start of seven days of feverish activity by everyone on board. Our training aircraft were gone and hundreds of lorry loads of stores were embarked. All our Bofors AA guns were de-cocooned and checked and many thousand rounds of ammunition were taken aboard for these.

More personnel were embarked to bring all departments up to full strength as well as maintenance staff for three squadrons of Seahawk jet fighters. Full spare part inventories for these were needed and large quantities of bombs, rockets, belt ammunition for aircraft cannon and a hundred boxed aircraft fuel drop-tanks. The last had to be placed in the hangar as well as other stores until they could be properly stowed. Finally, the ship had to be fully reprovisioned for a further three months and, of course, fully fuelled. Seldom have men worked so hard over seven days to turn a training ship into a fully operational warship. There was no grand send-off, but Admiral Creasy who had great affection for, and pride in, *Bulwark*, came down and wished us Godspeed. Also, many of the Dockyard civilian workmen, who had themselves worked very hard, were there to see us on our way. Although weary, I am sure every officer and rating aboard felt proud of our ship as we steamed out of Portsmouth. Once at sea, Squadron Nos. 804, 810 and 895—thirty Seahawks—and the Ship's Flight (Avenger and Helicopters) were flown aboard and we set course for the Mediterranean.

About to be refitted, *Bulwark*'s underwater hull was badly fouled with weed and barnacles—slowing us too much for war service. Accordingly, the ship steamed straight into the dry dock at Gibraltar. In forty-eight hours, the ship was given about the quickest bottom scrape and anti-fouling in history and we were on our way again, to join *Eagle* and *Albion* at Malta.

All this rushing had given many people the impression that we could expect to be in action within days. Realistically, however, we had to work-up and practise operating as part of a Carrier Task Force, and working with the two French carriers *Lafayette* and *Arromanches*. Further-more, negotiations to try to get Colonel Nasser to be reasonable were still proceeding. Our training programme continued for two months until 13 October. Tension eased slightly and the ship had an enjoyable few days at Marseilles in late September and also two at Syracuse, Sicily—yet all the time *Bulwark* was becoming ever more efficient and better prepared for fighting. For me, there were two incidents I will not forget.

Although still having minimal TAS responsibilities, I was now the ship's Operations Room Officer. For this, I had much to learn during our work-up, in preparation for taking part in large scale fleet operations. I found the role interesting and stimulating. But when not working with the other carriers I was relatively lightly employed, and so, available for odd jobs.

One such was Range Officer, in radio contact with, and spotting for, rocket-firing Seahawks practising on a marker offshore, from a bare cliff-top at Marsaxlokk, Malta. I was landed by boat in the early morning at the little harbour where my MFV had been all but wrecked eight years before, and driven to my cliff-top look-out. All went smoothly and I was impressed by the precision of our Seahawk's rocket-firing. On completion, rather than the lengthy road and boat ride back to the ship, a helicopter was sent for me. This chopper could easily have landed on the flat rock, and I could have stepped aboard. But my alleged mate 'Hogie' Carmichael was not going to let me off as easily as that. He insisted on lowering the lifting strop and wire. I had not been so lifted before, but knew the drill. I placed the harness round me under the armpits, pulled down the grommet and gave the hoist signal. But instead of telling his crewman to winch up, Hogie had him do nothing. He lifted the aircraft and proceeded to fly around the southern end of Malta a few hundred feet above the ground, while I dangled thirty feet below the chopper. I was powerless to do more than shake my fist at Carmichael as he looked down from the plane with a huge grin on his face!

While the ship was at Syracuse, I joined with James Clarke, the Captain of Marines (a close friend) and another officer to lead a MEDFOBA party up Mount Etna. We took the first thirty of many volunteers, from all departments. It will be recalled that I had made this ascent before and so there were no problems. However, there was no stay at the Grande Albergo Etna this time—we slept under the stars at our 'base camp' at

5,000 ft. Everyone made the summit and came back well pleased with the outing.

Months later, on paying off, my Permanent Loan List was found deficient of one blow lamp—classified as an attractive ('pinchable') store item. I was served a form demanding I show cause why I should not be debited £1 on the ledger. This no longer represented many Mars Bars. However, I had avoided all such charges in my career to date and felt I should try and talk myself out of this if possible. In fact, I had no idea what fate had befallen my blow lamp but, with a grain of truth behind the story and speculation as to what happened, I wrote: 'Blow lamp accompanied a MEDFOBA expedition up Mount Etna on date given, where it was required for brewing tea above the tree line where no wood was available for kindling [grain of truth—the odd blow lamp was taken for this]. Blow lamp was taken by party on final assault on the summit— 10,927 ft. [omitting to say last part of the ascent is a gentle walk], from which it never returned. It can only be supposed [no definite assertion] that blow lamp slipped from the rim of the crater into the molten lava, disappearing without trace.' The Stores Officer wrote his minute that, in his twenty years of naval store-keeping, 'Lost down Volcano' was the most ingenious story he had yet seen and felt it deserved Lost by Accident. The Captain concurred.

On 13 October, *Bulwark* and *Eagle* arrived back at Gibraltar. Our ship had been facing a major refit before we left UK. Not only had we foregone this, but we had since put in two months of almost continuous steaming and exercising and the ship had to have a week's self maintenance. *Eagle* was similarly placed so both ships were intensively worked on at Gib.

All the unscheduled movements of *Bulwark* had really upset the personal plans of an old Term-mate of mine, George Freer. He had taken over as the Gunnery Officer half way through the commission. I do not think I had seen him since Dartmouth, but as shipmates we soon became good friends. George had planned to be married back in August, just as soon as the ship paid off. Frustratingly for him, it was now well into October with no sign of the ship returning to UK. In desperation, he and his fiancée decided to be married while the ship was at Gibraltar, and the Captain agreed he could have six days leave for his honeymoon.

Arrangements were quickly made for the wedding in Gibraltar Cathedral. It was terribly one-sided, with the bride supported by only her mother and one bridesmaid. The groom, on the other hand, had about a hundred officers from *Bulwark* and *Eagle* and I was his best man. Nevertheless, the wedding was a great success—everyone felt like a glimpse of the realities of life after our intensive exercises—and, predictably, the bride, Shellagh, looked radiant. For me there was the pleasure of taking Shellagh's charming bridesmaid, Joyce Hirst, out to dinner at a Spanish restaurant at

La Linea. Ironically, George and his new wife were no sooner married than word came that *Bulwark* was to complete her week's self maintenance and return to UK after all. Further extension of the commission away from UK with the ship nominally still on Home Sea Service, could not be justified. The Freers were probably unmoved by this. At least they were now married and might as well make the most of six days honeymoon on the Costa Brava—they would soon meet again on the ship's return to UK. In the event, things turned out very differently. It was a case of 'Man proposes but God (or higher naval authority) disposes' and poor Shellagh would not see her man again for two months.

Bulwark reached Portsmouth on 18 December, four months late. George no doubt bade a breezy farewell to Shellagh who immediately emplaned for UK—happy in the thought that George would be in Portsmouth very shortly. Once on board, however, he was told that *Bulwark* was sailing next day—not for UK but to rejoin the other carriers at Malta.

BULWARK IN ACTION—SUEZ 1956

Our ship reached Malta on the afternoon of Friday 24 October for topping up with fuel and final briefings. Since 1946, I had spent three years in Med. Fleet ships, based Malta, but had never seen so much activity in the dockyard and around Grand Harbour, Valetta. The two biggest ships were *Eagle* and *Bulwark* but there were destroyers and frigates by the score as well as troopships, LSTs and a variety of Royal Fleet Auxiliary vessels. Figuring among the last were four or five Fleet Oilers, all fully-laden. Normally fuelling at sea was unnecessary in the Mediterranean as oil fuel supplies were nearly always available close by, but this and provisioning at sea were routinely exercised. In operations off Egypt there would be no chance to nip off to a friendly port for more fuel, stores or provisions. We might well have to remain on station for a month. Accordingly, Replenishment at Sea had been thoroughly exercised, and not always in the classic smooth seas, associated with the Mediterranean (see accompanying photo). In fact the closure of the Suez Canal by Nasser was already affecting world oil supplies. In those days there was neither Alaskan nor North Sea oil, and petrol rationing had been established in UK. However, as part of the elaborate logistic preparations, Malta was well stocked with oil fuel for all contingencies and also all the aviation spirit that might be needed.

The carriers sailed from Malta early Monday 27 October and the aircraft from *Eagle*, *Albion* and *Bulwark* were in action against the Egyptian Air Force at dawn on 31 October. I will not attempt to retell the whole story of the operations or the political background—although, as *Bulwark's*

Fleet Oiler Olna *in heavy seas in Mediterranean, 1956. Last seen by author up River Congo back in 1943. (Photo by author on superstructure of* Bulwark—*trying to fuel at sea.)*

Operations Room Officer, I had a fuller picture of what was happening than most. In the briefest terms, the Anglo-French forces were given a job to do, and did it with spectacular success, only to see all our achievements practically nullified by the political mismanagement of the whole affair. The Egyptian Air Force was seen as the biggest threat and had to be tackled almost unaided by our carrier aircraft. The RAF did what they could but, with their base at Akrotiri in Cyprus, their Hunter jets could only spend five minutes over Egypt and have enough fuel to get home. The Egyptian aircraft posed a serious threat as they outnumbered our Fleet Air Arm planes two to one, and in theory at least, our Seahawk jets should have been no match for their Mig 13s and 15s. Nevertheless, in three days the Egyptian Air Force was virtually destroyed on the ground at their three main bases of Abu Swer, Helwan and Cairo West. *Bulwark* lost one pilot through a deck landing accident resulting from the arrester hook breaking, and two other friendly planes were lost but the pilots recovered. I was in my Operations Room (where I kept watch-on-watch-off) while the drama of both these pilot recoveries unfolded. The story of these is told in the extract from the brief account of the operations taken from the First Commission Souvenir Pamphlet quoted below (again, this was written by the author thirty-nine years ago):

> . . . as is now well known, the ground attack aircraft from the three carriers
> played a major part in the virtual destruction of the Egyptian Air Force. Later
> operations by *Bulwark* aircraft included the sinking of three MTBs, the destruc-
> tion of a considerable number of tanks and military 'soft-skinned vehicles',

knocking out of coast defence batteries at Port Said, and finally the provision of intensive close ground support for first the paratroops, and then the sea-borne forces, that landed at Port Said. All this was achieved without loss in aircraft or personnel, as the result of enemy action, although unfortunately one pilot was lost in a landing accident on return from one of the sorties. During the first five days of the operation the number of sorties flown broke all records for an operational carrier. Furthermore, at the end of this time the service-ability rate was as high as ever, reflecting the greatest credit on all maintenance personnel.

. . . On two occasions when pilots of friendly aircraft were forced to bale out—in one case two miles from the coast close to Port Said, and the other twenty-eight miles behind the enemy lines at El Kantara—*Bulwark*'s aircraft provided immediate and effective cover until the pilots could be recovered by helicopter. In the Port Said rescue the aircraft silenced a 6-inch battery which opened fire on the dinghy, and at El Kantara enemy troops were prevented from approaching the pilot, although he had landed only a short distance from a military camp.

At one stage, while the carrier aircraft were supporting the paratroops in action near Gamil, Seahawks of 895 Squadron provided direct support for a company attack as part of their prepared fire plan. All arrangements were made and briefing carried out by R/T. Six aircraft then carried out continuous rocket and cannon strafing for exactly 9½ minutes. This was followed by thirty seconds of intense mortaring and enabled the paratroops to attack across open ground and carry a strong position which had previously barred their advance.

Throughout the day the co-operation between the two services was of an exceptionally high order. Whilst we in *Bulwark* were filled with admiration for the resolute fighting qualities of the paratroops, they in their turn were highly appreciative of the magnificent support they received from the cab rank which was constantly overhead. This spirit of comradeship was given practical ex-pression next day when our Avenger was flown into Gamil with 1,100 cans of beer, 30,000 cigarettes and quantities of 'nutty' (chocolate) for distribution to the troops as a gift from the ship's company of *Bulwark*.

Near the conclusion of the Port Said fighting the following signal to the British and French carriers was received from Vice Admiral Power, Flag Officer Aircraft Carriers:

'The first round is just about over. You have done all and more than you were asked to do, culminating in a really super performance yesterday when the carriers and paratroopers of both nations virtually captured Port Said unaided.

Thank you all. I am more than proud of my Command.'

Shortly after the capture of Port Said, Vice Admiral Power transferred from *Eagle* and for a week we were privileged to fly his flag in *Bulwark*.

At the present time no one can foretell the outcome of the tangled situation in the Middle East, but there is no doubt that *Bulwark* has played an important and honourable role and has fully lived up to her fine reputation for efficiency and *esprit de corps*.

Bulwark's Sea Hawk jets lined up for review on return to Malta after Suez operations, with 30 fighters all still 100% operational.

One or two footnotes to the above may be of interest. All co-operation with the Israelis was banned as we were by way of stopping a war between them and the Egyptians. The Israelis, however, quickly routed the Egyptian Army in Sinai. A result was a disorderly rabble of fleeing tanks and lorries all mixed up with Mercedes cars and other civilian vehicles choking the road from Ismailia to Cairo. Had our aircraft strafed this motley column, there would have been a scene similar to that on the road from Kuwait after the 1991 Desert Storm campaign.

We were ordered not to attack because a) this would be seen as assisting the Israelis and b) there were civilians amongst the fleeing army. From the outset, we were told in as many words to win this war but try not to kill any Egyptians if possible and to avoid knocking over any bricks and mortar for reporters to photograph. Few armed forces have ever been sent into battle under such constraints! Indeed, enormous care was taken to minimise civilian casualties. The defensive position our planes helped the paratroopers carry was a graveyard on the isthmus between Gamil Airfield and the western outskirts of Port Said. The Egyptians had had a month to fortify this cemetery with pill-boxes, dug-in tanks and self-propelled guns, barbed wire and minefields. The defences were manned by about five thousand Egyptian troops. Yet the position was carried by eight hundred British paratroopers with minimal casualties. However, one unfortunate Egyptian happened to be in the cemetery burying his dead father. He was not spotted by our aircraft, which could hardly hold up the attack until he was finished. As a result, the poor man was bowled over by a rocket by one of our Seahawks and had a leg shattered. The Army had cleared the cemetery in minutes and had no casualties requiring surgery aboard *Bulwark*, so our rescue helicopter picked up the injured Egyptian civilian and, within minutes, he was on the operating table of *Bulwark*'s sick bay, having the remains of his leg amputated and tidied up—undoubtedly saving his life.

Even with such care the incident was raised in Parliament and written up in the press—how the brutal British Armed Forces would not even respect the sanctity of a cemetery but took pleasure in mowing down innocent civilians trying to bury their dead! Can it be wondered that the Defence Chiefs decided it was in the nation's best interest to keep reporters as far from the actual front as possible for the Falklands War? One hears much about official misinformation. Can it be said that the media are never guilty of counter misinformation?

On a professional note, conventional wisdom held that in carrier operations one should plan for two days of intensive activity, based on 2½ sorties per plane per day. Thereafter, one should expect to achieve only 1½ a day because of unserviceability. In *Bulwark*'s case, 600 sorties were flown by 30 aircraft in six days—in other words, over three sorties per plane per day for six days and ready to go on at that rate. No wonder 'all known records' had been broken!

One other incident is worth recounting because I do not remember it being reported at the time. The Navy had a task force in the Red Sea (the cruiser *Newfoundland*, two *Daring* Class destroyers and the frigate *Crane*). This involved some risk as even the carriers in the Mediterranean were too far away to provide air cover. Earlier, the Egyptian frigate *Domiac* had been foolish enough to put to sea—the only Egyptian warship (other than four MTBs) to do so—and more foolish still in ignoring the call to surrender and, therefore, having to be sunk—in about five minutes flat. Some days later, in my operations room I heard an 'Enemy Report' from *Crane*, saying that she was under attack from four hostile jet aircraft, believed Mig 15s. No more was heard and I feared she had been sunk, the risk of operating ships without air cover having been accepted. This certainly gave rise to concern but I was surprised that any Egyptian planes had been brave enough to take to the air at all—our first news of any such daring. Two hours later, I was immensely relieved to intercept a further message from *Crane*, advising (apart from the obvious fact that she had not been sunk) that a) casualties and damage suffered were minor, although her radio was briefly out of action, b) she had shot down one of the attacking aircraft, and c) the planes were not Egyptian Migs but Israeli Ouragon jet fighters!

This incident was notable, as involving probably the only Israeli plane to date shot down by the RN. It was also a creditable performance by the brave little *Crane*, shooting down an attacking jet fighter with old World War II AA Guns. But it was not a fluke. Nor was it coincidental that *Crane* subsequently won the Far East Fleet AA Gunnery Trophy.

To end this chapter, one incident may counter any impression that the author had felt rather pleased with himself aboard *Bulwark*. One morning, our Seahawks found four MTBs venturing out of Alexandria and sank three of them but spared the fourth to pick up survivors. That night we were to have a scare. I had just reached my cabin, having come off watch at midnight, when the alarm buzzers sounded. This was unexpected as aircraft carriers do not normally go to Action Stations—they carry out more-or-less continuous operations from a distance. So we had not exercised any drill of that nature. On this occasion, my relief in the Operations Room had had his attention drawn to some curious small 'blips' on the radar and reported these to the bridge. It was suggested they might just be Egyptian MTBs. Having failed utterly by day, perhaps they were seeing what they might achieve at night—when they should have been used, if at all. If this should be the case, *Bulwark* had better be ready for them; we had no night-fighters, with which to hit them in the dark. In fact, these were almost certainly 'anaprop' (phantom) echos, but our Captain thought we should be on our guard.

Having no organisation for Action Stations, someone pointed out that we did have so-called Repel Aircraft Stations, to which everyone should respond if the alarm buzzers were sounded. Almost in terms of 'Let's see what happens if we press the button for the alarm buzzers', it was pressed. Although we had never exercised this, the whole ship's company knew (from other ships) that such buzzers called them to take up duty stations. For me, this meant back to the Ops. Room, if only to find out what was going on! I had to go outside into the darkened starboard gangway 'shell opening' and up double ladders to the gallery deck *en route* to the island superstructure. At these ladders, I ran into chaos with about a hundred men headed down to take up Damage Control duties and another hundred trying to get up to man anti-aircraft guns—all in the dark. At this point, I thought of Kipling's 'If' (If you can keep your head when all around you are losing theirs . . .). Clearly, the steadying influence of seasoned and mature Lt. Cdr. Seymour was needed here. So I called out with a loud voice of authority, 'Steady there. We'll have up traffic on the right—down traffic on the left.' There was a moment's stillness, then worse chaos than ever, as everyone moved to the same side. It had sounded fine when I said it!

CHAPTER 23

GANNET—ROYAL NAVAL AIR STATION, EGLINTON, NORTHERN IRELAND

BY EARLY MAY 1957, I was at last allowed to leave *Bulwark*—six months late. In fact my designated successor David Hallifax had been grabbed back, in the previous August, to be First Lieutenant of an LST for the Suez operations. In other words, he was given the job I had had aboard LST 11 as a Sub Lieutenant back in 1946. Such was the shortage of ships and superfluity of officers. However, David, whom I had long known and rated as a friend, was not disadvantaged and went on to reach the rank of Admiral.

I again wondered where I would be sent—and no one asked me where I would like to go. My appointment was to RNAS Eglinton, near Londonderry. The rationale, I was later told, was that, having just had a commission as TAS Officer of a carrier, I must now be an expert in naval anti-submarine aviation. Clearly, therefore, I was just the man to send to Eglinton where Fleet Air Arm Anti-Submarine pilots and observers were trained. This was a lot of rubbish as I had had virtually no TAS responsibilities at all aboard *Bulwark* and certainly no Aviation TAS. My enthusiasm was very limited by this prospect. I had made a number of friends in the FAA but I really longed to get into small ships again—anywhere, except perhaps, the Portland Local Flotilla. However HMS *Gannet* * at Eglinton it was to be, so I resolved to make the best of it. I reached Londonderry and Eglinton on 20 May 1967. The Air Base was very much a wartime-built establishment and most of the accommodation was in Nissen huts. It reminded me depressingly of RNAS Arbroath where I had had such a miserable time on Sub Lieutenant Courses. However, at least I was now a Lieutenant Commander and in late spring, the lush green fields of the Emerald Isle looked attractive. I would soon learn that the country was so green because it seldom stopped raining. We were on the south side of Loch Foyle (between Londonderry and the sea). I was told, 'If you can see the hills of Donegal across the water it's going to rain. If you can't see them, it is raining!'

---

* *Gannet* was the 'Ship Name' of the Air Station. But Gannets were the chief A/S aircraft flown there. This was purely coincidental.

As it turned out, the job was interesting and satisfying. Before I could teach aircrew about Air A/S operations I had to learn about them myself. Accordingly, I spent many hours up in Gannet aircraft practising dropping Sonobuoys, which detected the sound of submarines. These were plotted on the tiny plotting table in the rear cockpit. Once the general movements of the sub had been established an attack was made by dropping an A/S homing torpedo. These last were exciting new weapons—Mk.30 (passive homing) torpedoes. They were ingenious 'fish' as they had the ability to determine whether the submarine was moving to the left or right and then take an arbitrary intercept course. The A/S homing torpedoes of other navies could only steer towards the sound detected, which meant following a 'curved course of pursuit' ending in a chase. This could easily lead to the battery-powered electric torpedoes running out of 'juice' before they could hit. Furthermore, once the signal reached a certain strength, the batteries were put 'in series' and the homing run completed at top speed.

We had been told about these torpedoes on our TAS Course but they were then still only experimental. Now I had dozens to play with and Eglinton was the only place (or ship) from which planes were routinely dropping them under operational conditions. As far as I was concerned, these fish were much more fun than the dreary old Mk.9** yet, even now, at *Vernon*, the diehards really did not want to know about them. 'Why bother about these new-fangled electric homing torpedoes? The Mk 9** will still be around long after the Mk.30 has gone out of service.' Indeed, this was the case!

In serious terms, my torpedoes were ingenious, cheap to produce and the first designed to be dropped by aircraft to sink submarines. They were much more effective than depth charges, yet aircraft had actually sunk as many U-boats in the Battle of the Atlantic as had surface ships. Furthermore, the six hundred Soviet submarines were still looked upon as the greatest potential threat to Western civilisation. Our present perspectives of the Communist Russian menace, both then and now, are very different. We could not then realise that Russian militarism, at least through Russian eyes, was largely the outcome of fear of being overwhelmed by the capitalist West. Whatever the true situation, we took things as we found them, and training personnel in the maintenance, handling and operational use of these weapons seemed important.

In the event, the Mk.30 torpedoes were almost out of date before they were in general service. Several factors contributed to their demise. By 1958, the decision had been taken (largely on economic grounds) to abandon 'fixed-wing' A/S aircraft, i.e. the Gannet, and rely solely on A/S helicopters. The Russians now had both atom and hydrogen bombs and, by comparison, their submarine fleet no longer looked so menacing. Submarine technology had advanced a long way and even conventional

submarines were now so 'quiet' that 'passive-homing' torpedoes were
becoming less effective. Finally, nuclear-powered submarines were appearing and these had underwater speeds great enough to outrun any torpedo.

This is the perception of hindsight. At the time, I had no inkling that
my exciting new toys were already on the way out. Such was the accel-
erating rate of developing technology that, increasingly, things would tend
to be obsolescent before they were 'off and running' (that was for everything but the tried and true Mk9** torpedo!).

So I threw myself into all this TAS technology with undiminished
enthusiasm. RNAS Eglinton had one-only brand new modern building.
This was the cathedral-size TAS Centre, which was equipped with superb
workshops and storages for torpedoes, Sonobuoys and even future equipment, yet to be developed. There were well set-up classrooms, and an
impressive perspex-enclosed 'cut-away' Mk.30 with functioning homing
electronics (one could shake a bunch of keys in front and watch the rudders
go over). This was such a fascinating toy, I recall demonstrating it to the
Governor of Northern Ireland and asking, 'Would your Excellency care
to "have a go"?' He did—with obvious enjoyment! There was an impressive office for the officer in charge, not to mention the most modern
washing facilities, etc. on the base. It is hardly surprising, therefore, that
this complex was known to all other departments as the 'TAS Palace'.
Furthermore, it was, of course, naturally satisfying to me personally, to
reflect that all this was 'mine'! I still had not served in a *ship* with either
torpedoes or sonar since my specialist course. However, I could reflect
with joy that I was now up to my eyes in real TAS, even though *Vernon*
seemed singularly unimpressed! I was disappointed by the lack of support
I received from that quarter, so I had to resort to subterfuge.

A major problem was that the torpedoes only had ordinary lead-acid
batteries for practice running, of about a quarter the output of the silver
bromide batteries (usable once only) in the war-shot weapon. Accordingly,
if a successful practice attack was made by an aircraft on an actual
submarine or a simulator target, the torpedo would no sooner start to
home than its battery would give out. I would assure aircrew that with
the war weapon, this would have ended with a 'kill', but it was hard to
be convincing about this. This had been recognised by the Directorate of
Underwater Weapons at Admiralty and a new practice battery had been
devised with performance approaching that of the war torpedo.

The Torpedo Depot at Armagh, which supplied my torpedoes, had
held sixty of the new practice batteries for months and were keen to supply
us. Alas, some misguided Supply civil servant had decreed that the new
batteries could only be issued when all the lead-acid batteries were used
up. Each of these had to be run six times and a quick calculation showed
that they would last for many years. By then, the torpedo might well be

obsolete and the smart new practice batteries, produced at such great cost, might be scrapped without ever being used. I 'had the honour to submit' this argument through the 'proper channels' but knew that in peace-time no early decision on this could be expected from Admiralty.

I discussed the matter with my Captain, as keen as anyone to demonstrate how effective his A/S aircraft were. Between us, we devised about as devious a letter as my submission on the lost blow-lamp, which at least implied that we had been authorised to start using the new batteries. The Torpedo Depot—on our side anyway—accepted this as authority and changed over to these. The improved performance of the torpedoes was immediate and dramatic. It was a sad reflection, however, on how the Navy then worked, that I next heard of this eleven months later. I was attending a routine Torpedo conference at the Torpedo Experimental Establishment at Greenock, Scotland. A senior Commander from Director of Underwater Weapons Department Admiralty drew me aside and told me that I had put persuasive arguments for using the new batteries. So much so, he said, that he had instructed the file be 'given a yellow jacket' (evidently calling for priority handling of the matter). He said that I could therefore confidently expect a favourable decision within the next three months! I thanked him profusely for his personal interest in the matter. I naturally refrained from mentioning we had been using the new batteries for nearly a year. No doubt, Their Lordships eventually learned about the unauthorised issue of the batteries, but this would have been after Eglinton was closed down, the Mk.30 torpedo abandoned and Philip Seymour had left the Navy!

I will not write too much on technology in this chapter on my last service appointment. But there was one minor development of interest. The abandonment of the Gannet aircraft had been hasty. Henceforth, the Mk.30 torpedoes would simply be dropped by helicopters, the submarines having been located and tracked by 'dunking sonar', lowered by cable from the chopper. The sonar technology was fully developed and successful; dropping Mk.30s from hovering helicopters was not. From Gannets, the torpedoes were released at 200 knots, and slowed by a small parachute on the tail (jettisoned automatically as the weapon entered the water). The trajectory through the air caused the torpedo to enter the water at about 45 degrees, still with considerable velocity. This took the weapon down to fifty feet, at which a hydrostatic switch activated the propulsion system and the torpedo started its search. Clearly, no parachute was needed for a fish dropped from thirty feet from a hovering chopper. Alas, however, the first trial proved a total failure. These torpedoes had slight positive buoyancy, facilitating recovery without a 'blowing head'. When dropped from a helicopter, with no forward velocity in a horizontal position, they merely did a 'belly-flopper'. The torpedo would make a slight splash and float on the surface, like a still-born baby whale.

There was near panic. The Navy had scrapped the Gannet—yet A/S helicopters appeared incapable of using its one anti-submarine torpedo of which hundreds were held. The problem, of course, was not insurmountable—one of my pet expressions is that 'all problems are only solutions in embryo'! The Chief Ordnance Engineer Officer and I put our heads together and devised a simple angle-grooved plate into which a fitted pin on the tail fin slid. As a result, the tail of the torpedo would only be released when a preset angle of tilt was achieved. Dropped at a sufficient angle, even without forward velocity, the half-ton torpedo could be relied on to reach the required 'ceiling switch' depth. Initially, a variable-angle release system was tested to determine what angle was needed. Thereafter, all torpedoes and helicopters were fitted with this minimal modification and we could all breathe easy again—civilisation had been saved! This Engineer Officer and I thought out the concept between us. He designed and made the actual fitting and I dreamed up a name for it. It was designated the Tweaker as this sounded descriptive of its operation. More importantly, however, I pointed out that the acronym TWEAKER stood for: Torpedo Weapon Entry Angle—Kudos for Eglinton Research!

I felt immensely gratified that I had at last contributed to a successful invention. I had been trying for years, without success. At Navy Office Melbourne, in cooperation with a scientist who had invented the wire-guided anti-tank rocket, I had outlined a technique for using the guidance system in a new concept long-range A/S weapon. This would have gone to the limit of the detection range of the very latest long-range sonar about to enter service. It was actually discussed at a meeting of the Imperial Defence Materiel Committee, presided over by Sir William Penny. Unfortunately, I was not invited to this meeting and my scientist friend had assumed that I would be. Sadly, he was quite unable to explain the envisaged application. My only satisfaction came when my old mate Pete Wilson (RAN) was personally prepared to give me some credit for initiating the concept of the Australian Ikara wire-guided A/S missile.

I also submitted a system for the Seaward Defence of Sydney Harbour against midget submarine attack, utilising fixed sea-floor located Harbour Defence Sonar and three A/S Mortars Mk.10. This idea also withered on the vine.

Thirdly, at Eglinton I had written a paper pointing out that a small increase in the effectiveness of the Directional Sonobuoys could be achieved. This could eliminate the so-called Northern Sector problem, whereby it was almost impossible to obtain bearings over an arc of 15 degrees through Magnetic North. It would be pointless to explain this now. But I submitted that the problem could be overcome by merely making tuning condenser plates in the sonobuoy a different shape and slightly modifying the monitors aboard the aircraft. It was accepted that my theory was sound but it was too late. The design of these Sonobuoys was 'sealed' and, anyway, the service life of these units was now considered limited.

So much for the technology with which I was involved, and which certainly fascinated me. I was, of course, still a Seaman Officer and any activities involving ships or boats, as opposed to planes, usually involved me. This was also true of going to sea for torpedo dropping practices controlled from patrol boats sent out from Londonderry. For these, I soon realised that I could save an hour and a half each way if a chopper carried me to and from the boat in the exercise area. Otherwise, it had to be via Londonderry and the long journey out to sea and back. Accordingly, I became well accustomed to being winched up and down from helicopters—fortunately none flown by Hogie Carmichael!

Such helicopter trips were not always premeditated. One day there was an accident that cost three lives, and mine was very nearly a fourth. I was teaching a class around 1100, when a phone call summoned me urgently to the control tower. On arrival, the Captain told me that one of the (Wessex) helicopters had crashed into the sea as the result of engine failure. All three crewmen on board appeared to have been lost. Obviously nothing could now be done to save them but the Captain felt a compulsion to do something, if only to prevent a recurrence of this mishap. The aircraft had been exercising in the open Atlantic to the north, in conjunction with a frigate and a submarine, which happened to be Dutch. The location of the crash was known to within a quarter of a mile. My Captain wanted me to go there at once, take charge of a sonar search, locate the wreck of the helicopter, and mark the spot with a buoy. Then a special diving and salvage team might recover the plane and investigators determine the cause of the engine failure. I knew it was a very tall order even to locate the wreck by sonar in 100 fathoms of water. Then it would be a major salvage operation and rare calm weather would be needed. However, I understood the Captain's concern to do anything possible. Accordingly, I certainly was not going to tell him this would be a waste of time and effort.

I donned a 'Mae West' and was airborne within minutes. Once in the exercise area, I realised how hopeless this task was—but I had, at least, to try. The wind was blowing at 30 knots and there was a heavy sea running as I was winched down onto the frigate. I consulted with the CO who agreed to do what he could with a sonar search but held out slender hope of success. I knew there really was no hope. An inshore minesweeper with special mine-hunting sonar in calm weather might have stood a chance, but not in 100 fathoms (600 ft.). But this CO also understood my Captain's feelings and said they would do their best.

I decided to leave them to get on with things and called for the helicopter to lift me over to the submarine, which was on the surface nearby. I could not see how the submarine could help as such can only use sonar when submerged, but I felt I had better make a call there anyway. Being winched up and down on the narrow flat foredeck of a submarine was going to be tricky but I had not realised just how hazardous. My pilot told the submarine to steer down wind, to minimise the waves over the foredeck and to give the helicopter the maximum wind to 'lean into' for hovering. With the chopper headed the opposite way to the submarine, I was lowered onto the foredeck without incident. I soon realised this visit was a waste of time. Apart from the fact that I knew they could do nothing to help the search, the CO spoke little English and I spoke no Dutch. I waved to the helicopter still hanging around to pick me up again. The pilot once again lined up over the foredeck and the wire and strop were lowered.

I quickly donned the strop, pulled down the grommet, signalled the winchman to hoist and was lifted off the deck. Unfortunately, at this very moment there was a flaw in the wind, causing the helicopter to lunge forward through some twenty feet. This left me swinging like a pendulum a few feet in the air. To my horror, I saw that I was about to be swung hard straight into the steel conning tower of the submarine presumably breaking every bone I had and killing me. There was absolutely nothing I could do but await the inevitable impact. They say that, in such moments, one's whole life flashes through the mind. Be this as it may, I was far too confused and worried for any such 'replay'. All I could think was, 'I simply don't want to know about this!' and closed my eyes. Obviously I did not die—nor break any bones. This was not because the pilot corrected in time, but because of some very quick thinking by the crewman on the winch. He saw what was happening and let off the wire completely. With my eyes closed, I did not know what was happening until I felt my legs hit and crumple on the submarine's foredeck. I was just recovering my wits and about to struggle to my feet, when the wire tightened again. The pilot had now corrected—or over-corrected—and the aircraft had lurched backwards. I was dragged along by the seat of my pants and plucked into the air once more—this time safely up and into the helicopter. As can be imagined, my enthusiasm for this winching business was rapidly diminishing. I saw little to be gained by returning to the frigate. I spoke to her Captain over the R/T, and suggested they carried on what searching they could for another half hour while I returned and reported to my Captain.

I was back in the control tower in twenty minutes and giving my appraisal to the Captain. He thanked the frigate CO and reluctantly called off their search. I must have looked a bit battered but no one asked what happened to me; I might have felt a little sorry for myself, but at least I was alive and unhurt, whereas three airmen had lost their lives.

I recall no other special drama at Eglinton affecting myself. Even in those days there was an on-going threat posed by the IRA although Londonderry was a truly staunch bastion of the 'Orangemen'. Each year they celebrated Siege Day, commemorating the lifting of the siege of the town by two warships back in 1690. This would involve a parade of some 40,000 people with umpteen bands—and no republican would dare show his face. I tried to avoid discussing politics with Irishmen of any persuasion—they nearly all seemed to be so emotional and irrational! I may have offended any Irish readers with the foregoing remark. But I feel the extreme national chauvinism of the Loyalists in Ulster underlines the futility of the Republican cause in Northern Ireland. How could the fervour of all the Orangemen be contained if the whole of Ireland was under the rule of Dublin republicans? However, the local tensions largely left us untouched. In my two years in Northern Ireland I never heard of any Navy man being attacked by the IRA or anyone else. In fact, we would often cross the border in search of better trout fishing and even drive down to Dublin for short week-ends. We always found the people friendly—as long as one kept off politics! I recall one night with a friend drinking the ubiquitous Guiness stout amicably with the locals in the pub at Sligo. Closing time came and there was a token closing of the front door but those inside carried on drinking as before. An hour later, we were joined by the local policeman—who presumably reckoned his constabulary duties for the day were over!

Notwithstanding the absence of obvious hostility towards us, the IRA would have an occasional raid, usually on an unmanned border customs post late at night, and would blow it up. If they felt like a greater thrill, they would make for the nearest police station of the hated Royal Ulster Constabulary. All these police stations, however, were heavily fortified with sandbags and barbed wire. As a result, the attackers, often themselves well 'fortified' with Guinness, would place themselves round the building and open fire with automatic weapons. The RUC would return the fire and for fifteen minutes there would be continuous noise of small arms and automatic weapons. A few more panes of glass would be broken but then reinforcements, summoned by radio, would arrive after the assailants had cleared out. They would consider that they had had a good raid—but seldom would anyone be hurt.

The situation of our air station was a strange one because our accommodation was wholly undefended as was the perimeter of the airfield, surrounded only by a dilapidated cattle fence. On the other hand there was a heavily fortified 'citadel' comprising the Admin. block and one or two other buildings. This was surrounded by a sandbag wall plus barbed wire and machine gun emplacements, with a handful of Royal Marine Commandos inside night and day. These Commandos also made periodic patrols round the perimeter in Land Rovers. Nevertheless, if they had really wanted to, the IRA could have blown up all our aircraft in the hangars. I recall being on duty in our mini-fortress, in radio contact with HQ in Londonderry, for the whole of Christmas Day 1958. There was no excitement and the duty was just plain dreary. I reflected on some other strange Christmases I remembered—seeing my first naval gun 'fired in anger' in Biscay in 1943 and coping with a drunken ship's company under the tropical sun in Singapore in 1945. However, this time, I really did not anticipate any trouble (there was none) and I would be away on leave, skiing in Switzerland, in a week's time.

I had some good friends in the Wardroom. On arrival, I found the Commander was Cdr. Peter Hoare who had been my CO in *Loch Eck* in the Far East back in 1946 and the First Lieutenant was Lt. Cdr. Dundas whom I had last seen when I was his 'fag' as a Dartmouth Cadet, and he had been a Cadet Captain. He was now a quiet reflective person having survived two of the worst naval disasters of the war. He was one of only three survivors—and the only officer—from the *Hood*. He had survived the torpedoing and subsequent 15″ magazine explosion of the battleship *Barham*, with the loss of over eight hundred lives in the Mediterranean and finally been sick in hospital in Alexandria, when the cruiser he should have been aboard was bombed and sunk on a Malta convoy. Peter Hoare had been almost a god-like figure to me as captain of *Loch Eck*. But, after eleven years, I was now much closer to him. We would go fishing, make sorties together across the border at week-ends, and were on first-name terms.

I often went fishing by myself—fly fishing in the River Faughan—until almost midnight when, at midsummer in Northern Ireland the sun only dropped 15 degrees below the horizon. This meant it was almost 'twilight all night'. I caught few fish but really enjoyed the solitude and peacefulness. The only sounds would be an occasional owl, a trout rising or the distant moo of a cow. Perhaps this could not be called 'communing with nature'—but it came close to it.

It should not be imagined that I became a recluse. In fact, I missed the social life I had known in Malta, Australia and even Portsmouth. There was very little to do in Londonderry.

Nearly all the other officers of my age and rank were married and lived in married quarters outside the base. Many of the couples would invite me to dinner but I really had no way of returning their hospitality. However, I tried to make the most of the life. I was named as the Mess Social Secretary and managed to arrange a number of social functions. A regular one became known as the 'Thirst after Righteousness' (not an original name) for officers, their wives, Wren officers and nurses foregathering in the Wardroom for drinks after church on Sundays. What was different was that we featured some special refreshments such as oysters and Black Velvets (stout topped with champagne).

Our most ambitious function was a full-scale Australian style barbecue amongst the sand dunes at the entrance to Loch Foyle. The problem was that one could not bank on the weather even forty-eight hours ahead. The only way to play it was to have everyone briefed in advance and all planning in place. A site was selected and barbecuing facilities set up, even to a stack of dry driftwood kept ready under a tarpaulin. Butchers were organised to have chops and sausages for 150 people ready at twenty-four hours notice. Kegs of beer were also assembled and stood-by. Likely starters were canvassed and lists, for participants to place their names on, were typed ready for pinning up and an outline plan for available cars prepared. Finally, the Operations Officer and the Chief Meteorological Officer had to monitor the weather charts. As soon as a rare high pressure system was seen to be approaching, X Day (decision to act) was declared. This was B Day minus two and the whole organisation would swing into action. We achieved our barbecue as planned, for a full 150 people, and the party was a great success. We only just made it, however, as it started to rain at about 2300 just when we were packing up!

Another initiative was to form our own little Sailing Club. We had acquired four ex-German 'Olympic' dinghies. Unfortunately, we had nowhere to sail them. The sea was too rough and Loch Foyle was so shallow that one had to cross hundreds of yards of mud to reach the water at low tide. But we found there was a small fresh-water lake, of irregular shape with an island, that had possibilities. This was named Enoch Loch and we resolved to construct a sailing club on its shores. A quarter of a mile was the furthest one could go in a straight line but we felt we could just get in some sailing on it. An enthusiastic team of volunteers was formed including Cdr. Peter Hoare, a site was surveyed and the Sailing Club planned. The four dinghies and the odd privately owned craft were painted, rigged and prepared. A small 'sea-wall' was built out of old railway sleepers; a launching ramp was constructed. A prefabricated corrugated iron hut was erected and painted, a fence (of about 20 ft. by 30 ft.) was installed and, of course, a white-painted flagstaff raised. Finally, good grass turf, from the airfield perimeter, was laid over smoothed earth. All this (including clearing the scrub and grubbing out the roots from the lakeside) was done over two week-ends. The 'Gala Opening Day Regatta of the Enoch Loch Sailing Club' was set down for the third Saturday.

Happily, on the day, the sun was out for once, and a festive occasion took place. The wife of our Captain Roberts (for whom I had now come to have great respect and affection) was asked to open the Club. Mrs Roberts and other ladies rose to the occasion, in their smart summer outfits and Ascot-type hats. Champagne and canapés were handed round by the 'members'. A rather ragged sail-past was made by the dinghies, and the Red Ensign 'broken out' at the Masthead. I was even declared to be the Commodore! In fact, of course, we had no Royal Warrant to use the Blue Ensign ('defaced' or plain), were not affiliated to the Yacht Racing Association (forerunner to the Royal Yachting Association) and had yet to think up a suitable Club burgee. In truth, this venture did little to enhance the sporting facilities of Eglinton. A few people had the odd sail on the lake but no races were held. Winter was soon upon us and, by the following summer, RNAS Eglinton had closed down. One could argue that it was a lot of work for nothing, but I feel it was worthwhile, if only for the fun of our Opening Day—no more festive occasion was ever held on the sacred lawns of the Royal Yacht Squadron!

Other breaks in our otherwise routine lives were the visits by first two Gannet Squadrons of the German Navy and then three squadrons of Dutch Avenger A/S aircraft. I have referred to the Germans and the two *Unterseebootejagstaffels*. (I was pleased with myself when I had mastered this mouthful.) One has to say the Germans were somewhat diffident and formal, perhaps as the result of presenting themselves for training by their former enemies. The Dutch, on the other hand, could hardly have been more exuberant. Their visit overlapped that of the Germans and the difference was striking. The Avengers were accompanied by two Dakotas (DC3s) said to be bringing Squadron spares, etc. In fact when we backed lorries up to these planes, the cargoes seemed mostly to comprise cartons of Bols gin! Their officers breezed into the wardroom and declared, 'The party is on us tonight' and wheeled in the Bols. Their German allies, who had come in bowing and clicking their heels, were somewhat flabbergasted.

I was now aged thirty-two and my rugby-playing days were coming to an end. But I did have two full seasons playing for Londonderry Combined Services (I think the team was called), with most of the players provided by RNAS Eglinton. I was, in fact, the leader of the forwards—no doubt in deference to my age and seniority! Towards the end of my time there, I played in the Inter-Services competition. We eliminated the RAF in Northern Ireland and played the final against the Army. The Navy (in Northern Ireland) were definitely the underdogs, or outsiders, for this match. The Army, rather than picking out all the talent they could find in Northern Ireland (where several regiments were garrisoned), decided to field the team of the Duke of Wellington's Regiment, which had won the Army Regimental Competition for UK and Germany. Their team included two (England) Internationals and four players for the Army. We could not even boast one Navy player let alone any Internationals. Also the match was played on their ground with a thousand or more spectators, whilst we could muster only one bus-load of miscellaneous supporters including Captain Roberts and a few loyal Wrens.

There was no comparison between the polish and skill of the two teams. But what we lacked in these areas we made up for in enthusiasm and will-to-win. The match proved a cliff-hanger to the end. In the last five minutes, to my considerable embarrassment, I had my shorts half torn off. I heard a loud shout from the sidelines, from Captain Roberts, 'Don't worry about your nakedness, Seymour—get on with the game'! I am happy to report the Navy won by a very small margin. I had not felt so happy about a football victory since defeating the *Richelieu* at Scapa fourteen years before! That was the last rugby game I ever played.

I should mention, as part of my job and of my recreational activities, my relationship with my small TAS unit of ratings. Over two years, about a third of them changed but, essentially, my team comprised an Ordnance Artificer (Tradesman Engineer), a Petty Officer, a Leading Seaman and eight Able Seamen—all except our 'Tiffy' being TAS ratings. Quite unreasonably, but because they were 'different' and constituted a small unit, my sailors regarded themselves as far superior to the numerous Naval Airmen at Eglinton. Certainly, they had a marvellous *esprit de corps*—something akin to that of the crew of my old MTB. I had a funny old car, an old London taxi, into which the whole TAS party could crowd and, with twelve up, once a month or so we would head off over the border for a TAS Department outing. We would find somewhere interesting, with spectacular views, or drive along the sands of the beach at Malin Head (once being cut off by the tide and having to get back round some rocks by manhandling the car through a foot of sea). We would end up with a hearty binge at some pub and copious quantities of the inevitable Guinness. I may say that my sailors included two 'skates'—men who had served sentences in detention quarters and were rated Second Class for Conduct. However, as I had found elsewhere, if one could 'turn' such people by showing an interest in them and persuading them the whole world was not against them, they could well end up representing the most dependable sailors one had, and almost become willing slaves. Certainly, my whole team showed me devotion I had done little to deserve. My battered old taxi was lovingly looked after for me—as if it had belonged to the men!

Whilst it has little relevance, I feel impelled to write briefly about my taxi. It will be recalled that I had had a smart little new Morris Minor tourer in Australia, bought with a loan from my father. Sadly, he asked for repayment on my return to UK—but that had been the deal. I felt I had to have some car whilst in *Bulwark*. But, even if I could afford one, it could not be a new car. I just needed a utility vehicle I could leave on the dockside when at sea, but which would work when I returned, brushed the snow off and pressed the starter. I bought this taxi, twenty-one years old, from its owner/taxi-river, when the London County Council finally refused to reregister it as a taxi. Based on average annual taxi usages, I estimated this vehicle was well into its second half million miles! Fortunately the engine was so primitive that there was practically nothing to go wrong—or nothing I could not fix or get some friendly Artificer to fix for me. I even repainted it and brought it back to almost as-new appearance. Very occasionally, when we were going somewhere without embarked squadrons, my Captain allowed me to take it on board *Bulwark*. As the Sports Officer, I did find it handy for piling in the whole ship's soccer team and taking them to and from a match.

On our visit to Cherbourg, as the Press Liaison Officer, I was showing the editor of the local *Presse de la Manche* round the ship. Unlike some, this was a friendly press-man and was tickled pink at the sight of my taxi in the hangar. He photographed me with it and wrote about *Le sympathique Lieutenant Commander Seymour, avec son vénérable taxi de Londres*!

I could almost write a book about this taxi (including the impressions it made on Russian officers from the *Sverdlov* we had to look after at one stage) but I must desist. I still had it shortly after leaving the Navy, when I chanced to meet the one and only Mike MccGwire doing the Staff Course at RNC Greenwich. I was ready to sell the car and Mike said his course would give me what I had paid for it nearly five years back (£70). However, it would have to pass the test of conveying six of them from Greenwich to Portsmouth and back for a week-end. I suggested this was almost insulting my car which had been through the Atlantic Ocean, round Malin Head, through hedges near Londonderry and many other trials! Sadly my faithful steed failed the test. It would not have done under my command but these unfamiliar 'masters' simply did not know how to treat such a venerable old machine. The initial defect was routine and trivial—a small leak from the 'honey-comb' radiator. Alas, no one noticed, or possessed the rudimentary repair kit needed—a stick of chewing gum! They ran the taxi with the radiator dry until the engine seized up and the poor old car died and was abandoned at the roadside. I eventually recovered her and sold her (for £10) to the local garage lad, who doubtless fixed her up, hopefully for another half million miles!

THE CLOSING ACT—FOR PHILIP SEYMOUR

Back to matters naval. The reader will have no doubt detected that, by now, the Navy had far too many officers chasing far too little work. The bracket for the author's contemporaries was particularly overcrowded. Back aboard *Bulwark*, one of the senior Lieutenants, who was something of a wag, had remarked, 'If all the Lieutenant Commanders in this ship were placed end-to-end—they still wouldn't reach a decision!' Earl Mountbatten of Burma (as 'Lord Louis' had become) had achieved his life's ambition as First Sea Lord and gone further to become Chief of the Defence Staff. Rightly, he had perceived that all three services were grossly overstaffed and morale was bound to suffer with lengthy queues for 'dead men's shoes' regarding promotions. Also, all officers had to wait a long time to be given more responsible duties. For a time, at least, it could be said that the Navy was at peak efficiency, as there was an experienced expert for every job. But this could not last, as young officers were simply not getting the experience and responsibility needed to fit them for higher command.

Sadly, I was also beginning to feel a sense of frustration and disillusionment with the TAS Branch. In 1958 I attended the annual TAS Conference at *Vernon*, to which all TAS officers who could get there were supposed to come and update their knowledge and thinking on all aspects of TAS. The idea was sound, but the occasion had degenerated into a well-managed 'talkfest' by officers concerned with different aspects of the specialisation, with little scope for discussion. In other words, it was something of a mutual admiration society meeting with social overtones. In 1958, there were two significant attempts made to 'rock the boat'.

The first was raised by one Lt. Peter Campbell, whom I had known since he and several bright young Sub Lieutenants (most of whom, including David Halifax, who had relieved me in *Bulwark*, happened to specialise in TAS) had taken passage to the Med. aboard *Gravelines* in 1950. Peter had early been recognised as showing exceptional promise, had done the so-called TAS 'Dagger' Course—restricted to two-only outstanding officers each year—and was now serving as an equerry at Buckingham Palace. A highly technical paper had just been presented on the very latest developments in Mine Counter-Measures, including methods for 'sweeping' sophisticated acoustic, magnetic and pressure-sensitive mines (each in a number of forms). Unfortunately, one major problem (explained, for those interested, in Appendix 5) had not been addressed. The speaker had resumed his seat, to polite applause, and the subject was opened for questions. Campbell stated his rank, name and current appointment and asked, 'Why are the Navies of NATO currently committed to building a total of four hundred coastal mine-sweepers, when these craft are incapable of clearing an area of mines?' He went on to explain that he spoke with authority on this subject having recently commanded one of the craft charged with clearing the approaches to Port Said. There followed a few minutes of mumbling obfuscation, which totally failed to answer the question, before the Chairman declared it was time to move to the next item on the agenda.

Shortly afterwards, a Commander who was the Director of the Tactical School (at Greenwich) presented his paper on how the Tactical School envisaged convoy operations in the North Atlantic in another war. He expounded, with unarguable logic, that with a given ratio of ships to be escorted to available escorts, the quality of the protection increased with larger convoys and more escorts. This was because the area of a larger convoy (and therefore the number of ships convoyed) increased with two dimensions, whereas the linear perimeter of escorts increased with one. I would have thought this point could have been made in two minutes—but the speaker took ten. He went on to say that they had concluded that the optimum size for future convoys was six hundred ships—pause for gasps of surprise. He followed up by saying, 'I expect some of you will ask if such a convoy would not make a good target for nuclear attack—the answer, of course, is that the ships must steam in "anti-megaton" formation. That is, each ship four miles from its neighbour. In this way an atom bomb could only sink one or two ships, rendering the convoy not worth using an atom bomb on'—pause for more gasps of astonishment. Without waiting for the implications to sink in, the tactical guru continued, 'Naturally six hundred ships in anti-megaton formation will take up a large area of sea.' He released a diagram showing the English Channel from Lands End to the Cherbourg Peninsula occupied by this proposed convoy, explaining this was only to show its size; such convoys would, of course, be headed for the Western Approaches ports of Glasgow and Liverpool. Yes, this would be a very long perimeter for the screen to protect and would require at least fifty escorts. However, the logic was inescapable that *if* the convoyed ships had to be in 'anti-megaton' formation regardless, the argument remained valid that larger convoys could be afforded better anti-submarine protection than smaller ones.

I waited a respectful five seconds before rising to speak. I refrained from asking where fifty escorts were coming from as the RN now had under thirty frigates, but did ask how it was envisaged these six hundred ships would be kept in anti-megaton formation for unloading on arrival in port. The speaker looked, not at me, but at the Captain of *Vernon* and, with an air of contempt, said, 'I will do the questioner the courtesy [implicitly undeserved] of assuming that this is not a frivolous question, but would remind him of what he should know, that the stated object of Convoy Operations—as set out in Allied Tactical Publications No.1 [ATP 1— NATO tactical bible] was "the safe and timely arrival of the convoy". Thereafter, the ships and their cargoes were not the responsibility of the Navy.' I was appalled by this blinkered attitude but no other answer was forthcoming. Sadly, few officers, by that time, had perceived the almost total irrelevance of another Battle of the Atlantic in any future unrestricted nuclear global war. I only trust that both Campbell's and my questions are recorded in the dusty archival minutes of long-ago TAS Conferences.

In fact, I had already seen the writing on the wall and had been thinking about starting a new life. I had been interviewed by the European

Agricultural Settlement Board of Kenya. The prospects of farming in the 'White Highlands' of Kenya were made to sound most attractive and I even completed the enrolment papers for the Egerton Agricultural College at Nakuru, Kenya. This project eventually fell by the way, overtaken by other developments.

On Mountbatten's initiative, a White Paper was prepared outlining proposals for substantial reductions in the establishment of officers in all three Services, and these were initiated in late 1958. Despite my feelers put out regarding Kenya, I was reluctant to seek early retirement. But I was fully conscious of the realism of the situation and had to ask myself what future the Navy offered me. The frank answer, I am afraid, was 'not much'. I badly needed some close confidante and friend, with whom to discuss all this.

Fortunately, when the prospect of a voluntary officer cut-back was being mooted, I was able to talk to my old friend, Michael Vaughan. We discussed the situation fully and frankly—particularly how far either of us could expect to go in the Navy. For myself, I was beginning to realise that my chances of any further promotion were poor. My feelings were mixed. I felt reluctant to opt out of the Service I had come to love so much. I was not conscious of having any blot on my copy book. Realistically, however, my future prospects were only fair, simply because the competition was so strong. Of our original forty Term members, fewer than a quarter ever reached the rank of Commander, and I could think of at least ten more deserving than myself. This meant that if I stayed on, I had little chance of ever getting a Command but appeared likely to become a 'passed-over' Lieutenant Commander with increasingly depressing appointments. In other words, I should leave.

As for Mike Vaughan, he had to regard his prospects as still bright if he stayed. This was a view with which I fully agreed. Since his Kings Dirk from Dartmouth, as far as I knew, he had done everything right. He had scored As in all his Sub Lieutenant Courses, qualified as a German interpreter, and sailed through all his Destroyer Command Exams (I still had one to go). I knew he had left every ship in which I had served with him with a glowing report and, with his known energy and reliability, these must have continued. If I had been asked to lay a bet on the officer I knew most likely to make Flag Rank, I would have backed Vaughan odds-on. Mike himself might not have had as much conviction as I had but had to admit his chances were good. So, although he seriously considered the option of early retirement, he chose to stay.

In passing, I should have recorded that I attended his wedding to his charming wife Gay in Yorkshire whilst on my TAS Course and, later on, I was privileged to attend their son's christening, as his godfather. At the time of writing, David Vaughan is a Commander in the RN and

commanding the Submarine School at Gosport, having previously commanded the nuclear-powered submarine *Triumph*.

So the decisions were made and my application went in. The run-down
was to be largely voluntary and generous retrenchment compensation was
offered. However, there was some flexibility. It was not guaranteed that
all officers applying to leave would be allowed to go. The Navy also
reserved the right compulsorily to retire officers if there were not enough
takers, or if any particular officer did not measure up. There was a rather
pathetic scheme to try to disguise the letters of notification so that no one
would know whether any officer 'had jumped' or 'was pushed'. All letters
were sent out in hand-addressed envelopes but, unimaginatively, one lot
were in blue envelopes and the other in white—but, of course, all had
the same postmark and bore the same handwriting. Accordingly, everyone
knew who had had their blue envelopes but the word would go around
that 'poor so-and-so has received a white envelope'. There was only one
forced retirement at Eglinton—of a 'Special Duties' Sub Lieutenant who
was a good officer but happened to belong to a very specialised branch
that was grossly over-manned. I was not aware of any officers who applied
to leave but were not allowed to go. However, there must have been quite
a number whose applications were rejected as it was said that the terms
offered were so generous that the Admiralty was 'bowled over in the rush'.

An unimaginative element was the concept that the run-down would
take place over a period of four years, but that Their Lordships would do
what they could to meet applicants' nominated dates for release. In fact,
of course, once an officer had opted for 'out', he was going to want to
start his new life as soon as possible. He would not want to hang on for
four years doing jobs no one else wanted. Accordingly, nearly everyone
opted for Day 1. Foolishly, I took this question seriously and literally. With
Eglinton due to close down in three months, I thought I was being helpful
in nominating the closure date for the base. This, of course, placed me
at the end of the queue and I was informed that my release would be in
four years time!

I regarded this as preposterous and represented my complaint through
the 'proper channels' (two Admirals up the Chain of Command to Admiralty). My submission was in the most studied respectful terms and
stressed that I would serve on with good heart if only I was persuaded
the Navy needed my services. I had been told I could not be spared earlier
because of a shortage of TAS Officers. I made a calculation based on the
announced projected strength of the fleet and was only able to detect
sea-going jobs for eleven TAS officers. Some would be needed ashore for
training purposes and a few at Admiralty but reference to the Navy List
revealed that the RN had no fewer than 403 officers qualified in TAS. I
respectfully went on to say that I was in no position to pass judgements

on perceived manning requirements but felt I could point out the lack of information available to me to enable me to understand the stated needs. I concluded with 'I respectfully submit that the Best Interests of the Service [always the note one had to strike—as opposed the the best interests of Philip Seymour] were not served by the retention of any Officer or Rating against his will, unless such retention was not only necessary—but manifestly seen to be unavoidable. I have the honour to be, Sir . . .'

My own Captain, 'Chiko' Roberts, and the two Admirals (Flag Officer, Flying Training and Flag Officer, Home, Air) all supported me and minuted my submission, commending 'Favourable consideration'. Alas, however, the reply came back from Admiralty (presumably from a Civil Servant), telling me that my submission had been noted but regretting that no variation to my advised four-year retention could be contemplated. Furthermore (to add insult to injury), there was a second brief paragraph telling me my facts were wrong—there were not (as I had stated) 32 TAS officers at Admiralty but only 30. I had somehow counted in my friend at Buckingham Palace and another officer who had left. It is hard to imagine that the writer expected me to exclaim, 'Ah, that explains it—in the light of this news, it is clear why the Navy will need me for a further four years!'

Captain Roberts and his friend, the Captain of the Joint (RN/RAF) Anti Submarine School at Londonderry, who was also designated Senior Naval Officer Northern Ireland, shared my dismay. 'SNONI' volunteered to have a word with the Fourth Sea Lord, who was a friend of his, on my behalf. I thanked him for this but declined his offer. My rebel streak was now surfacing and I felt that, having hitherto scrupulously followed the proper channels without satisfaction, I was now free to make this another 'Crichel Down' *cause célèbre*. If this was to be raised on the Floor of the House, I was anxious it should be seen that I had made no attempt to pull any strings. My selected 'Champion', whom I had yet to approach, was a certain Vice Admiral Sir John Hughes-Hallett KCB DSO RN MP, who was a formidable officer. When Captain of *Vernon*, he had made his name by sweeping out most of the 'deadwood' members of the establishment there and acquired the nick-name of Hughes-Hitler! He had been on his feet in the Commons several times on the subject of excessive manpower for Britain's now tiny fleet.

Anyway, Christmas 1958 came and went (as I sat dispirited in my armed citadel at Eglinton) and in the New Year I was off for two weeks of leave skiing at Klosters in Switzerland. I had been prepared to forget about my future problems and enjoy my skiing, down the Parsenn from the Weissflujoch. But, a week later, to my amazement, a telegram arrived from Eglinton advising that the Admiralty had relented and I would be released in three months time. I may never know who had brought about this change of heart—but at least I now knew where I stood, and there need be no 'Crichel Down'!

It now only remained to tidy things up. There were no missing blow-lamps as the TAS department was wound up. I left Eglinton a week before the place closed down, having had a splendid farewell party. My last service to the Navy was to take one of the Torpedo Recovery Boats from Londonderry to Milford Haven. My whole TAS party volunteered for the trip—which could be tough in a small boat in the notoriously rough Irish Sea. Eventually I took our 'Tiffy' (most likely to be able to fix the engine if it broke down), my Petty Officer and the two '2nd Class for Conduct' ABs who excelled themselves with the cooking *en route*.

We made an overnight stop at Peel, Isle of Man, and reached Milford Haven next evening after a smooth passage. With sadness we hauled down the White Ensign on the only Command I had ever had in the Navy (except for my train, which, of course, wore no ensign!) and so ended my naval career—and half my working life.

CHAPTER 24

BROTHER OFFICERS

IT SEEMS APPROPRIATE, at this point, for me to recount where various people whose names have kept recurring, had been and now were at the time I left the Navy. My contacts with several of them had been limited by my absence in Australia for two years (although, as reported, I had run into MccGwire and Kersey there) and away from most of my Seaman Officer mates whilst with the Fleet Air Arm aboard *Bulwark* and at Eglinton. But here again, I also found some old shipmates and my old Term-mate, George Freer, aboard *Bulwark*, and Commander Peter Hoare.

By now, several members of the original Term had died. These included Peter Harris—a very promising officer who, in 1950, as Senior Pilot of a Sea Fury squadron aboard *Glory*, had flown into a cumulo-nimbus cloud and was never seen again, nor was any trace of his aircraft. Another casualty was William ('Willum') White who had been very popular with us all. He had died as the result of an accident on the fo'c'sle of the cruiser *Aurora*, whilst still a Lieutenant in 1946. This was a strange affair. I understand he was knocked over by a steel wire rope that parted and picked himself up, seemingly uninjured—but died from brain injury that night. Also lost at sea was Derek Foster, who went down with the submarine *Affray*, which disappeared whilst exercising in the English Channel in April 1951. Despite the most elaborate search ever mounted for a missing submarine, the craft was not located for six weeks. *Affray* was eventually found in nearly 300 ft. of water, in the Hurd Deep near Guernsey, in practically the only area of such depth in the English Channel. Positive identification was finally made through reading its name on underwater television. We are most unlikely to ever know what caused the loss of this submarine, with not only her crew but a year's Submariner's Long Course (including our Term-mate Foster).

Thus the known number of the Term lost on actual sea service was five (Ryland, Nicholson, White, Harris and Foster). Perhaps 12½% lost was not high over twenty years which had included two and a half of World War II and minor hostilities such as Korea and Suez. But one in eight is still a higher rate than is to be expected in most professions for duty-related deaths under the age of thirty.

Four others: Cogswell (who changed his name to Nutting), Hollyer, Prince and Sington, died from other causes (not known to the author) and

Rear Admiral Sir Nigel Cecil KBE CB. Dartmouth Term-mate and friend of over fifty years—partner in 'bomb' of car on Sub Lt. Courses.

two or three simply vanished with no known address (that is in Ministry of Defence [Navy] records)—after leaving the Navy.

Several had been invalided out, including our colleague who later became a 'contrabandier'. One, 'Bonzo' Ransome, had left the Navy early on and subsequently had a colourful career, mostly in the Army. I will return to him in the Epilogue which follows. One of the top members of the Term at Dartmouth had to leave the Executive (or Seaman) ranks, because of deteriorated eyesight but somehow found himself in the Legal Branch of the Army, in which he achieved distinction. He finally retired as Judge Sir David Hughes-Morgan.

Amongst my closer friends was Joe Lungley, whom I had first encountered on the train to Dartmouth in 1939. I attended his wedding in Reading whilst on my Long TAS Course in 1952 after he had been serving in a ship in the Korean War. Sadly, that was the last time I saw him. Not long after that he elected to leave the Navy and moved with his family to Australia, where a year or two later Mike Vaughan, aboard a ship visiting Brisbane, chanced to meet him. They no doubt swapped reminiscences about Mombasa as Midshipmen, Happy Hooligan Days in MTBs at Ostend and other encounters. Thirty years later I made a determined effort to trace Joe in Australia. I did pick up his trail and heard from several Australians who had known him in Queensland, but I failed to re-establish contact. Again, more detail will appear in the Epilogue. Mike Kersey by 1958 was serving in the RNZN and I did not see him again until my arrival in Australia, with both of us as civilians, after which our lives became quite inter-woven.

Mike Vaughan's life had been interesting, since I had known him aboard *Chieftain* in the Med. Fleet. The years 1950 to 1953 found him in the RN Rhine Flotilla—where he was doubtless able to put his fluent German to good use. Next came the Fleet minesweeper *Rinaldo*, followed by two years at RNAS, Yeovelton. For 1956–7 he was back in destroyers—first *Comus* and then *Cossack*, of the 8th Flotilla. It was aboard *Cossack* that he met up with Joe Lungley in Brisbane. When I came to leave the RN, Michael was serving as Assistant Staff Officer, Operations, to C-in-C Mediterranean. We will return to Vaughan in the Epilogue.

Gavin Wemyss had a time as an Applications Officer at the Underwater Detection Experimental establishment (UDE) at Portland. His job was to try to steer the efforts of the 'boffins' towards inventing what the Navy needed, as opposed to what the former fancied. This evidently proved a hard job as he found that ideas put forward by himself, or any other Applications Officer, would only be taken up with great reluctance. This led Gavin (always ready with a *bon mot*) to coin the phrase which has become widely used in the English-speaking world—'The NIH Syndrome'—for Not Invented Here, and therefore, implicitly, No Good! The truth is that this is something to which all of us are, to some extent, prone!

Later Wemyss was one of the first of my contemporaries to have his own Command. It was HMS *Plover*, about the oldest, smallest, and arguably ugliest and least impressive ship in the RN. She was pre-war built as a small train ferry and had her rolling stock deck converted to carry mines, which could be laid by running them out through ports in the stern. Whether she ever saw operational service as a minelayer, I do not know. For years, she had only been used for training purposes (in relation to mines) by *Vernon* and was Portsmouth-based—with a miscellaneous collection of ships, of which the mighty *Bulwark* was the most impressive. However, I am sure that in Gavin's eyes, *Plover* was the pride of the Royal Navy! Needless to say, he managed to instil a great *esprit de corps* among the crew, whilst displaying an element of the eccentricity one would expect from this man. For instance, I have described the ritual of saluting all ships commanded by more senior officers as one entered Portsmouth. In the case of *Plover*, this meant all other warships. Her CO would ensure this was done—but in his own way. Gavin, wearing a top hat for entering harbour, would doff his 'topper' with a flourish in salute to everyone up to and including C-in-C Portsmouth flying his flag aboard *Victory*! No Staff Officer was ever game to tell Wemyss that this was not what was expected of the most junior CO of all at Portsmouth.

This brings me to my friend Harry Hawkins from the TAS Course. He had turned up aboard *Ceylon* when I was in Australia and we had enjoyed a happy reunion. Where should he next appear, but as Wemyss's predecessor as CO of *Plover*, which he made a happy ship (before she became Gavin's command), despite the lack of glamour of the ship and her role.

What about Mike MccGwire? After MTBs, he had a colourful time serving aboard *Armada* (later to be a consort of my ship, *Gravelines*, in the Med.) in the Pacific in 1946. Whilst out East, he was sent to the frigate *Whitesand Bay* and helped evacuate the Indian Army from Padang, Sumatra. He played a part in the acquisition of another jeep, which he felt his ship had as much claim to as the newly-arrived Dutch, who actually fired on them to try to thwart the pinching of this vehicle. The jeep remained with the ship for a year but subsequently, in MccGwire's words, they found that 'peacetime morality had broken out' and jeep-stealing was no longer acceptable behaviour. Accordingly, they contrived to acquire a bill of sale from an army surplus dealer in Japan, rendering their jeep not only legal but privately owned. Together with a similarly acquired motorbike, it was eventually swapped in Trieste for a German Mercedes car—really civilian!

Whitesand Bay had been *en route* to Japan, when without warning she had been ordered to proceed forthwith to the Med. They were to reinforce the Palestine Patrol, whose duties intercepting illegal immigrants have already been described. Mike was the designated Boarding Officer, but never had to fight his way aboard a vessel like Exodous 47, which took 250 boarders five hours to subdue. It was around this time that Kersey and I had our 'run ashore' with him in Malta that nearly saw the three of us arrested.

August 1948 found MccGwire at Cambridge starting to qualify as a Russian interpreter. This later involved his living in extraordinary squalor with an impoverished White Russian family in Paris. Mike then found himself navigator of a Fisheries Protection Service ship, mostly cruising the waters of the Frozen North (in marked contrast to Sumatra or Palestine). This, however, enabled him to exercise his Russian on fishermen of Soviet trawlers encountered. Subsequently, after two years service at sea with the RAN in Australia, he was made Assistant British Naval Attaché in Moscow. No one could say that the RN did not offer a varied life.

We return to Joe Brooks—who had not had a happy time. It will be recalled we last heard of him about to train as a Clearance Diving Officer. As predicted, he soon established himself as one of the most proficient all-round divers in the Navy. In due course, he was put in charge of a small diving team, working out of the Helford River in Cornwall. Aircraft from RNAS *Culdrose*, nearby, were still doing development work with the Mk.30 torpedoes, with which I would shortly be so involved at Eglinton. The assignment for Brooks's team was to dive for, locate and recover from the seabed, any torpedoes which failed to surface at the end of their runs. All went well for a time until his divers started to be harassed by sharks (which are surprisingly prevalent off South Cornwall). Joe might perhaps have fished for these using hooks baited with raw meat—but more sharks might have been attracted. Instead, being a TAS officer, well trained in the use of explosives, he tried a novel approach—with regrettably disastrous results. He made up a 'line charge' of plastic explosives on a length of Cordtex—white line as thick as an electric extension lead but which is itself an explosive. On this, he crimped a detonator and a short length of safety fuse with igniter. He then got in a dinghy (from the Motor Fishing Vessel—their diving base), managed to lasso the particular large shark they were worried about, and ignited the fuse. The maddened shark attacked the dinghy and the explosives went off just as the creature reached the boat. The shark was killed but the men in the boat were also seriously injured. The upshot was that Joe had to have amputations on both legs, one just below the knee and the other just above the ankle.

Needless to say, Brooks had to be invalided from the Navy, but this was far from the end of him. He was back underwater in a wet suit and Scuba gear with artificial legs in six months, and being filmed for the underwater sequences of a film called *The Frogmen*. Thirty years on Joe was still living a full and useful life. Frankly, I suspected Brooks would have to be cut in small pieces before there was no part of him still moving—and asserting itself. He commanded the Sail Training vessel *Winston Churchill*—for handicapped sailors. Sadly, Joe proved mortal after all and died in 1994, after an heroic and unselfish life. No man I knew had been more ready to lay down his life to save others.

Before closing this chapter, I will report on the later lives of other people in this book, with concluding information on them, where I have no more to add in the epilogue.

My first Captain, G. B. Middleton of *Revenge*, who had been keen to see the first albatross as we headed for South Africa, reached the rank of full Admiral (CB & CBE) before he retired.

Captain Harold T. W. Grant of *Enterprise* returned to the Royal Canadian Navy after the war. He was promoted to Rear Admiral and, aged forty-four, to Vice Admiral in 1947. He was appointed Chief of the Canadian Naval Staff in 1949 and awarded the CBE, retiring in 1951. He was a brilliant Captain. I was inspired by his performance under intense fire—having been on his bridge throughout his principal surface action.

Our well-loved Captain of *Bulwark*, J. M. Villiers, was promoted to Rear Admiral and became the last RN Chief of Naval Staff of the RNZN. His final appointment was as Fourth Sea Lord. 'Mike' Villiers' daughter married John Webster, who had been the Sub Lieutenant of the Gunroom for *Bulwark*'s first Commission (under the Command of Villiers). John Webster himself went on to attain Flag Rank. Finally, at least one other officer of that Commission made Admiral. One of Webster's Midshipmen—presumably involved in the mouse-throwing at poor Peaches Page—was Ben Bathurst. As a full Admiral he was made the First Sea Lord in 1993.

Lt. F. H. W. Foord, whom I was appointed to assist and so much admired aboard *Enterprise*, was promoted to Lieutenant Commander and retired in the 1950s. He acquired no further gallantry awards (to add to his MBE) for his part in the Biscay Action. This was probably because no one but myself noticed what a fine performance of his duty he had given under heavy fire and his modesty was such that he would not have mentioned this to anyone.

My Term-mates Mark Terrell, Malcolm Skene and Mike Vaughan were shipmates with me throughout our time aboard *Revenge* and *Enterprise* and, later, were all in the 17th Destroyer Flotilla. Sadly, I was not to see Terrell or Skene again in the Navy, after *Enterprise*. I know next to nothing of Terrell's later life except that he took early retirement about the same time as myself and set himself up as a professional diver and surveyor/ marine consultant in Greece. I have not seen him since 1944.

I was not to see Skene again until our 1989 Reunion. However, subsequent information revealed that we had followed an almost identical pattern of appointments but at different times and often on different sides of the world.

On becoming Sub Lieutenants, I went to MTBs while he went to the Hunt Class destroyer, *Quantok*. Next, as the war ended, Skene went to MTBs and I joined the Hunt Class destroyer *Lauderdale*, spending most of my time in that ship in South Africa. A little later, I was aboard the light fleet aircraft carrier *Ocean* and Malcolm aboard her sistership, *Glory*—in the Mediterranean and Far East (I believe) respectively. Subsequently, after I had had a year around UK in *Flint Castle*, etc., during which Skene was in the Battle Class destroyer *Camperdown*, I found myself aboard the Battle Class destroyer *Gravelines*. By this time, my friend had started the 1950 Long TAS Course—the same course that I would start a year later. In mid 1951, Malcolm had qualified as a TAS Officer, taken passage to Australia and been appointed to HMAS *Rushcutter* (the RAN's TAS School). One year later, I had completed the course, moved to Australia and was installed at *Rushcutter*! My colleague must have been somewhere in Australia but I did not know this, or even that he had specialised in TAS. By my second year with the RAN, Skene was back in UK in a fleet minesweeper developing new mine-countermeasures. Late 1954, I was home again, 'standing-by' *Bulwark*, completing at Belfast and about to commission. But by early 1955, Malcom was headed back to Australia for another two years with the RAN. For my last two years, I was at RNAS Eglinton, Northern Ireland. Accordingly it is not surprising that we never met despite following almost identical career paths.

After I had left the Service, Malcolm had the appointment I would have loved—Staff TAS Officer to the First Destroyer Squadron, aboard *Daring*. He must have been looking well placed for promotion to Commander, but this was not to be. He had two years with Naval Intelligence and finally eight in charge of the Sea Trials Department and other Administrative Duties at *Vernon*—retiring in 1972. Like me, he had become a dedicated yachtsman—passage sailing to Gibraltar and around the Mediterranean and skippering a yacht from Capetown to Sydney in one of the early Round-the-World races. His last employment was with the Royal Yachting Association, training and examining Yacht Masters, etc.

With so much in common, I am only sorry I lost touch with Malcolm Skene for forty-four years.

We come to Ian Scrymgeour-Wedderburn, whom I had known as 'Scrym' when I was a Midshipman aboard *Orwell* and he a junior Lieutenant and our Navigating Officer. Together, we had manoeuvred the ship with gay abandon in the convoy lanes leading to the Normandy Beaches—and got a kick out of it, although incurring our new Captain's displeasure. I was not to encounter him in the Navy again. However, whilst writing this story, I chanced to hear word of him in 1992 and learnt that he retired in 1967 as a Commander. It was with great pleasure that I was able to open correspondence with him after forty-eight years. Only then did I learn that when I had been Operations Room Officer of *Bulwark* off Suez in 1956, Scrym had been Staff Navigating Officer to Admiral Power aboard our flagship, the mighty *Eagle*. We might well have spoken to each other (from Ops. Room to Ops. Room on so-called Combat Information Primary Wave) without knowing to whom we were speaking. Through Ian, I am able to report more information about our CO of *Orwell*.

John Hodges (of *Orwell*) retired as Captain J. M. Hodges DSO in 1956. He was awarded his DSO for playing a significant role in the capture of the naval base of Antisarine, Madagascar in 1942, despite determined resistance by Vichy French Forces. With the main assault held up outside Diego Saurez a daring attack was made on the enemy rear with fifty Royal Marines landed in the harbour of Antisarine from HMS *Anthony* (Lt. Cdr. Hodges), under fire, after a night dash of 120 miles in foul weather. This audacious move caused the French resistance to crumble. Had the Japanese been allowed to take Madagascar (as they did French Indo-China) the round-the-Cape supply route to the 8th Army would have been seriously endangered. (My Midshipmen colleagues and I would not have had nearly as happy a voyage through the Mozambique Channel aboard *Christian Huygens*—with her Wren passengers—a year later!) More detail of the Antisarine operation is given in Appendix 6.

Captain Hodges died in 1987 and, in his obituary in the *Daily Telegraph*, was described as one of the most notable destroyer officers of his generation. His last appointment in 1956 was still as a destroyer man—as Captain (D) of the Londonderry Flotilla.

Scrym submitted a eulogy on Hodges in 1987, which, however, was not published by Fleet Street. I would like to take this belated opportunity of issuing Commander Scrymgeour Wedderburn's personal tribute to a much-loved officer:

> I had the good fortune to serve under John Hodges during the 18 months he was in command of the destroyer HMS *Orwell* in 1943/44. He was an inimitable character, larger than life, sometimes incorrigible but eminently likeable, gregarious, amusing and imbued with the common touch.

He quickly endeared himself to the ship's company by typically accepting responsibility for an accident for which he was not to blame. They loved him not only for his integrity and his own rather eccentric brand of leadership but also for his irreverent respect for authority and his keen sense of the ridiculous which made people laugh when they wanted to cry.

I guess I am not alone in remembering John Hodges with nostalgic affection, tinged only with sadness for the long illness he suffered at the end of his life.

Ian was certainly not alone in such memories. I count myself privileged to have served under him—even if only for four months, as an insignificant Midshipman. I would simply add that Hodges 'irreverent' streak could have been related to his being a product of Darmouth—and his sense of the ridiculous illustrated by his attempt to signal the French destroyer *Combattante* with our time-honoured, '*Monsieur je regrette . . .*' (Little, I imagine, could C. H. Grenfell have anticipated his rigamarole apology would become so nearly universal among naval officers.) I would also note that, in my own view, Scrym himself was a fine, creditable—almost archtypal—product of Dartmouth.

Lt. Cdr. J. H. A. Benians DSC. My CO in *Lauderdale* retired as a Lieutenant Commander in 1960, aged forty-five.

Commander P. J. Hoare, under whom I had served aboard *Loch Eck* and at RNAS Eglinton, received no further promotion, but served on in Naval Intelligence in Washington until retirement in 1966, aged fifty. MccGwuire tells me he was a great success in Washington. He died in 1984.

I have no information as to what became my captain aboard *Flint Castle*. Happily, Jack Maidwell (the 'No.1' of that ship) made Commander and retired in 1970, aged fifty.

C. D. Newton DSC, our popular First Lieutenant and Social Secretary aboard *Gravelines*, took early retirement (as a Lieutenant Commander) in late 1958. I have no later news of him.

W. D. (Bill) Shaw, our much-loved captain of *Gravelines*, was promoted to Commander shortly after leaving that ship and then took early retirement in 1955, aged thirty-six. I would not see him again until 1994, when I dined with him near his home in Surbiton, close to where Michael Vaughan lives.

Nigel Fawcett, good friend aboard *Gravelines*, specialised in Navigation and reached the rank of Commander before retiring in 1973, aged forty-six. Again we met once more in 1994 for a mini-reunion of the officers of *Gravelines*' First Commission.

Another of my *Gravelines* mates, Mike Wilson, followed me into the TAS Branch, made Commander and was awarded the OBE—retiring in 1981 at the age of fifty-five.

I have already mentioned that David Brown who, with Fawcett, Wilson and myself made up our 'Four Musketeer' team aboard *Gravelines*, went on to a distinguished career. He seems to have worked his way up through successively larger vessels after he left *Gravelines* (as the No.2—the position I'd had)—MTBs, mine-sweepers, to command of *Cavendish* (it will be recalled that *Cavendish*, as an almost new destroyer, had transported me from Colombo to Singapore, eighteen years earlier in 1945, but had been almost re-built and modernised). On the way, he took the Long TAS Course and the Staff Course. He had various Staff Appointments. including Fleet Operations Officer and, later, Director of Naval Op-erations and a NATO appoint-ment in Naples. He had two further Commands—*Hermione* and *Bristol*. As a Rear Admiral he was Assistant Chief of the Defence Staff (Operations) and served out his time, as a Vice Admiral, as Flag Officer, Plymouth, retiring in 1985. David attended our mini reunion.

A contemporary of David Brown who also made Flag Rank was David Hallifax, who took over from me for the second commis-sion of *Bulwark*, and whom I had known since he was a Sub Lieu-tenant. He had also specialised in TAS. I do not have the details of his brilliant career, except that he was Chief of Staff to C-in-C (Fleet) Admiral Fieldhouse at Northwood during the Falklands operations. His quiet good humour and con-

Admiral Sir David Hallifax KCB, KCVO, KBE. A very distinguished officer, whom I had known since his Sub Lt. days and counted as a good friend. Succeeded me as TAS Officer of Bulwark and, after my retirement, sailed with me in 12-metre yacht Flica II. Played a major role in Falklands War as Chief of Staff to C-in-C Fleet. Well remembered for his wit and good humour. In crisis of Falklands War, signalled the Battle Group Commander who had a query regarding the Total Exclusion Zone, 'Tiz TEZ'! After retirement, was Constable and Governor of Windsor Castle. Died tragically in 1992 of motor neuron disease.

fident efficiency did much to sustain the morale of local commanders in the war zone, particularly when disasters struck. He retired as Admiral Sir David Hallifax KCB KCVO KBE and was appointed Governor of Windsor Castle, which position he occupied until June 1992, when ill health made him relinquish this post. Sadly, David died in late 1992. At least it was a blessing he did not live to experience the Windsor Castle fire.

Commander Peter Campbell LVO, DL—A brilliant officer who had been a friend since his Sub Lt. days. Fellow 'stirrer' at TAS Conference, 1958. Equerry to the Queen.

Yet another contemporary of Brown and Hallifax, and another TAS Officer, Peter Campbell, whom I had also known since his Sub Lieutenant days, and, like myself, enjoyed doing some stirring at the annual TAS conference of 1957, had a spectacular career including a position as an equerry at Buckingham Palace, marrying Moyra, daughter of the 4th Duke of Abercorn (who had been a lady in waiting to the Queen at her Coronation). He retired in 1966 and was made High Sheriff of County Antrim in Northern Ireland. Naturally, as he had been born and bred in Ireland, he had more love of that land than I had had at Eglinton!

It will be noted that a large number of officers mentioned in this story were Torpedo or TAS Officers. Such go right back to Captain Robert Falcon Scott (of the Antarctic), Foord (of *Enterprise*), Commander Charles Emerson DSO and Rear Admiral Hughes Hallett—all Torpedo Officers (before the formation of the TAS Branch). TAS Officers included Brooks, Wemyss, Kersey, Skene, Woolley, Barratt, Mylchreest, Hawkins, Wilson, Brown, Campbell and Hallifax. This is no more surprising than would be the case of a retired Army Officer mentioning many officers of his Regiment or Corps. I would merely add that many worthy fellows specialised in TAS!

INTERACTIONS

At this point, it is worth noting how a number of people's stories become interwoven. In early 1939 we have seven people who had never met each other before. Five are thirteen-year-olds about to start their careers as Royal Navy Officer Cadets; one had started eight months before; and one was in his twenties and a Lieutenant RN having transferred from the Merchant Marine. They are respectively Messrs. Kersey, Lungley, Seymour, Vaughan and Wemyss, Cadet MccGwire and Lt. Hoare.

We will now see the kaleidoscope of their lives as they interact in groups of two, three, four and five over the next half century. Until the end of 1941, all but Peter Hoare are together at Dartmouth. April 1942 finds MccGwire, Kersey and Seymour in war-torn London to represent the RNC in the Inter Public Schools Sevens Rugby, but achieving little except a three-day spree in London. One year later, the five of us (excluding MccGwire and Hoare) are to be found in the Eastern Fleet at Mombasa, East Africa—Kersey, Lungley and Wemyss aboard the cruiser *Newfoundland* with Vaughan and Seymour in the battleship *Revenge*. All seven would see action in the Atlantic, North Sea, Mediterranean and/or Far East.

In early 1945, MccGwire, Lungley, Seymour, Vaughan and Wemyss are to be found together in the 30th MTB Flotilla at Ostend in Belgium. Another year on, all seven are out in the Far East. Seymour meets Vaughan at Singapore and later joins the frigate *Loch Eck*, under the Command of Lt. Cdr. P. Hoare at Tanjong Priok—port of Batavia where the rest of Lungley's family were killed by the Japanese, four years earlier. This time, however, Seymour finds himself proceeding by jeep to Batavia with armed Japanese military escort, with no means (or desire) to find out if any of his escorts had been responsible for the murder of his friend's family.

Seymour has been seeing something of Sumatra (Palembang). MccGwire, after service in the destroyer *Armada* (a name that crops up again later) of the British Pacific Fleet, has visited Australia. But MccGwire now transfers (in 1946) to *Whitesand Bay*, hoping to revisit Australia but, instead, also finds himself in Sumatra (Padang)—involved in pinching another jeep!

On to 1947, with Kersey, Wemyss, Vaughan, Seymour and MccGuire all serving aboard ships in the Mediterranean Fleet, based Malta—with sundry reunions occurring. By 1948 MccGuire is at Cambridge, learning Russian, followed by a period of living in squalor with an impoverished White Russian family in Paris. Around this time Vaughan, smartly dressed in his starched white uniform aboard his equally smart destroyer *Chieftain*, on berthing in the Vieux Port, Marseilles, hears a hail from the shore of 'Hi Mike!' He identifies a scruffy-looking MccGwire in sandals, shorts and T-shirt—still supposedly learning the language from his Paris White Russians. Vaughan himself would soon be taking an interpreter's course—in German. M. Vaughan, however, is luckier than MccGwire—he is sent to the family of a German Count with a *Schloss* in Bavaria and an attractive daughter! This leads, not to hitch-hiking to Marseilles, but to a luxury stay in Milan to view performances of the opera at La Scala! To illustrate the luck in such courses, another friend of mine took Serbo-Croat and had to do his 'practical', lifting potatoes amongst Jugoslav refugees in England.

By 1950 we find another destroyer—the equally smart *Armada* (last heard of in the Pacific Fleet)—also in the Vieux Port, Marseilles with a scruffy-looking Seymour in motorcycling garb struggling over the guardrail as the ship is just departing for Malta.

The previous year (1949) had seen Kersey and Wemyss doing the Long TAS course together in UK whilst Seymour was serving aboard *Flint Castle* at Portland. This has afforded Kersey and Seymour their first chance to go sailing offshore—on their cruise to the Channel Isles.

1952 finds Seymour disembarking in Sydney and being greeted on arrival by Kersey and MccGwire. The three see quite a lot of each other in the next twelve months.

Moving on to 1956, we find Vaughan again smartly turned out aboard yet another smart destroyer—*Cossack*—berthing at Brisbane, and hearing another hail from shore of 'Hi Mike!' This time, the cry comes from Joe Lungley, down from his farm in central Queensland to see the visiting RN warship.

In 1957 Seymour finds himself at RNAS *Eglinton*, Northern Ireland where his Executive Officer proves to be now Commander Peter Hoare (last mentioned commanding *Loch Eck* around Java, etc.). In 1959 *Eglinton* closes down, Seymour leaves the Navy and later migrates to Australia. Hoare takes up an Intelligence appointment in Washington DC where he subsequently gets to know MccGwire, and where both spend quite a few years. Finally, as will be recounted in the epilogue, Seymour is greeted by the cheery hail of MccGwire on arrival at Washington's International Airport in 1989—*en route* to a reunion involving Kersey, Vaughan, Wemyss and many others in London.

Not all the meetings between the seven persons named have been listed but enough to show just how kaleidoscopic were their lives, involving recurring ship names, in places as varied as Dartmouth, London, Portsmouth, Mombasa, Ostend, Singapore, Batavia, Marseilles, Sydney, Brisbane, Malta, Northern Ireland and Washington. Of the group, all saw varying degrees of action, three identified with the TAS Branch of the Navy, two became Interpreters, two spent some time with Naval Intelligence, six, if not seven, came to Australia at some time with three settling there and two spent at least eight years in North America. I feel it can be said that not one of us has had a dull or dreary life—even if not exactly what thirteen-year-old Cadets Lungley and Seymour had envisaged on our train to Dartmouth in 1939.

Thirty Years On

Having left the Royal Navy in 1959 and moved to Australia the following year, I more or less put the Service behind me. However, not all past links were cut. In Sydney, I found my old friend Mike Kersey, also recently retired, living with his Australian wife and three children. We have maintained a close association ever since: he was best man at my wedding and then godfather to my son. Some fifteen years later, Kersey's marriage broke up and he followed a roving life aboard a cruising catamaran in the Greek Islands. Around 1980, he sailed this craft across the Atlantic and based it in the British Virgin Islands. However, he paid quite frequent flying visits to UK and, occasionally, Australia. Each visit to Sydney has involved us in a happy reunion.

Other old friends and Term-mates have turned up in Sydney from time to time. Gavin Wemyss appeared commanding *Apollo*, the 'mother ship' for all Far East coastal minesweepers, which were now under his command. It will be recalled that I had last seen this vessel in Stockholm, flying the flag of C-in-C Home Fleet. Gavin was now 'passed-over' as a Commander, but was thoroughly enjoying his wide-ranging responsibilities and, at least to some extent, living like an Admiral! He was then appointed the Resident Naval Officer for the Clyde, based Greenock. For this he had few naval personnel under his command but a fleet of small civilian-manned craft. He performed diverse administrative duties, all in his beloved native Scotland. I learned from independent sources that, with his dry humour and unmatched inter-personal skills, Gavin was a great success in this unusual posting. He was the only officer I knew who would get to know—and remember—the names of every sailor in his ship in just a week or so.

He never married, but was truly wedded to the Navy. Can it be wondered that he was so well-loved by his men? No man ever had more naval blood in his veins than Gavin Wemyss. In a little show-case at his home in Fife are medals, including the Victoria Cross, won by his great great grandfather, who led a naval detachment that played a vital part in the Relief of Lucknow in the Indian Mutiny. Gavin's mother was a Wren Officer during the War, while his father, who lived to the age of eighty-nine, also retired as a Commander after winning two DSOs and three DSCs as one of the most successful Anti Submarine aces of World War II.

He was CO of HMS *Wild Goose*, and 2 i/c of the famous Second Escort Group under Captain Walker, from whom he took over, after the death of the latter in the later stages of the war.

Gavin was a distant relative of Admiral of the Fleet, 'Rosie' Wemyss, who was First Sea Lord for the greater part of World War I, in which Gavin's father found himself in action, aged sixteen, aboard the battleship *Valiant* at Jutland. His action station was on the bridge assisting the Navigating Officer writing up every detail of the ship's movements, and chronicling the action. He must have watched the devastating blowing-up of two of Admiral Beatty's battle-cruisers, *Indefatigable* and *Queen Mary*. However, young cadet Wemyss never faltered from his precision writing up of *Valiant*'s log in his minute hand with the use of a mapping pen. This very Log Book may now be seen, open on the page for that fateful day in 1916, in a glass case at Gavin's home. It should also be recorded that Gavin's younger brother, Martin, retired as a Rear Admiral. We will return to the Wemyss family in Fife shortly.

Michael Vaughan continued to give the Navy devoted service. From 1960 to 1962, he was back at another Air Station—RNAS *Brawdy*. Then came two years at Admiralty on the staff of the Second Sea Lord, followed by two more staff appointments—with Flag Officer Gibraltar and FO Scotland and Northern Ireland. In 1972 he was Defence Adviser to the British High Commissioner in Sierra Leone. I recall our first visit to Freetown aboard SS *Antenor* in 1943—more interested in the Wrens aboard *Strathaird* than the West African Scene. Vaughan's last appointment was i/c Sea Cadets throughout the London Area.

I would again see Michael Vaughan and his family, both before and after his retirement (as a Commander), on a number of visits I made back to UK. I usually stayed at least a few days at his hospitable home in Surbiton. In civilian life, Mike secured himself a good job with the steel fabrication company, Condor Group plc, of which, for some years, he was the Market Development Manager.

On visits to UK I would often also visit my Long TAS Course mate, Harry Hawkins, who had taken early retirement at the same time as myself. Strangely, we found ourselves briefly working for the same company—even at the same work-place. I had been lucky in finding early employment with the Boyden Group of companies, as a Management Trainee. I quickly came to know the young chairman, Tony Boyden, who had made me 'Sailmaster' of his newly-acquired twelve-metre yacht. In fact, there was an element of truth in the notion that I secured my job because I was said to be a specialist spinnaker/foredeck hand! Be that as it may, shortly after I was signed up, independently, Harry answered an advertisement for another position as a Management Trainee, with Boydens. This led to the odd situation of Tony Boyden asking me if I had known a Lt. Cdr. Harry Hawkins in the Navy—and, if so, what did I think of him? Harry contacted me and said, 'Isn't this the crowd you are working for? Do you think I should join the group?' I could only reply, 'I can't say, Harry; I have only been with them a few weeks—but at least I look like getting some sailing!'

As it turned out, things went well for me and, eighteen months later I was in Australia, almost my own boss, with the group's Australian subsidiary. Harry was less fortunate. He found himself stuck—notionally being trained in management—in one of the less successful and, one must say, less well-run ventures of the group. After two years, Harry had had enough. He resigned and joined another company of which he became the Managing Director. However, Harry's time with the Boyden Group had not been totally unrewarding. He was not as keen as me on sailing but was a seasoned and competent naval officer, retaining his love of the sea. Accordingly, when Tony Boyden went ahead with his challenge for the America's Cup with *Sovereign* in 1962 (after I had moved to Australia), Harry was to find himself at sea again. He was not a member of the crew of *Sovereign*, but of the large steel-built motor yacht Tony had as 'mother ship' and HQ for his challenge at Newport Rhode Island. This craft had to make the double Atlantic crossing and take in a holiday for the owner at Bermuda *en route*. A handful of experienced mariners were needed and Management-Trainee Hawkins was seconded from his printing works to keep watch again on the bridge of a ship in the Western Ocean! In the event, it was as well Boyden had a stout crew as the vessel ran into a full gale and had a very rough outward passage. The sequel to this little adventure occurred some months later. A weather-beaten and sun-bronzed Harry was back in Portsmouth attending a TAS reunion dinner at *Vernon*. Our old contemporaries, seldom getting to sea in the oil-fuel economy-starved Navy of the sixties, and then mostly shut up in dimly-lit Operations Rooms, all looked decidedly pale. Harry chided them with, 'The trouble with you lot is you are not getting in enough sea-time'!

The last of my old buddies, on whom I have not reported fully, was Joe Lungley. I related that Joe had been last seen in Brisbane after leaving the Navy several years before myself. When I arrived in Sydney, in early 1961, I tried hard to locate him. I engaged an agency to trace him for me, from his last known location in the town of Theodore in Queensland (as reported by Mike Vaughan). A week later, I received a letter from my agents advising a certain address in Theodore and presenting a bill for ten pounds. With joy, I wrote at once to this address to ask Joe how we might get together again (notwithstanding the fact that Theodore is about 1,000 miles from Sydney). Sadly, I had no reply.

Nearly thirty years later, I made a determined effort to trace him once again. As the result of a notice, widely circulated at Theodore, I received letters from several old-timers, who remembered Joe and his family—with affection. It seems, however, that I must have just missed him in 1961 as they had moved to New Zealand shortly before that. His wife, I learnt, had been Matron of the hospital at Hastings in NZ and one of his friends from Queensland enquired after the Lungleys at that hospital whilst on a visit there. Alas, the only news was that the family had moved out, back to Reading in England, where his wife's family lived, and where I had attended Joe's wedding many years before. My only hope now is that Joe, or one of his family, will read this and contact me or one of his old naval mates. I still recall (despite my slight alcoholic haze at the time), the unhelpful grin on Joe's face near me as I played out the oxymoronic farce involving two inebriated RAF officers in the brothel that was our Mess in Ostend, in 1945!

During 1988, I started to receive advance warning of a planned 50th Anniversary Reunion in London of my contemporaries joining the Navy, as thirteen-year-old Cadets in May 1939. Term-mate John Carlill who had been one of the last to retire, as a Rear Admiral, was the convenor and organiser, and made a tremendous success of this undertaking. With my wife Pat, I immediately started making plans to attend. I found that Michael Kersey aimed to travel from the Caribbean and most of my old comrades would be there. It was at this time that I initiated my determined, but unsuccessful, second search for Joe Lungley.

As this was strictly a reunion of our own Term, I would not be seeing Mike MccGwire. However, as I had now tracked him down to Washington, and reopened correspondence after not having seen him for thirty years (and then only briefly when I had tried to sell him my old taxi for £70 at Greenwich), I wrote and asked him if we could stop over with him in Washington *en route* to England via North America. This elicited a warm invitation to stay with Mike and his wife and led to the hearty shout of 'Hi Bigshot' at John Foster Dulles International Airport! Suffice it to say, no two old friends were ever reunited for such a happy get-together after three whole decades. The endless reminiscences would, of course, have been very tedious for my wife—who had not known me as a Navy man—but, fortunately, Mike's charming wife Helen more than took care of Pat.

At this point, I should bring readers up to date with MccGwire's life—having last reported him in a Fishery Protection Ship in northern waters. For two years, he was Assistant Naval Attaché in Moscow before promotion to Commander. Later appointments included being Commander of the Submarine Depot Ship *Adamant*, Staff of SACLANT (Supreme Allied Command Atlantic) and heading the Russian Division of Naval Intelligence. He took early retirement in 1967, then spent ten years in the Chair of Strategic Studies at a Canadian University and eleven at the Brookings Institution, where my wife and I caught up with him in 1989. By 1990, he was into 'head-to-heads' with prominent figures on TV in UK and USA, testifying at Congressional hearings and being listened to by the Defence Secretary and other high-profile US Administration figures. Thus, MccGwire came to play a more important role on the World Stage than if he had remained in the Royal Navy–even as an Admiral.

The rest of our group played minor parts and tried to 'do our bit' around the world in, and out of, the Service. Peter Hoare, also in Washington, worked to strengthen Anglo-American bonds. Gavin Wemyss with his fleet of minesweepers stood by to clear international waterways of South-East Asia and the Far East for shipping, a capability, sadly, no longer extant and not replaced by any other maritime power (see Appendix 6). Joe Lungley was dairy-farming in Queensland, with his wife a hospital matron. Mike Kersey produced wool in New South Wales to clothe people in colder climes. Mike Vaughan was helping the establishment of newly independent Sierra Leone and passing on some of the values of the former Raj—that there were more commendable endeavours than 'tiefing' (thieving). He also earned the devotion of his servants, with his Head Boy naming his daughter 'Commander'! The author visited Beijing to promote Anglo-Australian trade and drink endless toasts in *motai* with a form of Pidgin-Mandarin: *Wei Au-Zhiong languo renmin yoyi, Ganbei!* (to friendship between the peoples of Australia and the Chinese People's Republic). We did not act out of pure altruism and were earning our living, but, at least, we were not *contrabandiers!*

All but Wemyss had families (and Gavin did much to encourage his nephews and nieces), all now making their own marks around the world. The author was least prolific with but one son, who is, however, becoming known in the field of hi-tech media activities in UK, USA and Australia, while his wife trains Philippinos and others in Mediation and Alternative Dispute Resolution. Roll on the six-billion-head Global Village–watch out, World, for further generations with the seven surnames (or a person named 'Commander'!)

On arrival in England in April 1989, we had usual stays with MSJ and other relatives and inevitable shopping at Harrods and Simpson's, Piccadilly. Then came the build-up for the Reunion. Our first contact was with George Freer and family and a delightful overnight stay at their home near Colchester. Next it was off to Scotland for the long-planned meeting up with the legendary Gavin Wemyss, now comfortably settled back as Laird of Luthrie, Cupar, Fife. We were joined by Mike Kersey, whom I had last seen in Australia a few years back. Also present was Gavin's eighty-nine-year-old father, Commander David Wemyss, already described.

The house, occupied by the widower and his bachelor son, had scant feminine touches to it but was packed with naval memorabilia—from the Relief of Lucknow, through Jutland, the World War II Battle of the Atlantic, and up to the end of Gavin's career. Commander Wemyss senior proved a charming old man, possessed of all his faculties. He would drive to the village for groceries and played a sharp game of bridge. Sadly, he died just two months after our visit.

We had a splendid three days together, with Pat somehow surviving being the only woman amongst four retired Naval Officers! At least, with us, she was able to enjoy the lovely countryside in spring. Gavin took us around St Andrews and across the Tay, and through Dundee into the beautiful highlands of Glen Clova, around which the hills were still capped with snow. The wooded and moorland country beside the fast running streams was of quite indescribable beauty. It was hard to realise that we had driven within fifteen miles of what had been Arbroath Naval Air Station, where I had been so miserable on our Sub Lieutenant Air Course in mid-winter 1944—thirty-five years before.

Finally, the time came for us to repair to London for the Big Day. The three sixty-three-year-old Term-mates and my wife had a hilarious train journey to London in one of British Rail's truly comfortable, but fast, Inter-City Expresses—a standard of rail travel comfort and efficiency I had not known when I had left UK for Australia. Because of the natural thrift of the Laird of Luthrie, we travelled Second Class, but it is hard to imagine what additional comfort we would have had First Class. On arrival in London, we went our different ways over-night. Pat and I stayed at the Royal Thames Yacht Club but were up bright and early next morning in glorious late spring weather, on 5 May 1989.

We had planned to proceed to Greenwich by water-bus but found that, for some reason, such were not running. Accordingly, we found ourselves at Charing Cross Station in the very heart of the great metropolis with time to spare to catch our train. We were turned out as smartly as we knew. I had ordered a new suit from Simpson's specially for the occasion and had polished my shoes until they shone. Being unhurried, we had time to watch the rush of truly cosmopolitan travellers coming and going to work, or sightseeing overseas visitors. For my wife, there must have been a feeling of some excitement and curiosity—about to be thrown into a wholly naval environment, such as she had never known. However, she was fortified by the knowledge that she at least knew Shellagh Freer. I personally felt relaxed with a sense of pleasurable anticipation. I was a very different person to the timid little thirteen-year-old who had stood on another railway station exactly fifty years before.

THE REUNION

On the steps in front of the main buildings at RN College, Greenwich, one after another, figures appeared who looked vaguely familiar but many of whom I found myself unable to place, after a lapse of up to forty-five years. I would have to keep asking Gavin, 'Who is that?' However, once told and having heard a distinctive voice, I found myself thinking, 'Of course—it couldn't be anyone else!' We managed to muster twenty-four of the original forty starters (and forty-four who finally made up the Term). I have named five who had died on service, another five who had died of other causes and there were three or four who had simply vanished like Joe Lungley. Several were in far-flung parts of the world—two in Canada, one in South Africa, Newnham in the USA, one or two were sick and unable to be present, and one was taking an exam that could not be deferred!

50th Anniversary Reunion 1994. Back Row (l. to r.): Michael MccGwire (Happy Hooligan), self, David Norman (contemporary of MccGwire, in 30th MTBs—also at Dartmouth in my time). Second row: Helen MccGwire, 'Whisky' Wemyss, Mrs Norman. Front row, centre: Peter Magnus (DSC and 2 bars), Senior Officer of 30th MTB Flotilla 1944–5.

The morning activities centred on a Memorial and Thanksgiving Service in the beautiful Wren chapel at Greenwich. Whilst few of my colleagues were fervently religious, I do not think any were atheists—very few sailors are. The service was deeply moving. Many of us were using the words of the Naval Prayer for the first time in a great many years:

> O Eternal Lord God who alone spreadest out the Heavens and rulest the raging of the sea, who has compassed the waters with bounds until Day and Night come to an end, Be pleased to receive into Thy Almighty and most Gracious Protection the persons of us thy Servants and the Fleet in which we served. Preserve us from the dangers of the sea and the violence of the enemy That we may be a safeguard unto our gracious sovereign Lady Queen Elizabeth and her Dominions and a security for such as pass on the seas upon their

lawful occasions; that the inhabitants of our Island and Commonwealth may in peace and quietness serve thee our God . . . '

In my own case and, it seems, a number of others, I was so choked with emotion that I was unable to finish this prayer, that I had known so well. Finally, it was again very moving to sing, kneeling (by naval tradition), the last verse of the hymn 'For Those in Peril on the Sea':

> O Trinity of Love and Power,
> Our Brethren's Shield in danger's hour.
> From Rock and Tempest Fire and Foe,
> Protect them whereso'er we go:
> And ever let there rise to Thee,
> Glad hymns of praise from land and sea.

After the service we assembled in the College Wardroom, mostly accompanied by wives, for drinks and a buffet lunch. Now I was able to meet again with Mike Vaughan and his wife Gay who had been so good to me on successive business trips to UK, George Freer and Shellagh and of course Gavin Wemyss and Mike Kersey. It was a joy to find Oswald Cecil—my car-owning partner of Sub Lieutenant days, Malcolm Skene—Midshipman shipmate from *Revenge* and *Enterprise*, and many others. Forty-odd years seemed to have been rolled back and I felt I was in a dream.

In the afternoon, wives were 'excused'. I went off with Mike Vaughan to his home at Surbiton, and changed into 'black tie' for our formal Naval Mess Dinner in the Wardroom of HMS *Belfast*, a 10,000 ton World War II cruiser, permanently moored in the Thames as a floating museum. Proceedings were predictable but emotional as well as heart-warming. For the first time in thirty years, I remained seated (by naval tradition) for the Loyal Toast. The exchange of messages with Her Majesty, mentioned at the start of this book, was read and we departed around 2300. Needless to say, most of us were 'feeling no

Commander Michael Vaughan MBE. One of the author's closest friends over 56 years. Term-mate, Dartmouth. Shipmates Revenge *and* Enterprise. *Together in 17th Destroyer Flotilla and 30th MTB Flotilla.*

Author with Gavin Wemyss (Cdr. OBE) at 30th MTB Flotilla Reunion, 1994. Dartmouth Term-mate and together in MTBs. No bravado or back-slapping here—just two very good friends enjoying each other's company after a number of years separation.

pain' by the finish. I was to spend that night at the Vaughans and have to admit that Mike and I had to assist each other on to a train at London Bridge, to change at Waterloo and take another train to Surbiton.

Next morning—another beautiful late spring day—I rose feeling a little the worse for wear, but Mike was filled with exuberance. After an early breakfast, we drove in his fine car, with the sun roof open, down the A3 to the submarine base, *Dolphin*, at Gosport. By arrangement, we were greeted aboard HMS/M *Osiris* under the command of Michael's son (my godson), David Vaughan. This was a great joy to me but a little unnerving to find the solemnity and deference to which we two Old Salts were treated in this naval heartland. I had last known this locality as a relatively junior thirty-one-year-old Lieutenant Commander.

After a drive back up the lovely Meon Valley, I parted with Vaughan—I hoped our next meeting would be in Australia—and rejoined my wife before flying off to a delightful week amongst the chateaux of the Loire Valley. Then I was off—back to Australia.

Regarding our reunion, it was natural that everyone would enjoy meeting each other again. Needless to say, some had fared better than others—with their Flag ranks, knighthoods, etc.—some had made names for themselves after leaving the Navy, whilst others had served out their full time in the Service without getting beyond Lieutenant Commander. However, no decorations were worn and place names at dinner had no ranks shown—we were just the Term-mates, as we had known each other at Dartmouth nearly half a century back. During the whole day, I did not detect even a suggestion of superiority by any individual towards another, nor, for that matter, any hint of envy or resentment by anyone who had been less successful in life. At this point, I would assert my own view, regarding promotion in the Navy. Whilst no system could hope to avoid all disappointment or heart-break, I believe the methodology used was as fair as anyone could humanly expect.

We had shared a truly memorable occasion, totally unalloyed by any unfortunate incident or ill-feeling. Apart from different fortunes befalling individuals, some had aged more visibly than others. Only a few, including Mike Vaughan, did not wear glasses but some were bald, some white-haired, some rotund and others surprisingly thin. But at the end of the night, I complimented 'Bonzo' Ransome on his hale-and-hearty appearance. He had left the Navy as a Lieutenant and had a harder life than most of us, working his way up through the ranks of a distinguished Cavalry Regiment to Warrant Officer. A wide grin, a full head of hair showing no perceptible greying and a small Cavalier-type beard, gave him a handsome swashbuckling look, and he seemed to have weathered the years rather better than any of us.

REFLECTION

My wife stayed on in England for another three weeks. This gave me time to collect my thoughts, not only about our reunion, but the broader view of our lives as a whole.

I found myself wondering, how would those following judge us? Would we be regarded merely as trained killers—who did not kill too many people because our nation was at peace most of our careers? This poses the question 'Is any military service honourable? Or, should we all be pacifists and unilateral disarmers? Are any causes worth fighting—and killing—for?' Few fighting men go into battle not believing in the justice of their cause. One might ask how the Germans, almost to a man, initially at least, were prepared to follow Hitler 'to hell and back' with his insane genocidal policies. Certainly, the officers and men of the Kriegsmarine, the German Navy, fought with remarkable bravery and determination. The story of the sinking of the *Scharnhorst*, fighting overwhelming odds, makes incredible reading.

I would be vain and 'blinkered' if I asserted that all hostilities involving Britain, even in my time, could be declared just causes. I feel Hitler's

Germany had to be resisted as had Japan's aggression. However, 'trailing a coat' before the Albanians in 1946, ready to 'blast hell out of them' if they fired a single shot, was uncalled for. The Korean War was morally supported by virtually the whole of the so-called Free World but the Suez operations were more questionable. The situation there appeared to us as entirely justifying Anglo-French military intervention. However, one should perhaps review the broad sweep of history in relation to Egypt and the Nile. This was a cradle of civilisation, back three thousand years— when Ancient Britons daubed their bodies with woad. Successive invaders conquered Egypt—the Cambyses, Greeks, Romans, Turks, Mamelukes, French (under Napoleon), British, Turks again, British again and, nearly in 1942, the Germans. Some invaders came and left quickly, like the British in 1803, whilst others left more evidence of their occupation. In passing, it may be noted that during the nineteenth century Britain conducted several major military operations with striking tactical success but achieved little lasting political gain. A classic was General Napier's highly successful Magdala campaign in Ethiopia in 1867/8. This was an operation on a larger scale than the Falklands War of 1988. The stated object (release of hostages from the clutches of the mad Emperor Theodore) was achieved and the whole force packed up and returned to India, leaving total anarchy in Ethiopia and thousands to be massacred in inter-tribal warfare.

Once again, the services executed a brilliant operation in 1956, capturing Port Said for the loss of under a hundred servicemen against superior forces in prepared defences. The stated object, of stopping a war between Egypt and Israel, was attained. But little was achieved and, a few weeks later, the whole force was withdrawn, leaving the Egyptians to spend the next month methodically scuttling blockships in the Suez Canal, unmolested. It is not for servicemen to query why they are being asked to fight. In many countries, military juntas have seized power. Nevertheless, I still believe that we are safer leaving elected governments to determine foreign policies—even if, with hindsight, some policies may prove to have been ill-judged.

The fleet had a great deal to do other than go round killing people. As a carry-over from the time when the British Empire was at its zenith and Britannia truly ruled the waves, the Royal Navy retained much of its role as the Police Force of the world. For many years between the wars, if trouble threatened anywhere, the arrival of a British cruiser (and the Navy had eighty) usually restored calm. Sometimes, a larger force was necessary and the presence of the Mediterranean Fleet at Constantinople in 1922 at least thwarted any massacres. Some people speak disparagingly of those days when the answer to most problems was said to be, 'Send a Gunboat'—in truth, however, this was not a bad policy. Worldwide policing did not always make the RN popular—as was the case with the

Palestine Patrol in the fifties. I do not suppose this sort of thing was in the mind of W. S. Gilbert, in his lyrics for *Pirates of Penzance*, writing 'When constabulary duty's to be done, A policeman's lot is not a happy one'—but there is some truth in this!

The Royal Navy was also expected to be something of a world-wide Ambulance Service—as in the case of Mountbatten's earthquake relief operation in the Ionian Islands. At other times the Service could simply indulge in making people's lives just a little brighter—by providing a Guard of Honour for the Coronation of His Serene Highness, Rainier of Monaco, or turning on a monster children's party in Oslo.

Some might regard Naval Officers as a bunch of dilettantes cruising in luxury around the world at the taxpayers' expense. It is true that, during the decades covered by this story, one certainly could 'Join the Navy and See the World', but this was seldom a luxury cruise. Except on occasional long ocean passages, every day—and night—at sea would be utilised for intensive training and exercising. Naval officers in foreign ports did enjoy a certain image of glamour and would often be royally entertained by the local hierarchy or wealthy British ex-patriots. Indeed, the author has recounted how, at times, his life was just a 'great big bowl of cherries'. Nevertheless, naval officers were never well-paid. Even Lord Louis Mountbatten declared that he would not have been able to make ends meet, but for the wealth of his wife. The naval life was, perhaps, thought to provide reward enough. In my case, I think it did. However, I believe that the nation got very good value for money out of its naval officers. The remark is often made, regarding highly-paid people in various professions: 'Remember they have to have long hard training before they are so rewarded.' This is true, no doubt, but no longer nor harder than that of a Captain of an aircraft carrier manoeuvring at high speed with the lives of a thousand or more ship's company dependant on his instant decisions and correct professional judgements. Such was the case of *Bulwark* in the English Channel in 1955. Even more expertise is expected of a Captain, or any officer, going into action against a determined foe. Yet a senior Captain would receive nothing like the remuneration of, say, a senior barrister or a surgeon in a hospital. However, one entered the Navy on the clear understanding that this would never make one rich—brilliant or otherwise.

I cannot pretend that we all joined out of sheer patriotism and desire to serve our country—yet there was always the notion that one was doing something honourable and worthwhile. Very definite rewards were the bonds of comradeship forged. In the RN these were not only with brother officers but also between officers and the lower deck. The other services may have had similar relationships in many instances—but not always. In the case of the Royal Air Force, it was inevitable that there would be lesser bonds between aircrew—mostly officers—who constituted the combatant spearhead and ground staff, who, although performing a vital role, generally performed non-combatant service. During, and since, World War II, Army officers have tended to lead their men into battle. However, in the appalling conditions of trench warfare of World War I, whilst there were officers in the front line trenches at Paschendale and the Somme, the higher ranking officers tended to be further from the enemy. This did not mean they were less brave—that was just the way things were. There was no such distinction or difference in exposure to danger between an Admiral at sea and an Ordinary Seaman. Admirals Holland-Martin aboard the *Hood*, Phillips in *Prince of Wales*, and others, had no greater chance of surviving the loss of their ships than anyone else on board, nor did Mountbatten when *Kelly* was sunk. In other words, fewer generals than admirals were lost.

Clearly, some ships with inspiring commanding officers were happier than others and morale could deteriorate when ships had nothing to do, as with my first LST rotting in Singapore. However, I never saw anything approaching a mutinous ship's company. The near-mutiny I did experience, aboard *Rocksand*, was of junior officers against their superiors.

Britain's naval heroes have not all been 'knights in shining armour'. Many Elizabethan 'Sea Kings' were largely 'in it for the money'—the bounty received when a Spanish treasure ship was captured or Cartagena sacked. Yet Sir Francis Drake had a sense of duty and knew how to keep the respect of his men, declaring, 'I must have the Gentleman haul and draw with the mariners . . . ' This perhaps inspired the concept that the Navy soon taught me—sometimes called the 'Law of Equal Misery' (perhaps a Wemyss *bon mot*). When the Commander of *Bulwark* stopped all leave at Invergordon, after the Ensign Staff Incident, he was wise enough to include the officers in the disciplining, even though it was inconceivable that any officer was to blame—other than, perhaps, having failed to thwart the alleged misconduct.

So much for the Navy, in general. My thoughts returned to the Naval Prayer. With humility and thanksgiving, but no claim to worthiness, I felt I had to acknowledge a measure of 'Almighty and most Gracious Protection', having survived at least seven potentially life-threatening situations, mostly unrelated to enemy action. These were: not being swept off my picket boat and drowned in the Congo; under intense fire from German destroyers in Biscay; my MTB, loaded with 100-octane fuel, almost impaled by the bows of a blazing tanker; car smash (as a passenger) in a tropical downpour in Malaya; splitting my head on a solid steel deck clench on the quarterdeck of *Ocean*; blood-poisoning at Aqaba in 115°F; motorcycle spill, in weakened state, on my TAS Course; and the submarine/helicopter incident off Northern Ireland (my 'closest call' of all)—not to mention being in distress in a yacht in a sinking condition, on a dark wintry night, with nearly all sails blown-out. Had events been only marginally different in any of these cases, this book would not have been written.

Such recollections inevitably give rise to philosophical thoughts. Any man believing, as I do, there is a God, inevitably asks himself, 'Why was I spared—when others demonstrably more deserving, such as Michael Ryland, were cut off in their prime?' Needless to say, such questions are asked by people in all walks of life. The truth is we simply do not know. Consideration of this matter quickly tells us that Merit, Good Works and Virtue cannot be considerations. People would not lay down their lives to save others. Furthermore, if survival were based on worthiness in any form, Darwinian Evolution of the Species, by now, would have given us a perfect world.

If one then examines one's own religious beliefs, it must soon be accepted that God is not specifically an Englishman—any more than he was ever Egyptian, Persian, Greek, Roman, Ottoman, French, German or even American. Yet Elgar may have been tempted to think Britain enjoyed some special divine privilege, with his plea, 'Lord who made thee mighty, make thee mightier yet.' We certainly cannot assume he is an RN officer (or 'Lord Commissioner for executing the Office of Lord High Admiral in the United Kingdom &c'), even if we do beg His protection from the 'Dangers of the sea and violence of the enemy'. The Serviceman simply accepts that he has a strong compulsion to 'do his duty'.

I would like to conclude by quoting Nelson's Prayer before Trafalgar:

> May the Great God that I worship Grant to my Country and for the benefit of Europe in general a Great and Glorious Victory. And may no misconduct in anyone tarnish it. And may humanity after victory be the predominant feature of the British Fleet. For myself individually I commit my life to Him who made me. And may His blessing light upon my endeavours for serving my country faithfully. To Him I resign myself and the just cause which is entrusted me to defend'.

Naval Officers have not been saints. Nelson's private life was reprehensible and he treated his wife abominably. Yet he was—and still is— regarded as one of the greatest leaders of all time. This was not just the view of the officers and men of his fleet but of the whole nation. Britain preferred to go into mourning at the news of his death than to rejoice at the winning of the most decisive naval victory in history. Also, Nelson largely deserves the credit for enabling William Pitt, after Trafalgar, to declare, 'England has saved herself by her exertions and . . . Europe by her example.'

Notwithstanding the disrespect we showed to pictures of 'the death of the immortal Nelson', he did achieve immortality. Nearly two hundred years after Trafalgar, when occasion permits, Naval officers will still hold a Mess Dinner on 21 October, and drink a solemn toast. The President will rise and pledge 'TO THE IMMORTAL MEMORY'. At the other end of the table, the Vice President will come back with 'VISCOUNT HORATIO NELSON' and officers will raise their glasses.

Nelson's dying words were, 'THANK GOD I HAVE DONE MY DUTY.' Can any of us aspire to make such an unqualified declaration when our time comes?

Royal Navy (RN), Royal Naval Volunteer Reserve (RNVR) and Royal Naval Reserve (RNR)

The reader may wonder why officers have been designated either RN, RNVR or, occasionally, RNR. This was uniquely significant for the Royal Navy. In the Army and Air Force, an officer was simply a Major, Squadron Leader or whatever—there was no distinction between regular and reserve officers. Only the Navy carried on through the war with peacetime-structured training of regular officers, through Dartmouth, Special Entry and Promotion from the Lower Deck, as well as through Sub Lieutenant Courses. In the Navy alone, therefore, was there any distinction. Notionally, a reserve officer (serving for the war only) had exactly the same authority as a regular officer of the same rank. In practice, however, commands of all ships from fleet destroyers up were held by regular RN officers (except in special cases of converted merchant ships).

This was only possible as the pre-war Navy was much larger than the Army and had a great many officers. Even so, in due course the regular RN officers were outnumbered by reservists. This was particularly the case in Coastal Forces, where there was only a handful of regular officers. Whether or not a distinction was desirable is debatable. However, the fact was that RN officers were given more responsible appointments, sometimes beyond the relative seniority of available reservists. In the narrative, it will be seen that the author, as a twenty-year-old Sub Lieutenant, was appointed second-in-command of an LST, even though there were reservists with greater seniority on board. All other LSTs had RNVR Lieutenants as their No.1s. Had the CO died, there might have been an argument as to who should assume command.

Whatever the merits or otherwise of the distinction, it existed; and was very visibly evident. RN officers had straight stripes on their sleeves, while RNVR had thinner wavy ones—hence the term the Wavy Navy. However, the distinction was not made in all Commonwealth Navies. For instance, one of our 30th Flotilla COs was an Australian Sub Lieutenant with a straight stripe. I concluded he must be a regular RAN officer, but this was not the case. Our Canadian had wavy stripes.

A futher variation was the Royal Naval Reserve (RNR). These were Merchant Service officers who had undertaken Naval reservist training in peacetime, but were, essentially, already professional mariners. These officer bore on their sleeves double (interwoven) wavy stripes. The quip in those days was, 'The RNVR are gentlemen trying to be seamen. RNR are seamen trying to be gentlemen, and the RN neither, trying to be both!'

Interestingly, the US Navy had no distinctions in uniform for regulars and reservists. However, regular officers from their Naval Academy would wear what was called the Annapolis Ring on one finger. Whether this was official or not, some distinction was thereby achieved.

The Gunnery Director System

At the turn of the twentieth century, the heavy guns of battleships were fired more or less independently, with minimal centralised control. By World War I, however, all the major navies had adopted the Director Control System, invented by a British Naval Officer named Percy Scott, who was regarded by many as the Father of modern Naval Gunnery, the principles of which remained valid up to the advent of anti-ship guided missiles.

The system comprised a Fire Control Director Unit, with remote sighting—removed from the smoke, flash and shaking of guns as they fired—which, through its own Director Layer and Trainer, generated a steady line-of-sight on the target. This was transmitted to a compartment in the bowels of the ship, known as the Transmitting Station, into which was also fed the range of the target as determined by optical range-finders and the inclination of the enemy ship as estimated by the Rate Officer. These factors and the estimated speed of the target made up the main input to the calculator—a mechanical form of computer—known as the Fire Control Clock. This equipment worked out where the other vessel would be at the end of the time of flight (which could be more than half a minute). This would be translated into the required elevation and training for all guns. Finally, the guns were actually fired, simultaneously, by the Director Layer, on the order of the Gunnery Control Officer. A buzzer would sound just before the shells were due to arrive to facilitate 'spotting' and adjustment for line and range. The author's Day Action Station aboard *Revenge* was as Secondary Rate Officer—charged with estimating and continuously updating the inclination of the enemy.

For big ships, fire would be opened with 'salvoes', usually of four guns, and patterns fired until line and length were established by a hit or a straddle. Only then would Rapid Broadsides be ordered. Thus, a battleship's turrets were expected to fire half a dozen times before a hit was expected (unless lucky—as was the *Tirpitz* in action with the *Hood*). Aboard destroyers like *Gravelines*, one opened fire with all guns from the start, with two or three broadsides in the air before the first landed. Spotting adjustments were made by the 'hosepipe' method. These (4.5″) turrets could fire up to 20 rounds per minute from each gun.

For older ships such as *Revenge* and *Enterprise*, the required elevation and training were transmitted electrically to the turrets or guns by 'M-type' motors which turned pointers on dials. It was then the duty of the Layer and Trainer at the gun to so elevate and train the weapon, that pointers on the dials (showing where the gun was actually trained or elevated) remained in line with the indicators controlled by the M-type motors as directed from the Transmitting Station (the TS). In this way, all guns would swing around ready to fire on receipt of the order, 'All guns follow director'. If the electrical circuit between TS and gun failed, such gun (or turret) could, of course, no longer 'follow director' or be fired by the Director Layer, and had to go into Local Control. Such was the case with all but one of the 6″ guns of *Enterprise* at the conclusion of her action with German destroyers in the Bay of Biscay.

As technology advanced (after World War II), the M-type motors were dispensed with and, at the flick of a switch, a turret, or gun mounting, would automatically elevate or train as directed by the TS. Also, by about 1943, range determined by radar was more accurate than that from optical range-finders. Later, direction could be determined by radar, permitting Blind Fire. However, visual laying and training remained more accurate— and reliable—until well after the end of World War II.

There was a similar system for predicting the location of aircraft targets, and therefore where to fire anti-aircraft guns. Such was, however, superseded by the Tachymetric Box system as fitted to the STAAG Bofors AA guns mentioned as fitted in *Gravelines* in which the author served after the war. This system simply measured the rate of movement of the sights (or radar) tracking the target aircraft—even allowing for the measured acceleration (first differential), of target movement.

The 30th MTB Flotilla 1944

THE FLOTILLA HAD AN EVENTFUL HISTORY from its formation at Lowestoft in mid 1944 until my contemporaries joined it six months later. Immediately after commissioning, the boats moved to HMS *Hornet*, the Coastal Forces base at Gosport from where they took part in the operations associated with the Normandy Landings. These included sorties of several days and nights, operating from the Mulberry Harbour. As the boats had no food storage facilities, they had to go round the Liberty ships begging a few loaves of bread! As the Army began to move up the French coast, the flotilla moved along the British coast—first to Ramsgate and then on back to Lowestoft. From Lowestoft, the boats were sent across to attack convoys on the Dutch coast or used to defend British East Coast convoys against marauding E-boats. This was unpleasant work in miserable cold weather and it was a long haul to the Dutch coast and back.

MTB 476 (which I later joined) had its share of the action, being hit one night by 20 mm shells, igniting the 2″ rocket flares. On another occasion, 476 had to take a disabled consort in tow, necessitating MccGwire hanging over the stern to secure the towing bridle in the dark. (It was typical of Mike that he tackled this himself, rather than tell a seaman to do it.) They were still close to the enemy coast when dawn broke and had a long, cold and dangerous journey back. Their arrival was so late that the base staff feared both boats had been lost, but everyone, including the Wrens, were out to cheer them into harbour— heroics!

The Captain of *Mantis* (the Lowestoft base) was a veteran RN Commander named K. B. Barnard who had had the misfortune to have lost an eye. He was affectionately known as 'One Fixed and One Flashing' (a typical description of the lights on a navigational buoy). He had seen the flotilla form up initially and its officers and men were his darlings. This unit was already regarded as a crack flotilla, had superb morale, and could be relied on to acquit itself with distinction at sea and in action—although the personnel had shown a tendency to high spirits and living it up when off duty (the result of a higher-than-usual Dartmouth element perhaps?)

Immediately after church parade on Christmas Day 1944, half the flotilla were sent on an offensive patrol off the Dutch coast. They set off, carried out their operation to the letter and returned to harbour on Boxing

Day all cold sober. This could not be said of the four boats of another flotilla that accompanied them. However, after the boats had been properly 'squared off' there was a certain amount of horseplay. One of the sailors nearly backed a lorry into the harbour and some flares were let off.

Sadly, 'Fixed 'n Flashing' had now been relieved by an unimaginative but self-important Commander RNVR who hated the 30th and was now eager to show his metal. He paraded all the officers and told them he had just rung Admiralty for permission to disband the flotilla! This was not granted, but all leave was stopped for a month and No.1s were made to sleep aboard their boats. This was harsh punishment for brave officers in wartime who had been risking their lives and fighting the foe valiantly and effectively for six months and whose Commanding Officers included some of the most distinguished—and decorated—officers in Coastal Forces. However, the worst punishment was the cancellation of the planned deployment to Ostend of the 30th as the specially chosen crack flotilla.

Instead, the Canadian flotilla at Felixstowe, who had also earned considerable renown, were sent over. Sadly, many crew would die in the explosion and conflagration at Ostend only a few weeks later. Thus it came about that the 30th was deployed to Ostend after all. However, as this had not been planned, the boats had to go over as soon as they were ready—in twos and threes. It was at this time that the author and his mates joined the flotilla.

APPENDIX 4

THE LORD CHAMBERLAIN

HAVING POSSESSED MINIMAL KNOWLEDGE of the duties and responsibilities of the Lord Chamberlain, I am deeply indebted to Mr and Mrs Russell Nash for lending me an admirable book giving all possible information needed. This volume was found and given by Elizabeth Nash to her father, General Sir John Northcott, then Governor of NSW in 1953, the year after it was published. It is *The Crown and the People* by Allan Machie, published by Secker and Warburg. This was close to the times about which I have been writing and, as well as fascinating reading, I am sure it is fully authoritative and definitive.

Allan Machie writes:

> By long tradition the senior official of the Queen's household is the Lord Chamberlain, at present the 76 year old sixth earl of Clarendon, the son and nephew of previous Lord Chamberlains . . . [Seemingly, therefore a hereditary office.]

Machie listed some of the duties of the Lord Chamberlain:

> He is the organizer of courts and levees and the reception and entertainment of visiting foreign dignitaries. It is his office which sends out the invitations to garden parties, scans the list of debutantes who seek admission to the court (now discontinued), arranges the closely timed procedure of investitures and sorts out the black sheep from the socially elite who apply for admission to the royal enclosure at Ascot racecourse . . .

I cannot help wondering how the butcher and dictator of Romania, Ceaucescu, got through this screening. If the Lord Chamberlain was in fact overruled by the government of the day, when given a State Banquet by the Queen, then it is arguable the Lord Chamberlain should be left to decide on such matters—as a hereditary septuagenarian office-bearer or not!

Allan Machie continues:

> Among his secondary duties are the appointment, on the Queen's behalf, of the royal chaplains, the royal physicians and surgeons [one might have imagined these would be more than 'secondary' duties], the Poet Laureate, the Queen's Bargemaster and watermen, and under his special eye come such officers as the Master of the Queen's Musick [sic], the Keeper of the Swans on the Thames, the Shower of State Apartments at Windsor Castle, the

Gentlemen-at-Arms, the Gentleman Usher of the Black Rod, the Lords- and Grooms-in Waiting as well as the pages of the back-stairs, the chamber and the presence. He is also the superintendent of the royal collection of art and antiques.

I have to say I had no idea the court employed all these people—perhaps I should have sought a post amongst these after leaving the Navy. Poet Laureate might have been beyond me. But, who knows? I might have performed well as Bargemaster or Waterman or even as a 'page of the back-stairs'!

Fascinating though the foregoing may be, it might well be asked, 'What has all this to do with Rules for Strippers?' Be patient, Dear Reader. Machie goes on:

> By a historical accident, the Lord Chamberlain is also responsible for censoring British Drama, a duty for which he is frequently criticised. His office has been connected with the theatre in England at least since 1574 . . . royal sponsorship for plays and actors, usually against fierce Puritan opposition . . . delegation to Master of the Revels [sounds a reasonable job—alas discontinued] . . . Licensing Act in 1739—the Lord Chamberlain was made dictator of the drama. This invidious post wished on him . . . appointed by the sovereign . . . now has two assistants—Comptroller and assistant Comptroller . . . no play publicly performed . . . without the Lord Chamberlain's license . . . in this century, works of Shaw, Ibsen and Maeterlinck banned . . .

If all this seems extraordinary, Machie records:

> Parliament has frequently debated his role as censor but has never been able to agree on the larger issue of censorship of the theatre and so the Lord Chamberlain has retained his anomalous prerogative. [It is worth noting that as the office was established in 1360, changes in its functions are not made over-night.]

An improbable facet of the office is that it terminates with the the death of a monarch and although in practice he remains in office for some six months, 'the tradition of an abrupt break in service is retained and at the funeral of a monarch his Lord Chamberlain unscrews his white staff and places half upon the coffin as a gesture of farewell' (in bygone times it was physically broken).

One might well conclude that the likes of Peaches Page would have a considerable interest in the health or otherwise of the sovereign, because a new monarch must mean a new Lord Chamberlain—with who knows what new rules for strippers to follow on stage!

It should be noted that the life and structure of the Court today bears little resemblance to that described in Allan Machie's book written in the early days of the reign of our Queen.

MINE WARFARE

MINE WARFARE AND MINE COUNTERMEASURES have always made for a battle of wits rather than problems that could be solved by 'throwing money at them'. The US Navy did and does many things with great energy, thoroughness and success—notably use of Naval Air Power. The subtleties of mine warfare, however, have not held much appeal in that Service.

To the Americans, mines have long appeared a matter of frustration rather than challenge. This goes back to Admiral David Farragut, at the battle of Mobile Bay in 1864. On hearing mines had been laid in his path, he made his famous cry, 'Damn the torpedoes [mines]! Full Speed ahead', happily without fatal consequences! Nearly a hundred years later during the Korean War, the landing of an American division at Inchon was delayed seven days because primitive nineteenth century mines had been laid by Chinese junks. This, reportedly, led to a (not so publicised) signal from the Commander, 7th Fleet to ComCinCPac: 'The enemy are laying mines of before 1900 from minelayers of before Christ—and this modern Navy can't sweep them!' I believe the final American answer in that campaign was to fill a dozen surplus World War II Liberty ships with concrete and steam them through with skeleton crews until all mines were detonated.

In World War II the Germans achieved enormous initial success with magnetic mines (mostly laid by aircraft in the Thames Estuary). These were ground mines, in relatively shallow water, which could not have mooring wires cut by conventional minesweeping methods. The only counter was to produce a magnetic influence similar to that of a ship and detonate the mines clear of the minesweepers. Before this could be done, a mine had to be recovered and dismantled at enormous personal risk—because of booby-trap devices in the mine—to find out how the magnetic firing mechanism operated. This was achieved by Lt. Cdrs. Ouvry and Lewis, who were each awarded the Distinguished Service Order for their efforts. With the secrets of these mines known, immediate steps could be taken greatly to reduce all vessels' magnetic influences by so-called De-Gaussing and to devise suitable magnetic 'sweeps'. This speedy countering of Germany's latest secret weapon undoubtedly saved hundreds of thousands of tons of shipping and countless lives. Not waiting until Germany had enough magnetic mines to seal all UK ports simultaneously was one of Hitler's greatest strategic blunders. He could then have virtually declared 'Check-Mate'!

This was, however, only an early chapter in the on-going development of ever more sophisticated mines and equally sophisticated mine countermeasures. The next magnetic mines had firing mechanisms actuated by horizontal magnetic fields instead of, or as well as, vertical fields. Then came acoustic mines, set off by the sound from ships' propellers. The counter for these was complicated by the fact that they could be triggered by pre-set 'signals' of sub-sonic or supersonic noise. Then came pressure mines and various combinations of these influences could be needed to detonate the mines. Another problem was posed by 'sensitive' influence mines, easily detonated but designed to destroy the minesweepers, and 'coarse' systems—not easily set off by influence sweeps and only detonated when a large ship passed overhead. The first sensitive magnetic mine was dismantled by my old mate Mark Ross, in the Korean war—for an MBE.

Almost the last straw came with a ship-count mechanism which could be set so that, even if all possible influences were synthetically produced, the firing mechanism would only tick over one notch. As a result, after two weeks of really comprehensive sweeping, an area might be declared safe, only to have mines go off under successive ships transitting the swept channel. It was such knowledge that led Lt. Campbell to conclude that the Coastal Minesweeper force charged with clearing the approaches to Port Said could have no certainty that they were safe. Fortunately, the Egyptians had negligible minelaying capacity.

Notwithstanding the daunting tasks of dealing with the mine problems outlined above, the Royal Navy has never accepted defeat in this ongoing battle of wits. The Normandy Landings would never have been possible without the unrelenting endeavours and constant vigil of the Mine Countermeasures Department at *Vernon*. As it was, mines claimed many victims including the destroyer *Isis* (and my friends Ryland and Nicholson), not to mention the disabling of *Ekins*—the controlling frigate for my MTB.

Efforts are now concentrated on highly sophisticated methods of locating mines on the seabed with very high definition mine-hunting sonar, underwater television, etc. Current technology is not even known to the author, although back in the fifties all these matters were the responsibility of the TAS Branch. However, it should not have passed unnoticed that, of all the navies involved in the recent Gulf War, the task of clearing the approaches to Kuwait was placed entirely on the Royal Navy.

ANTISARINE

IN CHAPTER 24 (Brother Officers), reference was made to the capture of Antisarine in Madagascar by Royal Marines landed from HMS *Anthony* (Commanded by Lt. Cdr. John Hodges, under whom I was to serve in Hodges' next command, the *Orwell*). Whilst the author was not present, this was a remarkable but little-known operation, earning Hodges the DSO. I have recently learned much more about this audacious action—in large part from a recent contribution to *The Naval Review* by Commander Lennox-King RNZN who as a Lieutenant was the Gunnery Officer of *Anthony*. I feel the reader might like some more background. Rather than quote Lennox-King's entire article I offer a digest of it:

> The assault landing of three brigades and a commando met little resistance and divided to make a two pronged attack on Diego Saurez and Antisarine. However, the Vichy French forces were not going to yield easily—they had recently repulsed an attempt to seize Dakar in West Africa. The force headed for Antisarine came quite unexpectedly upon the French defence line—a deep tank ditch which stopped our light tanks completely—also 'seventy fives' and machine guns which pinned down the infantry.
>
> A bold plan was suggested by General Sturgess RM, in charge of the land operations—to put a detachment of Royal Marines (from the battleship *Ramilles*) ashore in Antisarine itself to take the French in the rear. This was a desperate plan, involving embarking them in the destroyer *Anthony* which then steamed at full speed through the night in high seas, round the Andraka Peninsula (northern tip of Madagascar). They had to rely on the element of surprise to pass powerful coast defence batteries at almost point-blank range to get right into Antisarine.
>
> The Marines, unused to being flung about in a destroyer at 30 knots in ten-foot waves, were miserably seasick but really showed their mettle. Hodges had no chart showing the wharfage at Antisarine. No alongside berth was available, but having run the gauntlet of the shore batteries, he managed to put his ship stern-to-the-wall and enable the marines to scramble ashore. This fifty-man force under Captain Price RM was then supposed to attack the rear of the French defence line—if they could find it. As it happened, they took the wrong route and found themselves in the town of Antisarine. Here they chanced upon the Army barracks in which the garrison were blissfully asleep! Having secured this building they moved to another which proved to be the telephone exchange. With brilliant initiative, Price got a line through to the

HQ of the defence line and his competent French-speaking junior officer passed the word that Antisarine had 'fallen to an overwhelming force' which was about to assail the defence line from the rear. Accordingly, the surrender of the French was invited—and given. The ultimate result was the virtual surrender of the whole island of Madagascar to fifty Royal Marines—who, presumably, had not fired a shot.

In fact, *Anthony* was heavily fired on as she withdrew, but not by the biggest and most threatening guns at the harbour entrance, their gunners having noted how effectively other batteries had been silenced by *Anthony*'s guns, directed by Lt. Lennox-King.

Upon rejoining the fleet *Anthony* was greeted by all ships flying the flag signal 'Well Done' and they were cheered by ship's companies of all the other ships as they passed. This might appear to have been a minor operation but it was of vital strategic importance that Madagascar was secured by the Allies before the Japanese, who had been roaming the Indian Ocean almost at will, could take possession.

A. P. HERBERT AND MARY CHURCHILL

THE FOLLOWING IS TAKEN from the obituary notice for Captain John Hodges DSO in the *Daily Telegraph* of 15 August 1987. Hodges' ship *Orwell* was escorting the battle cruiser *Renown* bringing Winston Churchill, Mrs Churchill and Mary Churchill back across the Atlantic after the Quebec conference in 1943. Aboard *Orwell*, Hodges had the well-known scholar, humorist, writer and politician—then Petty Officer—A. P. Herbert as a passenger, who used his poetic talents to signal *Renown*:

Return Ulysses soon to show
the secret weapon of your bow
return and make your riddles plain
to anxious Ithaca again
and you Penelope the true
who have begun to wander too
we're glad to greet you on the foam
and hope to see you safely home.

To which *Renown* soon replied:

Ulysses and Penelope too
return their compliments to you
they too are glad to wend their way
homewards to Ithaca after a stay
with friends from where the land is bright
and spangled stars gleam all the night
and when he's mastered basic Greek
Ulysses to the world will speak
about the plots and plans and bases
conferred upon in foreign places
we thank you from our hearts today
for guarding us upon our way
to chide these simple lines be chary
they are the first attempt of Mary.

Concluding footnote by the author:

At last my odyssey is ended
I hope no one has been offended
Under Ulysses I fought
not just another Argonaut.
Ithaca now at peace may rest
I feel my wanderings have been blest